An Imaginary Trio
King Solomon, Jesus, and Aristotle
Yaacov Shavit
Edited By Anthony Uyl

Devoted Publshing
Ingersoll, Ontario, Canada 2023

An Imaginary Trio
King Solomon, Jesus, and Aristotle
Yaacov Shavit
This edition edited by Anthony Uyl ₘₜₛ

This book was originally published by Walter de Gruyter GmbH, Berlin/Boston.

The reformatted text of An Imaginary Trio is all protected under Copyright ©2023 Devoted Publishing. The covers, background, layout and Devoted Publishing logo are Copyright ©2023 Devoted Publishing. This edition is published by Devoted Publishing a division of 2165467 Ontario Inc.

Note on Creative Commons 4.0 Attribution status: Although all the text in this document is from the CC-BY, the layout, formatting and note changes makes this book a copyrighted work. The original document remains in the CC-BY and can be found here:

https://doi.org/10.1515/9783110677263

For details on CC-BY go to to http://creativecommons.org/licenses/by/4.0/.

Unless written permission is given for any material, all use of this material to be reproduced, stored in a retrieval system, or transmitted in any form by any means, electronic, mechanical, photocopying, recording or otherwise is forbidden. All rights reserved.

Drop Cap and Table of Contents fonts are AnglicanText by Typographer Mediengestaltung and used under a Free For Commercial Use License (FFC).

ISBN: 978-1-77356-451-7

Contact Us Online:
Email: office@devotedpub.com
Facebook: @devotedpublishing
Editors' Twitter: @AnthonyUyl
For more information on Biblical Demonology and issues with the occult in modern evangelicalism, check out the editors' Substack Blog Reformed Demonology: reformeddemonology.substack.com

Table of Contents

Acknowledgements - 5
Introduction - 9
Chapter One: Biographies Correspond - 23
Chapter Two: Solomon and Jesus—Two Sons of God, and of David? - 41
    Pagan polemic - 48
    The Sages' polemic - 49
    Christian polemic - 52
    Medieval Jewish Polemic - 55
    The Broken Dynasty: Solomon and Jesus—two sons of David? - 58
Chapter Three: Solomon—His Actions and Books: Prefiguration, Typology, and His Teachings - 65
    Solomon's Temple - 68
    The Queen of Sheba's Visit as a Typological Event - 73
    The Theological and Allegorical Interpretations of Solomon's Books - 74
    The Song of Songs - 76
    Proverbs - 80
    Ecclesiastes - 82
Chapter Four: The Divine Presence and a Heavenly Voice Come to Solomon's Aid—On Sin, Repentance, and Absolution - 85
    Solomon's Sins and Downfall in Jewish Tradition - 88
    Heaven comes to Solomon's Aid - 93
    Christianity on Solomon's Sins and Repentance - 95
Chapter Five: "How is Jesus Greater than Solomon?" Solomon and Jesus as Magicians (Healers and Exorcists) - 105
    Magic and Occultism - 105
    Magic and Healing - 107
    Jesus as a Healer and an Exorcist - 112
    The Riddle of Solomon's Ring - 118
    Solomon's After-Life as a Magician - 121
Chapter Six: Miracles and Wonders: Magic, Satan, and Demons - 127
    Sorcerers and Magicians - 130
    Satan and Demons - 135
    Asmodeus and the Demons Build the Temple - 139
Chapter Seven: Solomon's Wisdom—From Hermes to Aristotle - 145
    Solomon's Wisdom according to the Sages - 152
    Solomon's Wisdom in the Middle Ages - 154
    Solomon's Wisdom in Christian Literature - 158

Jesus' Wisdom - 160
  From Thoth-Hermes to Aristotle - 162
  Solomon and Aristotle - 167
  Wisdom versus Wit - 175
Chapter Eight: Solomon, *Aristoteles Judaicus*, and the Invention of a Pseudo-Solomonic Library - 179
  The Invention of a Pseudo-Solomonic Library - 192
Afterword - 199
Bibliography - 201

ACKNOWLEDGEMENTS

The research and writing of this book took place over a long, frequently interrupted, period. My original idea was to write about King Solomon as a timeless legend and myth in various cultures. Yet the more headway I made in the vast amount of source materials, the less I could avoid acknowledging that this was a Sisyphean task. The abundance of sources and the extensive research literature that has emerged over the last century or so regarding diverse aspects of the figure of Solomon led me to relinquish my original plan and to limit its scope. This book, then, is not intended to retell even a small portion of the legendary traditions about Solomon.[1] Instead, it focuses on those places and instances where his (imaginary) legendary biography intersects with those of Jesus Christ and of Aristotle, the Greek philosopher. Solomon is the axis around which this trio revolves and is the thread that binds it together. The book is based on the premise that there exists a correspondence, both overt and implied, between these three biographies—a correspondence that has taken shape within a vast, multifaceted field of texts for more than two thousand years.

First and foremost my thanks goes to Chaya Naor for her endeavor in translating the first version of the book. Throughout my years of research and writing, particularly in the final stages, I have been fortunate to receive assistance, insights, and input—both gentle and stern—from colleagues and friends. I am very grateful to all of the following: Professor Sara Klein-Braslavy, Professor Yuval Rotman, Dr. Yuval Haruvi, Dr. Maya Shabat (Pinhas), Dr. Yuval Rubovitch, Itamar Levin, Dr. Maoz Cahana, Professor David Katz, Razia Geselson and JeanLuc

---

1. See Faerber (1902); George Salzberger (1907, 1912); Seymour (1924); *Legends of the Jews*, by Ginzberg (1909), which as of 2003 has come out in six editions; and Bialik and Ravnitzky (1931-1934), which since its second edition has been the most popular and influential collection of Talmudic legends (taken largely from the Babylonian Talmud) in modern Hebrew culture. I should also mention here the most bizarre book on this subject, by the radical American author Moncure D. Conway (1832– 1907): *Solomon and Solomonic Literature*, 1899; see review by Tyler (1990).

Allouche (to whom I am grateful for his generous and indispensable help), and to Michal Engel and Carl Yonker for improving the final version.

Without the nearly daily assistance of Avital Ginat and Irit Halavy, I could not have brought the idea of this book to fruition.

I owe a special debt of gratitude to Professor Manfred Oeming of Heidelberg University for the fruitful months during which he hosted me at the Wissenschaftlich-Theologisches Seminar and introduced me to the statues of Solomon and Jesus at the Strasbourg Cathedral. My gratitude is also due—not for the first time—to Professor Günter Stemberger:

טוֹב פִּרְיִי מֵחָרוּץ וּמִפָּז וּתְבוּאָתִי מִכֶּסֶף נִבְחָר

("My fruit is better than gold, even fine gold. And my yield than choice silver", Proverbs 8:19)

Finally, but in truth first and foremost, this book could not have been written without Zohar, who once again has accompanied me along the entire journey, every up and down. Of such a partner Solomon must have thought when he wrote:

וְרָחֹק מִפְּנִינִים מִכְרָהּ

("she is more precious than jewels", Proverbs 31:10).

Early versions of several chapters of this book have appeared in the *Culture and Literature* supplement of the newspaper *Ha'aretz*; in the book *Books and Libraries* published by the Zalman Shazar publishing house, Jerusalem; and in the *Festschrift* in honor of Professor Peter Schäfer (thanks to Dr. Reimund Leicht, one of its editors, for his important comments). Those chapters appear here in expanded and supplemented form.

The book is dedicated to the memory of Tamar Dror.

Fig. 1 South portal of Notre-Dame de Strasbourg, Christ and King Solomon by Jean Vallastre, photo by Jean-Marc Pascolo, © Wikimedia Commons.

INTRODUCTION

Two statues stand on either side of the south transept portal of the Strasbourg Cathedral, one personifying the Church in the figure of the triumphant Ecclesia, the other representing Judaism as the humiliated *Synagoga*. Between the two sits King Solomon on his throne, the sword of "Solomon's judgment" resting on his knee;[1] above him, Jesus holds an orb, symbolizing his cosmic status as the arbiter on the day of the Last Judgment.[2] This is apparently the only work of art placed in the public sphere that brings Solomon and Jesus together.[3] It presents the Christian side of what I will call the "encounter" or "correspondence" between these two figures, who are linked by a diversity of connections and contexts.[4] Their "correspon-

---

1. This is the sword mentioned in 1 Kings 3:24–25: "So the king said, 'Bring me a sword', and they brought a sword before the king. The king said, 'Divide the living boy in two; then give half to the one, and half to the other'".

2. See Rowe (2008, pp. 179–202), especially p. 182, according to which the image "alludes to the divine regulation of heaven and earth" and the figures depicting *Ecclesia* and *Synagoga* appear in many European cathedrals, but those of Solomon and Jesus are unique to Strasbourg. Three responses to an article I published in the "Culture and Literature" supplement of the Israeli newspaper *Ha'aretz* on December 24, 2010, added several details about the cathedral and the statues. Dr. Margo Stroumza-Ozan wrote that the cathedral had been built in two major stages. The first took place in the 1230s and included the eastern portal, across from which was the yard that served as a public court; Solomon and Jesus served to underscore the authority of the local judges. Ruth Almog wrote that the creator of the statues may have been the builder-sculptor Sabina von Steinbach, the daughter of the architect and main builder of the cathedral. In the seventeenth century the originals were replaced by copies. In art, the sinful Temple often symbolized the *Synagoga*. See Pinson (1996, pp. 147–174).

3. The two appear in a painting of "The Descent of Christ into Hell" (*Descensus Christi ad Infernos*) from Byzantium c. 700. See Trumbower (2001), as well as paintings from the eighth century and later.

4. Two more figures could, in theory, be added to the trio. The first is Hermes Trismegistus, a legendary and perhaps mythical figure. It was said of Solomon that he had "all signs of a perfect Hermetist". See Ebeling (2007); Idel (1988, pp. 59–76), the quotation is from p. 129. The second is the neo-Pythagorean philosopher and miracle worker, Apollonius of Tyana. The *Ars Notoria* refers to him as the friend and successor of Solomon (see in chapters five and seven). There is little substance to the "parallels" drawn between Apollonius and Jesus, but what is important for my purposes

dence" is, of course, an imaginary one. Even if we accept the idea that Solomon and Jesus, and not merely Aristotle, were, in fact, historical figures—or at least that their biographies contain a historical core—that core has over time given birth to a vast assortment of myths and legendary traditions, and it is within these myths and legends that the correspondence takes form.

The correspondence between Solomon and Jesus, or perhaps more accurately between Jesus and Solomon, is part of a long-standing correspondence between Christianity and Judaism, at times direct and at times less so: In some cases both Christianity and Judaism are addressed clearly, while they constitute a latent presence in others. Here it is necessary to warn against the trap of over-analysis, in which nearly every biographical account of Solomon and Jesus is interpreted as a trove of concealed parallels or contrasts between the two and between the ideas they represent.[5]

What do Solomon, the biblical king, and Jesus, the Christian messiah, have in common with the Greek philosopher? What have the three to do with one another? They lived, after all, in periods far removed from one another: Solomon in the tenth century B.C.E., Aristotle in the fourth century B.C.E., and Jesus in the first century of the common era. While Jesus was familiar with Solomon's biblical biography, he apparently never heard of Aristotle; the latter knew nothing of the existence of King Solomon and was, necessarily, unaware of Jesus.

The response to this rhetorical question is that centuries of legendary biographical traditions have joined the three figures in an *imaginary trio*; creative imagination has woven links and correlations. The correspondence this book will describe exists within a broader cultural field wherein the three figures—and the correspondence between them—express, represent, and symbolize a vast range of phenomena in human existence and culture.

***

The principal figure in this trio is King Solomon, not only because he antecedes the others but mainly because of his multifaceted image, replete with contradictions. Both earthly and atemporal, he is trans-cultural in status and function, assuming complex and disparate

---

is that neither does the Christian literature express any need to reject that comparison.

5. See Brezis (2018). I will not delve into the subject here and will only note that the theory on the subject of a "hidden debate" on the part of the Sages is an example of how radical modern interpretations impose themselves on ancient texts, and that it is unclear why it would have been necessary to conduct such a veiled debate, when its audience or readers would have been unlikely to discern it.

roles within Judaism, Christianity, and Islam. However, why was Solomon granted so rich an afterlife in such diverse cultures? Is it due to a deep-seated tendency in the ancient world to credit new ideas to figures from the distant past, anchoring new views in *prisca sapientia* (ancient knowledge)? In such a context, might Solomon have been the most appropriate—or even the sole—biblical figure to serve that function? Or did his fame spread because the eventful episodes that characterized his long life, the biblical accounts of his virtues and actions, and, of course, the books he was said to have written inspired and fueled the creative imagination, making Solomon a complex figure— and, as such, accessible and available for various purposes? I have no precise answer to the question; it would require a Solomon, the wisest man, to settle.

Solomon's biblical biography expanded and proliferated beginning in the Hellenist and Roman periods, evolving into a plethora of legendary traditions that traveled from culture to culture and across literary traditions. He was cast in myriad roles, as an ideal king, exemplum, symbol, *topos*; he was, at the same time, a judge of great wisdom and justice, a sage of all sages, a magus of all magi;[6] a prophet,[7] a great builder,[8] an artist,[9] a poet, and a philosopher; a miracle worker, a fool, and a beggar;[10] a man to whom God revealed himself twice in a dream;[11] a sinner and a penitent; the prolific author of far more than the Song of Songs, Proverbs, and Ecclesiastes; and a man active in realms both earthly and supernatural, "not only king in this world,

---

6. Butler (1993, pp. 35–43).
7. *Sotah* 45b; *Seder olam rabbah* 17.
8. Van Leeuwen (2007, pp. 67–90).
9. In romances of the twelfth and thirteenth centuries there is mention of the term *L'Uevre Salemon*; the term represents the technique of engraving material like gold, attesting to the popularity of the term and to an assumption that Solomon himself engaged in that craft, based on the Vulgate translation of Song of Songs 3:10: "King Solomon made himself a chariot of wood of Lebanon. He made the pillars thereof of silver. The bottom thereof of gold, the covering of it purple", (*Ferculum fecit sibi rex Salomon de lignis Libani*; *columnas ejus fecit argenteas, reclinatorium aureum, ascensum purpureum*). See West (1954, pp. 176–182).
10. Fleg (1959, p. 8). Fleg writes that Solomon was "alternately a wise man, or a fool, prince or beggar, philosopher, master of the demons or their dupe, at once the pattern of faith and humility, and a monster of impiety and arrogance; warrior, tyrant, or apostle of peace, in whom already the justice of the Messiah is incarnate". And to all these, one can add that the legendary Solomon was a philosopher, the author of many books, a great builder, a just judge, an alchemist, astrologer, horseman, and more.
11. 1 Kings 5:5–15, 9:2–9, and parallels in 1 Chronicles 29. Origen stressed that as these revelations occurred in a dream, they were different than the communication between Jesus and God. See Young (2007, p. 134).

but in the next world as well".[12] The course of his life was likened to that of the moon, waxing full and subsequently waning, and came to represent various existential, theological, and moral questions, as well as the blurred boundaries between philosophy and faith, magic, and natural philosophy.

The Hebrew Bible does not present Solomon purely as an exemplar, but also as one who sinned and led others to sin, his reign simultaneously a golden age and a prelude to a schism within the nation. Hence the ambivalent attitude towards Solomon in Jewish and Christian cultures, and why his biography has long been the subject of a theological and philosophical debate touching on issues of sin, punishment, and atonement. The Solomon depicted in aggadic *Midrashim*, in Christology, in sermons, and in theology differs from the Solomon of occult literature and various genres of "secular" literature. One may well refer to him in the plural; he was a "Solomon for all seasons". Yet it seems to me that the widespread attempt to find hidden meaning in every Solomonic verse, and deliberate inter-textuality in every sentence, is often excessive. At least some of the *Midrashim*, legends, and folklore about him are simply an outcome of *Lust zum fabulieren*—that is, the urge to amuse and be amused, which discovered in Solomon an unparalleled protagonist.

***

The correspondence between Jesus and Solomon apparently grew out of the story about the Queen of Sheba—who came from the "uttermost parts of the earth to Jerusalem to hear the wisdom of Solomon and behold, something greater than Solomon is here".[13] The "something greater than Solomon" is Jesus, who is also, in the people's appeals to him as a healer of the sick and exorcist of devils, referred to as "the son of David". Perhaps this is the origin of Jesus' description as "the true Solomon" by Athanasius (c. 296–373), the bishop of Alexandria known as the "father of orthodoxy", in his work *Expositiones in Psalmos*.[14] Origen (c. 185–254) wrote in the prologue to his *Commentary on the Song of Songs* that "It is, I think, unquestionable that Solomon is in many respects a type of Christ" (*typos Christi*);[15] others offered similar sentiments.[16] The Solomon-Christ typology—that

---

12. From the *Second Targum to the Book of Esther*, a collection of *midrashim* in Aramaic evidently from the eighth century. See Grossfeld (1994). For a modern German translation see Ego (1996, pp. 59–137).
13. Matthew 12:42; Luke 11:30–31.
14. Hanig (1998). See also Perkins (1998).
15. Origen (1957, p. 51).
16. The Dominican friar Lorens of Orleans, who served in French royal court,

is, the Christian predilection to view the figure of Solomon through the lens of Jesus, and even more so vice versa—made Solomon a vital figure in the Christian polemic; this predilection was rooted in the fact that Christianity, like Second-Temple Judaism, was a text-based religion and, like Judaism, drew upon the same inexhaustible wellspring[17]—the Bible, which in Christianity came to be termed the Old Testament—as a sacred textual authority.[18] This exegetical reading of the Bible played an important role in the shaping and self-definition of both rabbinical Judaism[19] and nascent Christianity, a process during which the boundaries between the two were delineated. On the Christian side, that process involved the appropriation of the Bible, with an argument that the role of Judaism was obsolete once Jews completed their historical task of passing the Bible to the Christians. Jews had once been, in the words of Augustine of Hippo, *custodes librorum nostrorum* ("custodians of our books"); that task was now accomplished. Christianity regarded itself as a "new covenant", deprecating its predecessor: "And what is obsolete and growing old will soon disappear".[20] But in order to be "new", Christianity had to imbue the Old Testament with new meaning, for Christianity's newness was only partial. Its God was the biblical God, and its cosmogony and history derived from the holy scriptures of the Jews—in other words, from the Old Testament. Hence the new religion turned to polemics and apologetics[21] to legitimize the use it made of that heritage. In the apologetics of the bishop Ambrose (c. 339–397) of Milan, for example, Christianity is depicted as having received "the clothing of the Old Testament", including "the royal Davidic clothing" and that of King Solomon; it was given to the Christians, who "would know how to use the garment they had received, since the Jewish people kept it without using it and did not know its proper adornments. This clothing was lying in shadow, cast off and forgotten [...] The Christian people put it on, and it shone brightly".[22] In truth, Christianity borrowed far more

wrote in *Somme le Roi* (The Book of Vices and Virtues, 1270), a book intended to help prepare penitents for confession: "These are the seven streams of the holy life that the true Solomon teaches us".

17. The New Testament contains about a thousand quotations from the Hebrew Bible.

18. Paul writes to Timothy: "Until I arrive, give attention to the public reading of scripture, to exhorting, to teaching…" (1 Tim. 4:13).

19. There is such an abundance of research literature on this subject that I will mention here only one recently published book: *The Invention of Judaism*: *Torah and Jewish Identity from Deuteronomy to Paul* (Collins 2017).

20. Hebrews 8:13.

21. On the difference between polemic, dispute, and debate, see Rokeah (1982, pp. 9–10).

22. *De Jacob et Vita beata*, 2,9,2 ("On Jacob and the Happy Life"). In Saint Am-

than a garment from the Bible and from Jewish culture of the Second Temple period: it absorbed and assimilated ideas, symbols, and rituals. As a "new" religion, it needed to construct and furnish a social and cultural structure, and to do so it borrowed many elements, primarily from Judaism, from which it had emerged and which it knew very well.[23] Thus, while Judaism was reshaping its world in the aftermath of the destruction of the Second Temple, it found that the Bible had been "appropriated" by others, and responded by creating and developing its ways of reading the text.[24] While the Church Fathers and their successors unreservedly accepted the Bible's historical accuracy and added few details of their own to Solomon's biography, the Jewish Sages frequently made additions to biblical lore (thus "confirming" the Christian polemic that "the Talmud nefariously deviated from the Bible and competed with it".[25] Rabbinic Judaism did not adhere to the "letter" in the literal sense of the word but instead saw "well beyond the veil of the letter"—partly in response to Christian exegesis and commentaries. The two camps contended over true "ownership" of the Bible and over which of them interpreted it correctly. This was a polemic at once overt and covert; it could not have existed if both sides had not held firmly to their belief in the sanctity and authority (*exousia*) of the Bible and were not both using similar strategies of intertextuality and *post-factum* argument in order to prove their case. In other words, each camp brandished supposedly overwhelming proof for its claim in the form of quotations from the Holy Scriptures. For the Christian side, it was essential to prove that the decisive evidence of Jesus' gospel, the *demonstratio evangelica*, existed in the Old Testament, while the Jewish side rejected such alleged evidence and even mocked it. Pagan philosophers, as we shall see,[26] also contested these narratives—both Christian and Jewish—but the Jewish disagreement was the greater challenge for Christianity throughout the ages.

The parallel development and historical relationship between Judaism and Christianity over the first centuries C.E. are well-known; I have nothing new to add here. My interest lies instead in the roles that Solomon was assigned in both Jewish and Christian traditions as part of the "correspondence" between them,[27] and in how and why the

brose (1972).

23. On this matter, too, the research literature is far too abundant to cite more than a small portion of it. And so, I mention only one book from which I learned a great deal: *Biblical Exegesis and the Formation of Christian Culture* (Young 2002).

24. Pelikan (2005).

25. On this, see *inter alia* Yuval (2008) and Cohen (1999, pp. 59–60).

26. In Athens, Paul was challenged by several philosophers from the Epicurean and Stoic schools but persuaded only a few in the audience (Acts 17).

27. Torijano (2002, pp. 113–114).

conflict of Jesus contra Solomon arose in Christianity. This conflict was waged both orally and in writing; Justin Martyr (c. 100–165),[28] for example, wrote that "select [Jewish] messengers" went forth from Jerusalem to denounce the Christians.[29] Works such as Justin's *Dialogue with Tryphon* and *The Dialogue of Timothy and Aquila*,[30] probably from the second century or later, are "dialogues" in which a Christian speaker defeats his Jewish interlocutor (Aquila is eventually baptized into Christianity).[31] Other early polemic works included the *Epistle to Diognetus* (c. 120–200) and the *Epistle of Barnabas* (between 70–200), as well as homilies by the Church fathers such as Tertullian's (c. 120–160)[32] *Answer to the Jews*, John Chrysostom's *Homilies Against the Jews* (387–389), and various works by Augustine of Hippo (354–430).[33] Horbury writes that these "seem to reflect genuine debate, and hence genuine common ground between Jews and Christians."[34] In some of these writings, particularly in the dialogues I have mentioned, Solomon and the books attributed to him play a major role.[35]

In contrast, we have no Jewish polemical works at all from the first centuries C.E., nor any echoes of sermons that may have been delivered in synagogues. Instead, the Jewish response and counter-biography of Jesus appears both within the text and between the lines of the literature of the Sages,[36] and, more explicitly, in later works against Christianity such as *Toldot Yeshu* (The Life of Jesus)[37] and *Sefer Nestor haKomer* (The Polemic of Nestor the Priest).[38] Jewish litera-

---

28. Justin Martyr (2003).

29. Acts 15 speaks of "certain individuals [who] came down from Judea".

30. Varner (2004); *The Dialogue of Timothy and Aquila* (1986). Also see Kraft (2009) and Lahey (2001).

31. Of the vast literature on this subject, see Lucas (1993 [1910]); Parkes (1934); A. L. Williams (1935); Limor and Stroumsa (1966); Rosenthal (1960); Lasker (1997, 2017, 2019); V. Martin (1995).

32. Tränkle (1964). To prove his claim that the Christians had taken over from the Jews as the people of God, he cites Zechariah 1:3 "Return to me, says the LORD of hosts".

33. Rokeah (1980, pp. 55–87).

34. Horbury (1998, p. 201).

35. The fact that there is hardly any mention of Jews in *Historia Ecclesiastica* (Rokeah 1982, p. 71) does not mean that the "Jewish question", in contrast to the "pagan question", was not an important item on the Christian "agenda" in the first centuries.

36. Schäfer (2016).

37. Regarding this book, apparently written between the third and fifth centuries and translated into several languages, see Deutsch (1997) and Schäfer, Meerson, and Deutsch (2011). For a scholarly edition of all these versions, see Meerson and Schäfer (2014). Also see Limor (1998a).

38. Originally written in Arabic in the ninth century under the title *Qissat Mu-*

ture openly sparred with the Christian historical narrative and Christology from the eleventh century onward. This literature included *The Kuzari* by Judah Halevi (c. 1040–1080), *Sefer Bitul Ikarei haNotzrim* by R. Ḥasdai Crescas of the fifteenth century,[39] *Sefer Behinat haDat* by R. Elijah Delmedigo (1490),[40] *Clipeus et Gladius* by Judah Arye of Modena (1571–1648),[41] and others. The polemic continued even after Christianity became the victorious religion and no longer needed to compete with Judaism; even then, the homiletic interpretation of the Bible persisted in order to vindicate "Christian truth" (*veritas Christiana*). Many explanations have been offered for Christianity's continued dependence on the Bible even after it ceased to be merely a persecuted sect and, having established a separate identity, developed into a universal religion; there is no need for me here to repeat those explanations and theories. For our purposes, what matters is that Christianity's adherence to the allegorical mode of reading the Bible made Solomon a cardinal figure in the Christian imagination.

It should be noted that the different characterizations of Solomon (and Jesus) are not merely a product of the Christian-Jewish conflict, but also of controversies and trends internal to both rabbinical Judaism and Christianity (controversies which, in the latter case, did not end with the Council of Nicaea). Nor was each religion's attitude towards Solomon and Jesus always, or necessarily, a response to their characterizations in the other religion, or a result of the influence of those characterizations. As we shall see, Solomon and the events and writings attributed to him inspired a cornucopia of interpretation and allegorization. His reign was perceived as both a positive and a negative exemplum, and the idea of Jesus' prefiguration in Solomon aroused substantial internal tension and controversy among both Jews and Christians.

Such dialogues and polemics were not conducted solely between Jews and Christians, but also between pagans and Christians. This latter type continued for about three hundred years; we know of it mainly from the surviving account in Eusebius's *Praeparatio Evangelica* of the writings of the "pagan" philosophers, which do not necessarily reflect the nature of the response of the general pagan public to Christianity. Celsus, Porphyry, and the emperor Julian were appar-

---

jadalat al-Usquf; the Hebrew version appeared prior to 1170. About the book and its author, see Chapter Two.

39. Crescas (c. 1340–1412) was the rabbi of the Jewish community of Saragossa; the book was translated into Hebrew from Arabic by Joseph ben Shem Tov in 1451. See Ḥasdai Crescas (1990).

40. Delmedigo (1984).

41. Arye Yehuda of Modena (1960).

ently well-versed in the Bible and in Christian writings (just as some of the Church Fathers were knowledgeable about anti-Christian writings). They also criticized the Old Testament, as it formed the basis for Christian claims, and exposed what they saw as the contradictions in both the Bible and the Christian interpretations thereof, including Christianity's interpretation of the figure of Solomon.

***

Within the broad trans-cultural space of Christianity Jesus gained immortality, as well as a totally different status than that of Solomon. The New Testament attributes several identities to him. He is the "son of Enos, son of Seth, son of Adam, son of God";[42] the "Rabbi, the Cosmic Christ, the Son of man, the Bridegroom of the Soul, the Universal man".[43] But he is also a teacher of morals, a miracle worker, and an expeller of demons. Canonical Christian literature did not embroider Jesus' biography with additional acts or exploits beyond those related in the New Testament; what additions did develop emerged in the Apocryphal and pseudo-Apocryphal literature and in folk literature. At the same time, Christianity was familiar with Jesus' counter-biography in rabbinic literature and with the name by which he is known there (Jesus ben Pantera); there are reactions to the rabbinical approach in Tertullian's *De Spectaculis*, as well as in works by Justin Martyr and others. In later generations, Christians knew of it from works such as *Toldot Yeshu* (*The Life of Jesus*), which we encountered briefly above and to which I shall return. The Christian polemic was directed against the Talmud, which it perceived as *id est doctrina*. Article 26 of the *Articuli litterarum Pappe*, a series of charges against Judaism written in 1239 by the convert Nicolas Donin and presented to Pope Gregory IX, is a reaction to *Sanhedrin* 43a, in which Christ's mother is said to have conceived Jesus "while whoring with a man they called Pandera"; Donin's charge led to the burning of the Talmud in Paris in 1242. Others, such as the Benedictine monk Petrus Cluniacensis (Petrus of Cluny) in *Contra perfidum Iudaeorum* (1146) and Petrus Comestor (?-1178) in his *Historia Scholastica*, which has been dubbed "the Medieval popular Bible", reacted in a similar manner.

***

How and why did a correspondence emerge between Aristotle and

---

42. Luke 3:23–38.

43. Pelikan (1999); Fredriksen (2000). There are no folk tales about Jesus like the ones about Solomon. On the "Jewish Jesus", see Garber (2001). And about Jesus in Islam, see Khalidi (2001); Parrinder (2013); and Akyol (2017).

Solomon—or, to be more accurate, between Solomon and Aristotle—and how did Jesus enter the mix?[44]

In the Middle Ages, Aristotle gained the status of the most learned and wisest man of all time—the very personification of all human knowledge. Did he, therefore, take Solomon's place as the "sage of all sages"? The answer may be found in a Jewish legendary tradition wherein Solomon was *magister omnium physicorum* (master of all natural things), his wisdom encompassing all branches of philosophy and science—and in which he was presented as a teacher to the Greek philosopher. This tradition first appeared in the thirteenth century, after Aristotle's writings were translated into Latin and became the basis of Christian Scholasticism and Thomism in the West, as well as an authoritative source for Christianity's worldview and understanding of the universe. The acceptance of Aristotelian philosophy (here we must distinguish between the acceptance of Aristotle's logic, metaphysics, ethics, and natural philosophy) evoked a piercing polemic in Judaism and Christianity, as it had earlier in Islam; theologians and philosophers in all three faiths were divided between Aristotelians and anti-Aristotelians. Against this background emerged the tradition of Solomon as Aristotle's teacher and of their wisdom as the product of natural wisdom; the spheres of knowledge in which Solomon engaged were now defined according to Aristotelian categories.

For Solomon to fill the role of "Aristotle's teacher", it was necessary for the idea of Solomonic wisdom to encompass both "occult wisdom" and comprehensive knowledge of what was then known as natural philosophy, or science. Thus, medieval and later traditions held that he was well-versed in all branches thereof, and the three books attributed to him were perceived as conveying views about the order and structure of the world that predated scientific or pseudo-scientific theories.

The legend that Aristotle studied with Solomon was intended to affirm and bolster such theories and grant them legitimacy and prestige. In this context, Solomon is one of the ancient wise men representing *prisca sapientia*—the wisdom of old, its antiquity a testament to its truth. It sufficed merely to mention his name, quote from his books, or ascribe aphorisms to him in order to endow a newer opinion with authority (in the words of Tertullian: "*Primam instrumentis istis auctoritatem summa antiquitas vindicate*"—"Supreme antiquity, then, claims for these books the highest authority").[45] In Solomon's case, this wisdom was either a gift from God, inspiration from the heavens,

---

44. On the various versions of Aristotle's biography, see Natali (2013), And see at length in Chapters Seven and Eight.

45. Tertullian (1984, pp. 92–93).

or a personal quality.

And what about Jesus and Aristotle?—for generations Aristotle continued to represent "philosophy" in Jewish internal polemics; this was true even after the sixteenth century, when Aristotle, Christianized Aristotelianism, and Aristotelian science were dethroned. In contrast, in its engagement with philosophy and the sciences and in its attitude towards Aristotle, from the twelfth century onward Christian scholasticism had no need to depend on the legendary story in order to ground its legitimacy in Solomon's wisdom or in legends of his teaching Aristotle, the *praecursor Christi* (precursor of Christ) and to become both *Aristoteles judaicus* and *Aristoteles christianus*.

From the "Jewish" standpoint, one might say that the legendary tradition in question closed an imaginary circle, since it claimed that Christian Scholasticism and medieval Jewish philosophy would never have come into being without the challenge and influence of Aristotelian philosophy—which was, of course, born of the wisdom of Solomon, King of Israel, whose writings Aristotle read and absorbed. (Jesus was not considered to have authored any texts). However, because this Jewish tradition ascribed to Solomon the authorship of a large pseudo-Solomonic literary corpus, apparently as a response to the existing pseudo-Aristotelian corpus[46] (but could only enumerate the names of the books, and not relate their content), the result was the creation of an imaginary Solomon as a counterpart to Aristotle—that is, Solomon as a philosopher and scientist, *a magister omnium physicorum* representing *sapientia*, *scientia*, and *intelligentia*.[47]

And is it convincible that Aristotle, like Solomon, was both an occultist and sinner? Well, as we shall see, at the margins of this correspondence, both Solomon and Aristotle's experiences with women—experiences that would lead to loss and humiliation for both,[48] and around the first century C.E. the imaginary Solomon became well-versed in the secrets of esoterica and, like Jesus, was attributed the power to heal the sick and exorcise demons. Aristotle too was said to deal in occultism, especially in the field of alchemy, which seeks ways to convert metals by transmutation. This belief emerged because of the putative similarity between that study and Aristotle's theory of the four elements, even though in his *Meteorology*, Aristotle described alchemy as a fantasy; the claim was that later in life Aristotle changed his mind.[49] Plutarch tells that "It would appear, moreover, that Alex-

---

46. On this corpus, see Thorndike (1964, pp. 246–278). I will return to this corpus in Chapter Eight.
47. Yates (1984).
48. See Chapter One.
49. For example, Petrus Bonus' *The Precious New Pearl* (*Pretiosa Margarita*

ander not only received from his master [Aristotle] his ethical and political doctrines, but also participated in those secret and more profound teachings which philosophers designate by the special terms 'acromatic' and 'epoptic', and do not impart to many".[50] According to Plutarch, Aristotle wrote—and published—esoteric writings, which, in Alexander's view, should not become public. The philologist, theologian, and critic of Aristotle's writing John Philoponus of Alexandria (c. 570–1198) asserted that Aristotle believed in demons.

Various apocryphal writings such as the *Secretum Secretorum* (Secret of Secrets) were attributed to Aristotle, yet the canonical and most widely-accepted view rejected the idea that he dealt in "esoteric doctrines".[51] Maimonides wrote of a book entitled *Istimachis* and attributed by others to Aristotle, though he hastened to add that "[Aristotle] can by no means have been its author";[52] the medieval philosopher and kabbalist Rabbi Moses ben Naḥman (Naḥmanides, 1194–1270) described Aristotle, "may his name be obliterated", as an obdurate rationalist because he rejected the existence of "demons and witches" and the like, and denied "spirituality"—while in contrast the wisdom of Solomon, the wisest of men, did encompass sorcery.[53] Roger Bacon (1215–1294), whose empirical approach to scientific discovery was influenced by Aristotle (*De Scientia Experimentali*), did his best to refute what he termed the *vanitas* of magic and its attribution to Moses, Solomon, Hermes, and Aristotle, as well as the authenticity of several apocryphal books about astrology that were credited to the latter.[54] Doctor Faustus, in Marlowe's play of that name, wonders whether to "live and die in Aristotle's works"— that is, whether to adhere to scientific thinking or to prefer Solomon's wisdom—the wisdom of magic—which rendered its possessor a kind of demi-god; or, alternatively, to adopt the wisdom of Solomon-Ecclesiastes, who discovered late in life that all study is the vanity of vanities?[55] The belief in occult powers—especially in astral magic (which

Novella). See Thorndike (1964, Vol. 3, pp. 147–162). Bonus was a late medieval alchemist; his book was first printed in Venice in 1546.

50. Plutarch (1958, Vol. 7, p. 241; 1973, p. 259).

51. See Chapter Seven.

52. Maimonides (1904, 3:29). The French-Jewish scholar Salomon Munk wrote that the book deals with the subject of magic; he added that in Moriz Steinschneider's view, the name of the book is a distortion of the Greek expression *stoicheiomatikos*–"an astrologist reading a horoscope". See Maimonides (2002), note 51 on p. 527.

53. Cited in Dov Schwartz (2004b), or Dov Schwartz (2005) for the English edition.

54. On these books, see Thorndike (1964, pp. 246–278). On Abraham Ibn Ezra (1089–1164) see Sela (1999), or Sela (2003) for the English edition.

55. See Hattaway (1968), pp. 499–530.

requires a knowledge of astronomy)—was perceived as an alternative to Aristotelian physics and rationalism,[56] and the imaginary trio, therefore, represented the blurred boundaries between "science" and "magic" until the seventeenth century.[57]

I do not intend to deal with the history of these texts, but rather how the texts impressed their readers. Nor, again, will I attempt to paint a complete picture of the pseudo-Solomonic or pseudo-Aristotelian corpora, for the book does not purport to be a collection of the depictions of Solomon, Aristotle, or Jesus, or of their countless representations in theological studies, *midrashim*, legends, sermons, *belles lettres*, and folklore. It touches briefly upon weighty themes such as the Jewish-Christian polemic,[58] the essence of magic and its place in Judaism and in Christianity, and the link between magic and science—but only to the degree to which these themes are reflected in the correspondence between the three figures in our trio. The few citations noted here from Islamic tradition do not reflect the extent of Solomon's status within it.

***

The underlying assumptions that directed my reading of the texts, and those at which I arrived after concluding my research, are as follows. First, appearances and representations of Solomon, Aristotle, and Jesus must be evaluated within the broad context of the array of texts contemporary to those representations. In quite a few cases, scholars dealing with the different instances of a tradition, a theme, a motif, or an image tend to assign status or value to the topic of their research without weighing it with other traditions, themes, motifs, and images of the same period. Second, the Solomon who emerged from sermons, *belles lettres*, legends, and folktales had a far more substantial presence than did the Solomon of theological or philosophical writings, which were known only to a limited circle. Third, the texts cited in this book are not representative of the whole of "Judaism" or of "Christianity", and not only because most of the cited Christian sources come from Western (i. e., Roman Catholic) Christianity. Hence, I claim neither that the texts cited here had a formative status in Jewish and Christian cultures, nor that most texts cited here, or their contents, were known to or understood by a large audience. Fourth, there is no doubt that at least part of what I describe as a "correspondence" between the three is the fruit of my creative imagination, and that at

56. On this, see Schwartz (2004a, 2004b, 2005).
57. See Greg (2015). Greg does not, however, deal with Solomon.
58. It suffices to mention two out of numerous books: Merchavia (1970) and Kraus (1995).

times I find correspondence in places where it does not exist. However, it is precisely the retrospective reading of texts that gives rise to today's comparative research literature examining the various presentations of Solomon in Judaism, Christianity, and Islam, and only from a later perspective can one argue for the existence of such a correspondence. Fifth, Solomon's biography has a monogenesis in the Old Testament Urtext, from which it developed into various branches. But in many cases, particularly when the ancient world is involved, it is difficult to reconstruct the way that stories and motifs developed, largely because much of the literature written in that time period has been lost. Hence, I have not attempted to reconstruct the often-circuitous ways in which themes and motifs were transmitted between cultures, texts, and versions; these transmissions often have missing links that can only be filled in by hypothesis. It is possible to perceive in Solomon a case study in the similarity, proximity, and affiliation between Judaism, Christianity, and Islam, expressed in the mutual flow of ideas between them and in the similar status they accorded their holy texts and exegetical methods. However, it is important to recall that similarity in terms of theological and philosophical inquiry, themes, motifs, and exegetical approach may not in itself create affinity, and certainly not affiliation, but may lead instead to hostility and competition.

***

During the rather long period in which I was writing this book, the body of research on nearly every one of the aspects mentioned above continued to expand[59] and to build upon the literature written on the subject throughout the twentieth century. Some of these works also discuss the imagined encounter between the three, and from these, I have learned much. Although a great deal of the material in this new research was already known to me, I see fit to mention it since on several matters at least it has expanded my horizons and my knowledge and referred me to many new sources. My hope is that, even after all that has been researched and written, this book may be of interest to the reader, and perhaps contribute a few new insights of its own.

---

[59] Among these books and articles, I will mention only some of the several that were published recently: Klein-Braslavy (2007); Sasson (2013), which is a comprehensive study on the figure of Solomon in the literature of the Sages; M. Bloch (1925); Verheyden (2013a); Shalev-Eyni (2006); Milstein (1995); Vanning (2002); Nitsche (2017).

Chapter One: Biographies Correspond

"He was from the beginning worthy to be a king in this world
And he shall be worthy in the world to come"
   - The Second Targum to Esther, II.

When King Solomon emerged from the pages of the Bible, he became the Solomon of legend—one of three figures (together with Moses and David) endowed with biographies in both biblical and post-biblical literature.[1]

Jewish literary culture, which developed under the influence of Hellenistic culture and consequently expanded to adopt new literary genres, was in search of a hero; in Solomon, it found one. Nor was Jewish culture alone in embracing him as a cultural hero: Solomon, mainly on the wings of legend, was destined to transcend borders of culture and of time. But this book deals with a trio, and, indeed, the lives of Aristotle and Jesus would expand similarly over time. Aristotle's status as a scholar and philosopher, his vast bibliography, and his connections with Alexander the Great inspired numerous biographies and pseudo-biographies; and, in apocryphal and pseudo-apocryphal literature, the life of Jesus took on new and varied forms beyond those depicted in the New Testament.[2] This great abundance of legends, and the versatile roles attributed to these three figures, made possible the correspondence that would develop between them.

Solomon's reign lasted between 967 and 928 B.C.E.—a period of nearly forty years[3]—and his biblical biography speaks at length of

---

   1. A ruler whose timeless and transcultural renown approaches Solomon's to some extent is Alexander the Great. See, among others Cary (1956); Royce Moore (2018) and Boardman (2019).

   2. See, for example, the *Protoevangelium of James and the Gospel of Pseudo-Matthew* (Infancy Gospel of Matthew).

   3. 1 Kings 11:23. According to Biblical historian, his main source was "the book of the acts of Solomon" ("Now the rest of the acts of Solomon, all that he did as well as his wisdom, are they not written in the Book of the Acts of Solomon?", 1 Kings 11:41).

his greatness, of the richness of international trade with his kingdom under his rule, of the patterns of his reign and administration, and, first and foremost, of his construction of the Temple. It is notable that no contemporaneous extra-biblical sources, however, make mention of his actions or his name.

The Bible provides Solomon with two parallel biographies. The first, and earliest, version of the story is given in 1 Kings 1–11. A second version appears in 1 Chronicles 8–29-2 Chronicles 1–15,[4] focusing on Solomon's glory and on the construction of the Temple while omitting the shadows that "would eclipse his kingdom". Beyond the pages of the Bible, versions of Solomon's life abound.

The profusion of appellations that have accrued to Solomon also attests to his status.[5] The prophet Nathan called Solomon *Yedidiah* ("Friend to the Lord");[6] the *Midrash* refers to him as *Kohelet*,[7] *Etiel* ("God is with me" because the spirit of God lay upon him), and *Yikhat*.[8] Rabbi Simeon ben Yoḥai, a Tannaitic sage, maintained that Solomon was one of three *tzadikim* (righteous ones), together with Isaac and Joshua, whose name was given to them by the Almighty himself ("Of Solomon, what does it say? Here a son has been born unto you, he will be a man of rest, and I have rested from all my enemies around me, for Solomon will be his name, and I will give peace and quiet to Israel in his days").[9] In Christian writings, his Latin name, *Salomon*, was also translated as *Pacificus*—a maker, or bringer, of peace; in Muslim literature, his name is *Suleiman*, and sometimes *Salim*.[10]

Few doubted the veracity of Solomon's biblical biographies prior to the nineteenth century.[11] One of the arguments put forth as evidence

---

4. On this matter, see Throntveit (1997) and Frisch (1991).
5. Stamm (1960).
6. 2 Samuel 12:24–25.
7. *Ecclesiastes Rabbah* 1:1; *Song of Songs Rabbah* 1:1.10.
8. Yik'hat yamim, Genesis 49:10; Ecclesiastes Rabbah 1:1.10.
9. *Mekhilta Pisha* 16 (Horovitz–Rabin, Jerusalem, 1960, pp. 59–60). According to the *Second Targum of Esther*, Solomon was called *ben* [son] "because he built the temple of the Lord". The translator understood the Aramaic word ben not as son but as 'built' [bana].
10. As with the names of biblical figures such as Moses, David, Elijah, and more, the name Solomon was not common as a given name among the Sages; like the others, it became more common in Jewish culture only c. 900 C.E.
11. In recent decades, research has emerged questioning the accepted tradition of the Hasmonean Revolt. In this new research, Solomon is described as a "Hebrew-speaking" Alexander the Great; it argues that the biblical tradition regarding Solomon emerged during the Hasmonean period and that his portrayal is based on that of the Macedonian king. T. L. Thompson (1999, pp. 202, 206) claims that the stories about a "Croesus-like" Solomon are not "about history at all, and that to treat them as if they were history is to misunderstand them". This notion may have been inspired by the description of Solomon as a "Hellenistic king" in Josephus' *Antiquities*. See Amir

of his historicity was that the patterns of rule and administration that characterized his kingdom, as described in great detail in the Bible, were modeled on those of the Egyptian kingdom;[12] some biographers even claimed to know the name of the daughter of Pharaoh that he took as his wife, or the locations of the various lands to which his fleet sailed. Another, more skeptical group, believed that these were simply various historical traditions that had, over the course of generations, undergone various stages of composition, compilation, and editing until their eventual collation into a single unit, perhaps after the destruction of the Temple.[13] Who, then, were the creators and composers of those traditions, and what guided them? One theory is that Solomon's biography in 1 Kings was composed in two main stages, in each case with entirely different goals. The early version, composed in the ninth century B.C.E., or before the end of the seventh, idealizes Solomon as a ruler and depicts his reign as the golden age of a great kingdom—of an empire, really—its capital large and fortified with a magnificent temple at its heart. The other version, written while Judah was weakened or after its destruction, presents Solomon as the *topos* of a sinful king, personally responsible for the destruction of Judah, Jerusalem, and the Temple. This version, then, was the creation of opponents of the renewed kingdom.[14] This hypothesis assumes an early text written as royal propaganda, to which a later author—or authors—added their own subversive, anti-monarchic take; it assumes further that readers of the new version could distinguish between it and its predecessor, and understand the subtext and its message.

Regardless of the course of its development, Solomon's biblical biography, at least part of which is itself legend, is the fertile soil from which numerous and varied legendary traditions have sprung forth, evolved, and merged, traveling tirelessly across cultures and across eras. This phenomenon raises several issues fundamental to the history of traditions as a field of study (*Traditionsgeschichte*): the identity of the primary sources of these legends; in what context and for what purposes they were created; in what manner they were disseminated; why and how they were absorbed in such disparate environments; and what roles and significance they assumed in the receiving environ-

(1968); Feldman (1976, 1997); and Verheyden (2003b).

12. Ash (1999); Brueggemann (2005); Weitzman (2011).

13. Torijano (2002, pp. 8–25).

14. See van Keulen (2004); Isaac Kalimi (2012, 2019); Frisch (1991); Finkelstein (2006; pp. 121–150, 175–208). This analysis of the two-stage composition of Solomon's biography raises the question as to why the editor or editors retained the earlier version. A discussion of this point, however, is beyond the purview of this book. On the hypothesis that the story developed in various stages, see Nadav Na'aman (2017, 2018).

ments and within the frameworks of various literary genres.

No wars or momentous upheavals marked Solomon's lengthy reign. In their absence, his biblical biography describes his supreme wisdom, his marriage to a thousand women, the famous "Judgment of Solomon" in which the fate of a child hung in the balance, and the no less famous visit of the Queen of Sheba; these evocative narratives proved fertile soil for the eventual emergence of Solomon's legendary biography. At the same time, his biblical biography comprises not only his life story but also the books of the Bible he is said to have authored: The Song of Songs, Proverbs, and Ecclesiastes, and Psalms 72 and 127. The very first words of the Song of Songs are "The Song of Songs, which is Solomon's"; Proverbs opens with "The proverbs of Solomon the son of David, king of Israel";[15] and Ecclesiastes offers "the words of the Preacher (*Kohelet*), son of David, king in Jerusalem", later proclaiming "I, the Preacher, was king over Israel in Jerusalem".[16] The attribution of these three texts to Solomon made it possible to embroider upon his biography and his persona, and to endow him with a variety of opinions on the nature of life and the relationship between humanity and God. A vast exegetical and *midrashic* literature took shape around the theme, expanding and sculpting his biography with new detail and revolving primarily around the "autobiographical" accounts found in Ecclesiastes and the Song of Songs. His literary output was similarly augmented: countless additional books were ascribed to his putative authorship, including *Sapientia Salomonis* (The Wisdom of Solomon), the *Psalms of Solomon*, the *Odes of Solomon*,[17] and others that have been lost over the centuries.

Solomon's biblical and legendary biographies became a topos of an ideal king—a *rex optimus*[18]—and simultaneously that of a king truly worthy of condemnation. These two conflicting aspects were summed up circa 180 B.C.E. by Ben Sira:[19]

> *Solomon, king in days of peace [[ ]] because God granted this to him by making the surrounding nations quiet.*
> *who established a house for his name [[ ]] and founded a sanctuary forever.*

---

15. Proverbs 1:1.

16. Ecclesiastes 1:1, 1:12.

17. The *Psalms of Solomon* date from the first century B.C.E., while the Odes consist of forty-two psalms from the turn of the second century; though like the Davidic psalms, they are attributed to Solomon. The literature on the subject is vast and I will mention only: Charlesworth (1985); Harris and Mingana (1916–1920); and R. B. Wright (2007).

18. Throntveit (1997).

19. Ben Sira lived in Jerusalem and wrote in Hebrew; his grandson would later translate his work into Greek.

> How wise you were in your youth [ ] For you overflowed as the Nile with instructions. The earth [ ] your [life] and you sang a heavenly song of pra[ise].
> in song, [parab]le, riddle, and proverb [[ ]] you astounded all peoples.
> You were called by the name of the glorious one, [[ ]] by which Israel was called and you amassed gold like iron [[ ]] and multiplied silver like lead.
> But you gave yourself in lust to women [[ ]] and handed over to them the rule of your body.
> And you [brou]ght corruption upon your glory [[ ]] and profaned your wedding bed wrath upon your descendants [[ ]] and regret to your deathbed.
> [ ] into two tribes [[ ]] and from Ephraim a kingdom of violence.[20]

In contrast, *2 Baruch*—written around the turn of the second century C.E.—was lavish in its account of the grandeur and glory of Solomon's reign, which it regarded as a model for the days of the Messiah:

> And the bright sixth waters which thru did see,
> This is the time [[in]] which David and Solomon were born.
> And there was at that time the building of Zion,
> And the dedication of the sanctuary,
> And the shedding of much blood of the nations that sinned then,
> And many offerings which were offered then in the dedication of the sanctuary.
> And peace and tranquility existed at that time,
> And wisdom was heard in the assembly:
> And riches of understanding were magnified in the congregations,
> And the holy festivals were fulfilled in blessedness and in much joy.
> And the judgment of the rulers was then seen to be guile,
> And the righteousness of the Mighty One was accomplished with truth.
> And the land [which] was beloved by the Lord,
> > And because its inhabitants sinned not, it was glorified beyond all land,
> > And the city Zion ruled then over all lands and regions.
> These are the bright waters which you have seen.[21]

To affirm Solomon's greatness as a statesman, Eupolemus, a Jewish Hellenistic historian and diplomat who headed Judah Maccabee's delegation to Rome in 161 B.C.E.,[22] cited "authentic" exchanges of let-

---

20. The existing Hebrew text of Ben Sira is fragmentary; instances where the translators have been obliged to guess at missing content remain unmarked in the quote above for legibility. See an original translation by Benjamin H. Parker and Martin G. Abegg: https://www.bensira.org/navigator.php?Manuscript=B&PageNum=33 (visited on October 1st 2019). See also M. Segal (1953); B. G. Wright (2013).

21. 2 Baruch 61:1–8. See Charles (1982 [1896]).

22. 1 Maccabees 8:17.

ters between Solomon and Vaphres (King of Egypt), and between Solomon and Souron (King of Tyre, identified with the biblical Hiram). In these letters Solomon demands that the King of Egypt immediately send him 80,000 laborers to build the Temple; his demand is met at once. He makes the same demand of the King of Tyre, who likewise accedes immediately and writes that he will furthermore contribute an architect to the undertaking.[23] Josephus, too, expanded Solomon's biography, adding new details.[24] He described Solomon as an "Oriental" king whose scores of horses were sprinkled with gold dust so that they might glitter on the Sabbath, and who rode in his carriage dressed all in white. Josephus compiled a long list of Solomon's sins—sins that would bring disaster upon Israel—and wrote: "But although Solomon was become the most glorious of kings, and the best beloved by God, and had exceeded in wisdom and riches [...]; yet did not he persevere in this happy state till he died. Nay, he forsook the observation of the laws of his fathers and came to an end no way suitable to our foregoing history of him. He grew mad in his love of women, and laid no restraint on himself in his lusts [...] and he transgressed the laws of Moses [...] He also began to worship [foreign] gods, which he did in order to the gratification of his wives [...]. Nay before this happened, he sinned, and fell into an error about the observation of the laws".[25]

Within the entire vast literary corpus of which Solomon is the protagonist there exist poems,[26] songs, and plays, but no epos; nor have I been able to locate more than one historical novel, which is in Yiddish.[27] This may be because Solomon's reign, relatively free of dramatic events, provided only a few motifs to inspire development; storytellers throughout the ages thus turned to the Song of Songs and Ecclesiastes in order to supply an inner world and a love story for his biography. The Sages dealt at length with Solomon's life,[28] but his legendary biography is scattered among many Aggadic *midrashim*; the only source that comes near to being a full biography is *Song of Songs*

---

23. Eusebius (2002, pp. 476–478), *Praeparatio Evangelica* IX, 30:5, 30:8); Josephus (1963, Vol. 8, pp. 50–57); Wacholder (1974, pp. 156–157); Bartlett (1985, pp. 65–69).

24. Thus, for example, Josephus wrote that Egyptian sources "confirmed" the fact that Solomon married a daughter of the Pharaoh (*Antiquities* VIII, 159).

25. *Ant*. VIII:7; See Verheyden (2013b, pp. 85–106); Feldman (1995).

26. *Tragische Könige*, for example, relates Solomon's life story in poetry and prose. Written by the Austrian poet Ludwig August Frankl Ritter von Hochwart (1810–1894) and published in Vienna 1876, it was translated into Hebrew by Shimon Bachrach in Budapest, 1881.

27. Sapir (1931).

28. Seligsohn (1925).

Rabbah.²⁹ Throughout the generations, Solomon appeared in various forms in the literature of the Sages, who employed him (and quoted from writings attributed to him) to convey their opinions on diverse matters. It is possible to view this invocation of "Solomon" as an indirect means adopted by the Sages to obscure their positions for and against various cultural and social phenomena and modes of behavior, including, for example, their own status in Jewish society, their attitude towards Hellenistic-Roman culture, and their reactions to Solomon's portrayal in Christian literature.³⁰

The Aggadic literature was dazzled by biblical descriptions of Solomon's wealth ("Judah and Israel were as numerous as the sand by the sea; they ate and drank and were happy";³¹ Solomon had "four thousand stalls for horses and chariots, and twelve thousand horsemen",³² in addition to a large fleet of ships that traded for valuable goods with far-off lands such as Ophir and Tarshish).³³ The legends seem to compete with each other as to which can add the most "color" to descriptions of Solomon's wealth. *Pesiqta deRab Kahana* reports that ten fat cattle and a large handsome fowl were placed daily upon his table,³⁴ while *The Second Targum of the Book of Esther* (Chapter One) relates that "demons and evil spirits were delivered under his control. Imps brought him all kind of fish from the sea and the fowl of the heavens together with the cattle and the wild beasts up to the slaugtherhouse".³⁵ *Yalkut Shimoni* assures us that "Solomon had forty thousand stables";³⁶ according to the *Tales of the Prophets* (a collection of Muslim legends from the Middle Ages) "Solomon's tables stretched for one mile, and he had a thousand cooks each of whom had a demon to help him slaughter cows and sheep, break up firewood

---

29. Neusner (1989, pp. 53–56).
30. Sasson (2003); Shimoff (1997).
31. 1 Kings 4:20.
32. 2 Chronicles 9:25–26.
33. 1 Kings 9:26–28, 10:1–11. Such words captured the imaginations of many who attempted to identify Ophir and Tarshish. Thus, for example, Spanish sailors dubbed an archipelago they reached in the Pacific in 1568 the "Solomon Islands".
34. *Pesiqta deRab Kahana* 6,1 (Mandelbaum 1962, pp. 113–114).
35. Grossfeld (1991). Also see p. 70 of *The Second Targum to Esther*: *The Zvi Cohen Edition*, 1991. See also Cassel (1888), which is a translation from Aramaic of a collection of Aggadic *midrashim*; and Ego (2001). Solomon was also "rich and powerful and acquired possessions, silver and gold in great abundance".
36. *Yalkut Shimoni on Kohelet*, § 967, 413. R. Hamah bar Haninah is quoted therein as saying: "Solomon's table was not lacking with beets in the summer and with cucumbers in the winter" (the *Yalkut* takes this quote from *Ecclesiastes Rabbah* 2,5 [Hirshman 2016, pp. 130, and Cohen (1939) for the translated edition], Ecclesiastes 5:6, and *Deuteronomy Rabbah* 1, 5, trans. J. Rabinowitz (1939)). In other words, costly, out-of-season vegetables were also served at Solomon's table.

and wash pots and pans. He had a thousand bakers, and in his kitchen were slaughtered every day thirty thousand head of camel, cattle, and sheep. The ascetics were seated on cushions of green silk, the genii on iron benches and the demons on benches of brass. The latter consumed nothing but aromas; and the birds ate wheat, barley, rice, beans, corn, millet, and lentils".[37] Even when Ibn Khaldūn, the great Muslim historian of the fourteenth century, expressed doubt on the veracity of the biblical accounts, he agreed that "in the days of Solomon, the Israelite state saw its greatest flourishing and their realm its widest extension". He was critical, however, of what he termed "nonsensical statements and untrue reports" that exaggerated Solomon's power and wealth (his army, for example, is described in 1 Kings 10:26 as numbering only 12,000 men, and his horses "only" 1,400).[38]

Solomon's life and deeds in these legendary traditions clashed with the image of the ideal king described in Deuteronomy: "… you may indeed set over you a king whom the LORD your God will choose. […] And he must not acquire wives for himself, or else his heart will turn away; also silver and gold he must not acquire in great quantity for himself".[39] On the contrary, the legendary tradition represented the very opposite ideal; it glorified Solomon's extravagant wealth and his royal conduct. Yet it was impossible for the creators of these legends to altogether overlook the negative aspects of his biography. As a result, his role in messianic prophecies was referred to indirectly under the general term "the house of David"; Solomon was not the *topos* of the ideal king, nor did he occupy an overt place in Jews' messianic hopes.

The Sages portrayed Solomon as an example of a great ruler's rise and fall; he, who once ruled over the earthly world and sat upon the "throne of God" would ultimately reign only over the "earthly realm". His fall occurred in stages: first, he reigned over the entire world, then over Jerusalem alone, and finally only over his own bed and his own scepter; even over his bed he was not truly a king, for "he feared the spirits". After his death, the power of the king in Israel waned, as the moon does after waxing.[40] Solomon, the Sages held, was "commoner and king, wise man and fool, prosperous and poor".[41] Due to this ambivalent attitude, the references in messianic visions are, as we have seen, to "the house of David" (*sukkat David*) and "a shoot

---

[37] Muḥammad ibn ʿAbd Allāh al-Kisāʾi (1997, p. 303); Abū Isḥāq Aḥmad ibn Muḥammad ibn Ibrāhīm al-Thaʿlabī (2002, p. 512).

[38] Ibn Khaldūn (1958, Vol. 1, p. 19).

[39] Deuteronomy 17:15–17.

[40] *Exodus Rabbah* 15,26 on Exodus 12:2.

[41] *Midrash Kohelet Rabbah* 1,12. See Hirshman (2016, p. 100). Also see Sasson (2003, pp. 163–173).

shall come out from the stump of Jesse, and a branch [...] out of his roots",[42] rather than to Solomon; in the pronouncement that "whoever contends against the sovereignty of the House of David deserves to be bitten by a snake",[43] it is unsurprising that David, rather than Solomon, represents an unimpeachable king.

Solomon's life of luxury is worlds away from Jesus' reply to a man who asked if he could inherit eternal life by observing only the first five commandments: "go, sell what you own, and give the money to the poor, and you will have treasure in heaven [...]".[44] It is no wonder that Augustine believed that Solomon's "prosperity, in fact, [...] did him more damage than his wisdom brought him profit".[45]

Christian theology would deal at length with Solomon's sins. It was true, St. Ambrose wrote, that a king was above the law, but Solomon sinned not only against the people but against God himself—a sin not forgiven to a king anointed by divine grace.[46] Solomon became a *topos* of a sinful king, and the question that resulted was whether he ultimately atoned for his sin, repented, and was absolved. John of Salisbury (c. 1115–1180), a theologian and philosopher who rose in 1176 to become bishop of Chartres, wrote in his book *Policraticus*— which dealt with the question of when a ruler might be regarded as a tyrant and justifiably be killed—that Solomon exemplified an upright king; his son Rehoboam, in straying from the straight path, strayed likewise from his father's teaching: "My child, if sinners entice you, do not consent".[47] John did not hold Solomon's great wealth against him; rulers were not forbidden riches but only avarice.[48] The Dutch poet and playwright Joost van Vondel (1587–1679) suggested a different take on the question in a five-act play titled "Salomon" (1648). In that play, Solomon is married to Sidonia, daughter of King Hiram of Tyre; he accedes to her request to build a temple to the goddess Astarte outside the walls of Jerusalem. Despite the protests of the people, he participates in the inauguration of the pagan temple and, in response to that sin, a great flood descends upon Jerusalem, causing the prophet Nathan to foresee the fracturing of the kingdom, the destruction of the Temple, and the exile to Babylonia. The play sees Solomon end his life an enfeebled and miserable king. Other works depicted him negatively as a king who became a limb of the Devil (*de magis curialium*), and

---

42. Isaiah 11:1.
43. *Sanhedrin* 110a.
44. Mark 10:21, Matthew 19:16–30, Luke 18:18–30.
45. City of God XVII:20, in Augustine (1984, p. 754). And see Chapter Four.
46. *Apologia prophetae David*, X.
47. Proverbs 1:10; Books III and V in John of Salisbury (2007). John refers to Aristotle as the "Prince of the Peripatetics".
48. Book IV in John of Salisbury (2007).

the iconoclastic Protestant Reformation employed him as the topos of an idolatrous king (while Hezekiah and Josiah were *topoi* of virtuous kings who destroyed the cults of idols and shrines).[49] In the anti-clerical and radical political views that prevailed in seventeenth-century England, Solomon was the model of a sinful king—a tyrant who inspired rebellion—and his marriages to foreign women were useful as a case in point for those opposed to the unions of English kings with foreign princesses.[50]

At the same time, both Christian cultures—whether in the Catholic West, in Byzantium,[51] or in Czarist Russia[52]—and the Muslim world[53] perceived Solomon as an exemplar of good ruler—a *rex optimus*, ruling with wisdom over a stable regime, a peacemaker, and a fair judge[54] (though David, and at times Hosea, were generally more esteemed). His kingdom was a model for the absence of the separation between Church and State (*sacerdotium and regnum*). Spinoza wrote that Solomon not only built the Temple but also established the rituals performed therein; he ruled absolute, in other words, on matters both sacred and civic.[55] Writings attributed to Solomon (and Aristotle) would inspire future conceptions of proper political conduct,

---

49. Aston (1993, p. 202).
50. Hill (1994, p. 69).
51. See Ville-Patlagean (1962).
52. Solomon was depicted as a model of supreme authority in Russian Orthodox religious literature, and as a hero in legendary tales that drew motifs from the Talmud. The sixteenth-century czar Boris Godunov supposedly wished to rebuild the Kremlin according to a model of Solomon's temple. See Raba (2014).
53. Muslim rulers associated themselves with Solomon and his throne, and their construction projects with his. Solomon, furthermore, appears frequently in Muslim iconography.
54. See Bose (1996) and Aston (1993, p. 38). The monk Notker Balbulus of St. Gall describes Solomon in his book *Gesta Karoli Magni* (884) as a wise king who served as a model for Charlemagne. He is furthermore lauded mainly as a great builder (such is his portrayal among the Freemasons). The bishop Isidore of Seville, in his *Historia Gothorum*, likened Sisebut, the seventh-century Visigoth king, to Solomon "the monarch, conqueror, and sage, who secured Israel's borders, united the twelve tribes, built a temple to God, and was known by his wisdom and eloquence". See J. Cohen (1999, p. 108). In the sixteenth century, Edward IV and Henry VII of England were depicted in paintings as Solomon, as was Philip II of France; the latter two were portrayed welcoming the Queen of Sheba (Henry by Hans Holbein and Philip by Lucas de Heere). A woodcut in John Foxe's *Acts and Monuments* (1583) shows Henry VIII in the guise of Solomon using Pope Clement as a footstool (See Brotton 2017, pp. 164–165). A book written in honor of the Ottoman Sultan Mehmed II ("The Conqueror") relates that the Topkapi palace in Istanbul once boasted a garden planted by the prophet Solomon. All these are only a sample of Solomon's extensive "appropriation" in many cultures.
55. Spinoza, Benedict (Baruch), *Tractatus Theologico Politicus* (1677, trans. Elwes [1883], pp. 245–257).

the violation of which was held to constitute a breach of the covenant with the people. When Locke, in his *Two Treatises of Government* (1679–1681), weighed the legitimacy of monarchy by inheritance, as well as the right of resistance to such rule, he referred not only to Aristotle's political philosophy but also to Solomon's personal example: "If Solomon," he wrote, "had a right to succeed his father, it must be by some other title than that of primogeniture."[56] Historical images, often passed down through literature, memorialized Solomon's reign as the golden age of the Israelite people. The Dutch philologist and jurist Petrus Cunaeus (1586–1638), for example, wrote in his book *De Republica Hebraeorum* (1617) that in the days of David and Solomon the Hebrew republic was at the height of its wealth; only after Solomon's death did it begin to decline.[57]

These ambivalent attitudes towards Solomon carried over into the modern age, as a few examples of his depictions in modern Hebrew literature will demonstrate. The first, dating from 1858, is "The Vision", a panegyric by the Jewish-Russian *maskil* Abraham Baer Gottlober (1810–1899) that expressed the Russian Jewish intelligentsia's attitude towards Czar Alexander II Solomon, in the poem, appears at Alexander's coronation and bestows the crown upon the new Czar's head; before doing so, he delivers a few words acknowledging the Jews living in Czarist Russia and their hopes for the new ruler. The poet foresees that the Czar will follow in Solomon's path:

> *Now you go his crown[58] to inherit*
> *And to fortify your kingdom on land and at sea*
> *You shall rush forth to the north, the south, the east, and the west*
> *You shall subdue and defeat all your opponents*
> *Every enemy and avenger shall you overthrow*
> *And banish from your land all conflict and war*
> *Affliction and evil will be ousted from your borders*
> *Only justice and peace shall dwell together*
>
> *Your people come to bow before you*
> *As they go, take heed to your way*
> *To do justice and act righteously…*[59]

In 1834, the *maskil* Wolf Meir published a German translation of Proverbs (but transliterated to Hebrew for Jewish readers). In the introduction, he wrote that Solomon, though spoiled since childhood, had erected marvelous structures and fashioned himself a throne of

---

56. Locke (1993, p. 67).
57. Cumaenus (2006, pp. 61–62).
58. The predecessor in question is Nicholas I.
59. Free translation of A. Gottlober (1858, p. 15).

gold-coated ivory. Lacking the ability to be content with little, he had built his kingdom not on a foundation of integrity and justice but on exploitation and marble columns. Solomon violated God's negative commandments ("thou shall not"); still, after all was said and done, "he studied and inquired into the traits of the finest of God's creations and in his wisdom fathomed the hearts of men, to know the secrets of their thoughts and their innermost passions". Solomon's reign is also extolled in the nineteenth-century book *Aseh pele*: "His kingdom grew more powerful than all the others and his wisdom was greater than that of all the sons of Machol".[60] The maskil Yudel Rosenberg (1860–1936) wrote in *Sefer Divrei haYamim asher leShlomo Alav ha-Shalom* (The Chronicles of the Life of Solomon, Peace Be Upon Him, 1914): "When Solomon ascended to the throne of his kingdom he instituted some fine measures in the land. He divided his kingdom into twelve regions in keeping with the number of the tribes of Israel […] He raised high the prestige of Israel and removed his people from poverty and disgrace, taking them to a life of glory and splendor […] the trumpet of war was not heard in the land and he amassed much wealth and luxury, until silver was as naught in the days of Solomon".[61] Legends and folktales continued to glorify his great wealth, but at the same time Jewish ethical (*musar*) literature pointed to his negative side; the *maskilic* worldview found Solomon a far from ideal king.[62] Wolf Meir, for example, criticized not only Solomon's arrogance but also the fact that he "made images of copper oxen under the sacred place of offering,[63] and figures of the lion around his throne" in violation of the commandment against idolatry. Moreover, Solomon relied too much upon his wisdom; hence, "the light of his mind grew dim, and he permitted his wives to raise shrines for their gods and allowed his ministers to oppress the people, and at the end of his life became a sick, angry man, so that the people did not mourn his death".

A further, significant part of Solomon's biography consists of those books and psalms he is purported to have written. According to one early account, the Holy Spirit rested upon Solomon in his old age when he was close to death and "he spoke three books—Proverbs, Song of Songs and Ecclesiastes".[64] However, these three books are generally thought to represent three distinct periods in his life—as a young king, a mature king, and an elderly king—or else three stages in the development of his *sophia* (wisdom), or of his decline: "in his

---

60. Yassif (2004, pp. 237–253).
61. Rosenberg (1914, p. 9).
62. Nonetheless, Solomon does appear in *maskilic* pastoral literature.
63. A reference to I Kings 7:23–26.
64. *Yalkut Kings* 1, § 172.

old age, he spoke vanities". In a poem by Micah Joseph Lebensohn (1828–1852), "Solomon-Ecclesiastes" appears as an aged and weary king, living out his days in a "palace overlaid with the finest gold, gleaming cedar and glowing capitals, among marble pillars pleasing to the eye, precious stones and rare treasures"—a monarch searching in vain for answers to existential questions:

> Then he searched and probed the laws of the earth
> From the hyssop on the wall to lofty cedars
> From the beasts of the forest to insects and vermin
> From the astute he learned as well, inquired of the wise
>
> And of the ancients, of the wise men of Egypt
> Of the idols their false knowledge
> He lent his ears to the secrets of their priests
> Perhaps to find light in the depths of the shadow of death
>
> In vain he sought of them wisdom and intellect
> They too knew how to ask, but to reply they knew not
> Hence his soul yearned to discover
> He sought words of truth, but concealed they remained

Weary of his fruitless inquiries, Solomon had a revelation:

> At once the king's eyes were opened
> He called forth: At last, you must all hear!
> Fear God, and keep his commandments
> For this is the whole duty of man![65]

We have seen that the Jewish Sages' messianic visions made no direct reference to Solomon, referring to the "house of David" rather than to the infamous sinful king. A similar approach exists in the Christian gospel. In Luke's account of the annunciation of the birth of Jesus, the angel Gabriel informs Mary: "And now, you will conceive in your womb and bear a son, and you will name him Jesus. He will be great, and will be called the Son of the Most High, and the Lord God will give him the throne of his ancestor David. He will reign over the house of Jacob forever, and of his kingdom there will be no end".[66] Here, too, the reference is to the throne of David, not the throne of Solomon; David's immediate successor is not mentioned. As we shall see, however, this did not prevent Christian tradition from identifying in Solomon the prefiguration of Jesus.

Solomon's popularity in folk literature and folklore inspired a

---

65. Lebensohn (1972, pp. 57–74); free translation by C. Naor. The poem "Hingegangen in den Wind", by the German poet and Indologist Friedrich Rückert (1788–1866) also ends on a pessimistic note. Rückert (1841, p. 370).

66. See Luke 1:31–33.

wealth of fantastic tales, many of which featured him as a magician and exorcist possessed of a complex relationship with demons and the devil. The twelfth-century story *Solomon and Morolf*,[67] for example, relates how Solomon abducted and married Salma, a pagan queen. The king of the pagans, her father, is able to rescue her; Solomon, disguised as a pilgrim, attempts again to abduct her and is instead captured and sentenced to the gallows. But he blows into a magic horn three times and his army hastens to rescue him.[68] Another fantastic tale is cited in a Russian work from the latter half of the seventeenth century, which achieved a significant amount of popularity. *A Tale of King Solomon's Birth and Exploits* follows two plots: the first tells of Solomon's expulsion from the palace and his wanderings, and the second of the abduction of his wife by the King of Cyprus.[69]

***

As with Solomon, Jesus' biography recurs throughout the four Gospels in several, and at times inconsistent, versions. For example, the story of Jesus' conception and birth by Mary through the Holy Spirit appears only in Matthew and Luke.[70] Similarly, the story of the holy family's flight to Egypt appears only in Matthew.[71] No wonder that in his *Against the Galileans*, the Roman emperor Julian the Apostate considered the Christians unable to invent a plausible genealogy, and saw Matthew and Luke as refuted by their disagreement concerning Jesus' genealogy. Furthermore, "Isaiah's prophecy that 'The scepter shall not depart from Judah, nor a leader from his loins' was most certainly not said of the son of Mary, but of the royal house of David".[72] Alternative biographies of Jesus appear in the apocryphal Gospels, which were not included in the Christian canon; these tell a different story about his life from his birth to his crucifixion.[73]

The "pagan" philosopher Celsus had a "Jewish" character[74] claim

---

67. See in Chapter Seven.
68. Kartschoke (1990) and Brunner (2003, p. 165). See Chapter Seven.
69. Lur'e (1964).
70. Matthew 1:1–25; Luke 1:26–38; 2:1–21. See Eusebius' (c. 260–449 A.D.) response to "the alleged discrepancy in the Gospels as to Christ genealogy" (1989; pp. 7–12, 20–22). Mani, the Manichaean (216–276), claimed that the two contradictory genealogies of Jesus are evidence of "Jewish padding". See Fox (2016, p. 127).
71. Matthew 2:13–15.
72. Julian (1980, Vol. 3, pp. 395–197). See also Schäfer (2008).
73. See Grabbe (2019); White et al. (2018); Pagels and King (2007).
74. See A. Baumgarten (2016). Baumgarten maintains that Celsus relied on Jewish polemical texts from before the second century C.E.; however, it is more probable that he was exposed to Jewish oral polemics against the Christians. Also see Pick (1911).

that Jesus had falsified his birth to a virgin mother [*parthenos*] and that, in fact, "the mother of Jesus was turned out by the carpenter who was betrothed to her, as she had been convicted of adultery and had a child by a certain soldier named Panthera".[75] Like Celsus, the Sages maintained that Mary was an adulteress who secretly gave birth to Jesus and similarly identified his father as a soldier named Panthera; according to R. Eliezer,[76] Jesus "brought forth witchcraft from Egypt by means of charms scratched into his flesh". Counter-biographies of this sort also appear in *The Polemic of Nestor the Priest* and in the book *Toldot Yeshu*. The *Polemic* was written in Judeo-Arabic in the mid-ninth century and its author, or editor, is presented as a Christian priest who converted to Judaism and lived in an Arab environment; a Hebrew translation appeared in twelfth-century Spain or Provence and contains mainly anti-Christian claims.[77] *Toldot Yeshu*, on the other hand, is an anonymous, apparently ninth-century work that was circulated in many manuscripts and relates alternative biographies of Jesus.[78] The Quran and medieval Muslim literature[79] present additional counter-narratives to the life of Jesus as portrayed in the Gospels. Much modern literature has been inspired by such alternative narratives, producing results that might be described as "counter-history"[80] or even "wild" history, and various genres of popular literature borrow content from apocryphal and pseudo-apocryphal literature on Jesus' life.[81]

What the "real" Jesus and the "real" Solomon have in common is that both spoke in parables. Yet, the parables in the Book of Proverbs differ significantly from those attributed to Jesus in the Gospels.[82] The "direct" correspondences drawn between Jesus and Solomon

75. Origen (1965, p. 31). See also Celsus (1987, p. 57); Rokeah (1969); and Abel (1969). Peter Schäfer's book *Jesus in the Talmud* (2007) supplies a comprehensive survey of Talmudic references to the life of Jesus.

76. *b.Shabbat* 104b; *y.Shabbat* 12:4 13d [both texts attribute the pronouncement to R. Eliezer!].

77. Lasker and Stroumsa (1996). See also Limor (1995). In the texts examined therein, Jesus is depicted as a chronic drunkard, a glutton, and a wastrel.

78. See Deutsch (1997, 2011).

79. See Introduction, note 45.

80. Among others: Aron (1990); Chen (1993); Arnheim (1984); Potter (1962); Aslan (2014). There is furthermore a rather bizarre book that evoked enthusiastic reactions and even inspired a film version: Strobel (2013); and Meggit (2015).

81. The best-known and most successful of these is Dan Brown's *The Da Vinci Code* (2006). I will not delve here into the subject of Hebrewand Yiddish-language literature about Jesus but will only mention Sholem Asch's book *The Nazarene* (1939), *Der man fun Natseres*, in the German edition, which provoked harsh criticism.

82. "Jesus' Parables and the Parables in the Literature of the Sages", in Flusser (1979), in Hebrew; Flusser (1981) for the German edition. It is important to note that Jesus does not quote from the Book of Proverbs.

were inspired by several verses in the Gospels, and they developed in different directions first within Christian theology and, later, in medieval Jewish literature. Chief among these correspondences is, of course, the prefiguration of several events of Jesus' life in the life of Solomon and, beginning in early Christianity, in Jewish-Christian polemic literature. That literature focused on the question "Who is the true Solomon?"—and the centrality of that question shows how prominently Solomon figured in the world of Christianity.

***

The main biographies we have of Aristotle appear in *The Lives of Eminent Philosophers* by Diogenes Laërtius of the third century C.E.; in the *Vita Aristotelis* by Ptolemy of Chennos (known in Arabic as al-Gharīb—"the foreigner");[83] and in the writings of Dionysius of Halicarnassus (c.60—c.7 BCE).[84] His private life and connections with Alexander the Great led to depictions of Aristotle at once favorable and disparaging.[85] Various pseudo-Aristotelian works also came into existence, including a treatise, the *Secretum Secretorum*, ostensibly written for his pupil Alexander; similarly there emerged poems and legendary traditions about alleged links between Aristotle and Solomon (see Chapter 8). One story that stands out among these is "Aristotle and Phyllis": here, Aristotle, like Solomon, is not only seduced by a woman—Alexander the Great's wife—but is also humiliated at her hands.[86] This popular fable "corresponds" with the biblical story

---

83. This was Ptolemy the Unknown, a cataloguer whose work was preserved in Arabic.

84. See Düring (1957, pp. 464–467); Chroust (1964, 1973); Natali (2013); Gutas (1986). See Chapter Seven.

85. Eusebius (2002), Book XV: Preface, Chap. II, p. 848. Eusebius writes that the names and books of Aristotle's detractors, during and after his lifetime, are deader than their bodies.

86. The research literature dealing with the evolution of this fable and its popularity, in France and Germany in particular, is extensive. See, for example, Sarton (1930). Sarton sees the story as an expression of the opposition to the "popular Aristotelianism" that arose in the Christian West in the thirteenth century, and Highet (below) writes that the fact that the story was popular during the period when Aristotelian philosophy attained a high status in universities is an example of the gulf between scholars and the public in the Middle Ages. See Matthews (2010); Highet (1970, p. 57). The scene in which Phyllis rides Aristotle is depicted with grotesque figures in several Gothic cathedrals in France. The story is mentioned in the book *Me'irat Einayim*, written by R. Yitzhak ben Shmuel of Acre (1250–1340), a commentator and Kabbalist who lived first in Acre and later in Navarre. See Ashkenazi (2000). In its Jewish form, the story is anti-Aristotelian and directed against the influence of Aristotelian philosophy. In fact, only the Hebrew version addresses his philosophy; in Christian texts, Aristotle is the personification of knowledge and wisdom, and the fact that he was tempted by a woman to the point of offering himself on all fours to be rid-

in which Solomon's wives lead him to sin, as well as with the Sages' descriptions of his trespasses, punishment, and humiliation.

The legendary biographies of Aristotle and Solomon correspond primarily in that both Jewish and Christian traditions dubiously attribute to each figure the authorship of numerous books. Both supposedly destroyed their writings; Solomon, according to an Armenian legend, ordered, before his death, that all his books be burned because: "The great number of my books is the cause that many people are lost, for they lose their faith in God, and cease to do good works". His servants fulfilled his commandment—but one hid in his bosom a book that the Church later preserved in three parts.[87] In a second version, Solomon ordered the destruction only of his books of magic, but two of these survived (*The Key of Solomon* and *The Testament of Solomon*); in yet another, he ordered all of his books to be burned, but the flames refused to consume Proverbs, the Song of Songs, and Ecclesiastes.[88]

It is said of Aristotle that his theory of the stars as "beings of superhuman intelligence, incorporate deities" who influenced life on earth, "provided for far later demonology".[89] In the Jewish legendary tradition that developed during the Middle Ages, Aristotle, who accompanied Alexander the Great on his visit to Jerusalem, took with him all of Solomon's books; having read them, he burned nearly all his own writings, leaving only his *Metaphysics* for posterity.

---

den upon bespeaks the weakness of rationalism. See Shavit (2018). In contrast, *Gesta Romanorum*, a fourteen-century collection of anecdotes, contains one anecdote (No. XXII) relating how Aristotle saved Alexander from death. The Queen of the North fed her daughter poison from infancy; Alexander fell in love with the daughter when she had grown into a beautiful maiden and was about to kiss her. Aristotle stopped him and suggested that she first kiss another young man; she did, and the man died immediately. Thus, did the wise philosopher save Alexander's life. The moral of the story is that a reasonable person knows how to restrain an arrogant person who knows no bounds and may teach him to choose the "middle path". In Russian popular literature, Phyllis was referred to as "the German woman riding the old man". According to W.F. Ryan, the story is "evidently a traditionalist attack on the westernizing policies of Peter the Great and his 'German' wife" (Ryan 1986). And see Chapter Eight.

87. Cited in Seymour (1924, p. 59).
88. Butler (1993. p 42).
89. Cited in Thorndike (1964, Vol. 1, p. 26).

Chapter Two: Solomon and Jesus—Two Sons of God, and of David?

Domine Fili unigenite Iesu Christe.
Domine Deus, Agnus Dei,
   - Filius Patris (Gloria)[1]

"*Solomon was a laughingstock,*
since he thought he was Christ"
   - The Second Treatise of the Great Seth (vii, a2)[2]

Solomon's presence in the polemic regarding Jesus' divinity as the Son of God can be traced to a single act of rhetoric in the Epistle to the Hebrews. The authorship of that text, which dates to the second century, was attributed to Paul[3] first by Eastern and later by Western Christianity, and this remained a commonly accepted view until the Reformation.[4] Some of the Church Fathers addressed the stylistic disparities between that epistle and others attributed to

---

1. "O Lord, the only-begotten Son, Jesus Christ; O Lord God, Lamb of God, Son of the Father", from the Christian hymn Gloria in excelsis Deo (English translation taken from the *Book of Common Prayer*, 1662).

2. Translation by Joseph A. Gibbons and Roger A. Bullard in J. M. Robinson (1988, p 363).

3. The existence of the Epistle was first documented in Alexandria in the second century; it was added to the Christian canon only several centuries thereafter.

4. In Luther's translation, the *Epistle* is relegated to the end of the canon to denote its scant importance in Protestant doctrine. Luther (and Calvin) believed the *Epistle* was not written by Paul or the other apostles. It has been attributed to various authors, including Apollos, a Jewish-Christian preacher from Alexandria who may have been influenced by Philo, and who arrived in Ephesus in 52 or 53, met Paul in Corinth (1 Corinthians 3:6), and apparently clashed with the latter on several matters. There were those who cast doubt on the Pauline authorship of the *Epistle* long before the Reformation. See K. Hagen (1974, pp. 19–30). The first annotated Hebrew translation of the *Epistle* was by Raphael Hirsch-Johann Heinrich Biesenthal (1800–1886), a converted Jew who worked in the service of the German mission (Berlin, 1853, with additions in 1858 and 1882).

Paul with the explanation that he had composed the former in Hebrew rather than in Greek, or that Paul strove to conceal his authorship for reasons of modesty.[5] The fact that many citations from the Bible are found throughout Hebrews has given rise to various hypotheses regarding the identity of its audience, which I will not present here.[6] But its audience was apparently thought to be well-versed in the Old Testament, and biblical quotations would not have been foreign to them.[7] Let us assume that it was indeed Paul, or Saul—a native of Tarsus in Lycia, formerly a Pharisee and a pupil of R. Gamliel the Elder who after a revelation in the mid-first century B.C.E. embarked upon a missionary journey in Asia Minor to spread Jesus' message among the Jews and the pagans to serve God, in his own words, "with my spirit by announcing the gospel of his Son".[8]

When addressing a Jewish audience, Paul injected verses from the Bible into his speech:[9] "To the Jews I became as a Jew, in order to win Jews. To those under the law I became as one under the law (though I myself am not under the law) so that I might win those under the law".[10] On the Sabbath, in the synagogue of Antioch in Pisidia, for example, he preached that Jesus had been brought into the world by God as a descendant of David: "Of [David's] seed hath God according to his promise raised unto Israel a Saviour, Jesus", and continued: "he has fulfilled for us, their children, by raising Jesus; as also it is written in the second psalm, 'You are my Son; today I have begotten you'".[11] Here, in other words, Paul employed the same phrase that begins the Epistle to the Hebrews, following it with an assertion that God

---

5. See J. W. Thompson (2008, pp. 3–10).

6. Attridge (1989). For a comprehensive discussion of the *Epistle* and a summary of the various views reflected in the research literature, see Ruzer and Zakovitch (2016). To accept that the Epistle to the Hebrews was not written by Paul one need only compare it to the other epistles. The Epistle to the Galatians claims that "when the fullness of time had come, God sent his Son, born of a woman, born under the law" (4:4).

7. Reading in public from the Holy Scriptures was one of the duties of community leaders (1 Timothy 3:13) and quoting from the Bible became easier with the adoption of the codex. See Gamble (1995, pp. 42–81).

8. Romans 1:9.

9. See Troiani (2017). In his second epistle to Timothy, whom Paul appointed Bishop of Ephesus in 65, he writes: "and how from childhood you have known the sacred writings that are able to instruct you for salvation through faith in Christ Jesus. All scripture is inspired by God and is useful for teaching, for reproof, for correction, and for training in righteousness" (2 Timothy 3:15–16). According to Snyder, Paul served as a mediator between the Bible and his audiences (Snyder 2001, pp. 194–195).

10. 1 Corinthians 9:20.

11. Acts 13:33.

had raised Jesus from the dead, "no more to return to corruption".[12] While the congregants at the synagogue first welcomed his words, urging Paul to return and teach the following Sabbath, they ultimately rejected his words. Upon their departure, Paul and Barnabas declared they were taking their message to the Gentiles.[13]

In the course of his third journey Paul arrived at Ephesus,[14] and there too he "spoke out boldly", preaching for three full months "about the kingdom of God".[15] To convince skeptics, he posed the rhetorical question that would connect between a onetime king and a new Messiah: For to which of the angels did God ever say, "You are my Son; today I have begotten you"?[16] The intended answer is clear: only to his son Jesus did the 'Father' (God) inform him of his birth", while his latter quote "I will be his Father, and he will be my Son" claims only that God will be a father to Jesus, and not that God has begotten him.

Here, Paul is referring to Psalm 2:7–8: "I will tell of the decree of the Lord: He said to me, "You are my son; today I have begotten you. Ask of me, and I will make the nations your heritage, and the ends of the earth your possession"—a verse that Paul maintains refers not to Solomon but to Jesus. One may, of course, wonder why a father should inform his son of the fact of his birth on that very day; the answer is that Paul's choice to open his appeal with a biblical reference was the rhetorical device that allowed him to claim Jesus' sole sonship to God, but in doing so, he unintentionally evoked the question of "double sonship".

Regardless of whether Paul or a later author composed the Epistle to the Hebrews,[17] it was unquestionably directed at Jews rather than pagans; only the former could have recognized its biblical references and ascertained "whether these things were so".[18] One may also assume that Paul's listeners, when told that after Jesus' baptism in the Jordan a voice from Heaven called forth "You are my Son, the Beloved; with you I am well pleased",[19] would not have found these words incongruous, since they are nearly identical to those of the prophet Nathan

---

12. Acts 13:34.
13. Acts 13:42–47.
14. Trebilco (2004).
15. Acts 19:8. Acts 17 tells of Jews from Beroea (Aleppo) who were able to refer to the Bible and evaluate the reliability of Paul's quotations from it.
16. Hebrews 1:5.
17. Richards (2004). In Larry W. Hurtado's view, "it is particularly significant that Paul describes his religious re-orientation as caused by a divine revelation to him of Jesus as God's unique 'Son'" (Gal 1:15). Hurtado (2005, p. 34).
18. Acts 17:11.
19. Mark 1:11.

about Solomon. Nor would it have seemed out of place that when his disciples suggested to Jesus that he erect three tabernacles on the mountain—"one for you, one for Moses, and one for Elijah"—a voice spoke from within a cloud saying "This is my Son, my Chosen; listen to him!"[20] they would not have been fazed by the use of the word son" (υἱός) but they would certainly have understood it metaphorically as a reference to Nathan's tidings concerning God's promise to David: "When your days are fulfilled and you lie down with your ancestors, I will raise up your offspring after you, who shall come forth from your body, and I will establish his kingdom. He shall build a house for my name, and I will establish the throne of his kingdom forever. I will be a father to him, and he shall be a son to me".[21]

The promise of fatherhood is repeated in Chronicles, where David states: "And of all my sons, for the Lord has given me many, he has chosen my son Solomon to sit upon the throne of the kingdom of the Lord over Israel. He said to me, 'It is your son Solomon who shall build my house and my courts, for I have chosen him to be a son to me, and I will be a father to him'".[22] This assertion is repeated in Psalm 2:7: "I will tell of the decree of the Lord: He said to me, 'You are my son; today I have begotten you'".

The Epistle to the Hebrews' "I will be to him a father" (Ἐγὼ ἔσομαι αὐτῷ εἰς πατέρα) may certainly be interpreted as referring to adoptive fatherhood ("I will be," rather than "I am"). Moreover, Hebrews refers to Israel as a collective son: "And you have forgotten the exhortation that addresses you as children—'My child, do not regard lightly the discipline of the Lord, or lose heart when you are punished by him; [...] for the Lord disciplines those whom he loves, and chastises every child whom he accepts'".[23] Thus, all those baptized as Christians become the children of God. The Gospels provide a similarly expansive vision of the divine family—"Blessed are the peacemakers, for they will be called children of God".[24] It would be possible, then, to interpret the Epistle to the Hebrews as describing two types of paternity: corporeal ("today I have begotten you", though here 'begetting' [*Ego semeron gegenneka se*] may also be viewed as a metaphorical

---

20. Luke 9:35.
21. 2 Samuel 7:12–14. See Sergi (2010); Avioz (2005); Chae (2006). Josephus does not repeat the words of the prophet Nathan that Solomon will be as a "son" to God, nor his words regarding David. He writes that Solomon is the heir "chosen by God", while the designation "my son" refers to the fact that he is the son of David (*Antiquities* VII: 373–74).
22. 1 Chronicles 28:5–6.
23. Hebrews 12:5–6.
24. Matthew 5:9.

personification)[25] and adoptive—a relationship between a father and his chosen, beloved son(s).[26] Thus, we may assume that a Jew would not have been disoriented by Hebrews' use of the terms 'father' and 'son',[27] but would have understood them as a metaphor for the biblical ideal code of rights and duties that exists between a people (or a king) and God (though in ancient Israel the perception of the kings as sons of God did not exist.[28] Biblical phrases such as "on holy mountains, from the womb of the morning, like a dew your youth will come to you"[29] make reference to a messianic future and the metaphoric nature of the God's choice of Solomon as David's heir is very clear from the language used: "Among the many nations there was no king like him, and he was beloved by his God".[30]

***

"Nothing may hinder us from confessing the absolute equality of the Father, Son, and Holy Spirit"
  - Augustine, *On the Holy Trinity*, Book VI:10.[31]

Is it possible that God had two sons—that both Solomon and Jesus of Nazareth were granted sonship? Perhaps Jesus' description as the son of God, like that of Solomon, was intended at first merely to invoke a prevalent metaphor, whose nature would change radically over time. (Pursuing this question would lead me deep within high Christology and I leave it to other studies to do so.) The figure of Jesus in the New Testament comprises several aspects, and in the four Gospels and the

25. See Lakoff and Johnson (2003). Maimonides' objection to the metaphorical perception of God probably stemmed from the understanding that a metaphor could easily become concrete. I should note here that Mary's virgin birth is not the only miraculous birth mentioned in biblical sources (See Kara-Ivanov Kaniel 2014). The writers of the Gospels required a woman's womb so that Jesus might be born of it, although the omnipotent God could have "created" a "human" son without such a need. (That, indeed, is what the Quran claims.) On an early polemic in relation to a virgin birth, see Chapters 63–79 of Justin Martyr (2003).

26. Matthew 10. The Syriac monk Aphraat (c. 280-c. 345) writes in his *Denomstrationes* 17: "On Jesus the Messiah who is the Son of God"; "While we grant them that he [Jesus] is a human being, however we also honour him and call him God and Lord. It was not strange to call him [so] and it was not a strange name that we have conferred on him, which they [the Jews] themselves have not made use of. But it is certain for us that Jesus our Lord is God, Son of God, King, Son of the King, Light from Light, Creator.... He is called with many names". Trans. from Syriac and Introduced by Valavanolickal (2005, p. 141). And see Gavin (1923).

27. On the concept of "sonship" in general and in the Kabbalah in particular, see Idel (2007).

28. On this matter A. Yarbro Collins (1999) disagrees. See also Cooke (1961).

29. Psalms 110:3.

30. Nehemiah 13:26.

31. Schaff (1995, Vol. 3, p. 102).

Epistles, these aspects are given different emphases and meaning,[32] just as differing versions exist of the story of the nativity. This multiplicity resulted from the various views contained in the New Testament itself and from the polemic on the true nature of Jesus that took place early in the process of Christianity's development during the establishment of the Christian canon; the polemic was settled by the Nicene Creed (*Symbolum Nicaenum*) in 325.[33] However, in the New Testament, Jesus appears as the son of God, is identified with God,[34] and is nonetheless at once a flesh-and-blood Messiah.[35]

Diverse meanings attached, in ancient Christology and onwards, to the idea of God's "divine paternity" and of Jesus as the "son of God"; this was a source of controversy and a cause for schism. Jesus was seen as, *inter alia*, the primordial son of God—"the firstborn of all creation", "He is the image of the invisible God".[36] According to the Gospel of Mark: "Then a cloud overshadowed them, and from the cloud there came a voice, 'This is my Son, the Beloved; listen to him!'"[37] And in John: "No one has ever seen God. It is God the only Son, who is close to the Father's heart, who has made him known".[38] And, moreover: "The Father loves the Son and has placed all things in his hands. Whoever believes in the Son has eternal life; whoever disobeys the Son will not see life, but must endure God's wrath".[39]

---

32. See the review by Ruzer (2016).

33. On conflicts in the canon see, e. g., Theophilos (2013). The First Council of Nicaea stated that "Christus is the only begotten Son of God, born of the Father before all ages […]". It rejected Arianism as a heresy (and established the dogma that Jesus' nature is identical to that of God the father (*homoousios*), i. e., consubstantial. *Documents of the Christian Church*, Selected and Edited by Henry Bettenson, Oxford University Press, 1963, pp. 36–37. The western Church had added the word *filioque* ("and [from] the Son"): "We believe in the Holy Spirit, the Lord, the giver of life, who proceeds from the Father and the Son…" The Byzantine Church regarded this addition "as illicit and possibly heretical". Pope Benedict XVI wrote that the word *homoousios* was "the only philosophical term that was incorporated into the creed" (Pope Benedict XVI 2007, p. 320).

34. Romans 1:1–4; Philippians 2:5–11; Colossians 1:15–20. Pliny the Younger (c. 61–113) testified that he heard Christian congregations singing psalms about Jesus as a god: *carmenque Christo quasi deo dicere secum inuicem*" (they were in the habit of meeting before dawn on a stated day and singing alternately a hymn to Christ as to a god" trans. J. Lightfoot. See R. P. Martin (1964). See also Dunn (2010).

35. This subject, on which there is a vast literature, is beyond the purview of this book.

36. Colossians 1:15.

37. Mark 9:7–24. On the use of "son of God" in John, see Dunn (2015, p. 77). Also see Hurtado (2005); Hengel (1976); Allen et al. (2019); Kofsky and Ruzer (2018, p. 13–34).

38. John 1:18.

39. John 3:35–36. In Ode 3, attributed to Solomon: "I have been united to Him, because the lover found the Beloved, because I love Him that is the Son, I shall be-

According to John, Jesus told the Jews that the Father teaches the Son, who does as he does: "The Father loves the Son and shows him all that he himself is doing; and he will show him greater works than these, so that you will be astonished. Indeed, just as the Father raises the dead and gives them life, so also the Son gives life to whomever he wishes".[40] And, furthermore: "For just as the Father has life in himself, so he has granted the Son also to have life in himself; and he has given him authority to execute judgment, because he is the Son of Man".[41] Peter, addressing the skeptics, exclaims: "For we did not follow cleverly devised myths when we made known to you the power and coming of our Lord Jesus Christ, but we had been eyewitnesses of his majesty. For he received honor and glory from God the Father when that voice was conveyed to him by the Majestic Glory, saying, 'This is my Son, my Beloved, with whom I am well pleased'".[42] Athanasius, the bishop of Alexandria, wrote in his epistle *De decretis* that the word "son" possessed two meanings in the holy scriptures: sonship by adoption and grace applied to any who adhered to God's commandments, while the second sense is that of "natural sons".[43] In any case, Athanasius wrote, it is impossible to ascribe a human nature to God.[44]

Jesus was also hailed as a "son of God" for his ability to work miracles and exorcise demons. After he walked on water and calmed a storm, "And those in the boat worshiped him, saying, 'Truly you are the Son of God'".[45] He was further perceived as the divine son by men under an evil spell, one of whom called out to him, saying: "What have you to do with me, Jesus, Son of the Most High God? I adjure you by God, do not torment me".[46] On yet another occasion, Jesus met two men possessed by devils; they called to him: "What have you to do with us, Son of God? Have you come here to torment us before the time?"[47] The demons Jesus exorcised likewise acknowl-

---

come a son" (trans. James Charlesworth 1985, p. 735).

40. John 5:20–21.

41. John 5:26–27.

42. 2 Peter 1:16–17. Luther maintained that there can be no redemption without faith in Jesus, son of God, and that Mary was truly the mother of God and yet remained a virgin (*theotokos*). As to Solomon, God does call him his son, but he will be his father, but this promise is dependent on the condition that he remain pious. Luther (2015, p. 73). It is worth noticing that the question here is not one of fatherhood, but rather of a promise to a grown man.

43. Young (2002, p. 31).

44. Young (2002, pp. 30–36). In the *Epistle to Diognetus* (c.1300?) by unknown Greek writer, Jesus is referred to as "son" and "child" of God. God sent him to reveal himself as man or the Designer and Maker of universe. See Lienhard (1970).

45. Matthew 14:33.

46. Mark 5:7.

47. Matthew 8:29.

edged him: "You are the Son of God!"[48] The claim of divine paternity led the Jewish High Priest in Jerusalem to state that Jesus "ought to die because he has claimed to be the Son of God".[49] Paul, meanwhile, expanded on the notion of paternity: "for in Christ Jesus you are all children of God through faith".[50] In place of the Torah came faith in the son, who was sent by God "in order to redeem those who were under the law, so that we might receive adoption as children".[51]

Pagan polemic

"Pagan" philosophers of the time argued that Christianity's claim regarding Jesus' sonship referred to corporeal paternity. Nor did they have reason to wonder at such a claim, since the notion of divine paternity of corporeal persons was not alien to pagan culture and may be found in far earlier Assyrian prophecies.[52] In *The True Word*, Celsus derided not the idea of Jesus' divine paternity but rather the "foolish quarrel" between Christians and Jews about the identity of the Messiah. He had a Jewish character voice the assertion that the Christian claim of virgin birth was hardly different than the various tales in Greek mythology of women who gave birth to Zeus' offspring. Jesus, then, was but one of many followed by disciples who collected "a means of livelihood in a disgraceful and importune way",[53] and went on asking "Could not the Great God, who had already sent two angels on your account, His own son, at the very place?" Familiar with the Bible, he quoted Moses in Deuteronomy 4:35: "To you it was shown so that you would acknowledge that the Lord is God; there is no other besides him", as well as in 6:4: "The Lord is our God, the Lord alone".

---

48. Luke 4:41.
49. John 19:7.
50. Galatians 3:26.
51. Galatians 4:5. On the Jewish background to the terms "son of God" and "sons of God" in Paul and their meanings, see Byrne (1979). Here "sonship" is a metaphor.
52. See Parpola (1997, pp. XXXVI-XLIV).
53. Origen (1965, p. 65); Celsus (1987, pp. 57–59); Wilken (1979, pp. 117–134); and Rokeah (1982, pp. 16–19). Mythological stories may have prepared the ground for the acceptance of the story of Jesus' birth by the pagans, who did not reject that type of narrative as Alexander the Great did (when a resident of Thebes tried to gain mercy for the city by saying that the king was a son of the god like Hercules and Dionysus, sons of Zeus, Alexander replied, "Do you believe you can deceive Alexander by concocting a myth?" Stoneman (1991, pp. 80–83). Plutarch recorded that Alexander wrote to his mother about a meeting in Egypt with a priest of the god Amun, who called him *O paidion* (son of the god), and afterwards the god addressed him as *O pai Dios* (O Son of Zeus; Plut. Alex. 27.5). In a Hebrew version of the book, Alexander was the son of the Egyptian queen Cleopatra and Amun-Dionysus (Dan 1969, p. 130) A fragment of Apollolonius of Tyana, cited in "The Life of Pythagoras II Porphyry", describes Pythagoras as the son of Apollo and of Pythais, "most beautiful of the Samians".

Two hundred years later the Roman Emperor Julian would write in a similar vein that "Moses taught that there was only one God, but that he had many sons who divided the nations among themselves"; nothing in the words of the Prophets, he maintained, suggested that Jesus was "the only son of God" or "the first born of all creation".[54] In his *Adversus Christianos* (Against the Christians), Porphyry, a Neoplatonic philosopher and scholar who slightly predated Julian, mused as follows:

> What use is the Son of God for us who have become flesh on earth? And why was he placed on the cross, and had to suffer, and was punished with another penalty? And what is the didactic purpose of the cross? Why did the Son of God, Christ, leave the body after a brief time? And since he is not capable of suffering, how did he come under suffering?[55]

In addition, in the first centuries of the common era, the Church Fathers found themselves confronting not only pagan philosophers but also—and primarily— heretical movements within Christianity itself. In opposition to the Arian "heresy", according to Arius of Alexandria (c. 256–336), Jesus' divinity stems from the divinity with which the Creator, who was not himself created, endowed him. This claim is based on, among other things, Acts 2:36: "know with certainty that God has made him both Lord and Messiah, this Jesus whom you crucified". The proselyte priest Nestor also offered outspoken critiques, inquiring why Christians were not ashamed to claim that Jesus had spent nine months in a place as repugnant as the womb: "And God said to Isaiah [66:1]…'What is the place that can contain Me, when the heaven is My is my throne and the earth is My footstool, so which place can contain Me.' The Lord says no house can contain Him, and you say that a woman carried him in her womb, in confinement and in the darkness of menstrual blood, in the place of filth…."[56]

The Sages' polemic

Apparently, Jews would have objected the idea of God's paternity.[57] When the author of the pseudo-Danielic fragment found in Qumran[58]

---

54. Julian (1980, p. 403, 290E-291 A).

55. Berchman (2005, p. 134, and see note 10). Porphyry, also known by his Syrian name Malchus, was a native of Tyre and lived circa 234–305 B.C.E. The fact that he was familiar with the Gospels and the Acts and pointed out internal contradictions in them predating the Jewish polemical literature, led the Emperor Theodosius II to order those books burned in 448. On Celsus see Berchman (2005, pp. 85–93).

56. "The Account of the Disputation of the Priest", in Lasker and Stroumsa (1996, p. 73).

57. John 5:18. See Lucas (1993, pp. 19–21); Klausner (1955, pp. 204–217).

58. 4Q246 [4QpsDand] 1:8–9.

wrote that "He shall be called son of God, and they shall designate him son of the Most High", he certainly meant it to be understood as a metaphor.[59] Moreover, in the Hebrew Bible, as well as in the literature of the Sages, God's "paternity" relates primarily to the entire Jewish people. When Simeon ben Shetaḥ, head of the Pharisees, is told that Honi the Circle-Drawer appealed to God saying: "Master of the Universe, Thy children have turned to me because [they believe] me to be a member of Thy house. I swear by Thy great name that I will not move from here until Thou hast mercy Upon Thy children", ben Shetah replies forgivingly: "Were it not that you are Honi I would have placed you under the ban... But what shall I do unto you who actest petulantly before the Omnipresent and He grants your desire, as a son who acts petulantly before his father?"[60] According to R. Akiva, of the second century C.E., "Beloved are the Jews that they are called sons to God; an extra love is made known to them that they are called sons to God, as it was said: 'You are children of the Lord your God'" (Deuteronomy 14:1).[61] In prayer, Akiva turned to "our father, our king".[62] Jews furthermore had the examples of Abba Hilkia and Ḥanina ben Dosa, who spoke of their relationships with God as that of a son with his father.[63] Yet, in contrast, we have the words of Solomon in Ecclesiastes 4:8: "the case of solitary individuals, without sons or brothers". Jewish theology did not reject the anthropomorphism of God, or more precisely the idea that the boundaries between anthropomorphization, materialization, and metaphor are blurred, and that God exists not alone but rather accompanied by mythological figures, such as Enoch and Metatron.[64]

Such supernatural entities may have been the inspiration for the Christian depiction of Jesus as supernatural. Unlike them, however, Jesus was depicted as human—as a man born of a woman, living an earthly life rather than rising from mythology or the distant past. It was consequently necessary for Christians both to explain how Jesus could be a son of God and to elucidate the Christological polemic about his divine nature. The Sages contended over the idea of this duality with heretics (whom they called *minim* (heretics)) while the Church itself did not address it, nor did it use the argument that Jesus'

---

59. Vermes (1987, p. 275).
60. *Ta'anit* 3:8
61. *Avot* 3:18.
62. *Ta'anit* 25b. In the literature of the Sages, "the son" is often not a singular but a plural reference to the people of Israel. Jewish prayer addresses "our father who art in heaven"—a father to the entire people of Israel. See Goshen-Gottstein (1987).
63. A. Yarbro Collins and Collins (2008); Flusser (2009, pp. 153–163).
64. See the detailed scholarly discussion in: Schäfer (2012, pp. 103–159); Hurtado (2005, pp. 111–133); and Alan F. Segal (1977).

"sonship" was confirmed by the Jewish (mythic) eschatological literature about 'lesser gods' existing alongside God. However, in response to Christianity's claims and to the fact it posited the actual "corporeality" of God's "son" rather than employing it as a metaphor, the Sages—particularly in the Jerusalem Talmud—denigrated the Christian story of Jesus' birth, the attribution of divine sonship to a man, and the perception of Jesus as a manifestation of God". Thus, when one of the *minim* asked R. Simlai[65] (a second-generation Palestinian *Amora* of the late third or early fourth century) how many gods had created the world, he encouraged the heretic to read Psalm 149:9: "The Lord of Hosts, it is not written but 'the Lord of Hosts is the God of all' and when the Holy One Blessed be He created Man in His image and His figure, the angels erred, thinking that he was like God, so the Holy One Blessed be He put man to sleep 'so that they all would know that he is man'".[66] In *Pesikta Rabbati* (a collection of Aggadic *midrashim* recorded in Palestine between the fifth and ninth centuries),[67] R. Ḥiyya bar Abba (a Babylonian *Amora* who spent most of his life in Palestine around the same period as R. Simlai) is said to have taught "If the whore's son should say to you, 'They are two different gods', reply to him, Scripture does not say 'The gods have spoken ... face to face' but *The Lord has spoken with you face after face*".[68] The reference here is to Deuteronomy 5:4—"The Lord spoke with you face to face at the mountain, out of the fire"—where the grammatical subject is clearly singular. In *Exodus Rabbah* 29:5, bar Abba employed Isaiah 44:6 ("Thus says the Lord, the King of Israel, and his Redeemer, the Lord of hosts: I am the first and I am the last; besides me there is no god") to address the question without explicitly referring to Christology: "I am the Lord thy God, thus said R. Abahu: An example would be an earthly king, who rules and has a father, brother, and son. God says: 'I am the last' [which means] I have no brother. And besides me there is no God' [which means] that I have no son".[69] Elsewhere Rabbi Abahu is said to have taught that "If man says 'I am God', he lies; if he says 'I am the Son of Man' he shall rue it; I will go to heaven' he saith, but shall not perform it".[70]

In contrast, the Sages makes no reference to Solomon as a corporeal son of God, nor as a messiah; certainly, he does not "ascend to the

---

65. *y.Berakhot* 9:1 12d.
66. *Genesis Rabbah* 8:9, ed. Theodor-Albeck (1936, p. 62).
67. The collection was sealed around the ninth century; it would appear in print in Prague in 1653.
68. *Pesikta Rabbati* (1968, 1:422).
69. *Exodus Rabbah* 29, 5, trans. S. M. Lehrman.
70. *y.Ta'anit* 2:1 65b.

heavens". Nowhere do they claim that Solomon is God's only son, and his role in Jewish polemic is not that of a counter-example to Jesus as the 'true son' of God; instead, he is used to repudiate thoroughly the concept of sonship. Solomon is accused of having failed to express himself with sufficient clarity upon this point: "R. Aḥa [a fourth-century *Amora*] said: God was angry with Solomon when he uttered the above verse. He said to him: 'Why do you express a thing that concerns the sanctification of My Name by an obscure allusion, [when you say] 'and meddle not with them that are given to change'? Thereupon immediately Solomon expressed it more clearly [as follows:] *There is one that is alone, and he hath not a second; yea, he hath neither son nor brother* (Eccl. 4:8); '*He hath neither son nor brother*', but HEAR, O ISRAEL: THE LORD [[IS]] OUR GOD, THE LORD IS ONE".[71]

Christian polemic

Unlike the Sages, Christianity engaged, from its inception, in an intensive polemic that is revealing of the extent to which the question of the "dual sonship" of Jesus and Solomon troubled Christian apologists.

Jesus' sonship is discussed at length in Justin Martyr's second-century apologia *Dialogue with Trypho*. Trypho, whom Justin describes as a Jewish refugee from the Jewish war against the Romans and as learned in Greek philosophy, negates the idea of divine fatherhood. Justin then invokes Solomon as a counter-witness, having him explain that the "king of glory" in Psalm 24:1–10 refers to Christ because

---

71. *Deuteronomy Rabbah* 2:33, Soncino transl. Deut. 62–63. According to a medieval *midrash* attributed to R. Eliezer Hakapar, a *Tanna* who lived at the turn of the third century: "God gave strength to his [Balaam's] voice so that it went from the one end of the world to the other, because he looked forth and beheld the nations that bow down to the sun and moon and stars, and to wood and stone, and he looked forth and saw that there was a man, born of woman, who should rise up and seek to make himself God, and to cause the whole world to go astray. Therefore, God gave power to the voice of Balaam that all the peoples of the world might hear, and thus he spake: 'Give heed that ye go not astray after that man, for its written 'God is not a man that he should lie'. And if he says that he is God, he is a liar; and he will deceive and say that he departed and cometh again at the end. He saith and he shall not perform. See what he took to his parable and said: 'Alas, when God doeth this'. Balaam said, alas, who shall live—of what nation which hearth that man who made himself God". *Yalkut Shimoni Numeri* § 765, ed. A. Hyman, Jerusalem 1986, 485 [Salonica sec. 725 on Num. 23:7, according to Midrash Yelammedenu Aaron (Adolph) Jellinek (1873, pp. 207–208). Quran 4:171 (Women) states: "The Messiah, Jesus, the son of Mary, was but a messenger of Allah... So believe in Allah and His messengers. And do not say, "Three"; desist—it is better for you. Indeed, Allah is but one God. Exalted is He above having a son. To Him belongs whatever is in the heavens and whatever is on the earth". Quran 19:35 ("Mary") states: "It is not [befitting] for Allah to take a son; exalted is He!" These two verses are inscribed on the inner octoganal face of the Dome of the Rock. See Bowersock (2017, pp. 140–159).

he rose from the dead, went up to heaven, and sat at the right hand of the father (Psalm 110:1). Christ was the "son of God", descended through virgin birth from the *genos* of Abraham and the tribe of Judah and David;[72] he "submitted to become incarnate, and be born of this virgin"Justin further cites the prophet Nathan in 2 Samuel 7:14–15, interpreting "I will be his father, and he shall be my son" as referring to Jesus: "Christ is the Lord, and God the Son, that in times gone by appeared by his power as man and angel, …"[73]

In his *First Apology*, addressed to the Emperor Antoninus Pius, Justin's aim was to prove that the Christians were neither atheists nor rebelling against the monarchy. To do so, he employed a dual strategy. On the one hand, he argued that the idea that Jesus was the first begotten son of God the Father, and not conceived as the result of sexual relations, was hardly novel or particularly different from the descriptions of several births in Greek mythology. Furthermore, even if Jesus had been born entirely "by common generation", he was still worthy of his divine sonship because of his great wisdom. On the other hand, Justin presented the Emperor with a series of "testimonies" from the Bible to persuade him that Jesus was indeed the "son of the living God, God himself". He quoted from, among others, Psalm 2:7: "you are my son; today I have begotten you",[74] on the naïve assumption that the pagan Emperor of Rome acknowledged the authority of the Jewish holy scriptures.

Origen (c. 185–254), for his part, rejected totally Solomon's status as God's "son," arguing that Jews could not have known the "Father" for there cannot be a "Father" without the existence of a "son". Lactantius (c. 240-c. 325), basing his interpretation on the *Epistle to the Hebrews*, wrote that the divine message in 2 Samuel 7:7–13: "I will raise up your offspring after you […] He shall build a house for my name, and I will establish the throne of his kingdom forever", could not have referred to Solomon, as his reign was not eternal; Solomon was the son of David, not of God.[75] Eusebius of Caesarea (c. 260-c. 339) similarly maintained that Solomon could not be the son of God since he was the son of a human.[76] Origen wrote that Solomon failed to attain an eternal throne because he succumbed to the passions of the flesh and to idolatry;[77] and according to Cyril, the bishop of Jerusalem (313–386), Jesus was "[God's] only begotten Son, our Jesus Christ, by

---

72. Justin Martyr (2003, pp. 176–177, 193–195). See also Barnard (1997).
73. Justin Martyr (2003, p. 193).
74. See Falls (1965, pp. 33–111).
75. Lactantius, *Divinae Institutiones* 4, 13.
76. *Quaestiones Evangelicae* 5.2.
77. Origen (1921, p. 192).

whom He made all things visible and invisible." He is not "an adopted but a naturally only begotten son, having no brother".[78] Augustine invoked Solomon himself as a harbinger of sorts: "Solomon himself in his own person merely gave notice of the coming of Christ, by a foreshadowing of the future [...] in Solomon there is a kind of shadowy sketch, while in Christ the reality itself is presented to us". Solomon was "the son of David, not the Son of God",[79] and all prophecies of the future were fulfilled in Christ.

The Dialogue of Timothy and Aquila[80] describes a "dispute" between a Christian named Timothy and a Jew called Aquila in which the Christian, naturally, has the upper hand and Aquila ultimately is baptized. Among other things, their dispute revolves around the correct interpretation of Psalm 2:7 ("[...] I will tell of the decree of the Lord: He said to me, 'You are my son; today I have begotten you'"), of Nathan's words to David in 2 Samuel 7, and of the prophecies of Isaiah. Timothy interprets these as referring to Jesus, and to establish the claim that the intended reference is not to Solomon, he emphasizes the distinction between Jesus and Solomon, reminding his Jewish interlocutor that Solomon succumbed to the temptations of demons while Jesus, in turn, overpowered them and controlled them for all eternity, and thus demonstrated that he was "greater than Solomon". To bolster his argument, Timothy cited Solomon himself, or at least a text attributed to him—the pseudo-epigraphical *Testament of Solomon*, which was written in Egypt between the first and fourth centuries C.E. and declares the supremacy of Jesus. Timothy did not deny that God regarded Solomon as a beloved son (*Jedidiah*), but he argued that God had revoked his love for this wayward "son" as punishment for not having adhered to his commandments; the true son of God was therefore Jesus. Aquila the Jew responds: "Then how do all the scriptures wish to call this Jesus the Son of David, but also in your Gospels we find the blind men crying out to him and also the Canaanite woman saying 'O Son of David'".[81] To this Timothy replies that the evil spirits that were expelled called out: "What have you to do with us, Son of God?"[82] Aquila is not satisfied, and Timothy adds

---

78. See Cyril (1995, xi). Jesus had two fathers: "one David, according to the flesh, and one, God". As a son of David, He is subject to time but as son according to the Godhead, He is not subject to time nor to place.

79. Augustine (1984, XVIII:8). And see the detailed discussion in *Contra Faustum* (*Reply to Faustus the Manichaean*), where he writes that Christ is "the true and truthful Son of God and the true and truthful Son of David" (Augustine 1984, p. 735).

80. See Pastis (1994). In Pastis' view, the Jews and Judaism function as heuristic devices in the Christian catechesis.

81. Matthew 9:27; 15:22.

82. Matthew 8:29.

that Jesus is said to be the son of David because it was necessary "for the things written in the law and the prophecies to be fulfilled".[83] Hence David's description as the father of Jesus and, moreover, as the harbinger of the latter's appearance and his status as the Messiah.[84]

The question of Jesus' sonship persisted in Christian polemics even after Christianity became ascendant, by which point the three-hundred-year long debate with the pagans had drawn to an end and Judaism was more an imagined rival than a real one. Nonetheless, Augustine, for example, felt compelled to remark that "the Jews realize that the son promised, as they read in this passage to King David, was not Solomon; but so amazing is their blindness that they profess their hope for another even when the promised Son has clearly manifested".[85] Hugh of St. Victor (d. 1149), for his part, inquired how the words in the first chapter of the Epistle to the Hebrews could refer to Jesus if the source of the quote in question was 2 Samuel 7:14. He concluded that the literal reference was to Solomon, while the hidden, more mystical reference was to Jesus.[86] Another example was Alfonso Tostado Ribera, Bishop of Avila (1400–1455), who asserted that Solomon was "an adoptive son. Christ was a son by nature".[87] Luther wrote: "And although God does call Solomon his son [...] and says that he will be his father, this promise is dependent on the condition that Solomon will remain pious [...] It is not at all rare that God calls his saints, as well as the angels, his children. But the son mentioned in 2 Samuel 7:14 is a different and special son who will retain the kingdom unconditionally and be hindered by no sin".[88]

Medieval Jewish Polemic

In the Middle Ages, the Jewish response to these arguments was not intended to defend the depiction of Solomon as the chosen son of the "Father," i. e., God, but rather to deride the sacrilegious Christian belief in the virgin birth and in Jesus as "son of God". Neither in rabbinical literature nor in the Jewish "disputation" literature from the twelfth century onwards was any attempt made to disguise the out-and-out re-

---

83. Varner (2004); Robertson (1986, p. 219).

84. Psalms 72:1. The verse continues: "Give the king thy judgments, O God, and thy righteousness unto the king's son. He shall judge thy people with righteousness, and thy poor with judgment [...] In his days shall the righteous flourish; and abundance of peace [...] Yea, all kings shall fall down before him: all nations shall serve him".

85. Augustine (1984, XVII: 8, p. 735).

86. *Quaestiones in Epistolas Pauli, in Epist. ad Hebraeos*, 14:11.

87. OPERA. In secundum librum, Regum Commentaria, Venice: Balleoni, 1728. (Reprints exist, as well as a digital edition).

88. Luther (2015, p. 73).

jection of Christian dogma. Yet, in Jewish polemical literature, Solomon is not pitted against Jesus in this context.

In the *Kuzari*, Judah Halevi wrote that the first man (Adam) was created a whole, perfect creature; hence, "We call him God's son, and we call all those who were like him also sons of God".[89] In his *Bitul Iqqarei Dat ha-Notzrim* [A Refutation of the Principles of Christianity], Ḥasdai Crescas (c.1340–1410), a philosopher and teacher of Jewish law, pointed out contradictions and illogic in ten principles of the Christian faith and in Jesus' biography, including the concepts of the Trinity and of Jesus as a son of God. To Jesus' declaration that "My teaching is not mine but his who sent me",[90] Crescas responded by asking "Is the messenger not equal to he who sent him?" He also wondered why it was necessary for Jesus to turn to his Father for aid if he himself were possessed of the same divine powers. Crescas claimed furthermore that verse 4:6 in Paul's Epistle to the Ephesians—"one God and Father of all, who is above all and through all and in all"—actually reiterates the Jewish belief, expressed in Deuteronomy 4:39 that "the Lord is God in heaven above and on the earth beneath; there is no other".[91] In other words, God was "Father of all, and Father to no other god".

Advancing a different argument in the summary to his commentary on Psalm 72, the grammarian and biblical exegete R. David Kimhi, also known by the acronym Radak (1160–1235), overturned Christian claims: peace did not predominate during Jesus' lifetime, sinners and evil men did not vanish from the land, Jesus did not reign over all the people. As for Jesus' divinity, he wondered how it could be possible to pray that a man live, for there was no reason to pray for a divine being's life; "[…] if they (the Christians) said: the son will pray to the father for all who believe in the son, to whom will he pray? For he is the son of God", and later, "if you [Christians] say: the son will pray to the father for the sake of his believers, to what purpose will he pray? Is not the son himself meant to be God?"[92]

Similarly, Leone Modena (Judah Aryeh), in his *Clipeus et Gladius* [Sword and Shield], asserted that if God had wished to appear in the flesh, he would have done so by means other than a human birth—just as he created Adam and Eve by other methods. He went on to

---

89. *Kuzari* 1:95.
90. John 7:16.
91. R. Ḥasdai Crescas, *Sefer Bittul Iqqarei ha-Notzrim*, trans. into Hebrew from Catalan in 1451 by Joseph Ben Shem Tov, ed. Daniel J. Lasker (1990). There were several Church Fathers who claimed the Sages knew of the triune nature of God but chose to hide that knowledge from the masses. R. Ḥasdai cites as an example Hippolytus, *Adversus haereses*, 100, n. 97.
92. Kimhi (1967, p. 62).

perform a linguistic analysis: the Hebrew root yod-lamed-dalet (יָלַד—"begat") actually meant *yatzar* (יָצַר—"created"); in other words, God created Solomon but did not physically beget him. Furthermore, the Hebrew word for God, *Elohim*, was grammatically singular despite seeming to possess a plural suffix, and in those places where multiple names of God appear ("the Lord God of hosts, the God of Israel") no allusion exists to a trinity. Modena repeated the main arguments of Nestor the Priest, namely that if God had desired a son, he surely would not have resorted to the unclean vehicle of the female womb but would have created him in purity as he did the angels or Eve. He also pointed out the contradictions in Matthew and Luke: if Jesus was not the son of Joseph, then perforce he was not of the seed of David. He further denied that the words in the Epistle to the Hebrews (which he attributed to Paul) refer to Jesus.[93]

The Dominican friar Raimundus Martini responded to such arguments in a book titled *Capistrum Iudaeorum*, written around 1267. To answer the claim, for example, that Jesus did not "have dominion from sea to sea, and from the River to the ends of the earth",[94] he quoted from the Mekhilta de Rabbi Yishmael[95] on Exodus 12:6 that "a man's agent is like the man himself", and from the Babylonian Talmud, *Sanhedrin* 99b, that "he who causes his neighbour to fulfil a precept, is regarded by Scripture as though he had done it himself". Jesus' disciples and apostles fulfilled the psalmic prophecy and disseminated Christianity "from the great sea in the south, where the Cushites live, to the great sea to our north".[96]

Medieval Jewish biblical commentators responded to the Christian allegorization of the Bible not with a counter-allegorization of their own but rather with a literal interpretation. In other words, they disputed what they perceived as the distortion of biblical sources by the Christian camp[97] and the lack of historical truth in Christology. It is particularly noteworthy that they did not cite Nathan's prophecy to David as proof that Solomon was a son of God; this was because

---

93. Arye Yehudah of Modena, *Magen vecherev*, 27–30 and 47–49. In his polemic work *The Reproach of the Gentiles*, Profiat Duran, a rationalist philosopher, points to the errors, lack of logic, and contradictions in Christology, among them the concept of sonship and the divinity of the son. Thus, for example, Jesus' words on the cross: "My God, my God, why have you forsaken me?" (Matthew 27:46) show that Jesus did not regard himself as God (here I will add: Jesus cried out: 'My God, my God' and not 'my father, my father'). Duran also cited the differing versions of Jesus' genealogy. See Talmage (1983).

94. Psalms 72:8.

95. *Mekhilta de R. Yishmael Pisha* 5 (Horovitz–Rabin 1960, p. 17).

96. Jeremy Cohen regards the book as a manual for Christian preachers and missionaries. Cohen (2001, pp. 279–294).

97. On this matter, see Chapter Three.

they did not attribute sonship to Solomon and because such a claim might indirectly have bolstered the Christian claim of Jesus' sonship. I should mention here that Islam, too, regarded the "corporealization" of the term *ben* (son) as evidence of Christianity's "polytheistic" nature and as a denial of the monotheistic principle. The Quran itself addresses the matter; in Quran 19, we find: "Such was Jesus, son of Mary: (this is) a statement of the truth concerning which they doubt. It befitteth not (the Majesty of) Allah that He should take unto Himself a son". God ordered the birth of Jesus but surely was not his parent.[98]

The Broken Dynasty: Solomon and Jesus—two sons of David?[99]

Jesus' divine sonship is a theological dogma, while his sonship in the genealogical sense is a historical matter.[100] The latter conception poses an inherent difficulty since the New Testament describes Jesus as a descendant of David. The belief in a "Messiah born of David", made David—rather than Solomon—the fitting candidate to be Jesus' "father according to the flesh".[101]

Solomon is mentioned only a few times in the New Testament: (a) in the story about the Queen of Sheba's visit to "a greater than Solomon"; (b) in Jesus' parable on humility: "Consider the lilies, how they grow: they neither toil nor spin; yet I tell you, even Solomon in all his glory was not clothed like one of these";[102] (c) in the Gospel of John relating that several men, amid a crowd in the courtyard of the Temple, once called out that the Messiah would rise from the seed of David and out of Bethlehem but, since Jesus was from the Galilee, a controversy then broke out.[103] Solomon's most important appearance is in Matthew's genealogy of Jesus, which begins with Abraham and continues on to David, Solomon, and their descendants.[104] This is in contrast to the Gospel of Luke, where Solomon is absent from Joseph's family tree and Jesus is the only "son of David" and heir

---

98. Quran 19:34–35 ("Mary"). See also Parrinder (2013, pp. 126–132).

99. Many scholars have dealt with this subject. See, *inter alia*, Charlesworth (1995); Hanig (1993); Fisher (1986); Green (1982); Burger (1970); Oeming (2007); Trotter (1968, pp. 82–97); Chilton (1982); Bock (1991); and Perkins (1988).

100. There may have been groups within early Christianity that were skeptical of David's messianic status. See Ruzer (2007).

101. Romans 1:1–4.

102. Luke 12:27.

103. John 7:40–44. Yet see in the same Gospel: "the scripture said that Christ came of the seed of David, and out of the town of Bethlehem" (7:42).

104. Matthew 1:1–16. See Eusebius polemic against the "alleged discrepancy in the gospels as to Christ's genealogy" in *The History of the Church* (Eusebius, 1989, pp. 20–22).

to David's messianic role. In Luke, for example, the angel Gabriel informs Mary: "Do not be afraid, Mary, for you have found favor with God. And now, you will conceive in your womb and bear a son, and you will name him Jesus. He will be great, and will be called the Son of the Most High, and the Lord God will give to him the throne of his ancestor David. He will reign over the house of Jacob forever, and of his kingdom there will be no end".[105]

Furthermore, the Gospel of Mark relates that when Jesus arrived in Jerusalem astride a donkey, those following him called out: "Blessed is the coming kingdom of our ancestor David! *Hosanna* in the highest heaven!"[106] The scene is described similarly in Matthew: "Hosanna to the Son of David! Blessed is the one who comes in the name of the Lord! *Hosanna* in the highest heaven!"[107] Upon reaching the courtyard of the Temple, Jesus is again received as the "son of David".[108] Matthew relates that Jesus himself asked the Pharisees, "What do you think of the Messiah? Whose son is he?" To which their reply was "The son of David".[109] "How is it then," Jesus continued in Matthew's telling, "that David by the Spirit calls him Lord, saying, 'The Lord said to my Lord, "Sit at my right hand, until I put your enemies under your feet"'? If David thus calls him Lord, how can he be his son?" No one was able to give him an answer, nor from that day did anyone dare to ask him any more questions".[110]

In other words, the Gospels present David as the father of Jesus in his earthly incarnation as a "son of man", leaving no role for Solomon.[111]

Thus, Jesus is both "son of God" and "son of David. As "son of David" he is the mortal, earthly Jesus, while as "son of God" he is atemporal and eternal. According to Luke, Jesus is typologically the "son of God" *because* he is the true "son of David" (in other words, the Messiah):[112] "When he had removed him [King Saul], he made David their king. In his testimony about him he said 'I have found David, son of Jesse, to be a man after my heart, who will carry out all my wishes'. Of this man's posterity God has brought to Israel a Savior,

---

105. Luke 1:30–33.
106. Mark 11:10.
107. Matthew 21:9.
108. Matthew 21:15.
109. Matthew 22:42.
110. Matthew 22:43–46.
111. Augustine explains that the Pharisees were unable to reply because they did not understand that Jesus appeared before them as a man while remaining hidden from them as the son of God—in other words, the mystery that Jesus was both son and lord of David, and that one might be both man and God. Sermon XLI.
112. Ruzer (2006).

Jesus, as he promised".[113] And again: "Our father David," who was a prophet, had foretold the resurrection of the Messiah; since David did not himself ascend to the heavens, the words in Psalm 110:1— "The Lord says to my lord, 'Sit at my right hand until I make your enemies your footstool'"—must be intended for Jesus, the Lord and Messiah.[114] Further, Paul's Epistle to the Romans refers to the gospel concerning his (God's) who descended from David Son Jesus Christ our Lord, which was made "of the seed of David according to the flesh";[115] and Timothy is told: "Remember that Jesus Christ of the seed of David was raised from the dead".[116] David, moreover, exemplified an ideal king and at the same time heralded the coming of Jesus and his teachings: "Friends, the scripture had to be fulfilled, which the Holy Spirit through David foretold concerning Judas, who became a guide for those who arrested Jesus".[117]

When Peter spoke to the inhabitants of Jerusalem on the festival of Pentecost, he assured them that "ancestor David […] both died and was buried, and his tomb is with us to this day" and that God had resurrected Jesus, the Messiah: "Since he was a prophet, he knew that God had sworn with an oath to him that he would put one of his descendants on his throne. Foreseeing this, David spoke of the resurrection of the Messiah, saying, 'He was not abandoned to Hades, nor did his flesh experience corruption'. This Jesus God raised up, and of that all of us are witnesses. Being therefore exalted at the right hand of God, and having received from the Father the promise of the Holy Spirit, he has poured out this that you both see and hear".[118]

In addition, in the Book of Revelation, Jesus is depicted as a lion: "the Lion of the tribe of Judah, the Root of David, has conquered",[119] and in *Psalms of Solomon*, Solomon undergoes a transfiguration into Jesus:

> *Lord, you chose David to be king over Israel*
> *And swore to him about his descendants forever*
> *that his kingdom should not fail before you.*
> *See, Lord, and raise up for them their king*
> *A son of David, to rule over your servant Israel* [120]

This is a fulfillment of Amos' prophecy: "On that day I will raise up

---

113. Acts 13:22–23.
114. Acts 2:24–36.
115. Romans 1:3.
116. 2 Timothy 2:8.
117. Acts 1:16.
118. Acts 2:29–34.
119. Revelation 5:5.
120. *Psalms of Solomon*, Psalm 17. Charlesworth (1985, pp. 189–197).

the booth of David that is fallen, and repair its breaches, and raise up its ruins, and rebuild it as in the days of old".[121]

The *Blessing of Jacob*, a text preserved in the Dead Sea scrolls, draws a similar connection between David and the Messiah: "Whenever Israel rules there shall [not] fail to be a descendant of David upon the throne. For the *ruler's staff* is the Covenant of kingship [and the clans] of Israel are *feet* until the Messiah of Righteousness comes, the Branch of David. For to him and to his seed was granted the covenant of kingship over his people for everlasting generations [...]".[122]

David was assigned an additional role as the herald of the coming of Jesus, as seen in Psalm 72—"Give the king your justice, O God, and your righteousness to a king's son. May he judge your people with righteousness, and your poor with justice"—and in other psalms referring to the son of David and depicting his eternal reign on earth. Psalm 110:1 ("The Lord says to my lord, 'Sit at my right hand until I make your enemies your footstool'") is seen in this way: "Of this man's posterity God has brought to Israel a Savior, Jesus, as he promised". Justin Martyr asserted that Psalm 72 could not have referred to Solomon, since the future it described was never fulfilled during his lifetime: "[...] that none of these things mentioned in the Psalm happened to him is evident. For neither did all kings worship him; nor did he reign to the ends of the earth; nor did his enemies, falling before him, lick to dust". On the contrary, Solomon flouted God's commandments, violated the covenant, took pride in his wealth, and committed grievous sins of the kind that "Gentiles who know God, the Maker of all things through Jesus the crucified, do not venture to do, but abide every torture and vengeance even to extremity of death, rather than worship idols, or eat meat offered to idols". In contrast, Jesus was the "king of glory", "the eternal king" foreseen in the psalm, whose kingdom spread over the entire globe and would endure for all eternity.[123]

Others took a similar approach. Origen similarly found that Psalm 72 referred to the "true Solomon"—that is, to Jesus—while Solomon himself merely symbolized the vacuity that derives from ostentatious wealth, rather than humility and the supremacy of the soul over the body. And Tertullian, in his *Divinae institutiones*, wrote that Nathan the Prophet's prophecy was realized not in Solomon, whose kingdom failed to endure even though he was the son of David, but rather in Jesus. Eusebius too declared that Psalm 72 and the promise in 2

---

121. Amos 9:11.
122. 4QPBless. in Vermes (1987, p. 261).
123. See Chapter 34 in Justin Martyr (2003, pp. 51–53).

Samuel could not refer to Solomon,[124] while, similar to Origen, a work attributed to Athanasius (*Expositiones in Psalmos*) described Jesus as the "true Solomon" (Psalm 72:1). Regarding Psalm 45:6–7, Augustine wrote: "No one, however slow of wit, could fail to recognize in this passage the Christ whom we proclaim and in whom we believe, when he hears of 'God, whose throne is for ever and ever', and to recognize God's anointed, to be understood as God's anoints—not with visible oil but with the spiritual and intelligible chrism".[125] According to Augustine, Nathan's prophesy[126] refers to Jesus—"We may be sure that 'the blessing of the words' on David's line is not something to be hoped for a limited period, like that which was seen in the days of Solomon; it is something to be expected to last for all eternity"[127]—while Psalms 45, 72, 89, and 110 show that "it is in Christ that we see the fulfillment of these words".[128] Hence, "the Jews realize that the son promised, as they read in this page, to King David, was not Solomon; but so amazing is their blindness that they go on to profess their hope for another, even when the promised son has been so clearly manifested".[129] It was only owing to Christ that the house of David was "destined to become eternal".[130]

Most of the Sages attributed the authorship of Psalm 72 to the Messiah, the descendant of David, and believed that the subject of the psalm, likewise, was not Solomon, though he was David's son, but the Messiah.[131] Similar beliefs held true for Psalm 122, which tells of "thrones of judgment, the thrones of the house of David" in Jerusalem.

---

124. Eusebius, *Quaestiones Evangelicae* 5:2.
125. City of God 17:16 (Augustine, 1984, p. 746).
126. 2 Samuel 7:12–16.
127. *City of God* XVI:2 (Augustine, 1984).
128. *City of God* XVII:8 (Augustine, 1984).
129. *City of God* XVII:8 (Augustine, 1984). The Benedictine nun, poet and musician Hildegard of Bingen (1098–1170) writes that the meaning of "Behold, the lion of the Judah, the root of David, has prevailed" is this: the son, splendour of the Godhead, is like a root, He also roars like a lion when he casts the first angel with his followers into the abyss (Revelation 5:5), Letter to the Abbess of Altena, before 1173 (Letter 49R) in Hildegard of Bingen (2001, p. 164). According to Luther, Jesus was of the seed of David but not of Solomon, and was furthermore the "renewer of the covenant" (*promissio Gratiae*): "Thus the dear Son of David, Jesus Christ, is also our King and Messiah, and we glory in being his kingdom and people…" (Luther 2015, p. 212).
130. *City of God* XVI:12 (Augustine 1984, p. 742). And on this matter, see Chapters 8–15, pp. 734–744. Calvin, for his part, was opposed to the exclusion of Solomon from David's line: "If Jesus was not descended from Solomon, he was not the Christ". (Radak) Kimhi, as we have seen, countered this idea with an observation that while various prophecies remained unfulfilled by Solomon, neither did the prophecies regarding universal peace, an end to evil, and more come to pass during the time of Jesus Christ. Kimhi (1967, p. 160).
131. Zakovitch (1982).

Solomon did not satisfy the description in Psalm 72—"He shall judge the poor of the people, he shall save the children of the needy"—and thus could not be the future Messiah. David, then, was the formative father of the Jewish people; the Messiah would be a son of David, but not Solomon. The Sages ignore Solomon and speak of the "House of David" without mentioning him;[132] Solomon plays no role in Jewish messianic expectations and is instead subsumed, as we saw in Chapter One, into the general term "House of David",[133] or "the booth of David that is fallen"[134] (but which will one day rise again).[135] When the Roman Emperor Julian considered the prophesy "the scepter shall not depart from Judah, nor the ruler's staff from between his feet",[136] he wrote that it was as clear as the sun that it did not relate to Jesus.[137] His attempt to revitalize Greek polytheism and ground it in a philosophical foundation, however, was doomed to failure. Even before the first Council of Nicaea in 325 adopted the creed that the Christian faith was based on belief in "one Lord, Jesus Christ, the only Son of God, eternally begotten of the Father [...], true God from true God, begotten, not made", the title "son of David" had largely given way to "son of God",[138] though it did not vanish entirely. The "House of David" became a symbolic "house" in triumphant Christianity and continued

---

132. Duling, based solely on the evidence in the Gospels, claims that early Judaism preferred to mention Solomon not by name but rather as "son of David". Duling (1975).

133. Because of Christian censorship, this interpretation was omitted from printed documents. See Grossman (2012). The Qur'an describes Solomon as "David's heir" (Sura 26:16), and he is counted among the prophets. Al-Kisā'i's *Tales of the Prophets* relates that when Satan (Iblis) hears a divine voice declaring that Bathsheba is pregnant, and that the fruit of her womb will bring him much sorrow, he gathers all his sons and demons (genii) from all corners of the earth to investigate. They return and tell him that Bathsheba is carrying Solomon in her womb, who will rule over all the kings of the world; when Satan asks the angels assigned to guard the tower of David "Who is this Solomon?" he is told: "He is the son of David who will be the cause of your disaster and that of your offspring. al-Kisa'i (1997, p. 289).

134. Amos 9:11. Mireille Hadas-Lebel suggests that the four parallel sayings attributed to Rabbi Yohanan ben Zakkai (head of the school of Yabneh) on his death bed, which referred to King Hezekiah as the "Son of David", i.e., the Messiah, are an echo of the first exegetical polemic between Jews and Christians concerning the Christian argument drawn from the Bible on the identity of the "true Messiah". See Hadas-Lebel (1999).

135. In Jewish practice, the *Mi-She Berakh* prayer is recited on festivals and Sabbath mornings to the person called up to the reading of the Torah: "He who blessed our forefathers, Abraham, Isaac and Jacob". When the blessing is for a sick person or a woman who has just given birth, the names of Moses, Aaron, David and Solomon are added.

136. Genesis 49:10.
137. Julian, 243E.
138. Burger (1970).

to occupy an important place both in the ascending Christology and in Christian biblical commentary throughout the generations. In contrast, Jewish polemics against the sonship of Jesus made no mention of that of Solomon, as they saw no resemblance between the two instances of fatherhood attributed to God. Nor am I aware of any Jewish source that rejected God's fatherhood with respect to Jesus by arguing that Solomon was God's "true son".

The correspondence between Solomon and Jesus on the subject of sonship exists, therefore, primarily on the Christian side; it was Christianity that strove to defend the uniqueness of Jesus' status as son of God and to claim, in doing so, that Jesus, as the one true son, was thus also the "true Solomon".

Chapter Three: Solomon—His Actions and Books: Prefiguration, Typology, and His Teachings

> Thou may well see it reason
> For as the wise Solomon
> in his proverbs bears witness
> that gold, treasure, and great riches
> a good name doth well all surmount
> who that last aright account.
> - Guillaume de Deguileville, *The Pilgrimage of the Life of Man* (1330, 1335)[1]

Though Solomon did not figure in the genealogy of Jesus, he was nonetheless regarded as a prefiguration of the Christian Messiah. Despite Solomon's negative image as a sinner, the three books attributed to him were a rich source of allegorical readings that treated them as a *demonstratio evangelica* of both the coming of the Messiah and of the Church itself. Such readings resulted from the Christian view of the Old Testament as a Christian asset, the correct interpretation and true meaning of which only the New Testament could supply.[2] This implies that without the Old Testament there is no New Testament. This perception spawned a polemic and a sense of competition concerning the rightful owners, and the true interpreters, of the Bible.[3]

---

1. Lines 15407–15412. Translated by John Lydgate (1426), edited by Furnivall, Millwood, New York, 1975. See S. K. Hagen (1990).

2. See, for example Barrett (1963); Chadwick (1963); and J. N. D. Kelly (1963). More recently, see Kalimi (2017). It is unfortunately not possible to include herein a thorough discussion of the "internal" rabbinic-Karaite polemic and its influence on rabbinical interpretations of the Bible.

3. Justin Martyr accuses the Jew Tryphon of being "ignorant of Scripture", and Tryphon casts the same accusation at Aquila. We should bear in mind that the Evange-

From a Christian point of view, the historical role of the Jewish people was merely to preserve the Bible for the Christians until they appeared—in other words, to act as *custodes librorum nostrorum*. Augustine formulated this dogma in the following way: "In the Old Testament the New is concealed, in the New the Old is revealed" (*Novum Testamentum in Vetere latet, Vetus Testamentum in Novo patet*).[4] The Byzantine Emperor Justinian's *Novella 146* (issued in 553)[5] described Jews as adhering to a denuded, literal interpretation of the Bible because they did not believe in the final judgment of Jesus, in the resurrection, or in the creation of the angels. Thus, they were unable to comprehend the spiritual meaning of God's words[6]—i. e., the "correct", Christian way of reading the Bible, which made use of typological, symbolic, and allegorical interpretation.[7] According to Thomas Aquinas, "certain things *de Christo* are prefigured in the Old Testament through, e. g. David or Solomon, the Old Testament is a *figura* of the New Testament and the Church, and the Church is a *figura* of heaven"[8]—hence Christianity's claim of figurative validity. In any case, Justinian's above-mentioned *Novella* was aimed against those who sought the exclusive use of Hebrew and allows the liturgical reading "in all the other languages, changing language and reading according to the different places... there shall be no license to the commentators they have, who employ the Hebrew language to

---

lists and the early Church Fathers based their arguments on the Septuagint and accepted the legend that that translation was divinely inspired; as a result, at times they were misled—or erred—in understanding the text. Thus, for example, the word "alma" (עלמה) in Isaiah 7:14 was translated as "*parthenos*", "virgin". On this matter, see Benoit (1974); and Rokeah (2012). Luther wrote that the Jews were robbed of a proper understanding of Scripture because they read the Bible according to the *midrash* and rabbinic commentary and not according to its literal meaning, and that they "use all of these books to blaspheme the son of God" (Luther 2015, pp. 91, 93).

4. See Bright (1999); K. Hagen (1974, p. 39); Cohen (1999, pp. 36–51).

5. *Novella 146*, 553. See de Lange (2017); Linder (1987, pp. 402–411).

6. See Schmeling. A lengthy discussion of Augustine on this subject may be found in *Contra Faustum*; Rutgers (2009, pp. 37–77).

7. In the fourth century, the dogma of John Cassian (c.360–435) was broadly accepted, and was summed up by Nicholas of Lyre: "*Littera gesta docet* [The letter teaches how one should act]; *Quid credas allegoria* [allegory, what one should believe]; *Moralis quid agas* [morals, what one should do]; *Quo tendas anagogia* [anagogy, whither one should strive]", thus assigning four meanings to the Scriptures: literal, allegorical, typological, and anagogic. Celsus pointed out the dualism (or internal contradiction) within Christian allegory when he wrote that Christians adopted the Biblical cosmogony and, by means of typological allegory, attempted to conceal their denial of Mosaic laws (6:29). Origen (1965, pp. 344–345). See also Guibert of Nogent (shortly before 1083), quoted in Minnis (2009, p. 34). In any event, the issue of the correct way to understand the Old Testament was controversial within both Judaism and Christianity. Young (2002, pp.189–192).

8. See K. Hagen (1974, pp. 47–48).

falsify it at their will…"; the reasoning was that Jews' knowledge of Hebrew would allow them an advantage in interpretation.[9] In doing so, Justinian interferes in an inter-Jewish *Kulturkampf* where radicals want to impose the Hebrew reading even in the diaspora.

Jewish and Christian exegetes read the Bible in similar ways, "rambling" through it, separating verses from their literal meaning and historical context (while simultaneously accepting the historicity of characters and events), and combining verses originally far apart in terms of time, location, and substance, imbuing them in this manner with new meaning. Their selection and combination of verses were not undertaken randomly. An exegete had predefined goals; he searched out—and found—those verses that suited and affirmed his goals. Thus, while Jewish and Christian exegetes read the same verses, they used them to support entirely different meanings.[10]

Medieval Christian polemicists, who encountered mainly Jewish *midrashim*, scarcely understood the hermeneutical techniques or meanings that Jewish *Midrashic* literature employed up to the end of the seventh century (ninth, if we include texts like Pirqe de-Rabbi Eliezer or Seder Eliyahu); these were fundamentally different from the hermeneutical techniques of Christian biblical commentators and theologians.[11] At any rate, the prodigious amount of writing devoted to interpretations and allegorizations of Solomon's life and, even more so, of the books said to be his, testify to his central place in the correspondence that took place between Christianity and Judaism over the centuries.

The first Christian allegorist was Origen. Lawson writes that he was "the first Christian scholar to systematize allegorical interpretations of Scripture based on the mystic concept that it has a visible and invisible element and that in the invisible it has hidden meaning and has a soul".[12] Based on this belief, Christian allegorical readings accorded Solomon the status of a *praefiguratio*—a presaging of Jesus; sections of Solomon's biography were thus subject to typological, symbolic, and allegorical interpretation. The kings of many nations who trav-

---

9. See Parkes (1934, pp. 392–393), and Rutgers (2009, pp. 67–77).

10. Modern commentators and exegetes continue in this manner and interpret ancient *midrashim* considering their own views and modern concepts, and, in this way, endow them with new meaning.

11. On this point I have learned a great deal from the insights of Daniel Boyarin's *Intertextuality and the Reading of Midrash* (Boyarin 1990).

12. Origen (1957, pp. 8–9). On Origen's exegetical methods, see Daniélou (1973, pp. 273–281). Aristotle influenced biblical criticism and oriented it toward a rationalist approach. See Smalley (1983, pp. 292–295). Ambrose, who read Origen, showed Augustinus the way of allegoric interpretation of scriptures as a way to conceal its hidden meanings.

eled to Jerusalem to hear Solomon's wisdom prefigured and symbolized the ultimate Day of Judgment and Jesus' universal, atemporal message. Isidore, Archbishop of Seville, found that by constructing the First Temple, Solomon "prefigures the image of Christ who raised the house of God in the heavenly Jerusalem, not with stone and wood, but with all the saints".[13] *Speculum Humanae Salvationis* (The Mirror of Human Salvation), a work of popular late-medieval theology, stated that Solomon enthroned was an image of Christ seated in the Virgin's lap: "The Throne of the true Solomon is the most Blessed Virgin Mary, in which sits Jesus, the True Wisdom".

Though the canonization of the three books attributed to Solomon once attracted a fair amount of controversy, Christian tradition did not, for the most part, doubt the idea of his authorship or of Solomon's divine inspiration in composing them. Tertullian, for example, stated that their "supreme antiquity endows these books with the highest authority".[14] As to whether it was fitting to grant authority (*auctoritas*) to Ecclesiastes—its author being given to wickedness and sin—the consensus was positive, as Solomon also exemplified the penitent sinner.[15]

Solomon's Temple[16]

Rabbinic Judaism regarded the construction of the Temple as Solomon's greatest deed—an eternal and even cosmic act. Some sources describe the building and inauguration of the Temple as second in importance only to the theophany at Mount Sinai. The Sages even viewed the construction of the Temple as an act that ensured Solomon a place in the next world. The *Midrash Song of Songs Rabbah* says: "all assist the king; all the more then do all assist for the glory of the king of kings, the Holy One, blessed be He, even spirits, even ministering angels".[17] According to R. Berekiah, during its construction, stones carried themselves to the Temple and arranged themselves row by row. The Sages were not, however, universally complimentary about Solomon's great creation: though he spent seven years building the Temple, he devoted thirteen to the construction of his extravagant palace. Not only that, but upon completion of the Temple, he married the Pharaoh's daughter, celebrating their marriage with an elaborate

---

13. Isidore, *Allegoriae quaedam sanctae Scriptura*, Migne, Patrologia Latina, Vol. 98, cols. 97–130.
14. "Auctoritatem litteris praestat antiquitas summa". Apologeticum, XIX. F1.
15. Minnis (2009, pp. 109–111).
16. Georg Salzberger (1912). On the Temple in the New Testament, see Hogeterp (2012).
17. I.1,5. The *Midrash* was compiled in the seventh or eighth century CE.

feast.[18] Several rabbinic midrashim, in fact, even hold Solomon responsible for the Temple's destruction.[19] Jewish (and Muslim) legends refer frequently to the Temple, its construction, and the role of demons therein.[20]

In medieval Jewish thought, the Temple was described as the 'image of the world', as (in conjunction with its vessels) a symbol of the heavens, and even as a means of influencing earthly events, foreseeing the future, and more.[21] Christian tradition, in contrast, assigned less importance to Solomon's Temple than to the Second Temple built by Herod, where Jesus preached. The Gospels depict the Temple's destruction in the revolt against the Romans as the result of the Jews' stubborn refusal to acknowledge Jesus as the Messiah: "Did ye never read in the scriptures, The stone which the builders rejected, the same is become the head of the corner: this is the Lord's doing, and it is marvelous in our eyes? Therefore say I unto you, The kingdom of God shall be taken from you, and given to a nation bringing forth the fruits thereof. And whosoever shall fall on this stone shall be broken: but on whomsoever it shall fall, it will grind him to powder".[22] The rejection of Jesus' teachings led to the Temple's ruin; when his disciples showed him its buildings, Jesus said to them: "You see all these, do you not? Truly I tell you, not one stone will be left here upon another; all will be thrown down".[23] According to the Gospel of John, the temple of Jesus' body was the true Temple,[24] and the Christian church the true realiza-

---

18. *Leviticus Rabbah* 12:5, where the feast and its aftermath relates to the destruction of the Temple.

19. Gilad Sasson, *King and Layman* (Hebrew).

20. Masonic fantasy had it that the building plan on which Solomon based the Temple had been given to Moses at Sinai. The Temple has, since the seventeenth century, symbolized the perfect building, which embodies cosmic and supernatural forces. On the idea that at Mount Sinai God showed Moses the design for the building, which had been kept in Paradise, see *Lost Vision of Baruch* 1:4, pp. 6–7, ed. Stephen Pidgeon (2015). On the Masonic order, see Stevenson (1988). As an example of bizarre literature on the Temple, see Christopher Knight and Alan Butler (2007). According to Masonic tradition, Solomon possessed Moses' secret plans for the Temple. There exists a pseudo-tradition that the Templars discovered the Holy Ark in the ruins of the Temple and found therein ancient secrets from the time of Moses, including information that helped Columbus find his way to America. See Pellech (1997). Medieval legend had it that the Temple was built of cedars taken from the Garden of Eden and carried into this world by flood waters that deposited them on Mount Lebanon, from whence they were brought to Jerusalem.

21. Schwartz (2005), *Studies on Astral Magic in Medieval Jewish Thought*, 2nd ed.

22. Matthew 21:44–46 and similar verses.

23. Matthew 24:2.

24. John 2:21.

tion of Haggai's prophecy.[25] Similarly, in Corinthians, the Church is the Temple in spirit, and Christians are the temple of the living God: "What agreement has the temple of God with idols? For we are the temple of the living God; as God said, 'I will live in them and walk among them, and I will be their God, and they shall be my people'".[26] In Acts, we find that "the Most High does not dwell in houses made with human hands";[27] in the Book of Revelation, that the new Jerusalem will descend from the heavens "prepared as a bride adorned for her husband".[28] The *Epistle of Barnabas*, written between 70–200 C.E., quotes Isaiah—"The heaven is my throne, and the earth is my footstool: where is the house that ye build unto me? And where is the place of my rest?"—as evidence that there can be a Temple to God only where he himself tells us that He is building it and perfecting it. Such a Temple will be erected only when we were made new men, created all over again from the beginning; and as a consequence of that, God is at this moment actually dwelling in us".[29] In his *Dialogue with Trypho*, Justin Martyr taunts his Jewish interlocutor, claiming that there are no grounds for the Jewish contention that Solomon is the subject of Psalm 24 ("Who shall ascend into the hill of the LORD? Or who shall stand in his holy place? [...] Who is this King of glory? The LORD strong and mighty, the LORD mighty in battle") and that the "King of glory" is, in fact, Jesus.[30]

In the Byzantine era, the hymns of the Jerusalem Christian liturgy for the eve of Palm Sunday included the words: "Corrupt and adulterous *synagoga*, you who have not kept faith with your husband, why have you held on to an inheritance to which you do not merit?"[31] The fourth-century poet Aurelius Prudentius Clemens, a native of Spain, wrote in his *Tituli Historiarum* (Scenes from History) that "Wisdom built a Temple by Solomon's obedient hands, and the Queen from the South [i. e., the Queen of Sheba] piles up a great weight of gold. The time is at hand when Christ shall build his Temple in the hearts of man".[32]

---

25. Haggai 2:9: "The glory of this temple shall be greater than the former".

26. 2 Corinthians 6:16, and see 2 Corinthians 5:1. "For we know that if the earthly tent we live in is destroyed, we have a building from God, a house with hands, eternal in heavens".

27. Acts 7:48.

28. Revelation 21:2.

29. *The Epistle of Barnabas*, in (Staniforth 1968, pp. 178–179).

30. Justin Martyr (2003, p. 212).

31. Athanasios Papadopoulos-Kerameus (1963, pp. 28–29).

32. "*Aedificat templum Sapientia per Solomonis\Obsequium; regina austri graue congerit aurum. \ Tempus adest quo templum hominis sub pectore Christus \ Aedificet, quod Graia colant, quod barbara ditent*" (Dittochaeon XXX). *Prudentius* (1979, Vol. 2, pp. 356–357).

In *Capistrum Iudaeorum*, his polemic against the Jews, the 13th century Dominican friar Raymond (Raimundus) Martini addressed a verse in Haggai according to which "The latter splendor of this house shall be greater than the former";[33] according to Martini, the prophecy would be fulfilled by the Messiah himself—"the treasure of all nations".[34] For this argument Martini cited putative evidence from the Bible and the Talmud.[35]

Eusebius's view was that while Solomon constructed a material Temple, Jesus created a Temple of believers—the body of Christ.[36] Augustine expressed a similar sentiment: "Jesus built a Temple, not with wood and stone, but with human beings";[37] "Now we build this house by living good lives, and God also builds it by helping us to live".[38] Hence Psalm 127—"A Song of Ascents, of Solomon: Except the Lord build the house, they labour in vain that build it"—refers not to Solomon, who presaged Jesus, but to Jesus himself, who from the hearts of his faithful built a Temple destined to become eternal.[39] The poem "*Das Lob Salomons*" (In Praise of Solomon), written in 1150, is a paean to the greatness of Solomon, the *Rex pacificus* (peace-loving king). Its anonymous author attributes the tale related to a man by the name of Heronimus who discovered it in a book called *Archely*, perhaps a reference to the *Ancient History* of Pseudo-Eusebius. The poem depicts Solomon as a great king, the predecessor of Jesus, and the bridegroom of the Song of Songs; verses 23–24 allegorically describe Solomon, the Queen of Sheba, and the Church and bishops as the teachers of Christianity, concluding with a prayer that Solomon's court be received in the Kingdom of Heaven. The poem tells of how Solomon caught a terrifying dragon who threatened the supply of water to Jerusalem; the dragon having fallen asleep, Solomon fettered it, and the captured serpent then revealed to the king how he might build the Temple in a single year by trapping a great beast that inhabited Lebanon and fashioning from the beast's veins a cord that would cut marble in two as cleanly as a razor. "Thus," the story concludes, "was the house at Jerusalem built without the use of iron [*ani alliz*

---

33. Haggai 2:9.
34. Haggai 2:7.
35. J. Cohen (1999, p. 347).
36. *Quaestiones Evangelicae, Supplementa ad Stephanum*, 9–10.
37. xvii:8 in Augustine (1984).
38. xvii:12, p. 734 in Augustine (1984).
39. Possibly this attitude may be the reason why in the iconography of the Orthodox Church there are no depictions of the construction of the Temple. It does appear in Muslim iconography, although the Quran does not mention its existence. See Eva Şarlak and Ruhiye Onurel (2014, p. 323).

isin]".⁴⁰

Thus, the earthly Temple symbolized *Synagoga* and the heavenly Temple, *Ecclesia*.⁴¹ Yet Christianity found a symbol for its victory over Judaism in the earthly Temples as well. "We have triumphed over you, Solomon [*nenikeka se Solomon*]", the Byzantine Emperor Justin I boasted (according to the historian Procopius of Caesarea) upon the final construction of the Hagia Sophia in Constantinople, a basilica larger and more elaborate than Solomon's Temple.⁴² Ahimaaz ben Paltiel (1017–1069?), a Jewish chronicler and poet from Capua, would certainly have been familiar with that claim when he related the story of R. Shefatia, who was ordered to travel to Constantinople and meet with the Emperor in order to debate with him about which edifice was more glorious. R. Shefatia requested that a Bible be brought to him, and therein located proof that Solomon's Temple far surpassed the new church. The Emperor was convinced and admitted: "R. Shefatia has triumphed over me in his wisdom"; to which Shefatia modestly replied: "My Lord, the Scripture prevailed against thee, not I".⁴³ Perhaps Judaism's "triumph" here related less to the relative magnificence of the Temple than to the fact that the Church, unsatisfied with its own spiritual offerings, resorted to emulating Solomon's "earthly" Temple in constructing elaborate edifices of stone—churches, cathedrals, and basilicas.

***

In *Nahar me-Eden*—a short history of the Jewish people for young readers adapted and translated from a Lutheran Christian collection of 52 tales from each of the Old and New Testaments⁴⁴—the writer David Samostz (1789–1864) adapted the original's moral regarding the Temple: "For the Lord of Hosts Solomon built our Temple / Such a magnificent edifice had never been built by a king: but I am a poor man, a simple weaver / I cannot build you a house for your eternal praise / Take instead my heart, where I will sacrifice my gratitude and offerings of peace".⁴⁵ Like Christian tradition (and Isaiah), Samostz

---

40. Brunner (2003, p. 92); Gevnents (1982, pp. 167–83). See further in Chapters Five and Six.

41. Schlauch (1939, pp. 448–464).

42. *De aedificiis*, 1, 1. This story is also related by the fifth-century Syrian monk and theologian Evagrius in his *Historia Ecclesiastica* I, 4, 31. See Paulus Silentiarius, *Ekphrasis of Sophia Church*; Evagrius, *Historia Ecclesiastica*, 1, 4, 13; Procopius, *De aedificiis*, book 1, 1.

43. *The Chronicle of Ahimaaz*, 17–18 (Salzmann 1966, pp. 70–71). See Bonfil (2009).

44. Hübner (1986 [1714], p. 150).

45. Samostz (1837, p. 154). Regarding the book, its author, and its aims, see the

wished for the reconstruction of the earthly Temple; nor was he alone in that desire.

The Queen of Sheba's Visit as a Typological Event

The event in Solomon's biography perhaps most popular in the Christian, Jewish, and Muslim traditions, as well as in Ethiopian tradition[46] and in folktales and *belles lettres*, is the story of the Queen of Sheba's visit to Jerusalem, as described in 1 Kings 10:1–13 and 2 Chronicles 9:1–12.[47] According to commentators, the story was mentioned in both the prophecies of Isaiah—"all those from Sheba shall come. They shall bring gold and frankincense, and shall proclaim the praise of the Lord"—and in Psalms—"May the kings of Tarshish and of the isles render him tribute, may the kings of Sheba and Seba bring gifts".[48] In Christian literature, the visit serves to foretell Jesus' universal mission; it is mentioned in Mark 10:1–11, Luke 11:29–32, and Matthew 12:42. In the latter verse, Jesus tells the Pharisees: "The queen of the South will rise up at the judgment with this generation and condemn it, because she came from the ends of the earth to listen to the wisdom of Solomon, and see, something greater than Solomon is here!"[49]

Christian tradition holds that the Queen's visit presaged the coming of the Magi[50] to the manger in Bethlehem, where they brought to the infant Jesus "gifts of gold, frankincense, and myrrh"[51]— clearly a parallel to Psalms 72:10 and to the prophecy in Isaiah. Her visit furthermore foretold the future acknowledgement of Jesus and his teachings by other nations,[52] and her pronouncement that God had appointed Solomon "to execute justice and righteousness"[53] was read as intended for Jesus. Bede the Venerable described the visit in his *Quaestiones super Regum Libros* (Questions on the Books of Kings),

M.A. thesis by Ran HaCohen (1994, pp. 47–63). The book was based on Hübner. Samostz did not translate the fifty-two New Testament tales.

46. See Silberman (1974); Schechter (1890); Stein (1993).
47. Lassner (1993); Milstein (1995, pp. 115–117).
48. Isaiah 60:6 and Psalms 72:10.
49. Matthew 12:42.
50. According to later tradition, these were three (because of the three gifts) "wise men" or "kings" (a trio appears in a mosaic in the sixth-century Basilica Di St. Apollinare Nuovo, in Ravenna); the traditions around them noted the various countries from which they came and their race or the color of their skin in order to underscore the universality of Jesus' teachings. Legendary biographies for the three were also composed, such as that by the Carmelite friar Johannes von Hildesheim (1315/20–1375), *Historia de gestis et translatione trium regum* (Die Legende von den Heiligen Drei Königen [The Legend of the Three Holy Kings]). See M. B. Freeman (1979).
51. Matthew 2:11.
52. Eusebius, *Commentary* on Isaiah 11.
53. 1 Kings 10:9.

as did Isidore of Seville, who wrote: "The queen from the south who came to hear the wisdom of Solomon is to be understood as the Church, which assembles from the utmost limits of the world to hear the voice of God".

The Theological and Allegorical Interpretations of Solomon's Books

The three books of *Sapientia Salomonis*—biblical books ascribed to Solomon— are the Song of Songs, Proverbs, and Ecclesiastes. All three have served, in every historical period, as a bottomless source for myriad commentaries, adaptations, and other uses. They have been employed by diverse authors to express diverse worldviews in numerous and varied contexts, including the conflict between Judaism and Christianity. The three books were furthermore believed to complement Solomon's biography and reflect the process of his spiritual development. I shall cite only a handful of the countless interpretations and commentaries on the subject, while noting that these commentaries were often forced to grapple with several internal contradictions, such as the different connotations of the Hebrew word "*chokhmah*" (wisdom) in the Song of Songs versus Ecclesiastes.

The Sages, characteristically, were divided in their opinions about the three books, supplying diverse arguments for—and against— their canonization in the Holy Scriptures. Some Sages drew distinctions between the books, divided on the question of which of the three should be considered holy or profane. The accepted view, however, was that all three were written in the divine spirit.

Rabbi Benjamin ben Levi stated that "the Sages wished to suppress the book of Ecclesiastes, for they found in it ideas that leaned toward heresy. They argued, was it right that Solomon should have said the following: 'Rejoice, young man, while you are young, and let your heart cheer you in the days of your youth'.[54] Moses said, 'and not follow the lust of your own heart and your own eyes (Num 15:39) but Solomon said, 'Follow the inclination of your heart and the desire of your eyes'.[55] What then? Are there neither judges nor justice? Is all restraint to be removed? When, however, he said, 'But know then that for all these things God will bring thee into judgment,' they admitted that Solomon had spoken well".[56] R. Yudan said […] that all who teach the Torah to the public…. the holy spirit rests upon him". *Song of Songs Rabbah* continues: "Said the Holy One, blessed be He, to [Solomon]: 'Thou dost seek out words of Torah; I swear that I will

---

54. Ecclesiastes 11:9.
55. Ecclesiastes 11:9.
56. *Leviticus Rabbah* 28:1.

not withhold thy reward. Because I cause the holy spirit to rest on thee'. Forthwith the Holy Spirit rested on him and he composed these three books".[57] And: "So the heart of Solomon was full of wisdom but no one knew what was in it but when the holy spirit rested on him he composed three books".[58] *Avot de Rabbi Nathan* provides a brief description of the controversy: "it is said, Proverbs, Song of Songs, and Ecclesiastes were suppressed; for since they were held to be mere parables and not part of the Holy Writings, [the religious authorities] arose and suppressed them; [and so they remained] until the men of Hezekiah [the Men of the Great Assembly][59] came and interpreted them".[60]

Early Christianity accepted the attribution of all three books to Solomon with scarce reservations;[61] they proved a wellspring of references to Jesus, his teachings, and the Church, and a fount of prophecies, moral teachings, and cosmology. According to Origen, each of the books dealt with a different area of knowledge: Proverbs taught moral science, or ethics; Ecclesiastes examined the natural sciences; and, in the Song of Songs, Solomon "instills into the soul the love of things divine and heavenly using for his purpose the figure of the Bride and Bridegroom".[62] Solomon-Ecclesiastes presaged Jesus, the "true Ecclesiastes", who would gather the Church into a unified flock. The Cappadocian Church Father and mystic Gregory of Nyssa (c.335-c.394) believed he had deciphered the philosophy hidden in Solomon's books, which conveyed a "philosophical way of life".[63] Thomas Aquinas relied on Plotinus when he wrote that the three books might be classified according to the three grades of virtue. The first was the political virtues, expressed in Proverbs; the second was the purgative virtues, described in Ecclesiastes; and the third was the purged soul, whereby a man, wholly cleansed of worldly cares, delights in the contemplations of wisdom alone; that virtue Aquinas identified in the

---

57. *Song of Songs Rabbah* 1,4–5. (According Neusner's numbering. In the Wilna edition, it would be 1.1.8–9.)

58. *Song of Songs Rabbah* 1,7.

59. The legendary Jewish legislative and administrative council during the early Second Temple period.

60. *Avot de-Rabbi Nathan* A 1.1 p. 2, trans. Judah Goldin, Yale University Press, 1955.

61. Augustine writes that "weightier authorities have no hesitation in rejecting the attribution. Nevertheless, the Church, and the Western Church in particular, has from early times accepted them [the three books] as canonical" (CD XVII:20), 354. The Catholic canon included *The Wisdom of Solomon* from the third to first centuries B.C.E.

62. Origen (1957, p. 41).

63. Pelikan (1993, pp. 180–181). For further discussion see Chapter Seven.

Song of Songs.[64] Isidore of Seville believed that Ecclesiastes taught natural philosophy (that is, physics) while the Song of Songs dealt with rational philosophy, or logic.[65]

The Song of Songs

Of the three books attributed to Solomon, the Song of Songs seems to have been the subject of the largest number of commentaries.[66] It would be no exaggeration to speak of a sea of commentaries, divided on the issue of whether the text should be considered "literally", as a mere love song, or allegorically; and if the latter, as an allegory of what? In any event, both Jewish and Christian commentaries employed similar hermeneutical principles and exegetical methods, and both consider the book as a theological and mystical allegory.[67]

It was R. Akiva, in the second century, who decreed that the book should not be read literally.[68] In the Mishnah, we find that "R. Akiva said: Heaven forbid, no man of Israel has ever disputed about the Song of Songs, claiming that it did not defile the hands. The whole world is not worthy of the day on which the Song of Songs was given to Israel, for all the Scriptures are holy, but the Song of Song is Holy of Holies".[69] The saying: "Had the Torah not been granted us, the Song of Songs would have sufficed to manage the world" was furthermore attributed to him. *Sanhedrin 101a* also expresses a view of the text as possessing religious significance: "He who recites a verse of the Song of Songs and treats it as a secular air, and one who recites a verse at the banqueting table unseasonably, brings evil upon the world. Because the Torah girds itself in sackcloth, and stands before the Holy One, blessed be He, and laments before Him, 'Sovereign of the Universe! Thy children have made me as a harp upon which they frivolously play'".[70]

The rule established by R. Akiva opened the gates to a plethora of allegorical, historical, and mystical interpretations of the book that created common ground with Christian[71] allegoristic and mystical commentaries. However, that is not the main point in the Midrash,

---

64. "Inaugural Sermons of 1256", in Aquinas (1998, p. 11).
65. Minnis (2009, p. 26). See also Smalley (1983).
66. See Bartal (2009, pp. 113–154).
67. In Ashkenazi synagogues, the Song of Songs is read on the Sabbath of the intermediate days of Passover, and in Sephardic synagogues on every Sabbath eve.
68. On the hypothesis that the Song of Songs is based on earlier writings, which also preceded Kings, see Zakovitch (2015).
69. *Mishna Yadayim* 3,5.
70. Modern Hebrew literature has violated this rule, having "secularized" Song of Songs and used its words as lyrics for popular songs.
71. Yonah Frankel (1994); Urbach (1961).

according to which the legitimacy and authority of the Song of Songs derived from its utility as a gateway to understanding the Bible.

The Jewish allegorical reading of the Song of Songs describes the eternal covenant between God and the People of Israel and conveys a message about the redemption of the Jewish people and the construction of the Temple. Mishnah *Ta'anit*[72] interprets the verse "come out. Look, O daughters of Zion, at King Solomon"[73] thus: "Go out, maidens of Jerusalem and look on King Solomon and on the crown with which his mother crowned him on the day of his wedding, and on the day of the gladness of his heart"—"'the day of his wedding' that is 'the giving of the Torah'". According to Maimonides, "Solomon, of blessed memory, inspired by the Holy Spirit, foresaw that the prolonged duration of exile would incite some of our people to seek to terminate it before the appointed time, and consequently they would perish or meet with disaster. Therefore he admonished them in metaphorical language to desist, as we read: I adjure you, O daughters of Jerusalem, by the gazelles or the wild does: do not stir up or awaken love until it is ready!"[74] The *Epistle to Yemen* (1172) aimed to hearten the Jews that they might avoid succumbing to either their oppressors or to messianic delusion. He further added that in the Song of Songs, Solomon metaphorically described the people of Israel as Shulamit, a woman of perfect beauty, marred by no defect.[75] In his own commentary on the Song of Songs, Rashi (R. Shlomo Yitzhaki, 1040–1105) regarded the book as an allegory of God's love for the Jewish people, where the latter is likened to a widow yearning for the love of her youth; Solomon, made prophetic through the divine spirit, foresees a harsh future before her, until her redemption at the End of Days. Thus, for example, "Let him kiss me with the kisses of his mouth" expresses the bride's longing for the bridegroom, in contrast to Origen's interpretation in which the Church yearns for union with Jesus. (Origen also interpreted "for thy love is better than wine" as referring to the love (*ubera*) of the groom [Jesus]; replete in wisdom and knowledge, it is superior to the earlier wine of the Torah and the prophets.[76]

The Middle Ages saw the development of a Jewish rationalist and allegorical exegesis, universal in nature. That exegesis read the Song of Songs in light of the "doctrine of intelligence; the "bride",

---

72. Chapter Four, *Mishnah* 8.

73. Song of Solomon 3:11.

74. Song of Solomon 3:5; Maimonides bases himself on b.Ketubbot 111a where the verse is quoted, but without naming Solomon.

75. Maimonides' "The Epistle to Yemen", in Halkin and Hartman (1985; pp. 104–105, 130), Kellner (1991).

76. I base this on an article by Sarah Kamin, "Rashi's Commentary on the Song of Songs and Jewish-Christian Polemics" (Kamin 2008a). See also Kamin (2008b).

for example, was understood as representing the soul, housed within a material form.[77] In "*Sefer Sha'ar ha-Ceshek*", the introduction to his book *Ceshek Shlomo* (The Delight of Solomon), the JewishItalian neo-Platonic scholar and biblical exegete Johanan ben Isaac Alemanno (c. 1434–1503)[78]—to whom I will return in forthcoming chapters—depicted the Song of Songs as a spiritual biography of Solomon and a parallel to his intellectual biography as a *homo universalis*: a scholar of wide-ranging pursuits, wellversed in many of the "natural sciences" and in religious law, magic, alchemy, and astrology.

Christian interpretations[79] held that if, in fact, King Solomon was the author of the Song of Songs, then he foretold the covenant between the Christian faithful (the *Ecclesia*) and Jesus. Origen wrote: "In this [book] he [Solomon] instills into the soul the love of things divine and heavenly, using for his purpose the figure of the Bride and Bridegroom, and teaches us that communion with God must be attained by the path of charity and love".[80] Solomon's bride in Song of Songs[81] is the Ecclesia, gathered from among the nations (*Haec sponsa, quae loquitur ecclesiae personam tenet ex gentibus congregatae*); and the "lily of the valleys"[82] represents the Church of the gentiles. The Torah brought no man to a state of perfection, and hence the word of God could not advance beyond the flower and achieve the perfection of the fruit; only in the valley of the gentiles did it become a lily. "But what sort of lily? Surely just such a one as that of which He Himself says in the Gospels that the heavenly Father clothes it, and that not even Solomon in all his glory was arrayed as one of these".[83] The Song of Songs, according to Origen, depicts the mystical ascension of the soul and the soul's relationship to Jesus: "[It] sings by the spirit the song of the marriage whereby the Church is joined and allied to Christ the heavenly bridegroom, desiring to unite with him through speech". It describes the union with perfection that occurs after everything is subjugated to God, who will then be called Solomon—He in whom lies Peace. According to Ambrose,[84] the words "I am black, but comely, O

---

77. Schwartz (1993; 2016). However, as we shall see further on, no description was given of the content of Solomon's "wise soul" or of the nature of the "wisdom" that he meant to disseminate to humanity.

78. See Chapter Seven.

79. See Astell (1990).

80. *Commentary*, Prologue. See Origen (1957, pp. 31–41).

81. Song of Solomon 3:11: "[…] come out. Look, O daughters of Zion, at King Solomon, at the crown with which his mother crowned him on the day of his wedding, on the day of the gladness of his heart".

82. Song of Solomon 2:1.

83. *Commentary in Canticum* (*Commentary of Song of Songs*), 177.

84. *Commentarium*, 1:4–5.

ye daughters of Jerusalem" symbolized the *Synagoga* as black because it lived in error and disbelief; yet it was still comely since, in the end, it would find faith. Augustine too considered the Song of Songs a representation of the marriage of Jesus and the Church; it expressed, he felt, "a kind of spiritual delight felt by holy minds in the marriage of the king and queen of the city, namely Christ and his Church".[85] Gregory of Nyssa maintained that the book expressed a sublime philosophy— the unification of all mankind, joined in yearning for a common goal. In the Song, Solomon appears "in the persona of the Bridegroom, the Word of God who, as Gregory saw the matter, brings the Bride step by step to ever greater and higher attainment. Indeed, Gregory saw the Song's successive praises and characterization of the believing soul (i. e., the Bride) as marking a series of steps or "ascents"".[86] And the Carolingian exegete Haimo of Auxerre (d. 875) wrote in his popular commentary *Commentarium in Cantica Canticorum* that the words "Return, return Shulamite, that we may behold you" are the words of *Ecclesia* to *Synagoga*, bidding her to accept the true doctrine.[87]

Scholastic and monastic commentaries differed only on the question of whether the connection in question existed between Jesus and the entire Church, or on a more personal level between Jesus and each believing soul. Bernard of Clairvaux (1090–1153), who wrote eighty-six sermons on two chapters of the Song of Songs, stressed its moral-tropological nature. The book, in his view, was an account of Jesus as the bridegroom of the soul by inspiration from heaven. In it, Solomon sang the praises of Christ and his Church, the grace of holy love, and the sacraments of eternal marriage, at the same time giving voice to the deepest desire of the holy soul.[88] For Bernard, the Song of Songs served as evidence that the truth lay in the allegorical, tropological, and anagogical reading, while the Jewish "literal" reading wrongly interpreted it as dealing with 'worldly matters' on the level of unripe figs (a reference to Song of Songs 2:13: "The fig tree puts forth its figs").

One exception to such commentary is Theodore of Mopsuestia (350–428), who belonged to the school of Antioch, active between the third and fifth centuries. Theodore rejected the allegorical interpretation; Lawson called him a jejune rationalist since he believed that Solomon had composed the book as a response to criticism of

---

85. *City of God*, XVIII:20 (Augustine 1984). According to Augustine, this was a mystical epithalamium; see *City of God*, p. 757. Also see Minnis (2009, p. 43 and note 22, p. 236).
86. Gregory of Nyssa (1994, p. xxxvi).
87. According to Monroe (2007, pp. 33–61).
88. Bernard of Clairvaux (1981) 1.4.8.

his marriage to Pharaoh's daughter. Theodore was condemned by the Second Council of Constantinople in 553 and was regarded as the father of Nestorianism.[89] His work was echoed a millennium later when William (Guillaume) of St. Thierry (c. 1330) also wrote that the Song of Songs was Solomon's celebration of the marriage in question.

Proverbs

Jesus' proverbs differ from Solomon's; the latter are aphorism wrapped in metaphor, and more greatly resemble the Sages' *midrashim* (homiletic interpretations), which are studded with proverbs themselves.[90] The *Midrash Song of Songs Rabbah* interprets Ecclesiastes 12:9 as follows: "And moreover, because the preacher was wise, he still taught the people knowledge; yea, he gave good heed, and sought out, and set in order many proverbs. And made ears [handles] for the Torah".[91] In other words, the proverbs are akin to handles on a pot or jug, that one may grasp in order to examine the contents.[92] Other Sages compared Solomon to one who has discovered the entrance to a vast palace: "Until Solomon arose there was no one who was able to comprehend the words of the Torah, but as soon as he arose, all began to comprehend the Torah". He is similarly likened to a man making his way through a grove of cane stalks or lowering a bucket into a pool of deep water; thus "from proverb to proverb, Solomon uncovered the secrets of the Torah". R. Yudan attributed a different order to the process: "Anyone who speaks Torah [to others], receives the blessing of being imbued by the holy spirit. And from whom do we learn this? From Solomon, who, having spoken Torah, was imbued by the holy spirit and was moved to speak his books".[93] Thus, Solomon's proverbs open the way to an understanding of the Torah; at the same time, it is through the communal study of the Torah that the spirit of God rests upon the learner.

In Augustine's view, the Book of Proverbs demonstrated that all men "have come to know that Christ is the wisdom of God" (Proverbs 9:1–5); 'Wisdom has built her house, she has hewn her seven pillars, slaughtered her animals, she has mixed her wine, she has also set her table. She has sent out her servantgirls' [...]". Here we recognize with certainty the Wisdom of God, that is, the Word, co-eternal with the Father who built, as a house for himself, a human body, in the

---

89. On Theodore see McLeod (2009).
90. Flusser (1979, pp. 150–209). However, Jesus' parables were recited orally before an audience.
91. Midrash *Song of Songs Rabbah* 1, 8.
92. Meir (2014); Boyarin (1990, pp. 105–116).
93. *Song of Songs Rabbah* 1, 8.

virgin's womb, and united the Church to hit, as a limbs are united to the head".⁹⁴ Clement of Alexandria quoted Proverbs 2:1–2: "For the soul, methinks, joined with soul, and spirit with spirit, in the sowing of the word, will make that which is sown grow and germinate. And every one who is instructed is in respect of subjection the son of the instructor".⁹⁵

Medieval Christian culture in Europe was "thick weaves of proverbs";⁹⁶ Michael Hattaway writes that "it is obvious that Solomon's moral philosophy was disseminated in countless collections of proverbs and adages",⁹⁷ which served as a form of speech in both high and popular literature,⁹⁸ as in the dialogue between Solomon and Saturnus.⁹⁹ At times, proverbs were attributed to Solomon—the "son of Sapience"—of which he was not the author.¹⁰⁰ These were quoted most often—but not exclusively—in the context of reflections on the correct conduct of rulers and others. In the dispute about the doctrine of two swords, Pope Boniface VIII quoted Proverbs 8:15 in declaring that "through Him the apostolic princes govern and kings rule".¹⁰¹ Prudence, Melibeus's wife in the *Canterbury Tales* "Tale of Melibeus", is another invoker of Solomon's aphorisms: "Solomon saith 'that right as moths in the sheep's fleece annoy [do injury] to the cloth, and the small worms to the tree, right so annoyeth sorrow to the heart of man'; When the condition of man is pleasant and liking to God, he changeth the heart of the man's adversaries, and constrains them to beseech him of peace of grace".¹⁰²

The saying in Proverbs 22:6: "Train children in the right way, and when old, they will not stray" was widely accepted as a pedagogical

---

94. *City of God* XVII: 20, (Augustine 1984, p. 755).

95. Clement of Alexandria, The Stromata (1955, 2nd ed., p. 299).

96. Ziolkowski (2008, p. 29); for further discussion see Chapter Seven. Proverbs was frequently quoted, particularly for pedagogical purposes. One example is "Garden of Delights" (*Hortus deliciarum*), a pedagogical tool for young novices in 336 illustrations by Herrad of Landsberg, the Abbey of present-day Mont Saint-Odile, Alsace in 1167–1185. See also Minnis (2009).

97. Hattaway (1968, p. 503); West (1954).

98. Zemon Davis (1975). Adelaid de Condet, the lady of Thorngate Castel (England), commissioned, in c.1150, a translation of *Proverbs* into Anglo-Saxon by Sanson de Nanteuil that was used in the education of her son.

99. See the introduction by John Kemble to *The Dialogue of Solomon and Saturnus* (Kemble 1848, pp. 104–113). Regarding that book, see Chapter Seven.

100. These proverbs were enormously popular. See, for example, *Proverbia Salomonis, quae sunt historiae tabellae*, 1517; *Proverbia Salomonis*, 1557.

101. Ullman (1965, p. 128).

102. Chaucer's tale is an adaptation of a French "treatise" in prose: "Le Livre de Me'libe'e et de Dame Prudence". Also see "The Merchant": "It was only that you are so full of wisdom \ that in your exalted prudence it does not please you \ to depart from the proverb of Solomon". Chaucer (1971, p. 253).

principle and given various interpretations in Jewish and Christian societies. One example is the sermon by the humanist Thomas Horn of Kings College-Cambridge, given in 1679 before the graduates of Eton: "When Solomon says, train up a child in the way he should go, we understand that as catechizing and informing him in the way of Religion in which everyone should go…".[103]

Ecclesiastes[104]

Ecclesiastes has always been an exegetical challenge,[105] interweaving as it does words of heresy, words of piety, and practical wisdom. According to Jewish and Christian traditions, the book—the last ascribed to Solomon—was composed in the king's old age and reflects his life experience: "But in his old age, king Solomon was near to his death. Then the holy spirit rested upon him and spoke three books—Proverbs, Song of Songs and Ecclesiastes",[106] though "[as] he aged he babbled foolishly".[107] Several verses were thus interpreted as supplementing what was known of his biography and explicating the lessons he derived from his life.

The question of whether the book merited canonization was controversial because it contained "matters that lead toward heresy" and "words that contradict each other". According to Rabbi Samuel ben Naḥman, the Sages intended to suppress the book of Ecclesiastes because they found ideas in it that leaned toward heresy. They said "Should Solomon have uttered the following: What profit hath man of all his labor? This might imply, might it not, that labor in the study of the Torah was also included? On the other hand, they argued, if he had said 'of all labor' and left it at that, we might have thought that he meant to include labor as well as the study of Torah, however, he does not say this but 'of all his labor' implying that in his own labor man finds no profit, but that he does find profit in his labor studying Torah".[108] *Kohelet Rabbah* makes an even greater effort to find Ecclesiastes "worthy": "I know that there is nothing better for them than to rejoice, and to get pleasure so long as they live. But also that every man

---

103. See in Heyd (2011). According to Hattaway, Erasmus uses ammunition texts from Ecclesiastes and Proverbs for his virtuoso paradoxes that opposed the childlike simplicity of Christ to the sophistical wisdom of the schoolmen. Hattaway (1968, p. 508).

104. The Hebrew appellation "Kohelet" [Ecclesiastes] derives, according to Kohelet Rabbah, from the fact that "[Solomon] spoke in the *kahal* [assembly]".

105. Bolin (2017).

106. *Song of Songs Rabbah* 1:1.10 (Neusner's translation counts it as 1:1. 6.17), and *Yalkut Shimoni Kohelet*, § 965.

107. *Yalkut Kohelet* § 965.

108. *Midrash Rabbah Leviticus* 28.1.

should eat and drink". R. Tanḥuma in the name of R. Nahman, the son of R. Samuel b. Nahman, and R. Menahem said; 'All the eating and drinking mentioned in this book refer to Torah and good deeds'".[109]

In Eusebius Sophronius Hieronymus' (342\7–420) view, Ecclesiastes taught of "the vanity in everything that touches upon our senses in the world". He interpreted the verse "one generation passeth away, and another generation cometh" (1:4) as meaning that "the first generation of Jews passed, and the later generation of Christians came; now that that the synagogue has disappeared, the land will survive as long until the Church has fully entered (*terra autem tamdiu stat, quamdiu synagoga recedente ecclesia omnis introeat*). In reply to which the Midrash reads: "R Isaak said: 'A kingdom comes and a kingdom goes but Israel abides forever'".[110] Gregory of Nazianzus (329–390) found in Ecclesiastes overwhelming proof that at the end of his life Solomon realized that philosophy was "futility, utter futility" (*mataiotes mataioteton*).[111] According to Augustine, Ecclesiastes was "concerned with the two cities, that of the Devil, and that of Christ, and with their kings, the Devil and Christ".[112] If, according to Bonaventure's commentary on Ecclesiastes (written in 1254–1257), its author was a wicked man, could it nonetheless possess authority, or was it rather written by a penitent man, and hence worthy? Like Hieronymus before him, the Franciscan theologian Bonaventure (1221–1274) replied that the epilogue, in which worldly vanity is renounced, was ultimately a declaration of faith.[113]

Is Ecclesiastes a book of wisdom? During the Renaissance, Hattaway writes, it "became a polemical instrument used by humanists who preached humility and skepticism in their attacks on the schools (scholasticism)".[114] One could argue that the words "The end of the matter; all has been heard. Fear God, and keep his commandments; for that is the whole duty of everyone"[115] demonstrate that faith is superior to wisdom and that there is no room for speculation on God's nature and deeds, or that faith and wisdom are intertwined.

Christianity links the prefiguration of Jesus in Solomon only to positive aspects of Solomon's biography, and one might argue that the canonization of the three books attributed to him, which became a fount of allegories, symbols, moral instruction, and world-views, was

---

109. *Ecclesiastes Rabbah* 3:12.
110. *Kohelet Rabbah* 1:4 (Hirshman 2016, p. 42).
111. Pelikan (1993, p. 178).
112. Augustine, xvii, 21, p. 756.
113. See Minnis (2009, pp. 110–111).
114. Minnis (2009, p. 504).
115. Ecclesiastes 12:13.

not necessarily an outcome of this attribution, but that they achieved immortality in their own right. Nonetheless, had the books not been attributed to Solomon they might not have attained such a lofty status. Nor would they have been perceived as guides in three separate spheres: in mysticism and esoterica (the Song of Songs), ethics (Proverbs), and philosophy (Ecclesiastes), which were putatively merged in the work of a single man—who was at once a king, poet, and philosopher. In such a context, the negative aspects of the author's biography were of no importance. Whenever a need existed for the formulation of a complete and unified theological or philosophical doctrine, Solomon's three books were the essential sources.[116]

This brief overview thus leads us to an ineluctable contradiction: Solomon, a king who sinned, nonetheless was perceived by Christianity as a prefiguration of Jesus, and the three books attributed to him revered as canonical authority and inexhaustible wellspring of wisdom.

---

116. In his *Solomon Among the Postmoderns* Peter J. Leithart (2008) goes so far to argue that the passage "Vanity of Vanities, all is vanity" should be translated "Vapor of Vapors, all is Vapor", and in the entire book of Ecclesiastes indicate that Solomon "resonated with the themes of today's postmodernism".

Chapter Four: The Divine Presence and a Heavenly Voice Come to Solomon's Aid—On Sin, Repentance, and Absolution

"*Hic bonis initiis, malos exitus habuit*"
　　Augustine, *De Civitate Dei*, XVII., xx[1]
"*If Samson had remained cautious and Solomon devout,
the one would not have been deprived
of his strength nor the
other of his wisdom*"
　　Vita Edwardi Secundi[2]

Solomon is not merely a prefiguration of Jesus, nor simply an ideal king. He is also a king judged by his own misconduct, for his sins against God; and in both Jewish and Christian tradition, his biblical biography occupies a central place in the debate on the nature of crime and punishment, repentance and forgiveness.

Nonetheless, Christian literature accorded far more attention to this aspect of Solomon's biography than did Jewish writers. The correspondence that existed here was not one in which each side responded to the claims of the other, but rather a seemingly shared interest in, or need to address, the biblical account of Solomon's life. In this chapter, I will present only a few of the many treatments of this subject by Jewish and Christian writers in an attempt to understand the roots of their intensive occupation with the idea of Solomon as a sinner—an

---

1. "He made a good start, but finished badly".
2. *Vita Edwardi Secundi: The Life of Edward the Second*, originally composed in the latter half of the fourteenth century (attributed to a monk of Saint Bertin). Childs (2005, pp. 214–215). According to the Vita Ewardi, Solomon's rule was "a rule of peace".

occupation that clearly reflects Christianity's attempt to grapple with the Bible and to do so through exegetical methods. More than one biblical king, after all, was held to account for his sins.

***

Fig. 2 Triumph of St. Thomas and allegory of the arts/Christian learning (1365), Andrea di Bonaiuto da Firenze, Fresco Cappella Spagnuolo, Santa Maria Novella, Florence, © Wikimedia Commons.

In the Spanish Chapel of the Dominican church Santa Maria Novella in Florence one may find a fresco by Andrea di Bonaiuto entitled "The Triumph of St. Thomas Aquinas and the Allegory of Christian Learning" (*Il trionfo di san Tomaso d'Aquino*). The eponymous theologian is seated at its center, upon a detailed throne.[3] In 1346, another Florentine, Dante Alighieri, who had studied at that very church, completed his *Divine Comedy*; in its final section, *Paradiso*, Aquinas assumes a major role and leads the poet to Solomon, who symbolizes

---

3. At the Church of St. Catherine in Pisa there is a painting by Francesco Traini from c.1349 also titled "The Triumph of St. Thomas Aquinas." There Aristotle and Plato are placed on St. Thomas's left, Averroes lies at his feet, and standing about him are Matthew, Luke, Mark, and John. On his knees he holds a Bible opened to Proverbs 8:7 ("For my mouth shall utter truth, and wickedness is an abomination to my lips"), the quotation with which he opens his *Summa contra Gentiles*. I am grateful to Dr. Sefi Hendler for drawing my attention to this painting.

the wisdom of the governing body.⁴ In Canto 10:109–111, Solomon is the author of Song of Songs, possessed of the highest wisdom. He is "the fifth light, the most beautiful among us \ breathes from such love, the whole world down there \ Desires vehemently to have news of it".⁵

In the fourteenth century, it was not yet certain that the theology of the Dominican St. Thomas would indeed triumph over that of the Franciscans, even though in 1321 the Vatican pronounced him a saint, and two years later the Bishop of Paris withdrew his accusations of heresy. In the fresco (one of the countless paintings that glorify him), St. Thomas is depicted as a victor—a man who has unified faith and wisdom (the latter encompassing Aristotelian philosophy and the sciences). He sits upon a Gothic-style throne wearing a black robe and holding an open book, surrounded by two sets of five figures representing the Old and New Testaments: David carries a harp; Moses, the Ten Commandments; Isaiah, the Book of Prophecies; Job, the book that bears his name; and Solomon, Proverbs. Nine figures of the ten have halos over their heads, and the only missing halo is King Solomon's.⁶

In denying Solomon a halo, Andrea di Bonaiuto expressed the duality in Christianity's attitudes towards him—a duality also reflected in Dante's work. Solomon—a prefiguration, according to Christology, of Jesus—was also a king who sinned greatly, did not repent, and never was forgiven. Hence, he did not merit the status of holiness granted to the other figures in the fresco (and it is both symbolic and ironic that the fresco decorates the hall of what was originally a monastery, whose monks came daily to confess their sins, hear words of reproof, and be absolved.

This ambivalent attitude towards Solomon, prevalent both in Jewish and Christian traditions, was an outcome of internal controversies within both religions regarding the nature of sin, proper expressions of penitence (*paenitentia*), methods of penance, and the significance of sinners' absolution and redemption (*actus iustificationis*). And, as in other contexts linked to Solomon's multifaceted legendary image, this duality gave rise to apologetics on the one hand and denunciation on the other. Although there were other kings in Judea and

---

4. "*[...] Regal prudenza e' quell vedere impair*", a reference to 1 Kings 3:9: "Give your servant therefore an understanding mind to govern your people, able to discern between good and evil; for who can govern this your great people?"

5. Dante Alighieri (1981, p. 394). In Henry Wadsworth Longfellow's translation: "The fifth light, that among us is the fairest, \ Breathes from such a love, that all the world \ Below is greedy to learn tiding of it". Dante Alighieri (2017, p. 36).

6. See Norman (1995, pp. 225–228); Norman does not address Solomon's missing halo. It is relevant incidentally to note the figures at the bottom of the fresco, which represent the liberal arts; among them is Aristotle, representing Philosophy.

in Israel who sinned, and whose wrongdoings were not forgiven, Solomon was the paradigmatic figure in the theological debate on these issues. In the Middle Ages— and long afterward—the definition of sin and the question of proper atonement formed both the subject of extensive theological discussion and a literary theme.[7] The debate had practical implications, namely the need to clarify the motive of a sin,[8] the question of whether a sinner who repented and atoned could achieve sainthood,[9] and the matter whether a ruler who sinned could atone and be forgiven.[10]

Solomon's Sins and Downfall in Jewish Tradition

It is ironic that the biblical author, in attempting to magnify and exalt Solomon as a king, attributed a thousand wives to his name, including a Pharaoh's daughter; what might be considered grandeur was no less a sin, whose gravity cast a heavy shadow on the construction of the Temple and on the composition of Solomon's three books. It was not the fanciful number of women that troubled Jewish and Christian thinkers (and certainly the latter could be excused for not excoriating the practice of gentile marriages) but rather the fact that these women preserved and imported their religious practices, among them the worship of idols. Thus, Solomon—the chosen of God, the architect of God's Temple, the prefiguration of Jesus—became, in both traditions, a sinful king.

Regardless of whether 1 Kings 11:3 ("Among his wives were seven hundred princesses and three hundred concubines; and his wives turned away his heart") exaggerates matters for the purpose of glorifying Solomon, or, alternatively, as a justification for his fall,[11] his heaviest sin lay not in accumulating wives but rather in building high places of worship for their religions and participating in their rites. Because he should have restrained his wives in their idolatry but did not, the Talmud says, "the Scripture regards him as though he sinned".[12]

The Bible recounts that Solomon "loved many foreign women [...] from the nations concerning which the Lord had said to the Israelites, 'You shall not enter into marriage with them, neither shall

---

7. See Ohly (1992).

8. Prudentius (2011).

9. On saints of the Church who sinned and atoned for their sins, see Dorn (1967, pp. 42–43).

10. Solomon's sins are rarely mentioned in debates on the question of whether it may be justified to murder a tyrant.

11. Zakowitch (2015).

12. *Shabbat* 56a. All these sources accept, without question, the fantastic number of his wives.

they with you; for they will surely incline your heart to follow their gods'".[13] Furthermore, "when Solomon was old, his wives turned away his heart after other gods; and his heart was not true to the Lord his God, as was the heart of his father David. For Solomon followed Astarte the goddess of the Sidonians, and Milcom the abomination of the Ammonites. So Solomon did what was evil in the sight of the Lord, and did not completely follow the Lord, as his father David had done. Then Solomon built a high place for Chemosh the abomination of Moab, and for Molech the abomination of the Ammonites, on the mountain east of Jerusalem. He did the same for all his foreign wives, who offered incense and sacrificed to their gods".[14]

The Book of Chronicles downplays the gravity of the sin, mentioning only Solomon's marriage to the Pharaoh's daughter and that he did not bring her to live in Jerusalem: He brought Pharaoh's daughter from the city of David to the house that he had built for her, for he said, "My wife shall not live in the house of King David of Israel, for the places to which the ark of the Lord has come are holy".[15] On the other hand, Ezra and Nehemiah found in Solomon's example validation for their campaign to convince Jews who returned to Zion to expel their gentile wives:[16] "Did not King Solomon of Israel sin on account of such women? Among the many nations there was no king like him, and he was beloved by his God, and God made him king over all Israel; nevertheless, foreign women made even him to sin. Shall we then listen to you and do all this great evil and act treacherously against our God by marrying foreign women?"[17] The Septuagint presages the apologetic line that would emerge in the future—Solomon did not at least, worship idols in the high places which he built for his wives.[18] Ben Sira does not deny Solomon's sins, but chooses to omit idolatry: "You did bow your loins to women, and in your body you were brought into subjection. You did blemish your honor, and profane your seed, to bring wrath upon your children; And I was grieved for your folly".[19] Josephus, in contrast, describes the king's sins at length. Not only did Solomon violate Mosaic law, marry many foreign women, and succumb in his dotage to their seduction (albeit only to gratify them), but he also placed images of brazen oxen in the Temple.[20]

---

13. 1 Kings 11:1–2.
14. 1 Kings 11:4–8.
15. 2 Chronicles 8:11.
16. Ezra 10.
17. Nehemiah 13:26–27. See Frisch (1997).
18. Gooding (1965).
19. Ben Sira 47:19–20.
20. VIII, pp. 192–193, in Josephus (1963).

As for the sages, they were divided in their attitudes towards Solomon's sins, or more precisely, in the ways they employed his image to transmit a theological and ethical message, or to express their views about monarchy as an institution, while other Sages sought explanations and justifications for his sins, yet also strongly condemned him. Others claimed that Solomon married many foreign wives "to draw them to the teaching of Torah and to bring them under the indwelling presence of God",[21] or even converted all of them to Judaism (Solomon converted only Pharaoh's daughter before marrying her, or did not marry her at all[22]); not only that but the conversion was valid.[23] A later *midrash* enumerated Solomon's sins: "'And King Solomon loved many foreign women and the daughter of Pharaoh (1 Kings 11:1). Now was the daughter of Pharaoh not included [among the women]?[24] Why, then, was she singled out for special mention? We hereby infer that she was more beloved than all, and, vis-à-vis sin, that she caused him to sin more than all".[25] In *Yalkut Shimoni's* version, Solomon transgressed the prohibition against marrying many wives and took seven hundred wives and three hundred concubines. His wisdom and his understanding failed to help him to learn from the experience of Adam that one woman was enough to deceive him.[26] On 1 Kings §172, it adds that although Solomon did indeed love God, he began building the Temple only a full four years after he was crowned, and simultaneously brought Pharaoh's daughter to the City of David. Citing Jeremiah 32:31 ("This city has aroused my anger and wrath, from the day it was built until this day, so that I will remove it from my sight"), it maintains that Solomon was thus responsible for the destruction of the Temple that he built.

Some sages denied the accusation of sin; others argued that although the foreign wives did try to draw the king into idolatry, they failed, and Solomon even prevented them from building high places for the worship of idols. Just because he did not strongly protest their intention to build such places of worship in Jerusalem, "Scripture regards him as though he sinned".[27] Other sages asserted that Solomon took foreign wives "to draw them to the teaching of Torah and to

---

21. *y.Sanhedrin* 2:6, 20c, attributed to Rabbi Yose. In the views of R. Simeon ben Yohai, R. Hanania, and R. Eliezer, however, his foreign wives caused Solomon to sin.

22. According to *b.Yevamot* 76a-b.

23. In Maimonides' anachronistic interpretation, the conversion could not be valid because it was not carried out before a rabbinical court (beit din) and the women thus remained idolaters. *Mishnah Torah, Hilchot Issurei Biah* 13:14–17.

24. *Sifre* Deuteronomy 52, (ed. Finkelstein p. 119).

25. Neusner (1987, p. 171).

26. *Yalkut Shimoni Proverbs* § 962.

27. *Shabbat* 56b.

bring them under the indwelling presence of God",[28] or even that he converted the daughter of Pharaoh before marrying her.[29] With regard to Ecclesiastes 7:7 ("Surely oppression makes the wise foolish, and a bribe corrupts the heart"), *Midrash Tanhuma*[30] has this to say: "When Solomon was engaged in matters in which he did not have to engage, they led him astray, for it says (in 1 Kings 11:4) 'For when Solomon was old, his wives turned away his heart after other gods'".[31]

Maimonides did not ignore the fact that the Bible denounced Solomon, but argued that it did so because he sinned in practicing idolatry, a sin that called for severe punishment.[32] According to the biblical commentator and philosopher Abraham Ibn Ezra (1089–1167), a king such as Solomon, who was wiser than all who lived before and after him, was incapable of being seduced into idolatry. The philosopher and statesman Isaac Abrabanel (1437–1508) also held that a wise man like Solomon could never have been beguiled by the senseless notions and abominations that "foolish gentiles" believed in. Such apologetics were at variance with the biblical account and have nonetheless endured to this very day.

Still, Solomon paid a price for his sins. According to Resh Lakish, a thirdcentury *Amora*, "At first, Solomon reigned over the higher beings, as it is written, Then Solomon sat on the throne of the Lord as king; afterwards, [having sinned] he reigned [only] over the lower, For he had dominion over all the region on this side the river, from Tifsah even to Gaza. But eventually his reign was restricted to Israel, as it is written, I Koheleth have been king over Israel etc. Later, his reign was confined to Jerusalem alone, even as it is written, The words of Koheleth, son of David, king in Jerusalem. And still later he reigned only over his couch".[33] Of Solomon's downfall R. Ḥiyya bar Abba, another *Amora* of the third century, said: "It would have been better for him if he had cleaned sewers, so that this verse would not be written about him".[34] The downfall was also described in *Song of Songs Rabbah*:

---

28. *y.Sanhedrin* 2:6, 20c. According to Rabbi Simeon ben Yohai, the book Deuteronomy "ascended, bowed down before the Holy One, praise to Him, and said to Him: Master of the Universe, You wrote in Your Torah that any disposition which is partially invalid is totally invalid, and now Solomon wants to uproot a ׳, from me! The Holy One, praise to Him, said to Him, said to it: Solomon and thousand like him will disappear but nothing from you will disappear". *y.Sanhedrin* 2:6.
29. *Yevamot* 76a.
30. The Midrash began to take shape in Palestine in the fifth century.
31. *Tanhuma Buber Vayera* 2 on Exodus 6:2.
32. *m.Keritot* 1a.
33. *Sanhedrin* 20b, trans. H. Freedman, London, 1938.
34. *Tanhuma Vayera* 6, and *Tanhuma Buber Vayera* 2.

"Solomon went down by three stages. The first descent was that, after he had been a great king, ruling from one of the worlds to another, his dominion was reduced, and he ruled as king only of Israel [...]. The second descent was that, after he had been king over Israel, his dominion was reduced, and he was king only over Jerusalem [...]. The third descent was that, after he had been king over Jerusalem, his dominion was reduced, and he was king only over his own house [...] But even over his own bed he did not really rule, for he was afraid of spirits [...] R. Yudan said, ' He was king, a commoner, hen king, a sage, a fool, and then a sage, rich, poor, then rich [...] R. Hunia said, 'He was commoner, king, and commoner, fool, sage, and fool; poor, rich, then poor".[35]

Yet another version appears in *y.Sanhedrin* 2:6:

"It is Written: the Holy One, praise him, said to Solomon 'What is this crown on your head? Descend from My throne! Rabbi Yose ben Hanina said, at that moment an angel came down looking like Solomon, removed him from his throne, and sat in his stead. He was going around in synagogues and houses of study, saying *I am Ecclesiastes, I used to be king over Israel in Jerusalem*'. They were telling him, the king sits in his chair of honor and you say, *I am Ecclesiastes*? They hit him with a stick and brought a dish of beans before him".[36]

The third-century sage R. Samuel ben Naḥman was adamant on the subject, attributing the following to his teacher R. Jonathan ben Eleazar:

"Whoever maintains that Solomon sinned is merely making an error, for it is said, and his heart was not perfect with the Lord his God, as was the heart of David his father' it was [merely] not as the heart of David his father, but neither did he sin. Then how do I interpret, For it came to pass, when Solomon was old, that his wives turned away his heart? That is [to be explained] as R. Nathan. For R. Nathan opposed [two verses]: It is written, For it came to pass, when Solomon was old, that his wives turned away his heart, whereas it is [also] written, and his heart was not perfect with the Lord his God, as was the heart of David his father, [implying that] it was [merely] not as the heart of David his father, but neither did he sin? This is its meaning: his wives turned away his heart to go after other gods, but he did not go. But it is written, Then would Solomon build a high place for Chemosh the abomination of Moab?—That means, he desired to build, but did not".[37]

Other traditions absolved Solomon of punishment, maintaining that the price of his sins was instead paid by the Jewish people: Solomon

---

35. *Song of Songs Rabbah* 1:6. Neusner (1989, pp. 51–52).

36. *y.Sanhedrin* 2:6 20c, trans. Heinrich W. Guggenheimer (2010): *Studia Judaica* 51, De Gruyter, Berlin, p. 100.

37. *Shabbat* 56b, trans. Neusner, Scholars Press, Atlanta, Georgia, 1996, pp. 242–243.

himself escaped penalty due to paternal merit: "I will not, however, tear away the entire kingdom; I will give one tribe to your son, for the sake of my servant David and for the sake of Jerusalem, which I have chosen".[38] R. Isaac (a second-generation Babylonian *Amora*), said on this matter "When Solomon married Pharaoh's daughter, Gabriel descended and stuck a reed in the sea, which gathered a sandbank around it, on which was built the great City of Rome"[39]—in other words, Solomon's sins led directly to the establishment of Rome, which would in future destroy Jerusalem and the Second Temple.

Heaven comes to Solomon's Aid

When the members of the Great Assembly were called upon to name Solomon among the three kings and four laymen condemned to have no part in the next world, the figure of David, his father, was invoked to plead his case, as well as God himself—for to forgive sins of this magnitude heavenly intervention was required:

> "R. Ashi: The men of the Great Assembly enumerated them. Rab Judah said in Rab's name: They wished to include another, but an apparition of his father's likeness came and prostrated itself before them, which, however, they disregarded. A heavenly fire descended and its flames licked their seats, yet they still disregarded it. Whereupon a Heavenly Voice cried out to them, 'O you see those who are skillful in their work? They will serve kings; they will not serve common people' (Prov. 22.29). He who gave precedence to My house over his, and moreover, built My house in seven years, but his own in thirteen, he shall stand before kings; he shall not stand before mean men. Yet they paid no attention even to this. Whereupon the Heavenly voice cried out, 'Should it be according to thy mind? He will recompense it, whether thou refuse, or whether thou choose; and not I…'".[40]

In other words, it was for God alone to decide who would have a portion in the next world, independent of the considerations of humans. According to another *midrash* on Proverbs, the *Shekhinah* intervened with the Almighty and said to him: "Master, have you ever seen anyone so diligent in doing your work? And yet they wish to count him among those consigned to [eternal] darkness! At that moment, a heavenly voice came forth, saying to them: 'He shall attend upon kings; he shall not attend upon those consigned to [eternal] darkness'".[41]

The gravity of Solomon's sins is secondary to the fact that the Bible does not record that Solomon repented of his transgressions and

---

38. 1 Kings 11:13.
39. *Sanhedrin* 21b, trans. J. Israelstam, Soncino Press, London, 1951, p. 188.
40. Job 34:33; *Sanhedrin* 104b.
41. *Midrash* Proverbs 22 (Visotzky 1992, p. 156).

begged for forgiveness, or that he was ever forgiven. No mention is made of his having divorced his foreign wives, destroyed the high places he built for their idolatrous worship, or asked for and received God's forgiveness. According to the Bible, God did not forgive Solomon, but only promised him that, for the sake of his father David, his kingdom would be divided only after his lifetime. One might have expected the Sages to address the question of whether Solomon atoned for his sins and whether he was absolved; in fact, they hardly discuss the issue of his repentance or his absolution. Those Sages who held that Solomon's sins had been absolved could only base their belief on the fact that he ended his life as a king or argue that he acknowledged his sins and repented ("because I questioned His actions, have I stumbled"[42]). They find evidence in the fact that "Close to his death the holy spirit rested on him and he composed three books—Proverbs, Song of Songs and Ecclesiastes".[43]

Medieval Jewish apologetics found it difficult to accept that Solomon's good deeds could compensate for his sins; hence, even if he regretted them, they were not absolved. In *Sefer Hasidim* (The Book of the Pious),[44] R. Judah ben Samuel of Regensburg (d. 1217) concluded on the basis of *Song of Songs Rabbah* that even though Solomon's books brought merit to his people, for him to escape being denied a part in the next world required a heavenly defense on the basis of his being David's son; the meaning, therefore, was that even meritorious actions that benefit the many do not suffice as defense against one's sins, or as a guarantee of a place in the world to come.[45] Bruno, Bishop of Segni (c. 1047–1123), voiced a similar judgment from the Christian tradition: "A righteous man who has sinned, can have no absolution".[46]

Over time, new elements were added to the array of punishments Solomon suffered for his sins. R. Isaac ben Samuel of Acre, one of the greatest kabbalists of the fourteenth century, combined mythological (Prometheus), Jewish, and Christian traditions, the latter of which he had learned of, according to his testimony, from a Christian who told him about a monk who once saw ravens in the desert pecking at a man's flesh. When he asked, "Why are you sentenced to this punishment?"

---

42. *Exodus Rabbah* 6:1.

43. *Song of Songs Rabbah* 1, 8, and parallels. The Quran also says about Solomon: "And to Dawud (David) We gave Suleiman (Solomon). How excellent (a) slave! Verily, he was ever oft-returning in repentance" (Q. 38:30) without stating why he needed to repent.

44. In fact, the book represents the combined teaching of the three leaders of German Hasidim (Pious Ones) during the twelfth and early thirteenth centuries.

45. Rabbi Judah ben Samuel (1998, p. 262).

46. Bruno of Segni, *Sententiae* 2 PL 165 \914B. See I. A. Robinson (1983).

the reply was: "I am Solomon, king of Israel". Then the monk asked: "But why are you made to undergo such severe suffering by divine decree and how long will you endure it?" Solomon replied: "Until the Messiah, who is of my seed, shall come and the Almighty will forgive me owing to him." The kabbalist interpreted this as meaning that Solomon's agony symbolized the *Shekhinah*, suffering because of the exile of the people of Israel and that the ravens were gentiles or the forces of defilement, fated to be overthrown by the Messiah.[47]

In his introduction to a German translation (in Hebrew transliteration) of the Book of Proverbs,[48] the *maskil* Wolf Meir offered an explanation for Solomon's sins: in his old age, Solomon "dove into the sea of metaphysics" and concluded that all is vanity and divinely predetermined; his wives were then able to take advantage of his resulting passivity and weakness and turn his mind their way. In allowing them to build high places where they worshipped their gods, he desecrated the Temple of the Lord which was treasured by the people, who after his death despised and did not mourn him.

Christianity on Solomon's Sins and Repentance[49]

"*Women, when nothing else, beguiled the heart*
Of wisest Solomon, and made him build,
And made him bow, to the gods of his wives"
 - John Milton, *Paradise Regained* (Book II, 169–171).[50]

Solomon's status in early Christianity is reflected in the writings of Emperor Julian, who mocked the "excuses" and apologetic tactics employed to explain away Solomon's sins. Despite the lofty virtues attributed to him and his great wisdom, Solomon was incapable of re-

47. Cited in Idel (1995). A Scottish tale maintained that Solomon was condemned to be devoured daily by ten thousand ravens until the end of the world (Butler 1993, p. 400). According another version appears in a story written in Germany at the end of the thirteenth century, in which Ashmedai, chief of the demons, plays a central role. God calls on him, commanding him to replace Solomon, who has sinned by marrying foreign women, and promises Ashmedai that he will not be harmed. Ashmedai pushes Solomon off his throne, takes his seal, and assumes the form of Solomon; the man himself walks about like a drunkard, begging for bread and insisting that he is Kohelet [Ecclesiastes] who once reigned as king in Jerusalem. He is mocked by everyone he turns to. Bathsheba, his mother, recognizes the pretender to the throne by his donkey feet, and informs Baneihu, who ascertains Solomon's identity. The tale ends with the lines: "Thus did the Almighty do for Solomon, who violated but one transgression in the Torah, and for anyone violating the words of the Sages, all the more so". On the manuscripts in which the tale appears, see Kushelevsky (2011). On this story therein, see Chapter Seven.

48. Verlag des M.I. Landa, Prague, 1834.

49. Vanning (2002) is a detailed survey of the subject. I have relied on it greatly throughout this part of the chapter. Also see Bose (1996), and M. Bloch (1925).

50. Milton (1994, p. 403).

straining his desires and was seduced by a woman's words. "Is their 'wisest' man Solomon at all comparable with Phocylides or Theognis or Isocrates among the Hellenes […] 'But', they answer, 'Solomon was also proficient in the secret cult of God'. What then? Did not this Solomon serve our gods also, deluded by his wives, as they assert? What great virtue! What wealth of wisdom! He could not rise superior to pleasure, and the arguments of a woman led him astray! Then if he was deluded by a woman, do not call this man wise".[51]

Julian's derision was directed at the Christians, but this did not prevent the latter from hurling similar claims against the Jews in order to aggrandize Jesus and ridicule Solomon. Justin Martyr, for example, wrote that "I do not hesitate to quote the Book of Kings, where it is written that Solomon committed idolatry at Sidon for the sake of a woman. On the contrary; the Gentiles who know God, the Creator of the world, through the crucified Jesus, would rather endure every torture and pain, even death itself, than worship idols, or eat meat sacrificed to idols".[52] In *The Dialogue between Timothy and Aquila*, the Jew Aquila maintains that Solomon did not sacrifice to the idols but crushed them in his hands unwillingly (26.5). To this, the Christian Timothy replies: "Will I then accept this one as a son of God, who did not move toward repentance as Manasseh did? […] He (Solomon) did not keep any of the commandments of God, and you know that! For he even built altars to each one of the idols his wives worshipped, which he had taken as foreigners […] know, therefore, that Solomon greatly provoked the Lord God of heaven, because he disobeyed him […] know, O Jew, that he worshipped and sacrificed grasshoppers to the idols".[53] The sinful king symbolizes the punishment of the Jews for their rejection of Jesus as the Messiah, and at times he is even viewed as the Antichrist.

In *The Testament of Solomon*, the king confesses that he took numerous wives from many lands and says: "the glory of God quite departed from me; and my spirit was darkened, and I became the sport of idols and demons. I became weak as well as foolish in my words.[54] Claiming that Psalm 72 does not apply to Solomon, the author writes that he does not hesitate to repeat what is written in the book of Kings that Solomon has committed idolatry for the sake of a woman in Sidon" (xxxiv), and Origen wrote in the same vein in his commentary on Song of Songs that although Solomon was most wise, he surrendered himself to "many wives" (referring to "many nations")

---

51. *Against the Galilaeans* 224D–224E. Trans. Wright, pp. 383–385.
52. Justin Martyr (2003, pp. 199–200).
53. 9.8–9.16, Varner (2004, pp. 157–159).
54. Conybeare (1898, p. 45).

whom he invited to his palace in order to study their diverse doctrines and varied philosophies; he could not keep himself within the rule of divine law, and went so far as to build temples for them and even sacrifice to the idol of Moab.

Christian writings also were divided among themselves concerning Solomon sins. "The changes in attitude to Solomon throughout the centuries", writes Vanning, "reflect concomitant developments in polemic, political attitudes, philosophical knowledge, Biblical exegesis, religious thought, and theology".[55] Indeed, internal conflict is evident beyond any quarrel with Judaism. Nonetheless, I will not survey the great corpus of debates on whether Solomon did in fact sin and repent, nor the corpus of allegorical interpretations of his rise and fall, in part because the size of both is greatly inflated by repetitions.

In *Adversus Marcionem Tertullian* (c. 160-c. 220) argued there was no need for Solomon to be lavish in his polygamy in order to sin since Solomon had lost the blessing of God the very first time he was "delivered up to idols".[56] Jerome (Hieronymus, 345–419/20) wrote: "Was there anyone wiser than Solomon? Yet he was made foolish by the love of women, having been overcome "by the flesh". According to Augustine "At the beginning of [Solomon's] reign he burned with a passion for wisdom, which he acquired through the love of the spirit and lost because of his love of the flesh".[57] As a result, his house "was full of foreign women who worshipped false gods; and the king himself, who had been a man of wisdom, was seduced and degraded to same idolatry".[58] "In the person of this man Solomon appears both astounding excellent and its equally astounding overthrow, what happened to him at different times, first the good fortune and afterward the misfortune, therefore, is nowadays evident in the Church all the same time. For I think that signifies the Church, and the evil that befell him signifies that it is beset".[59] Pope Gregory I (540–604) compared Solomon to Judas and to the people of Sodom because he received his wisdom at night.[60] According to Isidore of Seville (c.560–636), Solomon's many good deeds failed to compensate for his sins,[61] while Walter Map (1140–1210), an English clergyman and author, wrote in his collection of anecdotes *De nugis curialium* (Courtiers' Trifles): "Solomon, the treasury of the Lord's delight

---

55. Vanning (2002, p. 355).
56. Vanning (2002, p. 5).
57. *De doctrina Christiana* LLL, xxi.
58. *City of God* XVII: 8 (Augustine 1984, p. 735).
59. *Contra Faustum Manichaeum*, 88:2.
60. *Moralia in Job*. 22.
61. *Questiones in Vetus Testamentum* 6–1.

... had the light of his soul obscured by the thick ink of darkness, lost the perfume of his renown and the glory of his house under the glamour of women, and in the end bowed his knee to Baalim, and from being the preacher of the Lord, turned to be a limb of the Devil".[62] The Benedictine reformer (and Cardinal) Peter Damian (1007–1072) wrote in a homily on 2 Samuel 7 that Solomon was redeemed of his sins and was necessarily holy since he was a prefiguration of Jesus. Philip of Harvengt (d.1183), abbot of the Bonne Espérance abbey, wrote in his *Responsio de damnatione Salomonis* that he found no indication in the Holy Scriptures of Solomon's atonement and absolution. He was contradicted by the author of the twelfth-century *Quod pentium Salomonis*, who asserted that there could be no doubt of Solomon's sins; after all, the *libri Hebraei* [Hebrew books] themselves record that Solomon was dragged through the streets of Jerusalem, beaten with switches in the Temple, and finally made to forfeit his throne. In *The Descent of Christ into Hell*, an apocalyptic text apparently written between 138–168, Solomon, alongside Adam, Eve, and others, is rescued from Hell by Jesus and led to Heaven. Similarly, the text *Acta Pilati* (Acts of Pilate) contained in the Gospel of Nicodemus, and later in Old English poetry, was inspired by Ephesians 4:7–11, which says that before Jesus ascended to heaven "he also descended first into the lower parts of the earth".[63] The Franciscan scholastic theologian Bonaventure (1221–1274) regarded Solomon as an "exemplum of the penitent sinner who received divine grace".[64] The question of sin, atonement, and absolution was at times a political issue. A letter from the bishop Fulbert (c.960–1028) of Chartres written in 1024 to Hildegar, the sub-deacon of Chartres, regarding a dispute that had arisen between Duke William of Aquitaine and his bishops cites various sources to persuade the bishops to peacefully settle the dispute. Fulbert quotes Bachiarius' (c. 350-c.425) *Liber de Reparatione Lapsi*:

> "Solomon, that wondrous man (*ille mirabilis*), who deserves to share in the wisdom that sits next to God, rushed into the embraces of foreign women; and he defiled himself by committing sacrilege when he made an image of Chamos, the idol of the Moabites. But since he was led by the prophet to acknowledge the error of his way, is he banished from the mercy of heaven? Perhaps you will say: Nowhere in the canon do I read that he was repentant [...] I have no doubt, brother, as to his repentance, though this was not recorded in the public laws, and he may have been a judge all the more acceptable because he did not do penance, not in

---

62. Map (1988, pp. 292–294).
63. Dorn (1967, pp. 42–43).
64. Minnis (2009, p. 111).

front of the people but in the secrecy of his conscience with God as his witness. That he obtained pardon we know from this: that when he was released from his body, scripture states that he was buried among the bodies of the Kings of Israel."[65]

Fulbert's proposed solution was entirely convenient for a leader accused of having sinned: his repentance need not be public since Solomon's example demonstrated that the matter of one's sins may be settled between oneself, one's conscience, and God.

A fourteenth-century Northumbrian poem, *Cursor Mundi* (The Cursor of the World), depicted a Solomon sorely repentant of his love for heathen women: "He summoned prophets and patriarchs and begged to be relieved of crown and kingly robes, announcing his purpose to flee, because of his sins, to a foreign country. To the patriarchs, kingship was divine, and they refused to listen to his plan. He then implored them to lay upon him a hard penance. Accordingly, he was scourged through the streets, the blood streaming from his back. He bore all patiently and won mercy, after which, lust all forgotten, he ruled well and contributed lasting works to posterity".[66] In the *Legenda Aurea* (Golden Legend), a collection of legends about the lives of the saints written c. 1260 and circulated in hundreds of manuscripts,[67] the Archbishop of Genoa, Jacopo de Voragine, wrote that "It is said, but I find it not in the Bible, that Solomon repented much of this sin of Idolatry and did much penance, therefore, for he let him be drawn through Jerusalem and beat himself with rods and scourges, that the blood flowed in the sight of all the people".

The idea that the biblical depiction of Solomon's downfall was borne out in observable reality is evident in Johannes of Würzburg's (1160–1170) *Description of the Holy Land*, wherein the author describes how he saw firsthand the place where Solomon worshiped Molech.[68] Similarly, the Russian Orthodox monk Arseny Sukhanov, who spent time in Jerusalem in the 1650s, wrote of visiting a site where King Solomon's "palace of pleasure" once stood, in which he had housed his "many wives and concubines, who were brought from diverse countries and faiths" and arranged for them places of worship. Moreover, "Solomon entered the temple of the idolaters, bowed down before them and burned incense. For all this, he was not absolved, in his old age he did wickedness in the sight of the Lord, and died".[69]

Christian theologians were preoccupied for generations with

---

65. *The Letters and Poems of Fulbert of Chartres* (Behrends 1976, pp. 164–169).
66. In Borland (1933).
67. Between 1470 and 1530 it was one of the most printed books in Europe.
68. Johannes of Würzburg (1971).
69. Raba (1986).

the question of repentance and absolution; indeed, this was a matter of greater concern than the nature of his sins and punishment. In his *Apologia prophetae David*, St. Ambrose asserted that as a king David was not subject to human laws, but that he sinned nonetheless by violating God's commandments, which even a king must obey.[70] Several Church Fathers expressed compassion for Solomon since he was tempted by women when he was weak and in his dotage; others absolved him entirely.[71] Yet, if Solomon did atone for his sins, how did he do so? After all, the Bible does not report that he divorced his wives and returned to full observance of God's commandments.[72]

Nor does any *midrash* attribute to Solomon the typical actions associated with a quest for absolution, such as prayer, fasting, or confession, while his father David did confess: "David said to the Lord, 'I have sinned greatly in what I have done. But now, O Lord, I pray you, take away the guilt of your servant; for I have done very foolishly'".[73] Similarly, Menasseh, the king who built high places and altars in Jerusalem, was taken prisoner by the Assyrians, during which time he repented; and after God returned him from his exile, he atoned by removing the high places he had built.[74] (This penance was made explicit only in the minor apocryphal work *The Prayer of Menasseh*.) The inhabitants of Nineveh also sought God's forgiveness for their evil deeds: "Human beings and animals shall be covered with sackcloth, and they shall cry mightily to God. All shall turn from their evil ways and from the violence that is in their hands".[75]

The Sages doubted the sincerity of the repentance of the people of Nineveh, and only *Teshuvat Yonah haNavi*, a *midrash* written between the eighth and eleventh centuries, describes their contrition as a model of repentance. As for Solomon, who committed the most grievous sin of all—the practice of idolatry—indeed, according to some sources he repented (not even inwardly), wore sackcloth, or prayed: *Yalkut Shimoni*[76] does relate that when Solomon was going from house to house begging, a poor man invited him to eat a simple "meal of vegetables" in his home, telling him: "this is the way of the Lord, to reprove and then reconcile… and the Lord will restore you to your kingdom." Yet, even in this tale Solomon, remembering the

---

70. This brief summary is based on Bose (1996) and Dorn (1967).

71. See Dorn (1967, pp. 42–43).

72. According to a 13th century Armenian manuscript, Solomon commands his chamberlain to burn all his writings, and, "having repented, he wept bitterly. And God reckoned it to him as repentance". Stone (1978).

73. 2 Samuel 24:10.

74. 2 Chronicles 33.

75. Jonah 3:8–10.

76. *Yalkut Shimoni* on Proverbs, § 953 (15).

days of his kingdom, weeps but does not repent. The seventh blessing in *Mishnah Ta'anit* 2:4 reads: "He who answered David, and his son Solomon, in Jerusalem, may He answer you, and listen to your cry on this day. Blessed art thou, O Lord, who has compassion on the earth!" The words are based on Solomon's prayer at the inauguration of the Temple: "Then hear in heaven your dwelling place, forgive, act, and render to all whose hearts you know" (1 Kings 8:39). Here Solomon, however, is asking forgiveness for the sins of the entire people, rather than for his own.[77]

The quote most frequently cited as evidence that Solomon was forgiven is "Close to his death the holy spirit rested on him and he composed three books—Proverbs, Song of Songs and Ecclesiastes". However, no Jewish source claims that Solomon followed in the ways of David, his father, who, after his sin with Bathsheba, asked of God to "Wash me thoroughly from mine iniquity, and cleanse me from my sin" (Psalms 51:2).[78] The Bible and the Sages do not overlook David's human failings or his transgressions because his confession of his sin only serves to underscore his greatness and his righteousness; yet, in Solomon's case, there is no basis for such a claim since he never admits his sin or betrays an awareness of his human frailty. Sages, preachers, and commentators who came to his defense[79] all defended his past, but not his future. Maimonides, for example, wrote that "there is no king in Israel" who was not the seed of both David and Solomon, and that

---

77. The question regarding who is repentant of a sin he committed by not restraining his earthly appetites preoccupied the Sages; one of the answers is that a repentant person is one who does not succumb to his urges or to temptation a second time. *Mishnat R. Shmuel HaHasid* states that self-mortification is also required. See Kushelevsky (2011, pp. 54–161).

78. In Muslim polemical literature against the Jews, the favorable attitude towards Solomon is called into question. Abū Muḥammad ʿAlī ibn Aḥmad ibn Saʿīd ibn Ḥazm (999–1064), a prolific scholar and native of Cordoba who, in his book *Refutation of Ibn al-Naghrija the Jew, May God Curse Him* addressed a book ascribed to Samuel HaNagid that disparaged the Quran, held that the original sin had already been committed at Solomon's birth: Solomon was an outcome of the adulterous relations between Judah and Tamar and David and Bathsheba. This was one man's opinion, and it ran counter to the Quranic descriptions above. The Quran clears Solomon of any sin: 'Yet Solomon did not disbelieve" (Q. 2:102 ("The Cow")). Elsewhere, it states that "he was even turning in repentance [toward Allah]" (Q. 38:30 ("Sad")). The eleventh-century *Tales of the Prophets* by al-Thaʿlabī contains several accounts of Solomon repenting. In one of them, Asaf b.Brakhya, Solomon's teacher, tells the king that his wife al-Jaradah, the daughter of King Saydun, who had conquered her father's kingdom, was secretly worshipping idols. Solomon shatters the idols, dons a garment of purification, and goes forth to beg for forgiveness. In another story, he covers his body with ashes, weeps, and begs forgiveness.

79. In contrast to Solomon, David admitted to his sins and thus was forgiven. See Knoppers (1995).

whoever disagrees denies the Torah and Moses. Such a position was probably a reaction to Christological descriptions of Jesus as a "son of David" and to the eradication of Solomon's memory as the second in that dynasty. Maimonides also wrote that the "King Messiah will arise and restore the kingdom of David to its former state", and that it would be at its finest when a "king will arise who will possess more wisdom than Solomon and meditate on the Torah, as did his ancestor David".[80]

It is David who serves as a model for the observance of the commandments and for meditation on the Torah, while Solomon is 'the wisest of all,' who spoke in the divine spirit. In *Mishnah Torah/ Sefer ha-Mada*, Maimonides discusses "the practice of repentance" and cites several quotes from Ecclesiastes ("Remember your creator in the days of your youth", 12:1) and Proverbs ("but the righteous are established forever", 10:25).[81] But Solomon did not adhere to these rules, "and only repented on the day of his death and died penitent, all his iniquities are pardoned to him, as it is said: 'before the sun and the light and the moon and the stars are darkened and the clouds return with the rain' (Ecclesiastes 12:2)".[82] The Sages ascribed many virtues and good deeds to Solomon, including the idea that by virtue of his proverbs and his study of the Torah, the people were able to delve into the more obscure meanings of the Torah.[83] Nevertheless, his sin of idolatry was not forgotten in Jewish tradition, and even though the days of his reign marked the peak period of the monarchy, he was excluded from its restorative visions of redemption. David is the "eternal" king of Israel, mentioned as a father of the nation alongside Abraham, Isaac, and Jacob in the version of the prayer *"mi she-be-rakh"* (He Who Blessed Our Fathers) spoken on the Sabbath, on festivals, for the ill, and for women giving birth.

The Sages, thus, do not cite Solomon as an example of a repentant sinner, even if "One hour of repentance and good deed in this world is better than all the time in the world to come".[84] In contrast, the Christian theological discussion of Solomon's sins held that his punishment symbolized that of the Jews for having rejected Jesus as the messiah. Yet, within Christianity, it is impossible to ignore Solomon's Christological role as the prefiguration of Jesus and as the author of Proverbs, Song of Songs, and Ecclesiastes. Thus, Andrea di Bonaiuto's fresco did not exclude Solomon from St. Thomas' entourage, but only

---

80. Maimonides, *Mishnah Torah, Hilkhot Teshuvah* 9b; *Hilkhot Melakhim* 11:1, 4. Maimonides, *Mishnah Torah*, Jerusalem, 2012 (Sefer Yad ha-Hazaka).
81. Maimonides, *Mishnah Torah*, pp. 218–250.
82. *Hilkhot Teshuvah* Chap. 2, 1.
83. *Song of Songs Rabbah* 1, 8 (Neusner 1989).
84. *Mishnah Avot* 4:17.

deprived him of a halo, and he was regarded as a symbol and ideal model of a king.

While Jewish tradition stresses that the women who seduced Solomon were gentiles, and thus forbidden to him, in Christian tradition the sin the women represent is that of the temptations of the flesh and the limits, or even the weakness, of wisdom vis-à-vis faith. It deals extensively with Solomon's sins in order to emphasize the great distance between him and Jesus and, in so doing, establish Jesus' place as the "true" son of David.

Did the Sages, for their part, wish to distance Solomon from Jesus in the story of Joshua ben Peraḥyah, Jesus' young "teacher"[85] who denied the former' request to return to study under him, insisting that "Anyone who sins and causes the public to sin, he is not capable of repentance"?[86] Here, Jesus' sin was that he "performed magic and led other astray toward idolatry".

It seems then that the Christian theologians' preoccupation with Solomon's sins was born of a desire to create distance between him and Jesus, though he prefigured the latter. In the Christian tradition, no heavenly voice arrives to ensure his place in the world to come.[87] He was not the "true Solomon" because Solomon was not, as Augustine wrote, innocent of all sin like Jesus,[88] whose death upon the cross bought forgiveness for all of humanity's sins.

The "correspondence" between Jesus and Solomon on the subjects discussed in the previous three chapters existed primarily on the Christian side and was expressed in a few contradictory aspects: (a) Solomon was not a "Son of God" like Jesus; (b) Solomon was expelled from the genealogy of the House of David, while Jesus was the "Son of David"; (c) Jesus was "greater than Solomon", the "true Solomon"; and (d) Solomon was a prefiguration of Jesus. Judaism responded to these claims by rejecting Jesus' "sonship", though without establishing Solomon's sonship as a counterpoint, and by rejecting Jesus' place in the House of David. Yet, Judaism did not argue that Christianity had appropriated Solomon's three books without claiming that their author was "greater than Solomon", and the correspondence did not end there.

---

85. See Chapter Six.
86. *Sanhedrin* 107b.
87. See Hägerland (2012).
88. "No sin could be found in Christ himself", *City of God* XVII:9 (Augustine 1984, p. 737).

Chapter Five: "How is Jesus Greater than Solomon?" Solomon and Jesus as Magicians (Healers and Exorcists)

"*A sound magician is a demi-god*"
    - Christopher Marlowe, *Doctor Faustus* (1704), 1, 1:59
"*Will you believe in antiquity?*
I'll show you a book where Moses and his sister
And Solomon have written of the art"
    - Ben Jonson, *The Alchemist* (1612)

Magic and Occultism

Did the image of Solomon as a magician appear as an inseparable part of Jewish occultism that developed during the Second Temple period (the Hellenist and Roman), or was it a reaction to Jesus' reputation as an exorcist and healer in an effort to prove that Solomon was greater than Jesus?[1] Or, perhaps, it was the other way around. Namely, when the people refer to Jesus, known for his ability to exorcise demons, as the "son of David", they do so because during the Second Temple period Solomon was famous as a healer and exorcist, and the authors of the Gospels wished to cite evidence that Jesus was, in this regard, greater than Solomon. Or, perhaps, both traditions emerged separately as an outcome of the extensive presence of magic in all the cultures of the ancient world. However, Solomon does not resemble Jesus and he is not described as having engaged in the practice of magic, namely in exorcising demons, and not as having written magic oaths and texts, or having possessed them. Jesus, on the other hand, is described as having engaged in the practice of magic, namely,

---

1. On this claim, see Sasson (2003, pp. 140–141).

in healing people and in exorcising demons, and not as the author of any text whatsoever. At the most, the two "meet" in the few magic texts in which they both appear.

Since the terms "magic" and "occultism" appear frequently in the research literature—and will appear in this chapter and in Chapter Seven as well—I will begin by relating the nature of the occult (or esoteric) sciences. The word first appeared in German (*Esoterik*) in 1792.[2] Magic is part of these sciences and generally refers to human activity in the supernatural sphere, namely to various practices such as astral magic, mathematical magic, natural magic, mechanical magic, and others.[3] By human means, an attempt is made to influence supernatural forces to come to one's aide, both for evil purposes (*magia diabolica*; necromancy) and for worthy purposes, i. e., "white magic" (*magia bona*). The former, known as "black magic" (*goetia*), has been denounced as "mendacious, loathsome vain acts" (*magicas vanitas*) because it employs false trickery (*miracula circumlatoris*) that deceives men and is used by itinerant witches who lead people astray. The latter, theurgy, instructs people how to harness supernatural forces for human benefit.[4] However, practical magic is not separate from the sciences of occultism because it is anchored in an all-embracing view (occult philosophy) about the structure and order of the world and about the forces and concealed mechanisms that act within it and operate it.[5] The polymath, legal scholar, and physician Heinrich Cornelius Agrippa's (1486–1535) definition of this kind of magic is: "Magic is a faculty of wonderful virtue, full of most high mysteries, containing the most profound contemplation of most secret things, together with the nature, power, quality, substance, and virtues thereof, as also the knowledge of whole nature, and it doth instruct us concerning the differing and agreement of things among themselves, whence it produceth its wonderful effects, by uniting the virtues of things through the application of them to one another[…]".[6] When Faust says he has despaired of theology, philosophy, and the sciences,

   2. Lynn Thorndike uses "magic" as a generic term to include all superstitious arts and occult sciences (Thorndike 1964, pp. 973–974).
   3. Birkhan (2010, pp. 33–114).
   4. Philo of Alexandria, for example, draws a distinction between "true magic", which is the "science of vision" or *theosis*, namely the study and interpretation of the actions of nature, on the one hand, and magic on the other. See Garin (1983, p. 91).
   5. On the terminology, see Copenhaver (2003, pp. 280–281). See also Hanegraaff (2013); Katz (2007).
   6. *Three Books of Occult Philosophy*, Book I. The book was translated into English in 1651. On it, see Lehrich (2005); And see Giordano Bruno, in the Third Dialogue, *Spaccio de la bestia trionfante* (The Expulsion of the Triumphant Beast). Agrippa, incidentally, does not count Solomon among the ancient authors of occult literature.

and decides to turn to magic in order to explore the wondrous and to understand *"was die Welt / Im Innersten zusammenhält / Schau' alle Wirkenskraft und Samen / Und tu' nicht mehr in Worten kramen"*[7] he is not referring to practical magic, namely to magic techniques, but rather to texts that suggest a religious or cosmological method,[8] such as neo-Platonic or Hermetic writings, which tell how the world was formed (*gnosis*) and what forces (*primae causae*) operate within it and how they influence humans. The two magi, Marsilio Ficino (1433–1499) and Pico della Mirandola (1463–1494) believed that magic is "the practical part of nature" (*magia est practica scientiae naturalis*). The idea that (occult) magic is no more than a collection of superstitions and speculations, or that it is an "irrational" belief, has not been the accepted view for a long time. I should like to quote the words of the scholar of ancient Egyptian magic, John Baines that "Magic and rationality do not conflict; magic is rational, its argumentation is often rationalistic".[9]

Magic and Healing

The belief in demons, magic, and magic practices does not acknowledge any boundaries between religions and cultures,[10] which were—and still are—transcultural, in many cases diffuse, dynamic, and syncretic in their nature.[11] It is more than a folk culture;[12] in fact, it is a deeply rooted phenomenon, existing continuously from the ancient

---

7. "That I might see what secret force / Hides in the word and rules its course / Envisage the creative blazes / Instead of rummaging in phrases" (I:82–85), Goethe (1963, p. 95). It is no coincidence that I cite Faust. Agrippa's doctrine in *Aus Meinem Leben: Dichtung und Wahrheit*, VI, resonates in Faust's above-mentioned words. Goethe stated that Agrippa's book was one of his favorites and "so set my young brains in a considerable whirl for a time" (Basel, 1949, 140). Agrippa is also one of the two magicians who come, in Marlowe's play, to persuade Faust to embrace esoterism: "The miracles that magic will perform \ Will make thee vow to study nothing else" (1.1: 130–131).

8. See Wasserstrom (2000). The article contains a lengthy bibliography and the issue contains other important articles on the subject.

9. Baines (1991, p. 165).

10. See Greenbaum (2016).

11. Bohak (2004, 2007, 2015); Hull (1974, pp. 27–37).

12. The number of books written on the subject of magic in general, and magic in the ancient world in particular, is so vast that I saw no need to cite more than a handful of them: Butler (1998); Wygant (2006); Kieckhefer (1990); Klutz (2004); Schäfer and Kippenberg (1997); Classen (2017); Fanger (1998); Dickie (2001); Paola Zambelli (2012). On magic and exorcism in the period of the Second Temple in general, see Bohak (2008, pp. 71–142); and in Josephus in particular, see Bohak (2008; pp. 83–85, 99–105). On its representation in art, see Battistini (2004, pp. 131–249); Page (2004). For a short bibliography on Egyptian magic, see notes 43 and 44 in my Shavit (2013).

era until the present day and it cannot be eradicated,[13] certainly not in a world in which magic is perceived as part of the created order, in which no distinction was drawn between it and "religion," in which magic was regarded as an effective means of achieving security in this world, which is constantly threatened by concealed forces;[14] a world in which "magic," "medicine",[15] and "science" were not thought to contradict one another. In all the cultures, practices were—and are—followed to expel evil demons.[16] These included incantations (*epoide*), curse tablets (*defixiones*), charms, gems with magic powers, amulets, curse bowls, and seals. These techniques passed from culture to culture, and along with them went magic rituals (*goetian*), magic texts, and a system of magic symbols. An endless number of testimonies document the circulation of magic texts and the use of magic practices in Mesopotamia, ancient Egypt, Greece, and Rome.[17]

It is not surprising, then, nor is there any need to cite evidence, that belief in the existence of evil spirits (the "spirit of Satan", or "spirits of malice") that harm humans was also prevalent in Jewish culture and that, at the same time, Jews believed there were ways and means of combating these spirits.[18] For example, the apocalyptic Book of Tobit [Tobias] (written and edited between the 2nd-4th centuries B.C.E.) describes the exorcism of a demon or evil spirit with the aid of incense from the liver, heart, or gall of a fish (I, 1–9). According to Josephus, the Essenes "display an extraordinary interest in the writing of the ancient, singling out those which make for welfare of the soul and body. With the help of these, and with a view to the treatment of diseases, they make investigations into medical root and properties of Stone".[19] And the Roman historian and geographer Strabo (64 B.C.E.—23 C.E.) based his view on Posidonius' when he wrote that the Jews were a "people of sorcerers who pretend to use incantations".[20]

However, Solomon was not depicted as having healed the ill or exorcised demons from the bodies of humans. He is not like Elijah,

---

13. Barb (1963, p. 125).
14. Assmann (2002, pp. 239–240).
15. See Jankrift (2005).
16. See Thräde (1962b).
17. Israelowich (2015); Meggitt (2006, pp. 109–114); and Tanman and Pitarakis (2018).
18. See Alexander (1986).
19. *The Jewish War*, II (6), 136.
20. Strabo, *Geography*, 16. 2.43 (Strabo 1930, p. 295). In the apocryphal book, *The Testament of the Twelve Patriarchs*, the narrator, Judah, is sad about the fact that his sons are being seduced by witches and spirits. And that is only one example that shows how widespread belief in magic was.

nor like his father David, who cured Saul of the evil spirit that had possessed him by playing on his harp.[21] Nonetheless, the source of his fame as a magician is in the wisdom attributed to him in the Bible: "And Solomon's wisdom excelled the wisdom of all the people of the east, and all the wisdom of Egypt".[22] It included, among other things, the ability to speak "of trees, from the cedar that is in the Lebanon to the hyssop that grows in the wall; he would speak of animals, and birds, and reptiles, and fish."[23] "He composed three thousand proverbs, and his songs numbered a thousand and five".[24] As for "the wisdom of Egypt", the allusion is probably to the wisdom literature such as *Instructions of Amenemhat* from the 11th to 12th centuries BCE.[25] Even if we read the verse in 1 Kings 4:33 as "**to** the trees, **to** the beasts, **to** the fowl," instead of "of the trees," etc., that would still not suffice to suggest that Solomon possessed the skills of a magician just as the words in the *Gemara* about R. Johanan ben Zakkai that he was well-versed in "the speech of the Ministering Angels, the speech of spirits, and the speech of palm-trees"[26] do not make him a magician.[27]

Putative evidence that Solomon engaged in magic is in "Song for the Stricken" from Qumran, which is attributed to David (11QPsAp).[28] It states that Solomon received from his father a hymn [a version of a curse] to exorcise an evil spirit, but it does not say he used it. And Josephus writes that "God granted him knowledge of the art used against demons for the benefit and healing of men. He also composed incantations by which illnesses are relieved, and left behind forms of exorcism which those possessed by demons drive them out, never to return".[29]

Moreover, Josephus finds it necessary to cite a concrete example of Solomon's power as a healer and an exorcist of demons. Another source may have been the Vulgate. Solomon was known as a writer of curses in the first centuries C.E. from a number of sources: the 1st

---

21. Plutarch writes about the playing of music to exorcise demons among Pythagoras' pupils: p. 371.
22. 1 Kings 4:30.
23. 1 Kings 4:33.
24. 1 Kings 4:32. We have no way of knowing what the wisdom of the three ancient wise men was (whom Josephus calls "ancients").
25. Which has several parallels in Proverbs 22:17 and 22:25.
26. *Sukkah* 28a.
27. On the other hand, according to the legendary biography of Apolloni Tyaneus, written by the Athenian sophist Philostratus (c. 170–247), he knew all the languages in the world, understood the language of birds, healed sick people who were possessed by demons, or were struck blind (III 3.38), and he also owned books of magic. Philostratus (1995, p. 277).
28. J. M. Baumgarten (1985). Nitzan (1985).
29. Josephus, *Ant.* 8, 45–46.

century fragment *Cithsrismus Regis David contra daemonun Saulis*, in which David warns the demons: "A son will be born to me who will rule over you"; and the work *Hydromatiae of Solomon*, namely divination through water, or hydromancy, which describes healing techniques in which the magician places the demons in a basin of water;[30] as well as at the end of the 3rd century C.E. by the alchemist Zosimus of Panopolis: "among the Egyptians there is a book called *The Book of Seven Heavens* but it is not true that it was written by Solomon, for these bottles were brought [from Jerusalem] many generations earlier by the [Egyptian] priests. But Solomon only wrote a single book about the seven bottles…".[31]

The Sages did not mention Solomon in the context of exorcism, though Talmud Yerushalmi[32] refers to a "tablet of remedies" that King Hezekiah ordered removed in order to cleansing the Temple of idolatry (גנז טבלה של רפואות).[33] The late secondary addition to *Mishnah Pesahim* 4:9 reads: "King Hezekiah did six things… He hid the book of remedies". In Maimonides's view, the tablet was a list of magical remedies.

The tradition that this book was composed by Solomon appears in Christian literature.[34] In *Quaestiones et responsiones XLI*, Anastasius Sinaita, the 7th-century monk, repeated the question posed by the Church father Hippolytus in the early third century in his commentary on Song of Songs. There, Hippolytus wondered where had the proverbs and psalms written by Solomon[35] disappeared to. His reply was that King Hezekiah feared the people might apply the incantations that appeared in those books instead of praying to God for a cure, and, hence, only a portion of Solomon's writings were copied during his reign and the rest were placed in archives. Among the latter, Hippolytus enumerates books on the physiology of plants, animals, flow and fish, as well as the healing of illness. According to the Byzantine writer George Syncellus (ca. 800), it was Solomon's writings that were engraved in the gate of the Temple that contained the remedy for every disease. McCown concludes that in the fifth century there were

---

30. According to Varo, who is cited by Augustine (1984, 8:38) the source of these techniques was in Persia. And see Livy, XI, xxix, pp. 91–93, and the discussion in Torijano (2002, pp. 209–309). The book was preserved in Persian under the name *Key of Mercy* and *Secrets of Wisdom*.

31. James (1893, pp. 195–196).

32. *y.Mishnah Pesachim* 9:1, 36c–d, p. 332; also see *b. Berahot* 10b, *Pesachim* 56a, *Sanhedrin* 47a.

33. Halperin (1982); Silverman (1976). This tradition is part of the attempt to glorify Hezekiah's image.

34. See Halperin (1982, pp. 117–126).

35. 1 Kings 5:13.

still Christian writers who related with admiration to pseudo-Solomonic texts on magic.[36] Even if we accept this view, the fact is that none of these texts from the Second Temple period and thereafter mention Solomon's magic practices, and the *Testament of Solomon* is apparently the only work in which the king not only rules the world of demons but also recruits them to construct the Temple while he also exorcises a demon called Urinus from a boy's body and calls other demons by name in order to exorcise them.[37] Jesus appears in this text as possessing more power to rule over demons than Solomon.

Would it be correct to state that during the Second Temple period a tradition about Solomon as an exorcist was widespread in Jewish society in Palestine and in Egypt, and that that tradition was also accepted by non-Jews? We have not come across more than a few magic papyri that use the name of Solomon before the 3rd century C.E. that can be attributed to Jews and can serve as evidence of a Jewish "popular tradition" about Solomon as an exorcist of demons and the use of Solomon's name for purposes of magic.[38] From the few examples of such use, we can mention the Paris magical papyrus from the fourth century, which states: "I adjure (*exorkizo*) thee [the demons] by the seal which Solomon laid upon the tongue of Jeremiah and he spoke".[39] The text of the papyrus is complex and in a later version, 'Jesus, the God the Hebrews', was added to it. And, written on another papyrus, Köln 338 (3rd century C.E.): "I adjure every spirit wicked and evil by the great God most high who created heaven and earth and seas and all things in them, to come out of Allous, whom Annis bore, the holder of the Seal (*sphragis*) of Solomon. Now! Now! Now! At once!"[40]

All this is not enough evidence of the existence of a widespread tradition about King Solomon, in contrast to Jesus, performing magic or healing.

---

36. McCown (1922a, p. 15).

37. *Testament of Solomon* had an influence on demonology in much later generations. For example, the Dutch physician and occultist, Johann Weyer (1515–1588) mentions 69 demons in his book *Pseudomonarchia Daemonun* (False Kingdom of Demons) and in the index to his book *De Praestigiis Daemonum et Incantationibus ac Venificiis* (On the Illusions of the Demons and on Spells and Poisons, 1563).

38. Torijano writes that: "The figure of Solomon as exorcist enjoyed enough fame among the gentile readers of Josephus to allow the adaptation of pre-existent patterns without much trouble" (Torijano 2002, pp. 104–105). However, there is no evidence that Solomon was famous among non-Jewish readers in the time of Josephus. Duling also writes that "the fascinating legend of Solomon's magical wisdom was widespread in Late Antiquity […]", Duling (1985).

39. Bibliothèque Nationale, Supp., grec., no. 564, 11, 3039 f. [PGM IV 3009–3009]. And see Bonner (1943); Kotansky (1995, pp. 261–266).

40. David R. Jordan and Roy Kotansky (1997); Duling (1975).

Jesus as a Healer and an Exorcist

The major achievement ascribed to magic is the exorcism of demons or devils from the body of an ill person using various techniques. All the cultures of the ancient world[41] believed that evil spirits (demons/devils) possessed the power to enter the body of a person, and in the power of a king, or a saint, to overcome the demon by the touch of his hand.[42] There are instances of healing without any magical practice in the Bible (the stories of Elijah and Elisha) and in *Genesis Apocryphon* (XX. 16–32), a work from the Judean desert scrolls (Qumran) that tells how Abraham cured Pharaoh after all of his sorcerers had failed and fled: Abraham: "prayed [for him]…and I laid my hands on his [head]; and the scourge departed from him and the evil [spirit] was expelled…".[43]

Similar testimonies are found in rabbinical literature. In the *Midrash Genesis Rabbah*, a tale is told about "Elijah of blessed memory who came to our master [Judah ha-Nasi], put his hand on his tooth and healed him".[44] Certainly, the Sages opposed healing by whispering spells, viewing it as a practice of the *minim* (heretics),[45] but their negative opinion was not adopted by the public. The belief in healing through the laying of hands of saints and kings endured at least until the seventeenth century.[46] This widespread belief aroused quite a lot of criticism and derision.[47]

Many episodes in the Gospels tell of Jesus' deeds as a healer and exorcist of demons, and they contain different versions of how Jesus explains the source of his power. I shall cite only a few.[48] Matthew relates that Jesus passed through all the cities and villages "teaching in their synagogues, and proclaiming the good news of the kingdom"

---

41. Jayne (1962); Bharyo and Rider (2017).

42. Flusser (1957).

43. Vermes (1987 edn.), *The Dead Sea Scrolls in English*, 255. See also Fitzmyer (2004, p. 103).

44. *Genesis Rabbah* 33:3; ed. Theodor-Albeck (1936, pp. 306–307).

45. See Schäfer (2007, pp. 52–62).

46. Uzbek, the Persian traveler in Montesquieu's *Persian Letters* writes: "This king is a great magician […] he even succeeded in making them [the French] believe that he can cure them of all sort of diseases by touching them." The King of France is a master sorcerer, whose subjects believe not only in the paper money he prints, but also in the healing power of the touch of his hand. The disease, scrofula, is called "kings evil" in English. Letter 24 in Montesquieu (1973, p. 73). And see Thomas (1973, pp. 227–242).

47. Lucian of Samosata mocks those who "purify themselves with holy potions and others who are deceived by imposters who sell them spells" and tells about a fool who was seduced into buying incantations from a Jew (*Iudaios eternon moron eksadei labon*). Lucian of Samosata (1973, p. 173).

48. See Duling (1978, pp. 392–410); Paffenroth (1999).

and that he also was "curing every disease and every sickness."⁴⁹ And he also tells how Jesus cured a girl by holding her hand, and two blind men, whose eyes he touched, and said: "According to your faith let it be done to you". And their eyes were opened.⁵⁰ Jesus also healed by exorcising demons: "Then they brought to him a demonic-possessed man who was blind and mute; and he cured him, so that the one who had been mute could speak and see. All the crowds were amazed and said, 'Can this be the Son of David?'"⁵¹ And when another presumed to cast out devils in his name, Jesus did not prevent him and said to his followers: "Do not stop him; for whoever is not against you is for you".⁵²

The only direct correspondence between Jesus and Solomon as exorcists is in Matthew 12:22–24, when the crowd, amazed at seeing Jesus cure a blind man possessed of a demon, cries out: "Can this be the Son of David?" The Pharisees heard it, and said, "It is only by Beelzebul, the ruler of the demons, that this fellow casts out the demons". And Jesus replied: "If Satan casts out Satan, he is divided against himself; how then will his kingdom stand? If I cast out demons by Beelzebul, by whom do your own exorcists cast them out? Therefore, they will be your judges".⁵³ There is also the story in Mark⁵⁴ about the beggar Bartimaeus, the son of Timaeus, who upon seeing Jesus began to call out: "Jesus, Son of David, have mercy on me!"⁵⁵ In these stories, the "true" Jesus does not appear as a magician⁵⁶ or a shaman.⁵⁷ However, he does not use healing herbs, roots, incantations, or a seal.

In these acts, Jesus is akin to Elijah the Tishbite, who resurrected the son of the woman in whose home he lived: "After this the son of the woman, the mistress of the house, became ill; his illness was so severe that there was no breath left in him. She then said to Elijah, 'What have you against me, O man of God? You have come to me to bring my sin to remembrance, and to cause the death of my son!'

49. Matthew 9:35.
50. Matthew 9:25–31.
51. Matthew 12:22–23.
52. Luke 9:50.
53. Matthew 12:24–27.
54. Mark 10:46–52.
55. Matthew 12:42; Luke 11:31. And the story about the "Queen of the south" (Queen Sheba) who when she came to hear the wisdom of Solomon, found that "something greater than Solomon is here!"
56. Unlike Morton Smith's claim in his book. See Smith (1978). See Birkett (2015); Twelftree (2007); Benko (1982); Kee (1986). In a thoroughly researched study, it is argued that healing and miracles contributed to the success of Christianity. See Ehrman (2019, pp. 131–159).
57. Craffert (2008).

But he said to her, 'Give me your son'. He took him from her bosom, carried him up into the upper chamber where he was lodging, and laid him on his own bed. He cried out to the Lord, 'O Lord my God, have you brought calamity even upon the widow with whom I am staying, by killing her son?' Then he stretched himself upon the child three times, and cried out to the Lord, 'O Lord my God, let this child's life come into him again'. The Lord listened to the voice of Elijah; the life of the child came into him again, and he revived".[58]

Jesus exorcises demons through his authority and faith. When he exorcises a foul spirit from the body of a child and commands it: "You spirit that keeps this boy from speaking and hearing, I command you, come out of him, and never enter him again!"[59] He said to them, "This kind can come out only through prayer".[60] And when, at the synagogue in Capernaum, where he taught as one that had authority, and not as the scribes, a foul spirit entered into one of the worshippers and Jesus ordered it to come out, those observing were all amazed, and they kept on asking one another, "What is this? A new teaching—with authority! He commands even the unclean spirits, and they obey him".[61] In this way, Jesus' power is greater and different from that of Philip from Samaria, who exorcised foul spirits and healed the lame, and from that of Simon (Magus), also from a city in Samaria, who used sorcery and bewitched the people of his city with his magic. But after they heard from Philip the tidings about the kingdom of God and the name of Jesus Christ, they were baptized, both men and women.[62] Hence, Matthew and Luke rejected magic practices and, in doing so, drew a distinction between Jesus as an exorcist of demons and other exorcists.[63] He is the antithesis of Simon Magus, who amazed the crowds with his sorceries *tais mageasis*[64] and in the Middle Ages became the archetype of a satanic magician.

Jesus works miracles without using incantations or other means. He is, therefore, a therapeutic Jesus, who exorcises demons that have possessed the body of a person, or heals the disabled, with the power that comes to him from God,[65] and works miracles the like of which have never been wrought before: "But if it is by the Spirit of God

---

58. 1 Kings 17:17–22.
59. Mark 9:24–25.
60. Mark 9:29.
61. Mark 1:21–29.
62. Acts 8:4–19. See also Butler (1993, pp. 63–83).
63. Butler (1993, pp. 73–83). According to Matthew (12:28), Jesus says: "by the Spirit of God that I cast out demons".
64. Acts 8:9–13.
65. Fisher (1968).

that I cast out demons, then the kingdom of God has come to you".[66] Jesus passes this power on to his apostles, whom he sends to heal the sick, to revive the dead, to purify lepers, to cast out demons.[67] But the use of Jesus' name to exorcise demons was already widespread during his lifetime, and "imposters" began to use his name. When his followers encountered such an imposter, they forbade him because "he does not follow with us".[68] During his journey to Ephesus, Paul came across several vagabond Jews who claimed they were casting out demons by using Jesus' name, but the possessed man fought them off and they fled, naked and wounded, and "the name of the Lord Jesus was magnified". Following this incident, "A number of those who practiced magic collected their books and burned them publicly; when the value of these books was calculated, it was found to come to fifty thousand silver coins".[69]

The power—and the authority—to exorcise demons lies only with the Apostles. In Lystra, Paul heals a cripple by calling out loudly: "Stand upright on your feet." And the man leaped and walked.[70] This deed caused the people of the city to regard Paul and Barnabas as gods who had come down to earth in the likeness of men. In Malta, when the father of the chief man of the island lay sick with fever and bloody flux, Paul prayed, laid hands upon the man, and cured him.[71] Timothy reminds Aquila that Jesus healed the many illnesses of those who were sick (7, 6b).[72]

Eusebius attests to Jesus' popularity as a healer when he writes that when Abgar, King of Edessa in southern Syria, fell ill, he heard reports about Jesus who healed the sick without using herbs and medicines, caused cripples to walk again and blind men to see, and cast out evil spirits and demons. The King understood that Jesus is a god who descended from heaven to work all these miracles, or that he is, perhaps, a son of God. Hence, he asked him to come to Edessa to cure him. The King also heard that the Jews were spreading malicious rumors about Jesus and trying to harm him. His city is small and pious, the King writes to Jesus, and there is room for the two of them. Jesus replies: "Those who have seen me will not believe in me" and "those who have not seen me will be saved". He says he will not come to Edessa for he must complete his mission, and then will be taken

---

66. Matthew 12:28.
67. Mark 6:13.
68. Luke 9:49; Mark 9:38.
69. Acts 19:19.
70. Acts 14:8–10.
71. Acts 28:7–9.
72. *The Dialogue of Timothy and Aquila*, 155.

up to heaven, but he will send to Abgar one of his apostles who will bring him a cure. Eusebius hastens to add that there is evidence of the existence of this exchange of letters in an Edessa archive.[73] This is, of course, a legend, but the fact that Eusebius believed that Jesus' healing powers furthered the spread of Christianity in Eastern Syria indicates that he regarded Jesus' powers of healing and exorcising demons as a significant element both of his divinity and of the attraction of believers to the new religion.[74] He writes that it is well known that we are accustomed to using the name of Jesus and pure prayers to repulse the actions of demons[75] and Justin Martyr writes in a similar vein.[76]

---

73. Eusebius, *Ecclesiastical History*, 1.13.1–10, in Cartlidge and Dungan (1980, p. 91). The reference is to Abgar V, King of Osrhoene in Mesopotamia 4–50 C.E. Another version of the story comes from Ioannes Damascenus (676–749), an Arab Christian monk and theologian. According to him, Abgar wrote to Jesus asking that, in case he will refuse to come, he will charge his ambassador to employ an artist to make a portrait of him (*Epistola ad Theophilium*). The letter is mentioned in a description of the journey of Egeria, at the end of the fourth century. She relates that the bishop of the city showed her the king's letter and Jesus' reply. Wilkinson (1999, p. 133). In the medieval apocrypha "Letter of Lentulus", the writer, Publius Lentulus, a fictitious governor of Jerusalem, Jesus "raises the dead and heals all diseases". See Lutz (1975).

74. On the vast literature on this subject, see Cartlidge and Dungan (1980, p. 9); as well as the bibliography in the article by Meggitt (2006, pp. 109–114).

75. *Preparation for the Gospel* III: 6, 35, in Eusebius (2002).

76. "…it is equally clear (as the word of prophecy) speaking in the name of His followers, metaphorically affirms, that We believers beseech Him to safeguard us from strange, that is, evil and deceitful spirits. We constantly ask God through Jesus Christ to keep us safe from those demons […]We call him our Keeper and Redeemer […] it is clear to all of us that His Father bestowed upon Him such a great power that even the demons are subject both to His name and to His ordained manner (the sign of the cross) of suffering" (Chap. 30), Justin Martyr (2003, pp. 191–192). Celsus also attests to the fact that Jesus was renowned as a healer and exorcist who learned certain magical powers in which the Egyptians excel, and when he returned to Palestine, he became arrogant and declared himself a god (1:28, Chadwick 1963, p. 28). He also mocked the Christians for materializing the demons, an act they had copied from various books of magic and compared the incantations and curses to an ode hummed by an old woman trying to put an infant to sleep. He adds that: "a certain Dionysus, an Egyptian musician […] told him that magical arts were effective with uneducated people but not with people who had studied philosophy with whom they were not able to do any effect, because they were careful to lead a healthy way of life" (VI:41. Chadwick 1963, pp. 355–356) that is, only among the uneducated because of its vulgarity and the utterly illiterate" (I:26). The miracles ascribed to Jesus are the actions of sorcerers, who promise wondrous things, but the belief that they cast out demons, heal illness and call up spirits is but a figment of the imagination. To that claim, Origen replied: "But as a Christian, and having a more accurate knowledge of the matter than he [Celsus], I must aver that these are not doctrines of Christians, but of those who are wholly alien to salvation, and who in no way profess Jesus to be either Saviour, or God, or teacher, or Son of God (VI:30, Chadwick, 346). Origen writes that Jesus overcomes the demons by his soul "and the divine power in him". Their power would be destroyed, since they are unable to withstand the light of the divine power"

According to Emperor Julian, Jesus "accomplished nothing worth hearing of, unless anyone thinks that to heal crooked and blind men and to exorcise those who were possessed by evil... can be classed as a mighty achievement" (CG, 191 E).[77] In other words, this was a common phenomenon, not a great achievement to boast of. These mocking words towards Jesus and his disciples are far more harsh (and derisive) than Julian's opinion of Solomon, who was, according to him, "proficient in the secret cult of God" (224c–d), namely in performing magic practices that created a link with the divine and also influenced him".

However, demons do exist and hence, Jesus, with his greater power, protects people from them through *exousia* in the spirit like that of Julian and Celsus. Nestor the Priest writes that the Christians worship Jesus "because he resurrected one dead man, but resuscitated two people; one before his own death and the one after he has died", Elisha "resuscitated two dead people: one before his own death, and one after he died. He walked in the Jordan River", and "Ezekiel resuscitated many dead in the valley" (13\15). And that is far more marvelous than what Jesus did by resuscitating one dead person on the third day after his death.[78]

The name of Jesus as a healer was also known among Jews because of the incident related about R. Eleazar ben Damma, of the 2nd century C.E., who was bitten by a snake. Jacob of Kfar Sama came to cure him by using the name of Jesus ben Pantera. When R. Ishmael refused to permit this, ben Dama told him he would prove him wrong, but "he did not have time to bring the [promised] proof before he dropped dead".[79] However, not all the Jewish healers used the name of Jesus, and the prohibition against magical healing was not only due to the fear that it might be associated with Jesus.[80] In any event, the prohibition did not keep Jews who were ill from seeking magical healing.[81] The Church unreservedly accepted the belief in the existence of demons that dwell in the soul and body of a man and control him.[82] It also adopted some magic practices, but endowed them with a new character by means of a version of prayers and incantations (*coniuro, adiuro*), in the name of

---

(I.60), Chadwick 1963, p. 54. Schäfer writes: "Casting out demons through the power of Jesus' name does not just mean through Jesus' authority (*exousia*), but, literally, through using the power (*dynamis*) inherent in Jesus' name:" In Schäfer (2007, p. 59).

77. Julian (1980).
78. *The Polemic of Nestor*, "The Account of the Disputation of the Priest". See in Lasker and Stroumsa (1996, p. 54).
79. *Tosefta Hullin* 2:22, trans. Neusner.
80. Schäfer (2007, pp. 105–106).
81. See in Bar-Ilan (1995) and Schäfer (1997, pp. 33–38).
82. Jenkins (1953).

the "father, the son and the holy spirit". Nuns also accepted the belief in the power of amulets.[83] For example, Anthony of the Desert (c251–356) was renowned for his ability to cast evil spirits from the bodies of the ill,[84] and the acts of healing and exorcism of the zealous Monophysite monk, Barsauma of the fifth century, were known to meet the standards of the established Church.[85] In *Summa Theologiae* (Book II, Question 96), Thomas Aquinas denounced the magic rituals intended to replace the grace of God as a way of achieving knowledge, and wrote that "magic art is to be absolutely repudiated and avoided by Christians"; nonetheless, he did not impugn the validity of some types of magic.[86] And it is a known fact that the use of the Scriptures for magic purposes was popular at least until the fifth century and John Chrysostom called them *theiai epôdai* (divine charms).[87]

The Riddle of Solomon's Ring

Although Josephus may not be the source for Solomon's image as a magician, he did make a significant contribution to the dissemination of that image.

Why wasn't Josephus content merely to praise Solomon's knowledge of magic and its practice? Why did he decide to add a story about a miracle that proves the power of the incantations written by Solomon? According to his well-known story, Josephus claimed that he saw with his own eyes a man (perhaps an Essene) named Eleazar who, in the presence of Vespasianus, his sons, and a number of other soldiers, freed men possessed by demons by putting "[…] to the nose of the possessed man a ring which had under its seal one of the roots prescribed by Solomon,[88] and then, as the man smelled it, drew out the demon through his nostrils, and when the man at once fell down, adjured the demon never to come back into him, speaking Solomon's name and reciting his incantations (*epôdai*) that he composed. The exorcism of the demon revealed to the onlookers the greatness of his [Solomon's] nature and how God favoured him, and that no one

---

83. In Underwood (1953, pp. 131–140) and Kieckhefer (1990, pp. 69–80).

84. "Life of Antony by Athanasius 64 (36)", in White (1991, pp. 48–49).

85. Kiperwasser and Ruzer (2013).

86. In the 17th century, the French scholar Gabriel Naude (1600–1653) rejected the claim that Aquinas had engaged in magic in his book *Apologie pour tous les grands personages qui ont esté faussement soupçonnez de magie*, published in 1625 and printed in four editions. He also defended Pythagoras, Socrates, and others against a similar claim.

87. See Gamble (1995, pp. 237–241).

88. Ring (*daktulios*) and seal (*sphragis*). They are sometimes one object (see Esther 3:12) a seal is attached to the ring, and they were attributed with magical powers. In the *Testament of Solomon*, the seal ring is given to him by the Archangel Michael so that he can control demons. Also see Barb (1963, pp. 112–113).

under the sun may be ignorant of the king's surpassing virtue of every kind".[89]

The addition of this episode to the description of Solomon's wisdom is a riddle of sorts that has aroused much interest among scholars, among other reasons, because it "revealed" the significant role of magic, magic practices, and astrology in Jewish culture and society. Josephus also wrote that there were books in circulation giving "recipes", and that he himself knew of a work under such a title ascribed to Solomon.[90]

It seems that the importance that Josephus ascribes to Solomon as the author of magic incantations is not sufficiently explained by the fact that exorcism was a widespread practice in Jewish society,[91] or that Nahor's father supposedly taught him the traditions of the Chaldeans so he could practice divination and astrology according to the signs as reported in the *Book of Jubilees* (9:8), or that it is written that "Noah wrote everything in a book just as we taught him according to every kind of healing, that the evil spirits were restrained from following the sons of Noah, and he gave everything which he wrote to Shem, his oldest son[...]".[92]

However, neither that nor the fact that exorcism was a widespread practice in Jewish culture, can explain why Josephus saw fit to ascribe to Solomon "magical wisdom",[93] which is not attributed to him in the Bible. One might also wonder why Josephus believed that the story of Eleazar's act of exorcism, in which he was helped by incantations and recipes written by Solomon, would impress the educated Roman reader, and why he did not cite a different concrete example of the depth and breadth of Solomon's wisdom. Bohak writes that Josephus "assumed his non-Jewish readers would share his own excitement about such a glorious manifestation of the supreme wisdom of an ancient Jewish king".[94] Josephus must have been cognizant of the harsh, even derisive criticism of faith in magic practices (*magikê technê*), which were thought to belong to *dedita supersti-*

---

89. Ant 7VII.45–9, Trans. Thackery with Bohak's modification, in Bohak (2008, p. 101). Also see Förster (2001).

90. McCown (1922a, pp. 1–24).

91. Eshel (1999).

92. *Jubilees* 9:10–14, trans. Wintermute, in Charlesworth (1983, pp. 35–142).

93. Contrary to Duling's view. See Duling (1985, p. 7).

94. Bohak (2008, pp. 100–101). Joshua Amir goes even further when he writes that Josephus sees in Solomon's ring "the greatness of Solomon", and also adds that if so, "it is no wonder, then, that in the eyes of the simple Jew of the time Solomon's magical power seemed to be one of the strong cards of Judaism in its great proselytizing campaign". Amir (1968, p. 17). Feldman's claim that Josephus added the episode because "exorcising demons was regarded as the sign of special power in a wise man", is odd. Feldman (1998, p. 584).

tiosa gens, to be *miracula circumlatoris* and *magicae vanitates*. Josephus lived and wrote in Rome at the time when the Roman authorities failed to suppress traditional Egyptian magical techniques and the circulation of magical texts.[95] The expulsion from Rome of astrologers and sorcerers in 33 B.C.E. was not effective, and the burning of thousands of magic books by order of Emperor Augustus in 13 C.E. was also to no avail (the church father John Chrysostom [c. 347–407] states that in the city of his birth, Antioch, soldiers searched for books of magic and set fire to them).[96] At the same time, in Egypt under Roman rule, "much of what had constituted public religion was driven underground, becoming a secretive and 'private' practice".[97] In any event, the persecution or even the execution of those using magic or possessing amulets or books of magic did not succeed in dissuading those who wished to avail themselves of such practices.[98]

If so, did Josephus have any reason to believe that the Emperor Vespasianus would be impressed by Eleazar's ability to cure a blind man, using a ring and incantations? Tacitus (56–120 C.E.) states that while the emperor was staying in Alexandria, a blind man and a man who had lost the use of his hand approached him and begged to be cured. Vespasianus at first ridiculed these appeals and treated them with scorn. However, when the men persisted, he "took precaution" and consulted his physicians "whether such blindness and infirmity could be overcome by human aid". Their reply treated the two cases differently: they said that in the first the power of sight had not been completely eaten away and it would return if the obstacles were removed; in the other, the joint had slipped and become displaced, but they could be restored if a healing pressure were applied to them. Such perhaps was the wish of the gods, and it might be that the emperor has been chosen for this divine service; in any case, ridicule would fall only on the poor supplicant. So, Vespasianus, believing that his good fortune was capable of anything and that nothing was any longer incredible, with a smiling face, and amid intense excitement on the part of the by-standers, did as he was asked to do. The hand was instantly restored to use, and the day again shone for the blind man".[99] In order to confirm the veracity of the story, Tacitus stresses that "both facts are told by eye-witnesses even now when falsehood brings no reward". It

---

95. Ritner (1993, p. 89).

96. MacMullen (1975, pp. 46–127); Kippenberg (1997).

97. Ritner (1995a, pp. 43–60). At the same time, Pliny the Elder writes, "magic rose to such a height that even today it has sway over a great part of mankind, and in the East commands the King of Kings", Pliny the Elder XXX.1–1–2 (trans. Jones).

98. See Barb (1963, pp. 100–125).

99. Books IV-V, LXXXI, pp. 158–163 in Tacitus (1969). Tacitus also writes that the Egyptians "are the most superstitious of nations".

is impossible to know what the truth is in this story, but it seems more reliable to me than Josephus' story, although the latter states that he himself was present at the act of exorcising the demon.

Why, then, would Josephus provide support, for example, for Posidonius' assertion that the Jews are a people of sorcerers who pretend to use incantations? Duling suggests that Josephus believed such a story would enhance Solomon's prestige within a public that believed in supernatural forces and was familiar with the traditions about Solomon's greatness and wisdom.[100] This explanation seems to me contrived.[101] The only reasonable explanation is that Josephus did not find in the historical tradition any concrete example demonstrating that Solomon was well-versed in all branches of "scientific" knowledge. Therefore, he decided to add the episode about Eleazar—and even to affirm it, declaring that he himself saw it with his own eyes. And perhaps the simple explanation is that Josephus, like many authors, wanted to introduce anecdotes into his story, a fruit of his creative imagination.[102] Whatever the reason, this episode certainly influenced the shaping of Solomon's legendary image as a ruler of demons, which dominated the imagination of the coming generations.[103]

Solomon's After-Life as a Magician

In *Commentary upon Matthew*, Origen wrote that "the Jews are regarded as adept at the adjuration of demons and they employ adjurations in the Hebrew language drawn from the books of Solomon". By "books", Origen was not referring to Song of Songs, Proverbs or Ecclesiastes, but rather to books of incantations. *Sepher ha-Razim*, apparently written in Palestine in the third century C.E., relates that an-

100. Duling (1985, p. 25); Förster (2001).

101. There is no evidence that "Solomon's ring" (or "seal") was known in Jewish history before the writing of *Jewish Antiquities*. Possibly, the motif appears under the influence of the book, which was quite popular. Tertullian writes: "The Jew Josephus, native champion of Jewish antiquities, must be consulted" (Tertullian 1984, xix, pp. 5–6). The motif was known, for example, to several Byzantine chronographers, such as Georgios Hamartolos (ca. 850), who mentions the exorcism carried out by Eleazar, and Cederes (c. 1000) who mentions the act of exorcism and the incantations composed by Solomon. See Torijano (2002, p. 87). However, it is impossible to prove that Josephus was the progenitor of this motif.

102. On the claim that Jews engaged in demonology was widespread in Byzantium see the Byzantine poet Johannes Tzetzes of the 12th century who wrote: "To the Jews, I say in a proper manner in Hebrew: Your blind house devoted to magic, your mouth, a charm engulfing flies [...]" in Herrin (2008, p. 242).

103. Solomon's ring appears on a glass paste oval amulet from the Byzantine period. In Maguire (1995, p. 39). Papyrus PGM XII, 261–69 states: "A little ring useful for every [magical] operation and for success. Kings and governors [try to get it]. Very effective". In Betz (1992, p. 161).

cient books of magic were passed down each generation to Solomon. Secrets of magic were passed down from Noah through the Patriarchs to Moses, and from him to the Prophets and Sages, until they came to Solomon: "And the *Books of the Mysteries* were disclosed to him and he became very learned in books of understanding, and (so) ruled over every-thing he desired, over all the spirits and the demons that wander in the world, and from the wisdom of this book he imprisoned and released, and sent out and brought in, and built and prospered. For many books were more precious and more honorable and more difficult than any of them".[104] In other words, these "books of secrets", which contained incantations and curses to exorcise demons and spirits, were not written by Solomon but were passed down to him in a chain of transmission, of which he was the last recipient. In contrast, according to the Sufi encyclopedia, *Rasāʾil Ikhwān al-Ṣafā*, compiled in Basra in the second half of the tenth century, the source of the magic texts is human—the Persians received the wisdom of astronomy from the Indians, and Solomon gained the knowledge of trickery and sorcery and curses and the uses of idols and talismans from the kings of other nations. In other words, not from the mythological Noah, the Patriarchs, and the Prophets. On the many incantation bowls against demons and evil spirits found in Babylonia, Solomon's name[105] is mentioned on some, for example: "Solomon the Son of David who worked spells on male demons and female liliths".

The longevity of this tradition is attested to by, among others, Don Isaac Abrabanel, the learned Jewish statesman from Portugal (1437–1508). In his commentary on 1 Kings based on Josephus' *Antiquities* (which he read in a Latin or Castilian translation published in 1492), he wrote that Solomon's magic power "in the matter of demons and their deeds and the spells to be employed against them" is an expression of his unique wisdom. And the German bishop, theologian, and scholar Albertus Magnus (1200–1280) cites the work *Speculum astronomiae*, which refers to "satanic books attributed to Solomon". The *Ars Notoria quam Creator Altissimus Salomoni reuelauit* from the 12th century (which was preserved in more than 50 manuscripts and attributed also to Apollonius) states: "Ista, inquit Salomon" (Thus said Solomon): magic is described as a "holy art" and a sacrament revealed by God to Solomon".[106] Many books from this genre known

---

104. Morgan (1983); Margalioth (1966, p. 16).
105. See Shaked et al. (2013); Shaked (1999).
106. Page (2004, p. 39). The 15th century *Liber Visionum* (Book of Visions) was, for example, "an attempt to reconcile the goals of a condemned medieval, ritual magic text, the *Ars Notoria* after which is was loosely modelled". See "Plundering the Egyptian treasure: John the Monk's Book of Visions and its relation to the *Ars notoria of*

as "Solomonic Grimoire" were disseminated in the West.[107] The most popular of these is *Clavicula Salomonis* (*Solomon's Key*), a collection of talismanic formulae for summoning demons.[108] Its source is unknown and it appeared in the West in the sixteenth century in Latin, Italian and French manuscripts.[109] When Faust says: "Für solche halbe Höllenbrut / Ist Salomon's Schlüssel gut" (I.1257–8), he is not referring to the ability to overcome a ghost with a real key, but with the help of a book that contains ritual diagrams. That also appears in the chapter Ars Goetia in the book *Lesser Key of Solomon* evoked by King Solomon.[110] In the two works, Solomon bequeaths the knowledge of magic he possesses, "the most precious of all", which shows how to introduce the celestial movement to his son Rehoboam. The four brass jugs in which Solomon imprisoned and sealed the demons are part of this sacred geometry. A key is mentioned in *The Second Targum to Esther*:[111] "Solomon was a wise man who knew the secrets of the heavens… To him was given a large key whereby to open the gates of wisdom und understanding the heart".[112] Here a key is not an object, but rather a metaphor ("the keys of heaven"). On the other hand, as someone engaging in magia naturalis, Solomon appears very rarely. For example, as such he appears in a 14th century work, *Jocalia Salomonis* (Diamonds of Solomon), where he is described as dabbling in alchemy.[113] In any event, as I noted, Solomon is famous not for the practice of magic, but rather as the author of magic literature, or as the possessor of such literature.

The use of a ring[114] was apparently not an "invention" by Jose-

---

Solomon", in Fanger (1998, pp. 216–249).

107. Among them: Liber *Salomonis libri de Tribus Figuris, Le Livre de Salomon, Herbarium Salomonis, Hygromantia Salomonis, Schemhamphoras Salomonis Regis*. On the "Solomonic Cycle", see Butler (1998, p. 48).

108. Yates (1984, pp. 42–43); Thorndike (1964, Vol. 2, pp. 279–290). According to a medieval Neapolitan story, the body of the poet Virgil was found in a grave perfectly preserved, and under his head, among others, was the Ars Notoria. Virgil also "possessed" the seal of Solomon. See Comparetti (1895; pp. 274, 318).

109. See Macgregor Mathers (2006 [1888]). His translation is based on a French translation from the eighteenth century. The Chivalric Romans *Sir Gawain and the Green Knight* (14th century) refers to the Pentangle, is a symbol that Solomon-formerly (conceived) as a "token of (holy) truth". Trans. Brian Stone (1974, p. 45) and Trans. S.W.A. Neilson (1999, p. 14).

110. This book was written under the inspiration of Johann Weyer's book, mentioned in note 34.

111. *The Second Targum to Esther*, II. Cassel (1888, p. 270).

112. Thus, also "key of David" in Revelation 3:7.

113. "Ergotzliche Experimente Salomons", Birkhahn (2010, pp. 52–53).

114. Ring (*daktulios*) and seal (*sphragis*) are often one object and a seal is attached to the ring. Milstein (1995, pp. 33–62). Another example is a glass paste oval amulet from the Byzantine period on which Solomon's ring appears. See J. Russell

phus, but he may have inspired the appearance of Solomon's signet ring (*sigillium*)[115] as a major item in the magic toolbox. In *Testament of Solomon*, it is related that after having prayed to the Lord Sabaoth, Solomon received from the angel Gabriel a signet ring from a precious stone on which a *pentalpha* was engraved to help him build the Temple. He brought to Solomon "a little ring, having a seal consisting of an engraved stone, and said to him: Take, O Solomon, king, son of David, the gift which the Lord had sent thee. With it thou shalt lock up all the demons of the earth, male and female; and with their help thou shalt build up Jerusalem". And Solomon called a boy, gave him the ring, and when the king ordered him to, he threw the ring at the chest of the demon.[116] On one side of a medallion from Smyrna, for example, the spell appears: "Flee, hated one: Solomon pursues you […] Seal of Solomon. Expel every evil from the bearer". When Timothy tells Aquila the Jew that a demon has entered his body making him belittle Christianity, he says, "make the seal of Christ that is the sign of the cross on his forehead and his heart" (II.2).[117] A ring also appears in esoteric texts attributed to Solomon, including *Sigillum Solomonis* (Solomon's ring). The "seal of Solomon" (i. e., signet ring) and "the ring of Solomon" became popular symbols and were widely disseminated. Egeria writes that during Easter week a crowd of worshippers came to the Church of the Nativity and, after kissing the cross, passed before a Deacon that held Solomon's ring and kissed it.[118] Priests in Catholic England used a "Solomon's ring" as well as "Solomon's staff" and the ring of the prophet Elisha.[119] From this very long tradition, the signet ring arrived at the roots of the plant whose botanical name is *Polygonatum odorum*, which was given the name "Solomon's ring" because it was used for healing wounds and fractures, and as a love potion. As for Jewish tradition, "Solomon's ring" did not become a talisman, a role that was filled by a Shield of David usually hung on the neck. But there are "Kabbalists" who call themselves "world renown experts", among other things, in writing amulets, "using the seals of King Solomon and the script of angels".[120]

(1995).

115. I will mention here the play *Der Siegelring des Salomo* (Berlin, 1820) by the rabbi, poet, and playwright from Strasbourg, Lippmann Moses Büschenthal (1784–1818).

116. Trans. Conybeare (1898, pp. 16–17).

117. Varner (2004, p. 43).

118. Wilkinson (1999, p. 155–156).

119. Thomas (1973, p. 323).

120. The (contemporary) "kabbalist" Yitzhak Mizrahi, whose name "precedes him and whose actions are well-known throughout the land and the whole world", offered his goods in a colorful newspaper ad in which a miniature photograph of the

While in the esoteric literature Solomon and Jesus compete as to which of them controls the demons, in the corpus of magic papyri, they do not compete, but at times act jointly. Most of these magical texts written in Greek come from the Roman period and those that originate in Mesopotamia are from a far later period. From about 600 C.E., we do not possess any magic papyri from the first century C.E., or from previous centuries, that can be attributed to Jews, and in which Solomon is mentioned. Among other sources, we know from *Sefer Hasidim* written by R. Judah he-Ḥasid, the rabbi of the Ashkenazi Chasidim in the 13th century, that curses and spells were widespread in the Ashkenazi society. It states that "he who deals in curses of angels or demons or in magical incantations will not come to a good end, and distressing things will occur to his body and his sons".[121]

Then, what Solomon did not write, or what was forbidden, is written (but not in Solomon's name) in Ashkenazi Jewish culture in *Guide to Exorcism of a Spirit*,[122] similar to guidebooks written in Christian society.[123] Hundreds of texts about possession by a demon and its exorcism, or about a *dybbuk* (a term that appears in Hebrew only in 1715) have been documented, and I will relate to only one of these, taken from the *Chronicle of Ahimaaz*. It tells the tale of R. Shefatia who cast out a demon that refused to come out of the body of the daughter of the Emperor of Byzantium. R. Shefatia told the stubborn demon he would cast him out with the help of the Almighty and said: "come forth, in the name of God, that he may know there is a God in Israel. It came forth at once and tried to escape; but he seized it and put it into a leaden chest; he then covered the chest on all sides and sealed it in the name of his Maker, dropped it into the sea, and let it sink into the depth of the mighty waters."[124]

Exorcism rituals are practiced to the present day in both Jewish and Christian societies.[125] In any event, Solomon's name was not used

seal appeared: "the strongest amulet today for couple hood, livelihood, physical and mental health." The "Beit haRuchot" site, www.israghost.co.il (last visited on October 1st 2019). See Bohak (2019).

121. Rabbi Judah ben Samuel (1998, p. 105). It is also written there: "If you see a man prophesying about the Messiah, know that he is engaging in an act of magic or of demons or using the explicit name", pp. 206, 175 (my translation).

122. Tzfatman (2016, pp. 187–202).

123. See in Kieckhefer (1990, p. 156). And in Tzfatman (2016, p. 189), n. 5 in the first "Guide to the Exorcist". *Thesaurus Exorcismorum* appeared in print in 1608. See, for example, Etkes (1995). And see a survey on this literature in the first half of the 17th century, in Feiner (2017, pp. 295–310).

124. Salzman (1966, pp. 71–72).

125. In 1972, Pope Paul VI forbade the use of exorcism. However, in November 2010, a committee of bishops in the United States that convened in Baltimore decided, considering the wide demand, to train priests to hold exorcism rituals. Ha'aretz, 14

in these rituals, but rather the name of Jesus, the cross, and holy water.

***

Supposedly, faithful Christians have no need for magic since Jesus protects them from evil spirits. God endowed him with such power that even the demonic forces are controlled by him. Jesus rules over the supernatural world. From the force of the name, Jesus Christ, Justin Martyr tells Trypho, the demonic forces shudder and are cast out. Christians have no need for the name of Jesus in formulae of oaths, or on amulets; they are replaced by the cross or by holy *reliqua*, which one only needs to show to the demon, and he vanishes.[126] Augustine writes that at the St. Ambrose Cathedral in Milan, where two martyrs are buried, not only people possessed by a foul spirit were cured but also a blind man, immediately after he touched his eyes with a kerchief that lay on the bier of the saints, which greatly enhanced the fame of the dead bishop (*Confessions* IX:16).[127] It was reported that St. Anthony, in trying to prove the power of faith to a group of philosophers who came to visit him, said: "There are some here suffering from the torments of demons […]. Now come on, use your syllogism and any wicked spell you wish, to drive out those whom you think of as your gods. But if you are unable to do so, hold out your conquered hands in supplication and take refuge in the signs of Christ's victory". The philosophers were amazed by the miracle that had been wrought in the name of Jesus.[128] St. Anthony overwhelmed the philosophers through his power of healing which he owed to Jesus. St. Francis healed the ill and cast out demons by prayer and touching, by the Cross and by virtue of holy obedience,[129] without curses or incantations. Thus, a charismatic, holy man can do these deeds in the medieval legend *Vindicta Salvatoris* (Revenge of the Saviour). Titus was healed thank to his decision to avenge the Jews for having crucified Jesus, and in the *Kaiserchronik* (1150–1160) Emperor Tiberius is healed by an image of Veronica wiping the sweat from Jesus' face on the sixth station on the Via Dolorosa.

November 2012 (trans. from the *New York Times*, 12 November 2012).
    126. See Jensen (2017).
    127. Augustine (1961, p. 191).
    128. White, *Early Christian Lives* (1991, pp. 58–59).
    129. Saint Bonaventure (2010, pp. 97–105).

Chapter Six: Miracles and Wonders: Magic, Satan, and Demons

Er erzählte mir aufs Neue,
Was mir schon Arabiens Dichter
Längst erzählt, wie Salomo
Einst bezwang den Todesengel
Und am Leben blieb—Unsterblich
Lebt er jetzt in Dschinnistan,
Herrschend über die Dämonen,
Als ein unbeschränkter König.
   - Heinrich Heine, "Atta Troll"

No intelligent person doubts the existence of sorcery.
   - Ibn Khaldūn, The *Muqaddima*

The correspondence between Solomon and Jesus also took place in the spheres of the esoteric and supernatural world of miracles and wondrous acts, even though, at this point, the two parted ways. Solomon did not work miracles or deal in magic, though he is a hero in many tales of wonders, while Jesus did work miracles and the mere mention of his name sufficed to overcome demons;[1] as a magician, he appears in both pagan and Jewish anti-Christian polemics.

In Mendele Mocher Sforim's[2] novel *Susati* (My Mare), a classic of Yiddish and Hebrew literature, the narrator encounters witches, demons, and the demon king Ashmedai in a forest. A demon, formerly one of King Solomon's servants, relates his account of 'What King Solomon Did': a mix of legends of the Sages and the author's imagination. Upon finishing his story, the demon informs his listener that "I have many more tales from Solomon's life; however, since I see in you signs of a non-believer—begging your forgiveness, one who

---

   1. Thus, for example, people arriving at the synagogue in Nazareth wonder "Whence hath this man this wisdom, and these mighty works?" (Matthew 13:54) Both Jews and pagans, however, regarded the claimed miracles as deception or witchcraft.
   2. The pen name of S.Y. Abramovitsh (1835–1917).

casts doubt on everything, and you do not believe the words of an old demon—I would do well to hold my tongue. And nevertheless, I am not angry at you. For, after all, you are a descendant of the sons of the sons of Solomon…".[3]

No one other than Solomon has so inspired the creative imagination to invent and create a plenitude of legends and fantasies and has become the hero of as extensive a variety of folktales and folklore.[4] He is famous for his ability to converse with animals and fowl. The source for the attribution of this skill is in 1 Kings 4:33: "And he spoke of trees…he spoke also of beasts, and of fowl, and of creeping things, and of fishes". That verse gave rise to the *Midrashic* understanding that Solomon knew "what an ass brays and what a bird twitters".[5] He has the marvelous ability to communicate with fowl, including wild turkeys and the hoopoe, and even ants, and make them his messengers. One story tells how an ant taught Solomon a lesson about humility: an ant warns her fellows to hurry into their nest to avoid being trampled by Solomon's army. The king calls the ant, places it on his palm, and asks its name. "Repentance" [*teshuva*], she replies, and when he asks whether there exists anyone greater than him, she replies that she herself is the greater: "If I were not greater than you, the Almighty would not have sent me to be held by you in your palm". Furious at the ant, Solomon throws it to the ground and declares: "I am Solomon, son of King David". The ant replies: "Know that you came from a putrid drop and that you should not be proud". Solomon falls on his face in shame and commands the wind to carry him away from there.[6] The ant parts from him with these words: "Go, but do not forget the blessed Almighty and do not take great pride in yourself".

Solomon was not alone in his ability to converse with beings of all kinds. Apollonius of Tyana is said to have learned the language of birds in his travels in "the East".[7] R. Johanan ben Zakkai was known to be fluent in the "speech of spirits" and the "speech of palm trees",[8] and it was said of Hillel the Elder "that he had not omitted to study any of the words of the Sages, even all languages, even the speech of mountains, hills and valleys, the speech of trees and herbs, the speech of wild beasts and cattle, the speech of demons and parables. Why [did he study] all these? Because it is stated the "*Lord is well pleased, for*

---

3. *Susati* (*My Mare*) in Mendele Mocher Sforim (1962, pp. 341–342).
4. Vol. 5, pp. 96–100, in Ginzberg (2003).
5. *Song of Songs Rabbah* 1:19, in Neusner (1989).
6. *Bet haMidrash* 5:11–13. On the Quran's version of this story, see Q. 7 ("The Ant").
7. Philostratus (1912, p. 329).
8. *Sukkah* 28a.

his righteousness' to make the teaching [*of the Torah*] *great and glorious*".⁹ Nothing, however, is said about the use R. Hillel or R. Yohanan made of this ability. The New Testament, for its part, does not attribute to Jesus the knowledge of the languages of animals. It was Christian hagiography that began to ascribe such knowledge to the saints: Francis of Assisi is said to have spoken with birds, and Anthony of Padua with fish.¹⁰

And what of miracles?¹¹ Unlike Jesus, neither the biblical nor the legendary Solomon walked on water, or turned water into wine, or worked a miracle like that of the bread and fish.¹² Jesus' fame spread with his miraculous demonstrations: "Then he got up and rebuked the winds and the sea; and there was a great calm. [The people] were amazed, saying, 'What sort of man is this, that even the winds and the sea obey him!'"¹³ Nor was fame the only result, but a confirmation of Jesus' holy status: "Truly you are the Son of God".¹⁴ *The Infancy Gospel of Thomas*, from the first or second century, relates another miracle worked by Jesus. As a boy, he was playing on the Sabbath and fashioned twelve sparrows from clay. A Jew who observed him at work hastened to tell his father Joseph that his son was desecrating the Sabbath. Joseph rebuked Jesus; the boy then clapped his hands and the birds flew away.¹⁵ The priest Nestor saw no reason to be overly impressed by Jesus' miracles or to call him Lord simply because he "turned water into wine¹⁶… and fed a thousand people with eight loaves of bread and fish". He notes that "Christ's deeds are no more marvelous than the deeds of Moses". Nor did Jesus outdo Joshua ben Nun, who "made the sun and the moon stand still in the sky a whole day. The Jordan River dried up for him and a flowing river, gushing with water, stopped in its course for him". The miracles of walking on the water and the miracle of the bread and fish were not equal to the

---

9. *Tractate of the Scribes* 15:9, in Cohen (1965, pp. 291–292).

10. Regarding St. Francis, see St. Saint Bonaventure (2010). On Anthony, see Heywood (1924, pp. 101–103). The collection is from the fourteenth century. This skill was also ascribed to others. See, for example, Bohak (2016).

11. See van Dam (1993); Theissen (1983 [1974]); P. Brown (1970). According to Ibn Khaldūn, "a miracle is a divine power that arouses in the soul [the ability] to exercise influence. The worker of miracles is supported in his activity by the spirit of God…miracles are found (to be wrought by good persons for good purposes and by souls that are entirely devoted to good deeds". Ibn Khaldūn (1958, Vol. 3, p. 167).

12. Matthew 14:19–20.

13. Matthew 8:26–27.

14. Matthew 14:33.

15. Gribetz (2013).

16. Jupiter, when visiting Philemon and Baucis, also performs a miracle in which a wine bowl is constantly refilled (this is only one of his many miracles). See Ovid, *Metamorphoses*, 8:679–680.

wonders worked by the prophet Elisha, who returned two people from the dead, walked atop the Jordan River, and made an ax head float. It is worth noting that Nestor did not count Solomon among the miracle workers.[17]

The Bible does relate miracles that happened to the Israelites, as does the Talmud. It is said of R. Simeon ben Yoḥai that he was "experienced in miracles",[18] and of the *Tanna* R. Ḥanina ben Dosa that, thanks to his blessing, a poor woman's meager cubits of wood sufficed to cover her house,[19] and that when he died, "miracle workers came to an end".[20] Miracles, however, do not occur to individuals, and the Talmud cautions against dependence on miracles: "A man should never stand in a place of danger and say that a miracle will be wrought for him, lest it is not. And if a miracle is wrought for him, it is deducted from his merits".[21]

Sorcerers and Magicians[22]

While the arts of sorcery were carefully kept shrouded, exhibitions of sorcery were often performed in public.[23] The reason for this, Ibn Khaldūn writes, was that the laws of religion forbade all types of sorcery; the purpose of acts of sorcery was usually to cause harm or damage, for example, to turn humans into animals, or to raise the dead from their graves.

The Bible condemns acts of sorcery and biblical law declares an all-out war against them: "No one shall be found among you who

---

17. Limor (1998a). According to Luther, the Jews called Jesus a sorcerer and tool of the devil "because they cannot deny his miracles" (Luther 2015, p. 148).
18. *Me'ilah* 17b. R. Shimon lived during the second century C.E.
19. *Ta'anit* 25a.
20. *Mishnah Sotah* 9 [trans. Neusner].
21. *Shabbat* 32a. See also Guttman (1947). The fantastic tales attributed to Solomon are numerous. One example, out of many: Solomon had a great robe "of green silk, woven of gold thread with all manner of pictures, sixty miles in length and sixty in breadth, and Solomon would sit wearing it and move with the wind throughout the world, eating breakfast in Damascus and supper in Medea…") in *One Thousand and One Nights*, the robe turned into a carpet).
22. For general survey see Harari (2017). On Solomon, see Sasson (2003, pp. 129–160).
23. *Sanhedrin* 67b. Ibn Khaldūn wrote that sorcery unlike magic was the science of imbuing human souls with the ability to influence the material world, without any outside help: "The sorcerer possesses a particular quality in potentiality, as is the case with all human powers. It is transformed [from potentiality] to actuality by exercise. All magical exercise consists of directing oneself to the spheres, the stars, the higher world, of the demons by means of various kinds of veneration and worship and submissiveness and humiliation". However, "sorcery… is found (practiced) only by evil persons and as a rule is used for evil actions": *The Muqaddima* (6:27), Ibn Khaldūn (1958, Vol 3, pp. 159, 167).

makes a son or daughter pass through fire, or practices divination, or is a soothsayer, or augur, or sorcerer, or one who casts spells, or who consults ghosts or spirits, or who seeks oracles from the dead";[24] it commands that "You shall not permit a female sorcerer to live".[25] Daniel regarded the acts of magicians, astrologers, and sorcerers[26] as dependent on unacceptable Chaldean wisdom, and when Simeon ben Shetaḥ was elected president of the Sanhedrin in the first century C.E., he sent eighty men wrapped in prayer shawls to capture witches and instructed them: "When you enter, each of you shall choose one and lift her from the ground, since the nature of this sorcery is that separated from the earth it cannot do anything... They lifted them, took them away, and crucified them".[27]

The severe prohibitions against sorcery indicate that belief in the power of magic was widespread among the Jews from ancient times. Hence, they fought against it, not always with success.[28] "R. Johanan said: Why are [sorcerers] called *Kashshafim*? Because they diminish the power of the Divine agencies";[29] "While R. Abbaye bar Nagri cited R. Ḥiyya bar Abba to distinguish magic performed through the agency of demons from sorcery, which was accomplished without external aid".[30] Yet, at the same time, Jews exhibited an ambivalent attitude towards acts of magic. The Talmud also contains many tales of magic:[31] some are humorous, and some tell of the power of those skilled in magic and of conflicts between them and witches.[32] The latter sort, for example, includes three stories about the power of R. Joshua ben Hananiah as a sorcerer. One presents a foreign magician as a trickster; in another, R. Joshua orders the ruler of the sea to swallow one *min* (heretic); in the third, he mocks R. Yannai, who became involved in acts of magic and was hurt.[33] *Sanhedrin* 17a contains a remarkable statement: "R. Johanan said: None are to be appointed members of the Sanhedrin, but men of stature, wisdom, good appearance, mature age, with knowledge of sorcery". The words may have been said in jest, or perhaps they gave rise to the tale (the source of which is other-

---

24. Deuteronomy 18:10–11.
25. Exodus 22:18.
26. Daniel 2:52.
27. *y.Hagigah* 2:2, 77d, trans. Guggenheimer (2015, p. 439).
28. Eshel (1999). The apocryphal *Testament of Judah*, probably from the early second century, tells of men who rebel against the (Hasmonean) monarchy using magic. See Charles (1908, pp. 92–93).
29. *Sanhedrin* 67b [trans. Neusner].
30. See Schäfer (1997).
31. See Urbach (2006).
32. Including *Baba Metzia* 59b, *Sanhedrin* 67b-68, and *y.Sanhedrin* 7:19, 25d.
33. See JLevinson (2006).

wise unknown) about the Sanhedrin that wanted to replace a sage who had died with another. But since the new sage lacked any knowledge of sorcery, the Sanhedrin decided to send him to Egypt which was "known for its witches and magicians". The owner of the inn where the sage stayed on his way to Egypt offered to teach him sorcery, and when the sage was doubtful, the innkeeper demonstrated his ability: a barrel of water turned into a river and the sage found himself in a boat sailing with men from Persia and Medea (countries also famous for their magicians) and arrived in their country where he was appointed a minister and judge. I will not relate all his adventures; suffice it to say that after spending three months with the innkeeper he returned to Jerusalem "more proficient in sorcery than his elderly brethren".[34]

One of many works that attest to the Jews' knowledge and practice of sorcery in the Middle Ages is *The Chronicle of Ahimaaz* (inspired by Apuleius's The Golden Ass), in which local witches, against whom none can protect themselves and who are respected even by the dead, rob graves to use the bones to cause harm to their neighbors.[35] It relates how Abu Aaron of Baghdad saved a boy who had been turned into an ass by a witch.[36]

Yet none of the tales of witches, sorcery, and magical acts that are found in Talmudic literature, where sages encounter witches in their daily lives and contend with them,[37] depict Solomon displaying his power at magic, as Moses and Aaron did in the palace of Pharaoh (though Josephus makes it clear that Moses did not practice magic, but rather worked miracles "by the providence and power of God".[38] Only the Quran states explicitly that Solomon did not engage in sorcery: "Solomon disbelieved not; but the demons disbelieved, teaching mankind magic"[39]). In the Middle Ages, the magical powers attributed to Solomon were used in the polemic against Aristotelianism and its denial of the "supernatural" and the "spiritual". For example, the Kabbalist and rabbi Naḥmanides (1194–1240) of Catalonia believed that sorcery was ancient wisdom that could not be denied, and hence

---

34. The tale, called "The Knowledge of Sorcery", is found in Berdyczewski (1913, pp. 166–165).

35. Apuleius, *The Golden Ass*, trans. Robert Graves (1951, pp. 62–63).

36. Salzman (1966, p. 64).

37. On this subject see Sperber (1994).

38. Josephus, *Antiquities* (1963, Vol. 2, p. 286). According to Philo in De Vita Mosis (in his comments on the section on Bilaam), "the craft of the sorcerer and the inspiration of the Holiest might not live together", *De Vita Mosis* I:278. Colson (1994, Vol. 6, p. 419).

39. In *The Tales of the Prophets*, it is the demons who document the secrets of magic and hide them under Solomon's throne; after his death they remove them and claim that Solomon had written and used them. See Q. 2 ("The Cow").

King Solomon's wisdom included sorcery.[40]

Sorcery and sorcerers have been present in the Christian world since the inception of Christianity,[41] and the name of Jesus was invoked as a means of combating them and their influence. Thus, for example, Father Euthymius of a *laura* in the Judean desert rescued his relative Romanus from the claws of a sorcerer who, acting in the service of a man who craved Romanus's property, infected him with a disease. When Euthymius opened Romanus's stomach, he removed from it a tin plate bearing magic letters; thereafter, he rubbed the sick man's stomach, erasing the incision in it, and Romanus was restored to good health. The tale is told by Cyril of Scythopolis, of the second half of the sixth century; he claimed that Eutumus worked the miracle through the power of God who is benevolent towards saints", and simultaneously maintained that the miracle was wrought with the help of magic, without noticing a contradiction between these claims.[42] Augustine, we will recall, regarded magic as deception and Tertullian considered it fraudulent trickery (*miracula circulatoris*).[43]

It was only in the tenth century that the Church began to persecute those accused of engaging in magic, particularly witches—launching an infamous chapter in western culture, which also produced writings that provided instructions on how to identify anyone dabbling in magic. The best-known of these are the tenth-century *Canon Episcopi* and the *Malleus Maleficarum* (Hammer of the Witches), published by the Catholic clergyman Heinrich Kramer in 1486.[44]

The pagan polemic against Christianity, meanwhile, accused both Christians and Jews of engaging in sorcery. Emperor Julian described Paul as "surpassing all the charlatans and all the magicians of every place and every time",[45] while according to Celsus, Jesus and his disciples were capable of working the miracles attributed to them only through sorcery, and that they learned magic from the Egyptians. Origen rejected that claim; he trusted in Jesus' superior power: Christians trusted Jesus' superior power as Savior, God, teacher, Son of

---

40. Schwartz (2004b, p. 135).

41. The sacrifices offered by the Gentiles are made to demons and not to God: "Ye cannot drink the cup of the Lord, and the cup of devils: ye cannot be partakers of the Lord's table, and of the table of devils" (1 Corinthians 10:19–22).

42. Cyril of Scytopolis (1991, pp. 76–77). In her translation to Hebrew (Yad Ben Zvi, Jerusalem, 2005) Leah di Segni adds that such plates were discovered in the entire Mediterranean basin, including in Palestine (pp. 135–136, n. 297).

43. *Apologeticus* xxiii, I, p. 122.

44. L. Martin (2010, pp. 114–145), and see the brief bibliography, pp. 146–148. The early sixteenth-century compendium *The Pseudomonarchia Daemmonum* (False Hierarchy of Demons) names sixty-nine demons.

45. *Against the Galileans*, p. 341.

God".⁴⁶ Of Solomon as a sorcerer, in any event, no mention is made in the pagan polemic.

In Jewish anti-Christian tradition, Jesus also appears as a sorcerer.⁴⁷ The "biography" of R. Joshua ben Peraḥyah recounts how Simeon ben Shetaḥ, a leader of the Pharisees in the first century CE, called upon R. Joshua, who had been forced to escape to Egypt, to come back to Israel. On his return, he was accompanied by Jesus, who according to the tradition was his student. A story in *Sotah* 47a also describes Jesus as R. Joshua's pupil and relates that the latter dismissed him: "A Master has said: The disciple practised magic and led Israel astray". All of Jesus' attempts to appease his teacher failed.⁴⁸ Perhaps the similarity between the two names Joshua and Yeshua inspired the creative imagination to link the two, who were not contemporaries; and perhaps this affinity was created because R. Joshua ben Peraḥyah is invoked as a person possessing magical powers on incantation bowls in Aramaic, Syriac, and Mandaic.⁴⁹ It seems, however, that the accusation that Jesus engaged in sorcery played only a minor role in the Jewish anti-Christian polemic, and was expressed mainly in the book *Toledot Yeshu*, which in its various versions contains several depictions of Jesus' study of magic during his stay in Egypt, whence he returned to Palestine with knowledge with which he tried to save himself at his crucifixion. He spoke words of sorcery, flew into the air, hid in a cave, turned himself into a rooster; ultimately, he was apprehended and taken to R. ben Peraḥyah. When Judah the gardener was questioned by Pilate, in the presence of ben Peraḥyah, as to whether he knew Jesus, he replied that Jesus dealt in magic and trickery by employing the books of the Egyptian magicians. There was, after all, no better place to learn magic than Egypt. About that country, it was said: "Ten measures of witchcraft were given to the world, nine taken by Egypt and one [by] the rest of the world…"⁵⁰ According to another version, John the Baptist was questioned by a group of sages led by Joshua ben Peraḥyah, who asked where he had obtained the magic writings in his possession, and John replied they had been written by

---

46. (6:30), Origen (1965, p. 346). On Origen and Celsus, see Thorndike (1964, pp. 436–461).

47. Schäfer (2007, pp. 102–105).

48. Tropper (2011, pp. 89–110).

49. Geller (1974); Ilan (2013).

50. *Qiddushin* 49b. That image is repeated, for example, by the third-century Church Father Clement of Alexandria, who wrote "it is said that mystery originated in Egypt" (*Stromata* 1960, p. 153), and by the tenth-century Muslim historian al-Nadīm, who stated that in Egypt many men and women were sorcerers and exorcists, who claimed they possessed seals, talismans, and the like. Rabbenu Gershom on *Menahot* 85a: "So to a land full of sorcery you bring sorcery".

Jesus and his disciples.[51] And in yet another account, Jesus wrought his miracles through the power of holy letters he had stolen from the Temple: "and wrote the [holy] name on paper, mentioned the Name so it would not harm him, and cut his flesh, hid in it the paper with the Name, again mentioned the Name, and put the flesh back in place. And using magic and the name of defilement, he entered the Temple…".[52]

Satan and Demons[53]

The power of Satan and the demons is said, in Jewish and Christian (and Muslim) traditions, to encompass more than the mere possession of mortals, and the imaginary biographies of Solomon and Jesus also correspond in this context, which stems from the extensive presence of Satan and the demons in those traditions. Satan and the demons differ from magicians and sorcerers in that the latter are humans; hence, demons and Satan (or in his other names: Asmodeus, Samael, and Lucifer) must be dealt with differently. Their existence explains why the forces of evil and sin exist in the human world and underscore the challenge they pose to the faithful. Their presence, and the struggle against their attempt to gain control of the human soul, intensifies the need to believe in God, or in Jesus.[54] Satan and the demons are material creatures active in human society, even conducting a dialogue with it.[55] It is no wonder then that they play an important role in theological discussions, in books of ethics, in legends, and in folklore.[56] One cannot say about demons "Thou shalt not suffer a devil to live" (as was written of witches) because demons are not humans. Like evil spirits (*mezikin*) and demons, demons are perceived as dating back to the Creation[57] and depicted as active in the environment and society of humans. They have been described as "the angels of service"; they

---

51. Yaacov Deutsch (1997, p. 8).
52. Limor (1998b).
53. See Giversen (1972); Särkiö (2004), Bohak (2017). According to Origen, Satan is "an adversary to the Son of God who is righteousness, truth, and wisdom: (6:44), Origen (1965, p. 361).
54. See J. B. Russell (1984, 1991).
55. Of the literature on Satan I will only cite here: H. A. Kelly (2006); Boureau (2013).
56. A God-hating demon entered into the Jew Aquila who went around the synagogues preaching that "the one whom we Christians now worship is not the Messiah, but he was a man even as we are. He was condemned to be crucified as a blasphemer because he said that he was God" (1.2–1.5, in Varner (2004, p. 141).
57. According to *Mishnah* Avot 5:6, the destructive spirits were created on the eve of the (first) Sabbath at twilight, populated the imaginary reality of the ancient world, and took human form. The insides of clay incantation bowls found in Iraq and Palestine and dating from the fourth to seventh centuries were decorated with incantations and drawings of Asmodeus, Lilith, and other demons. See Vilozny (2017).

"have wings, fly from one end of the world to the other, know the future, and like human beings they eat and drink, procreate like human beings, and die like human beings".[58] It has been said that there are three times as many demons in the world as humans; they live in deserts, forests, ruins, and the like, and "can change into many colours" and they employ various tricks in attempts to incite humans to engage in evil acts, but also have been recruited to assist them. Demons are mentioned in the Bible, and the Israelites are denounced for sacrificing to demons (false gods).[59] Belief in their existence and activity spread throughout the Jewish culture apparently under Persian influence,[60] and their attributes and actions are frequently mentioned in the literature of the Sages.[61] In medieval Jewish philosophy, demons were regarded as real creatures, but also as a personification of internal forces acting within a person.[62]

The struggle between the rule of God and the rule of Satan[63] takes on various forms and in it, Satan appears in various guises. The Akkadian sage Saturnus asks Solomon: "How many shapes will the devil and the *Pater Noster* take when they contend together?" Solomon replies: "Thirty shapes" and describes them (the last is the "likeness of death"), and the *Pater Noster* does not win out over him.[64] In the Bible, it is Satan who suggests to God that he ought to test Job;[65] in the New Testament, he appears to Jesus in the desert and challenges him to work a miracle ("If thou be the Son of God, command that these stones be made bread", to throw himself from a high place, and to bow down to him, in return for which he will gain all the kingdoms of the word. Jesus rejects Satan and leaves him, whereupon "suddenly angels came and waited on him".[66]). It is told that the Pharisees claimed Jesus was exorcising demons with the aid of Beelzebub, and Jesus replied to them: "And if I by Beelzebub cast out devils, by whom do your children cast them out? Therfore they shall be your judges. But if I cast out devils by the Spirit of God, then the kingdom of God is come unto you". Luke relates that when the seventy-two messengers sent by Jesus to "every town and place where he himself intended to go" returned, they reported: "Lord, in your name even the

---

58. *Hagigah* 16a.
59. Deuteronomy 32:15–18, and more.
60. For a detailed description see Eshel (1999).
61. Day (1988).
62. Schwartz (2004a, pp. 189–199).
63. Theissen (1983 [1974], pp. 90–91). On demons in medieval Hebrew literature, see Rotman (2016). On Solomon and the demons in art, see Shalev-Eyni (2006).
64. *The Dialogue of Salomon and Saturnus*, (Kemble, 1848, pp. 145–149).
65. Job 1:6–12.
66. Matthew 4:1–11; Mark 1:12–13; Luke 4:1–13.

demons submitted to us". And Jesus said: "I watched Satan fall from heaven like a flash of lightning".[67] Satan is mentioned in Revelation: "When the thousand years are ended, Satan will be released from his prison...and will come out to deceive the nations at the four corners of the earth".[68]

Satan figured frequently in the Christian world of the imagination.[69] St. Anthony, for example, struggled against Satan's various efforts to forcefully divest him of his belief in Christ's suffering,[70] and Cyril describes the hermit Father Cyricus, who in a vision saw Satan gaining control over two monks and saved them, since Satan and the "tricks of the devils" are merely a personification of sorrow. And there is also the crowd of demons who hid on a hill near the Castellion monastery and were driven out by the monk St. Sabbas, who anointed the place with "the oil of the most revered cross".[71]

It is difficult to reconstruct the development of, and the various forms taken by, the demonological tradition. In any event, at a certain stage, stories about Solomon and the demons were in broad circulation. For example, in *Citharismus Regis David contra daemonum Saulis*, King David warns the demons that a son was born to him who will rule over them.[72] This tradition appears at great length in the syncretic and enigmatic *Testament of Solomon*, which was perhaps written in Roman Egypt in the first or second centuries C.E., and expanded and edited over several centuries thereafter. The book is an "encyclopedia of demonology", containing numerous tales and at least three thematic elements: belief in the existence of the world of spirits and demons as part of human existence, the exploits of King Solomon in the wondrous supernatural world, and the construction of the Temple in Jerusalem. Solomon's control over demons is also mentioned in the Gnostic literature found at Nag Hammadi, in the *Epistle to Rehobam*, and *The Apocalypse of Adam*, which enumerates thirteen false explanations for the birth of the redeemer, *Photor*. According to the fourth explanation: "Solomon himself sent his army of demons to seek out the virgin. And they did not find the one whom they sought, but the virgin who was given to them. It was she whom they fetched. Solomon took her, the Virgin became pregnant and gave birth to the child there".[73] In *The Testament of Solomon*, Jesus displays greater power over the demons

---

67. Luke 10:1.
68. Revelation 20:7–8.
69. J. B. Russell (1981).
70. Gibson (1995).
71. Cyril of Scythopolis (1991, pp. 25–27. 119–121).
72. Charlesworth (1983, Vol. 1, p. 546).
73. Trans. G. W. MacRae and D. M. Parrott in J. M. Robinson (1988, p. 282).

than does Solomon. When the devil is asked who drove him away, he replies: "He who was born of a virgin and was crucified by the Jews". The king also states in his "testament" that he commanded each of the thirty-six demons and interrogated them. "Tell me, O demon, to what zodiacal sign thou art subject?" Later, he commanded thirty-six other celestial bodies and questioned them, revealing his knowledge of astrology. They said: "We are the thirty-six elements, the world-rulers of this darkness. But, O King Solomon, thou wilt not wrong us nor imprison us, nor lay command on us; but since the Lord God has given thee authority over every spirit, in the air, and on the earth, and under the earth, therefore do we also present ourselves before thee like the other spirits".[74] Later, Solomon imprisons the demons with the aid of a ring and recruits them for various tasks, including building the foundations of the Temple. Solomon supposedly composed the *Testament* before his death so that the Israelites "might know the powers of the demons and their shapes, and the names of their angels, by which these angels are frustrated,[75] and that Jesus was Solomon's successor and would rule over the demons.[76] In the *Dialogue Between Timothy and Aquila*, Jesus is depicted as greater than Solomon: Solomon submits to the demons while Jesus subdues them and will rule them forever.[77]

In the Talmud, Solomon rules over Satan and the demons, but is also ruled over by them; he is at once stronger and weaker than they are. Perhaps this is meant to express the view that even a ruler like Solomon, who reigned over both the lower and the upper realms, has human weaknesses that overpower him, weaknesses that Jesus does not possess. Thus, the Talmud (as well as the Quran)[78] relates that Satan ousts Solomon from his throne and replaces him and that Satan is sent to punish Solomon, to humiliate him and succeed him.[79]

An encounter between Satan and Solomon appears in a medieval Christian folk tale about a trial at which Satan is the prosecutor; Mary

74. *The Testament of Solomon*, 18:1–3.
75. *The Testament of Solomon*, 18:14–15.
76. This text was widely circulated in the first centuries C.E.; whether it was the source for the tales about Solomon and the demons in the literature of the Sages (and later in the Quran), Conybear (1898); Duling (1983, p. 987); McCown (1922b); Schwarz (2007); and Klutz (2005).
77. *Ancient Jewish-Christian Dialogues*: *Timothy and Aquila*, Varner (2004, pp. 14–15.)
78. In the *Tales of the Prophets*, Satan hears a divine voice telling him of the birth of Solomon, David's son, "at whose hands will be your destruction and your seeds", al-Kisā'ī (1997, p. 289).
79. On the scores of versions of this story that appeared in the thirteenth and fourteenth centuries, see Kushelevsky (2011, pp. 272–288). For further detail, see Sasson (2003, pp. 129–160).

or Moses are witnesses for the defense, and Solomon is the judge. Though Satan quotes from the Holy Scriptures, he is sentenced to Hell.

Demons are not always depicted as negative characters. In the medieval *Musare Haphilosophim* (The Teachings of the Philosophers), Solomon learns of an island where wise demons live. The king, who wishes to hear what they have to say, commands the wind to carry him there. On his arrival a hundred and twenty demons gather around him, each speaking a profound thought. And "when they were through, Solomon son of David wrote down their words of wisdom and returned to his home".[80]

Asmodeus and the Demons Build the Temple

Demons brought water from India to the King's gardens and orchards: "Solomon made use of the spirits and sent them to India from where they brought him water with which to water [the pepper-plant] here [in the land of Israel] and it produced fruit",[81] and others were part of Solomon's army, who helped assist in constructing the Temple that Solomon built for the Almighty—a temple whose construction was perceived as the completion of the six days of the Creation. Solomon was said to have been aided by demons, while one of the sins of the Israelites was that they sacrificed to them ("They sacrificed to devils, not God"[82]). In addition to the 30,000 demons who worked in three shifts of ten thousand a month cutting down trees in Lebanon, others worked on the construction of the Temple ("besides Solomon three thousand and three hundred, a supervisor who were over the work").[83] Josephus adds, based on the account in Chronicles according to which the reference is to all those who remained in the land who were not Israelites, "Then Solomon took a census of all aliens who were residing in the land of Israel (2 Chronicles 2:16) that the workers who quarried the huge stones and carried them and the 'other materials' to the city were "strangers who were left by David".[84]

Legends of how the Temple built itself, quarried stones lowering themselves into position, or of how birds, spirits, and thousands of angels participated in the construction, were intended to imbue the undertaking with a wondrous aspect, rather than to simply say that the Temple was really built on the labor of a great many workers, often at the cost of their lives. One account claims that over the course of the seven years of construction, not a single builder died; after the

---

80. *Musare Haphilosophim*, Part 2, Chapter 21. And see Chapter Eight.
81. *Midrash Rabbah*: Ecclesiastes, II.2, § 4–5, § I, 55. Cohen (1939).
82. Deuteronomy 32:16.
83. 1 Kings 5:16.
84. *Antiquities* 8:59. Josephus (1963).

work was completed, however, all the rest died so they would not be tempted to build palaces for the practice of idolatry, and they received their wages from the Almighty in the next world.[85] This story about the workers perishing may have come into being to explain how the Temple was built without making use of iron: "The house was built with stones finished at the quarry, so that neither hammer nor ax nor any tool of iron was heard in the temple while it was being built".[86] It seems more likely the intent was to claim that the Temple was not built by forced laborers, but rather by demons. *Midrash Rabbah on Song of Songs* describes how spirits and angels helped Solomon construct the Temple: "all assist the king [...]; even spirits, even demons, even ministering angels". R. Berekiah said: "the stones carried themselves and placed themselves on the row".[87]

According to the fourth-century Gnostic work *The Gospel of Truth*,[88] Solomon built Jerusalem with the help of demons; after they completed their work, he held them captive in seven jugs, from which they escaped after the Romans conquered the city. *The Testament of Solomon* expanded its account of the construction by integrating various elements from the Bible and from Egyptian and Hellenist astrology with magic formulae. According to that work, Solomon received from Lord Sabaoth, via the archangel Michael, a signet ring made of a precious stone, on which a pentagram was engraved. With the aid of that ring, Solomon defeats the demon Ornias, who offers, in exchange for his release, to bring to the king all manner of demons, male and female. The king recruits the demons for various jobs—digging the foundations for the Temple, quarrying the stones, carrying them, creating gold and silver, and more. Some of the demons are sealed in jugs. One, Ephippas, the wind demon, is caught in the Arabian Peninsula to set up a huge cornerstone, too heavy for the other demons to lift; he carries out the task with the help of the demon of the Red Sea.[89] These versions of this text were circulated in the first centuries C.E. is evident from its citation in *The Dialogue between Timothy and Aquila*. A popular Jerusalem tradition from the early Byzantine period further shows how prevalent the motif of Solomon's rule over the demons and their participation in the construction of the Temple was at the time. An anonymous pilgrim from Bordeaux, for example, recounts his journey in *Itinerarium burdigalense*: he arrived in Jerusalem in the year 333, where, in the area of the Temple ruins, he saw

---

85. Josephus (1963).
86. 1 Kings 6:7.
87. *Song of Songs Rabbah* 1:1,5. Neusner (1989).
88. Trans. H.W. Attridge and G. W. MacRae, in J. M. Robinson (1988).
89. Duling (1988, pp. 81–91).

the vault "where Solomon used to torture 590 demons".[90] We have no way of knowing whether he knew the stories of Solomon's rule over the demons before he arrived in Jerusalem, or first heard them in that city. In any event, the brevity of the description may suggest that the author assumed his readers would be familiar with the tradition that Solomon sealed demons in a cave and tormented them. Another description of a journey in the early sixth century contains the information that "a dozen silver jugs in which Solomon sealed the demons" were found in the Church of the Holy Sepulcher (related in *Gospel of Truth*, and that the ring "with which Solomon sealed the demons" was found at Golgotha.[91]

It is difficult to trace the path by which the legend of Solomon's rule over the demons found its way into the *midrashim* and *aggadot*. At any rate, since demons and spirits were part not only of the popular culture but of the Sages' general understanding of the world, accepting the help of demons was not regarded as a wrongful act if done for the sake of Heaven: "Huna in the name of Rabbi Yosef said: Everyone helps the king, so even more so everyone helps for the honor of the King of Kings, the Holy One blessed be He. Even the spirits and even the demons and even the angels".[92] Solomon himself, in a letter he was said to have sent to the Queen of Sheba via a hoopoe bird, boasts about the fact that the Almighty appointed him to reign over the demons and spirits.[93] In the long Talmudic tale about Solomon and Asmodeus,[94] Solomon learns from a male and female demon that only Asmodeus knows the secret of the *shamir*,[95] namely how it may be used to split building stones without the aid of iron tools. He sends Benaiahu, son of Jehoiada, to obtain it by trickery and bring it to him. Thus, Asmodeus was (after a variety of digressions and sub-plots) cunningly trapped and brought before Solomon, upon which he disclosed the whereabouts of the *shamir*—a hoopoe bird that possessed the power to split and chisel stones, without which it would have been impossible to build the Temple".[96] The Talmudic legend regarding the iron-less construc-

90. Wilkinson (1999, p. 29).
91. Wilkinson (1999, p. 199).
92. *Song of Songs Rabbah* 1:1,5. Neusner (1989).
93. *Targum Sheni Esther*, 1:2.
94. *Gittin* 68a-b.
95. The reference is probably to a diamond. *Mishnah Avot* 5:6 has it that the *shamir* was created on the eve of the Sabbath.
96. In *Tales of the Prophets*, the story is extended by elements from Gnostic literature, the *Testament of Solomon*, and Talmudic literature. According to al-Kisā'ī, the angel Gabriel convened for Solomon four hundred and twenty groups of all types of demons and devils, males and females, that he instructed to engage in various work "in iron, copper, wood, and stones, as well as in building villages, cities and fortresses". Finally, he set them to work building the Temple. In this version, the residents of

tion of the Temple found its way, probably from Byzantium, into the Paleia, a collection of tales based on the holy scriptures and apocrypha from the fourteenth century. In this version of the tale, Asmodeus transformed into a *kitovar* (a centaur). Solomon sent someone to trap the kitovar and get him drunk. He was then brought before Solomon to inform the king how to build the Temple from stones not chiseled with iron tools. He claimed there was a *kokot* (a rooster) who, with the divine help of the *shamir*, knew how to split rocks and plant trees on desolate mountain tops, and was hence known as the "artist of the mountains"; this rooster knew where to find the *shamir*. The King's messengers arrived at the rooster's nest and smeared it with white glass; when the rooster wanted to return to his chicks he found the nest sealed, and flew off to bring the *shamir* in order to cut the glass. The King's men yelled to frighten it, and when the wondrous worm fell from its mouth, they took it and brought it to Solomon.[97]

It is tempting to read many of these legends about Solomon as an expression of his greatness, as seen in his control over demons and Satan; they may also be interpreted as an explanation for the destruction of the Temple. Yet, in their own discussion of the destruction, the Sages do not mention the use of demons to build it,[98] nor is their assistance why the Sages reject the idea that God requires a physical home in one specific place (a view that inspired Christianity's attitude towards the Temple, as well as the idea of the *Ecclesia* as a temple). Nor is the aid of Asmodeus and the demons described in the Gospels or Christian literature as a flaw that marred Solomon's Temple from its inception.

Why it was Solomon specifically who became the protagonist of

the city complained about the noise made by the cutting of rocks, so Solomon sent for Sakar, a demon who had rebelled, who told him of an eagle who knew where to find a mountain of diamonds. From there the demons brought the necessary quantity of diamonds with which the rocks could be cut without making any sound. In this version, the construction took forty days, since each day Solomon employed "a thousand demons, a thousand devils and a thousand human builders". al-Kisā'ī (1997, pp. 516–517). On the Islamic traditions on this subject see Soucek (1976, pp. 73–123).

97. Raba (2014, pp. 152–155). The late Dr. Joel Raba generously provided me with the texts. The monstrous bird appears in part of the Old English poem "Solomon and Saturn II". A Babylonian sage, Saturn, asks Solomon to tell him about a mourning spirit (*gemorende gast*) which had aroused his curiosity for fifty years. Solomon responds with an obscure reference to a monstrous bird called *vasa mortis* held in chains in the heart of Philistine until the sound of Judgment Day is heard. Several suggestions have been offered in the research literature regarding the source of this text's inspiration and its meaning (see Chapter Eight).

98. It would be only a conjecture to infer that these tales were inspired by Augustine and his successors, who described the *Synagoga* as "the bastion of Satan" and the "domicile of demons and idolatry". See "The Synagogue as Foe in Early Christian Literature", in Rutgers, *Making Myth* (2009, pp. 79–115).

numerous *midrashim* and tales of occult adventure is a mystery. Be the reason as it may, such tales belonged primarily to Judaism's inward-facing literature, rather than to its correspondence with Christianity. However, between the figure of Solomon as the author of the Song of Songs, Proverbs, and Ecclesiastes, and the figure of Solomon who consorted with demons and Satan, there lies an abyss; no less an abyss divides Solomon from Jesus. The latter rejects Satan's temptations, and the mere mention of his name suffices to overcome the devil.

Chapter Seven: Solomon's Wisdom—From Hermes to Aristotle

"*Wisdom has built her house,*
She has hewn her seven pillars"
    - Proverbs 9:1
"*Von Osten bis zum Westen,*
wer ist so weise wie Salomo?
wer wie Israels Köning ist gesegnet'
wer so würdig eines Könings Thron?
[*From the east unto the west,*
Who so wise as Solomon?
Who like Israel's king is bless'd
Who so worthy of a throne?]"
    - Händel, "Solomon"

Various definitions of "wisdom" appear in the Bible, and the concept continued to accrue new meanings and understandings in post-biblical literature.[1] The idea of Solomonic wisdom and knowledge (*chokhmah* and *madda*) thus also attracted new interpretations under the influence of Hellenistic culture. *The Wisdom of*

---

1. From the rich literature on various types of wisdom in the ancient Near East. See John G. Gammie and Leo G. Perdue (1990); Noth and Thomas (1955); Crenshaw (1976); Hurowitz Yona (2011); Scott (1969); Kalugila (1980); Wälchli (1999). The terms *sophia* (Greek) and *sapientia* (Latin), or wisdom, intelligence and knowledge, are laden with many connotations in the Bible and in post-biblical Jewish literature. Wisdom is attributed to God ("The Lord by wisdom founded the earth; by understanding he established the heavens", *Proverbs* 3:19). It is personified ("Does not wisdom call, and does not her voice?", Proverbs 8:1); it is both the gift of God and an individual quality. Latin literature makes use of the terms *sapientia* and *prudentia*; the latter is a translation of the Greek *phronesis*, or "practical knowledge", in contrast to the former (sophia), a form of wisdom which is an end in itself (Aristotle, *Nicomachean Ethics*, Book Six). Clement of Alexandria writes that "Scripture calls every secular science or art the one name wisdom there are other arts and sciences invented over and above by human reason"); see Vol. 3 of Clement, *The Stromata*, in Roberts and Donaldson (1995, p. 304).

Solomon (*WS*), a work apparently written in Palestine and Egypt in the second or first century B.C.E., holds that wisdom is "the breath of the power of God, and a pure influence flowing from the glory of the Almighty: therefore can no defiled thing fall into her. For she is the brightness of the everlasting light, the unspotted mirror of the power of God, and the image of his goodness".[2]

Wisdom is also the wisdom of jurisprudence and just rule;[3] the wisdom that Solomon demonstrates in solving the riddles posed by the Queen of Sheba[4] and Hiram king of Tyre;[5] and that contained in the three sapiential biblical books attributed to him, as well as the *Book of Solomon*.[6] In the Septuagint's (henceforth *LXX*) translation of 2 Chronicles 1:11–12, the words *sunesis* and *sophia* are used as a pair to render the Hebrew *chokhmah* and *madda*; in its translation of 1 Kings 3:12, LXX speaks of "a heart of understanding and wisdom" (*kardian phronimên kai sophiên*)".[7] In apocryphal and pseudo-epigraphical literature, wisdom (*sophia*) takes many forms: a divine summons to man; a means of revelation; world-reason (*logos*); an omnipresent cosmic element; a way of life; a body of knowledge; and more. According to *WS*, "wisdom" teaches Man to understand the secrets and traits of

---

2. *The Wisdom of Solomon* 7:25–26.

3. Thomas Aquinas informs Dante that Solomon was a king who sought wisdom the better to merit his position (*Paradiso*, XIII, 94–95: "[…] clearly he was king who asked for wisdom \ That he might be sufficient a king", Dante Alighieri 1981, p. 46). Solomon's illustrious wisdom, in other words, was the wisdom of proper governance and jurisprudence.

4. *Midrash Proverbs 1*, which was apparently edited in Palestine between the seventh and eleventh centuries, contained more riddles. See Visotzky (1990, 1992); Lassner (2007); Stein (1993). According to al-Kisā'ī's version: "God said to David, 'wisdom is in ninety parts, seventy which are in Solomon and the other twenty in all the rest of the people", al-Kisā'ī, *Tales of the Prophets*. Another story has it that when Solomon turned seventeen, the angel Gabriel descended from Heaven and brought his father a golden page, saying: Oh, David, Allah sends you his greetings and commands you to collect all of your sons in order to read to them the questions written on the page. The one who can answer them will be your heir." David fulfilled the instructions and read the seventeen questions to his sons. Only Solomon knew how to answer them, and David received the approval of the sages to pronounce him his heir. al-Kisā'ī (1997, pp. 294–296).

5. *Antiquities* 8.5.4, Josephus (1963, pp. 143–149); *Against Apion* 1.1.17, pp. 111–115.

6. The Solomon of legends, folklore, and literature is generous with his wisdom and shares it with hoi polloi [the people]; in Boccaccio's *Decameron*, for example, he provides two young pilgrims to Jerusalem with advice on amorous matters "of great privacy and complexity". *Decameron* IX:9, Boccaccio (1975, pp. 721–736).

7. The discussion in Torijano (2002, pp. 29–30), suggests the two words refer to both "practical wisdom" including political judgment and physical science, and "knowledge of divine things", that is, of unchanging entities in philosophical terms. Torijano (2002, p. 29).

the world.⁸ Wisdom is "omnipotent, omniscient, and puts all the attributes into action";⁹ it is bestowed by God, or by the angels. As a body of knowledge handed down to an Elected One, wisdom appears, for example, in the *First Book of Enoch*: "After that he gave me instructions in all the secret things [found] in the book of my grandfather, Enoch, and in the parables which were given to him, and he put them together for me in the words of the book which is with me".[10] Aristobulus, a priest from Jerusalem from the second century B.C.E., who later settled in Egypt, wrote in his *Commentary on the Law of Moses* that "Solomon said clearly and better that wisdom existed before heaven and earth".[11] Ben Sira, in contrast, depicts Solomon as a poet and wise man in the sense of a teacher and educator who formulates rules of behavior in all areas of faith, morals, and justice: "Thy soul covered the whole earth, and thou fillist it with dark parables. Thy name went far unto the islands; and for thy peace thou was beloved. The countries marveled at thee for thy songs, and proverbs, and parables, and interpretations".[12]

WS and Josephus' *Antiquities* expanded on the biblical references to Solomon's great wisdom, making use of the new understandings of wisdom itself. They attributed to Solomon supreme proficiency in the "wisdom of nature" (tôn ontôn / *rerum natura*) alongside with the command of magic (healing and exorcism). In *WS* the king himself—the reputed possessor of all wisdom—describes his extensive knowledge, imparted to him by God:

> "For it is he (God) who gave me unerring knowledge (*gnôsis*) of what exists (*tôn ontôn*), To know the structure of the world (*sustasis kosmou*) and the activity of the elements (*energeia stoicheiôn*),
>
> The beginning and end and middle of times,
> The alternations of the solstices (*tropôn allagai*) and the change of the seasons,
> The cycles of the year and the constellation of the stars,
> The nature of animals and the temper of wild animals (pneumatôn bias),
> The powers of spirits (*pneumatôn*)[13] and the thoughts of human beings,
> The varieties of plants and the virtues of roots delet
> I learned both what is secret and what is manifest,

---

8. *The Wisdom of Solomon* 7:17–19.
9. Föhrer (1976); Charles (1913, Vol. 1, p. 527); Collins (1997 [1966]).
10. 1 Enoch 68:1.
11. Eusebius, *Praeparatio Evangelica*, 13.12.11, in Eusebius (1985, p. 841).
12. *The Wisdom of Solomon*, 47:14–17.
13. The reference here may not be to "evil spirits" but rather, according to some scholars, to the Egyptian *akhu*, or powers of the soul.

For wisdom the fashioner of all things taught me".[14]

In *WS*, Solomon's wisdom is said to encompass extensive knowledge of ontology, cosmology, physics, astronomy, biology, botany, zoology, and esoterica.[15] The philosophical vocabulary of *The Wisdom of Solomon* was influenced by GrecoHellenistic-Roman "scientific" and philosophical language—an influence manifested, for example, in the use of the terms *dynamis*, *energeia*, and *stoicheia*[16] (which also appear in Hermetic texts). The origins of *WS* itself are unknown, as is the nature of its intended audience. At any rate, although the book was widely disseminated in Greek, Latin, and other languages, it seems to have had scant influence in shaping the image of Solomon as a wise man—at least until the Renaissance.[17]

Antiquities of the Jews, written at the end of the first century C.E., also describes Solomon as well-versed in *rerum natura*:

> Now so great was the prudence and wisdom which God granted Solomon that he surpassed the ancients, and even the Egyptians, who are said to excel all men in understanding, were not only, when compared with him, a little inferior but fall far short of the king in sagacity [...] There was no form of nature with which he was not acquainted or which he passed over without examining, but he studied them all philosophically and revealed the most complete knowledge of their several properties.[18]

Josephus was apparently unacquainted with *WS*, and unlike it, does not describe in detail the nature of Solomon's research and discoveries. Despite that, and unlike *WS*, he explicitly compares Solomon's wisdom to that of the Egyptians and highlights Solomon's dominion over the supernal world.[19]

---

14. Trans. Grabbe (1997, p. 64). See also the translation by Winston (1979, p. 172), and Charles (1913, Vol. 1, p. 546). A description of "wisdom" also appears in 2 Enoch (the 'Slavonic Enoch'), which records the knowledge given to Solomon by God, as a result of which he is "all-knowing" (2 Enoch 13).

15. Pico della Mirandola, however, sensed an absence of detail regarding Solomon's occult knowledge and wrote that the version of *The Wisdom of Solomon* that had been preserved was different than the original, in which Solomon does explain "the nature of things".

16. Scholars found in *WS* the influence of Middle-Platonism, "in which many Stoic notions were incorporated", Alexander (1986, pp. 579–586).

17. The book was translated into Hebrew by Naphtali Herz Wesel (Wessely) in 1780.

18. *Ant.* VIII.42–44, Josephus (1963, pp. 693–695). In *Targum Sheni*, Solomon "explained parables, resolved mysteries, and made known secrets of infinite nature". Trans. Grossfeld (1994, p. 106).

19. Josephus attributes to Solomon not only the authorship of a thousand five hundred books of odes (*ōdai*) and songs (*melos*) and three thousand books of parables (*paroimiai*), but, as we saw in Chapter Five, also knowledge of the art used against

Josephus' purpose, it seems, was to depict Solomon as a royal sage. In the ancient Near East, quite a few kings were described as sages endowed with wisdom and knowledge, and the *topos* of Solomon as a "royal sage" could well have been inspired by traditions about who boasted of their profound wisdom (*hasisu palku*). Assurbanipal (668–631 B.C.E.), for example, bragged about his skills as a diviner and scholar various talents and declared himself a scholar learned in science and books and well-versed in both theoretical and practical wisdom.[20] It is far more likely, however, that the *topos* as it appears in Josephus' *Antiquities* was influenced more directly by the image of several kings of Pharaonic Egypt. For instance, King Tuthmose III (1479–1425) was praised for his wisdom:

> "Behold, His Majesty knew what has come into being. There was nothing at all which he did not know. He was Thoth in everything; there was not any subject of which he was not knowledgeable [...] after the manner of the Majesty Seshat. He could construe (or 'divide') a sign according to its value (or 'use') like the god who ordained it and created it".[21]

The Egyptian king is compared to the god Thoth (*mr-rh*)—"he-who-loves-knowledge", or "he-who-wishes to-learn", later known as Hermes Trismegistus ("Thrice-great one")—would be endowed, over the generations, with a panoply of qualities and functions. Egyptians and Egyptian-Hellenistic literature considered him, among other things, the author of numerous books on magic, theology, and philosophy (Manetho ascribed 525 books to Thoth, while according to Seleos the number was 20,000). He was regarded as the creator of cosmic order, the lord of knowledge, he who knew all that is hidden under the heavenly vault and beneath the earth,[22] the first measurer of time, and the inventor of hieroglyphic script. Esoteric wisdom, however, was his particular preserve.[23] *The Book of Thoth* is a title applied to numerous distinct texts; these were probably created by scribes associated with

---

demons (*Ant.* VIII.45–46). See Chapter Five.

20. "Marduk, the wisest (*apkalla*) of gods, gave me the wide understanding (*uznu*) and extensive intelligence (*hasisu*), and Nabu, the scribe [who knows] everything, granted me his wise teaching (ihzī nemeqi) [...] I learned the art of the Sage Adapa [so that now] I am familiar with the secret storehouse of all scribal learning (including) celestial and terrestrial potent". See Na'aman (2019, p. 79); Sweet (1990, p. 55).

21. In Jasnow and Zauzich (2005, p. 62), after Redford (1986, pp. 166–167). King Sesostris I (1917–1872 B.C.E.) is praised by Sinuhe as "the master of knowledge", and King Ramses II (1279–1213) is said to be "wise in knowledge like Thoth, knowing how to instruct, skilled in craftsmanship".

22. P. Graec. Mag. VIII.15–15, in Fowden (1993, p. 75).

23. Trans. Duling, in Charlesworth (1983, Vol. 1, 935–987); Fowden (1993, p. 23).

the "House of Life" (*pr-'nh*), the library of the temple. In various renditions of this 'book', Thoth emphasizes special branches of knowledge: "'What is its nature'? 'What is the shape of the papyrus plant'? [...]"[24] At the same time, *The Book of Thoth* revolved around the acquisition of knowledge, mainly the topography of heaven and the underworlds; it is prominent in underworld theology and "excellent in magic".[25]

Josephus was familiar with legends regarding the early origins of human wisdom. In *Antiquities* he wrote that the sons of Seth had "discovered the science of the heavenly bodies and the orderly array",[26] and that Abraham had "introduced [the Egyptians] to arithmetic and transmitted to them the laws of astronomy".[27] In other words, Abraham was the conduit of astronomical knowledge from Mesopotamia to Egypt.[28] Yet, while Jewish-Hellenistic apologetic literature attributed various "inventions" (*de inventis*) dating to the dawn of history to the patriarchs of Israel, Josephus himself made no such attributions to Solomon. Instead, he credited to him encyclopedic wisdom, in which "he surpassed the ancients, and even the Egyptians".[29] In other words, since Solomon's contribution to humankind could not be expressed in "inventions" from ancient times, Josephus attributed to him "wisdom" as it was understood in Hellenistic-Jewish literature and personified in the figures of the Egyptian god Thoth and Hermes Trismegistus.[30]

---

24. Jasnow and Zauzich (2005, p. 64).

25. It is important to note here that Thoth is not only omniscient but also an "inventor" (for example, of writing), an ability not attributed to Solomon. In *The Admonition of Ipuwer* (the Middle Kingdom c. 2040–1640 B.C.E.), the writer laments: "Lo, the private chambers, its book are stolen \ The secret in it are laid bare.... Lo, magic spells are divulged". In Lichtheim (1975, p. 155). On Egyptian magic see Pinch (1994); Hornung (2001, pp. 55–66); Ritner (1995b, pp. 3333–3379).

26. *Ant*. I., Josephus (1963, pp. 69–70). Josephus, however, describes Solomon as a "Hellenistic king".

27. *Ant*. I., Josephus (1963 pp. 167–168).

28. See Siker (1987, pp. 188–208). From the description ascribed to Eupolemus, probably from the first century B.C.E., of Abraham as the inventor of astrology who taught it to the Egyptians (in Charlesworth 1983, Vol. 2, pp. 861–879), and from several other mentions, some scholars have leapt to the exaggerated conclusion that "the Jews were known in the ancient world not only as miracle workers, magicians, fortunetellers and the like, but also as astronomers". In any event, they both shared the view that the universe was a "defined structure of directly related bodies". See Long (1982, pp. 165–192).

29. *Ant*. VIII.42–44. Josephus (1963, pp. 42–44).

30. The anonymous author of *Expositio totius mundi et gentium* (which dates to the second half of the fourth century) wrote, as if in response to Josephus: "It is impossible, in whatever matter you may wish, to find such a wise man as the Egyptian; and so of all philosophers and men versed in the wisdom of letters, the best have been those who have always dwelt in this country". On the literature about the "first discoverers" (*prōtoi heuretaī*), see Thräde (1962a); Sarton (1993, pp. 280–433).

Thus, in asserting that "there was no form of nature with which he was not acquainted or which he passed over without examining, but he studied them all philosophically and revealed the most complete knowledge of their properties",[31] Josephus ascribed not only broad "scientific" knowledge and philosophical understanding to Solomon but also a command of occultic wisdom.[32]

Since Thoth-Hermes was among the most popular of the Egyptian gods[33] and was regarded in Greek magical papyri as a cosmic power, the creator of heaven and earth, and an almighty world-ruler,[34] it is entirely likely that Josephus was familiar with his mythological image. There is no evidence, however, to affirm whether he had access to any of the versions of *The Book of Thoth*, which was "restricted knowledge" in the possession of temple scribes (although excerpts were copied and circulated). Thus, Josephus portrayed Solomon in Antiquities as, in Torijano's words, an esoteric king: "As seems clear from the above analysis, the lore that is described in the *Wisdom of Solomon* has little to do with biblical wisdom or purely scientific disciplines [...] as a matter of fact, each of the points listed is at the core of Hermetism, astrology, or magic in general".[35] Torijano also suggests that it is quite probable that Josephus knew of a tradition that connected Solomon with philosophical and Hermetic conceptions of four elements, and it was for that reason that he chose to present the king as a scientist or philosopher. Moreover, Torijano argues that Josephus' depiction of Solomon is an echo of a popular tradition of Solomon as a Hermetic sage.[36]

Be that as it may, neither *WS* nor Josephus constitutes sufficient evidence that Solomon was recognized by Jews in Egypt as an occultist, and it is difficult to believe that Josephus would have chosen to compare Solomon to a mythological figure or god. If anything,

---

31. *Contra Apionem* II.36, pp. 255–261. See Bar-Kochva (2010b).

32. He could have written about Solomon in the same vein that Philo described Moses in *De Vita Mosis* (I, 5–21); the claim was that the latter was tutored in Pharaoh's palace by Egyptian, Chaldean, and Greek scholars in subjects as diverse as arithmetic, geometry, the lore of meter, rhythm and harmony, music, philosophy conveyed by symbols, and astrology—comprising the so-called "encyclopedic subjects". Philo, Vol. VI, trans by Colson (1994, Vol. 6, pp. 229–287).

33. Fowden (1993, p. 22). Also see Bull (2018). In 2010, a colossal statue of Thoth, in the shape of a baboon, was discovered in Luxor, dating back to the 18th dynasty.

34. Fowden (2003, p. 25).

35. Torijano (2002, p. 93).

36. Torijano (2002, pp. 99–100, 103–104). Indeed, Solomon's name appears in four tractates of the corpus of Nag Hammadi. In one of these, *The Book of Solomon* is mentioned. See *The Origins of the World from Nag Hammadi*, in J. M. Robinson (1988, p. 117).

it seems more likely that Josephus' Solomon is akin to Egyptian kings, who in turn were compared to Thoth in order to glorify them. However, since Josephus and the author(s) of *WS* were, in all likelihood, unfamiliar with Egyptian, Hellenic, or Greek science, it would probably be correct to define the form of wisdom they attributed to him as occultism.

Further, in this chapter, we will see how, during the Middle Ages and the Renaissance, Solomon would come to be seen as an ancient magus—a figure like Hermes Trismegistus, the Hellenist incarnation of the Egyptian god Thoth.

Solomon's Wisdom according to the Sages

The Sages posited various reflections regarding the scope of Solomon's wisdom and the manner in which it was expressed. At times their approach was skeptical, though they also showcased Solomon's wisdom in numerous legendary tales about his prowess as a judge and searcher of all hearts, even in controversies between animals.[37] *Pesiqta of Rab Kahana* says: "It is written, God gave Solomon wisdom and understanding in large measure […] even as the sand that is on the seashore (1 Kings 5:9). R. Levi and the Rabbis say, "He gave him as much wisdom as all the rest of Israel had put together". Said R. Levi, "Just as the sand serves as the fence for the sea, so wisdom served as the fence for Solomon".[38] The *Second Targum of Esther* has it that "Solomon was perfect and honest, shining evil; he perceived the mysteries of heaven and was knowledgeable […] To him was given the great key whereby one can open all gates of wisdom and understanding of the heart"[39] Other *midrashim* are seemingly less abstract. According to *Midrash Tanhuma Buber* (*Qodashim* 10), Solomon "was wise and knew the root of the foundation of the world. […] Now Solomon knew which vein went to Cush and planted peppers on it".[40] Solo-

---

37. Zer-Kavod (1977, pp. 203–207).
38. *Pes. deR. Kahana 4.3*, in Neusner (1997, p. 50). That source also describes Solomon's wisdom as the wisdom of foresight: "You find when Solomon planned to build the house of the sanctuary, he sent to Pharaoh Neccho saying to him, Send me craftsmen. for a salary. For I am planning to build the house of the sanctuary. What did he do? He gathered all the astrologers of his court, who looked into the matter and picked out those men who were going to die that year, and those he sent to him. And when they came to Solomon, he looked into the matter through the Holy Spirit, realizing that they were going to in that year, and he gave them shrouds and sent them back to him. He sent and wrote to him, "Did you not have enough shrouds in Egypt to bury your dead? Here are they, here are their shrouds". PesK 4.3; trans. Neusner (1997).
39. Trans. Grossfeld (1994).
40. Trans. J.T. Townsend. In *Tales of the Prophets* by al-Kisā'ī, Solomon's wisdom is revealed in his youth as a reader of books. When he was twelve, David dressed him in the "garb of the prophets from white wool" and permitted him to mount the

mon, in other words, had mastered not only matters of agriculture but also the structure of the world.

Some sages argue that Solomon could be credited with both a profound knowledge and understanding of the Torah and with guiding others towards such understanding: *Song of Songs Rabbah* likens the Torah to a deep well whose waters Solomon learned to draw to the surface: "So proceeding from one thing to another, from one parable to another, Solomon penetrated to the innermost meaning of the Torah".[41] Solomon was a sage who instituted regulations: "When Solomon instituted *'erubin*[42] and the washing of the hands, a Heavenly Echo came forth and declared, My son, if thine heart be wise; My heart shall be glad, even mine".[43] The Solomon of *Ecclesiastes Rabbah* (7.23,4) states: "Concerning all these [ordinances of the Torah] I have stood and investigated [their meaning], but the chapter of the Red Heifer I have been unable to fathom" while in *Sanhedrin 21b* we read: "R. Isaac also said: Why were the reasons of [some] Biblical laws not revealed?—Because in two verses reasons were revealed, and they caused the greatest in the world [Solomon] to stumble. Thus, it is written: He shall not multiply wives to himself, ['That his heart turn not away', Deut. XVII, 17.] whereon Solomon said, 'I will multiply wives yet not let my heart be perverted.' Yet we read, When Solomon was old, his wives turned away his heart.[I Kings XI, 4] Again it is written: He shall not multiply to himself horses; [Deut. XVII, 17] concerning which Solomon said, 'I will multiply them, but will not cause [Israel] to return [to Egypt].' Yet we read: And a chariot came up and went out of Egypt for six [hundred shekels of silver]" [I Kings X, 29] (Soncino transl.). According to *Exodus Rabbah*, he was responsible, together with seven other elders, for the addition of the thirteenth month to the Jewish calendar; the seven elders plus Solomon, the prophet Nathan, and the seer Gad were together ten persons, as was the norm for the intercalation of a month.[44] R. Simeon ben Yoḥai interpreted Ecclesiastes 2:12 ("And I turned myself to behold wisdom, and madness and folly") as follows: "Solomon said: 'Because I tried to be wiser than the Torah and persuaded myself that I knew the intention of the Torah, did this understanding and knowledge turn out to be madness and folly [...] Who is permitted to entertain doubts about the ways and decrees of the King of Kings, the Holy One, blessed be He,

---

pulpit. And the boy Solomon "read to them from the books of Seth, Enoch, Abraham and Moses." al-Kisā'ī (1997, p. 350).

41. *Song of Songs Rabbah* 1.1.8.
42. 'Erubin for regulating Sabbath limits.
43. *Shabbat* 14b.
44. *Exodus Rabbah* 15.20.

whose words issue from before Him like solid blocks. [...] because I questioned His actions, have I stumbled'".[45] In contrast, R. Samuel ben Naḥman read the words of Ecclesiastes-Solomon—"walk in the ways of your heart, and in the sight of your eyes" (Eccl. 11:9)—as "words that tend towards heresy": "there is no judge, no laws!" Yet because Solomon continued the verse "know thou, that for all these things God will bring thee into judgment," the Sages found that "Solomon spoke well".[46]

As a judge, Solomon is unlike the judges of the gentiles: "I am not like all the other judges. A mortal king sits on his tribune and issues judgments for execution by the sword, by strangulation, by burning, or by stoning, and it means nothing [to him]. I am not like this. If I (unjustly) find a person guilty in monetary matters, I am held to account for it as if it were a capital case".[47] Solomon, endowed with an understanding of the natural and the spiritual, was also blessed with the wisdom of sound government and the ability to discern good from evil, and so with an ability to "impose order and judgment on to the entire world".

While the Sages had different views about 'Greek wisdom' (*tes hellenikos Sophias*), namely logic and natural sciences, they did not depict Solomon's wisdom as legitimation a of "Greek wisdom", and find no need to posit a resemblance or a distinction between the wisdom of Solomon and that of Greece.[48]

Solomon's Wisdom in the Middle Ages

Celsus wrote that the Jews "never did anything of worthy its names" (IV:31) and the emperor Julian wrote: that the wisdom of Solomon cannot be comparable to the wisdom of Hellens". In fact, God has not granted them to invent any science (*episteme*=knowledge) or any philosophical study (*mathema philosophon*). "Why is it? For the theory of the heavenly bodies was perfected among the Hellens, after the first observations had been made among the barbarians in Babylon, and the study of geometry arose in the measurement in the land of Egypt, and from this grew to its present importance. Arithmetic began with the Phoenician merchant, and among the Hellenes in the course of time acquired the aspect of regular science" (178 A-B). Indeed, we don't know about any institutionalized "scientific" activity, or any individual "men of science in Jewish society until the Middle

---

45. *Midrash Rabbah Exodus* (*Va'Era*), VI:1, trans. S. M. Leherman, London, 1961, pp. 104–105.
46. Ibid., XI:9.
47. Hammer (1986, § 10, 34).
48. See Shavit (1999, pp. 79–95).

Ages. Only with the mediation of the Islamic world, the Middle Ages saw the rise of a two-way interchange between Jewish thought and the heritage of Greek-Hellenist philosophy and science. "Wisdom" came to be seen as a matter of natural philosophy, (i. e., "physics") and Solomon was depicted as an occultist, philosopher, and man of "natural philosophy.[49] As this "wisdom" was divided into divine wisdom, natural wisdom (physics) and scholarly wisdom (mathematics, logic, etc.), it was Solomon who could become a king-philosopher engaging also in "science" and thus serve as personification of the ancient wisdom of the Jews and as legitimation to deal with philosophy and the sciences.

According to Judah Halevi's apology, Solomon's judicial fame was wellknown throughout the world, but the wisdom he revealed to the Queen of Sheba and other rulers remained a closely kept secret and hence was lost with few exceptions. In other words, much of Solomon's wisdom was "concealed wisdom"—known only to select individuals, never recorded, and eventually lost. Its substance could be extrapolated from various books of wisdom by the gentiles, who translated Solomon's books and so preserved them for the coming generations.[50]

In Maimonides' view, Solomon was an esoteric philosopher, his words intended for an intellectual elite and not for the "common people". Solomon was well-versed in the highest possible levels of natural and metaphysical knowledge, but he communicated his philosophical teachings and their metaphysical contents in an esoteric manner, by means of parables[51]—though he was nonetheless also a "practical wise man" who set forth concrete rules of moral and religious behavior. Abraham Ibn Ezra (1089–1167) found in Solomon's books knowledge of the "laws of heaven" (i. e., astronomy): "I know that whatever God does endures forever; nothing can be added to it, nor anything taken from it".[52] The statesman, philosopher, and biblical commentator Isaac Abrabanel (1437–1508) wrote, in his commentary on 1 Kings 3, that Solomon had excelled in several types of knowledge: "natural, scholarly, divine, and religious",[53] and that he had acquired this knowledge not gradually by way of induction, but "wondrously,"

---

49. In both Islam and Latin Christianity in the Middle Ages, the heritage of the ancient world was not only Aristotelian, but also included writings on various spheres including astronomy, medicine, physics, mathematics, and more. On this, see two popular works by John Freely (2010, 2015).

50. *Kuzari* 3:63. And see Chapter Eight.

51. I rely here on Klein-Braslavy (2007). And there are apologetics that explained that since *hoi polloi* were too ignorant to understand Solomon's wisdom, he conveyed it through parables.

52. Sela (1999, p. 45, note 38). See also Sela (2003).

53. Melamed (2003, p. 159).

which rendered him superior to Aristotle and all the sages who came before and after him.⁵⁴ Naḥmanides (1194–1270) wrote that King Solomon had so mastered the entirety of natural wisdom, history, even the strength and qualities of herbs, that he wrote a book of medicine. The thirteenth-century physician and scholar Shem Tov ben Isaac of Tortosa was of the opinion that Solomon's wisdom encompassed all of the natural sciences and that his medical knowledge derived from a divine power within him.⁵⁵ R. David Messer Leon (c. 1470–c. 1526), also a "Renaissance man", held that Solomon was fluent in every sphere of wisdom and possessed knowledge of all matters included in the natural sciences, among which he numbered physics, astronomy, and astrology.⁵⁶ *The Sefer haMesshiv* (*Book of the Responding Entity*), a late fourteenth-century collection of the visions of a group of Kabbalists from Spain, and which has been only partially preserved, relates its authors' discovery of the lost books of Solomon. It notes the names of these books and declares that they contain the original, true theory of nature and science, whose origin lay in divine revelation rather than philosophy or science, which are the products of human reason.⁵⁷ Spinoza, in contrast, interpreted Proverbs 16:22 ("Wisdom is a fountain of life to one who has it, but folly is the punishment of fools") to mean that Solomon's was a "natural wisdom"—an inner quality—and that Solomon's idea of God was a product of his wisdom, which is praised in the Holy Scriptures. Yet, this wisdom led Solomon to consider himself above the law of the Torah and to disdain the laws of the king⁵⁸ even to the point of violating them.⁵⁹ In Rabbi Jacob Emden's (Ya'avetz, 1687–1776) view, a scholar and posek (arbiter) from Altona, Solomon was the father of alchemy based on a passage in the Gemara: "When King Solomon built the Sanctuary, he planted therein all kinds of [trees of] golden delights, which were bringing forth their fruits in their season and as the winds blew at them, they would fall off [...] and when the foreigners entered the temple they withered".⁶⁰ Emden wrote that "now there are concealed secrets regarding the nature of plants and minerals that are known to a select

---

54. Cohen Skalli (2017, pp. 178–189). In the author's opinion, Abravanel was influenced by Hermeticism and the notion of natural magic.

55. Muntner (1958, p. 326). Shem Tov based his views on al-Zahrāwī, Kitāb al-Taṣrīf (Sefer haShimmush), a thirty-volume encyclopedia of medical practice composed between 1261–1264, or earlier (around 1000).

56. *Sheva ha-Nashim*, in Tirosh-Rothschild (1991, pp. 71, 280).

57. Idel (1994).

58. Deuteronomy 17:16–17.

59. Spinoza, *Tractatus Theologico Politicus* (see Chapter Two). See also Israel (1995).

60. *Yoma* 21b.

few, like the praises of the alchemists regarding the power of all-purpose healing medicine [...] I believe they learned this from the Book of Healing of King Solomon [...] when the sages said that Solomon planted a forest of gold, I maintain they are hinting at the conversion of metal into gold, which increases by means of the seed it contains".[61] In *Sefer haBrit* (*Book of Convanant*) by the Kabbalist Pinhas Eliyahu Hurwitz (1765–1821),[62] Solomon was described as having anticipated the scientific thinking of the west, and his assertion that "the earth remains forever" (Ecclesiastes 1:4) served to refute Copernicus.[63]

For the Haskalah movement in the nineteenth century, Solomon represented the ideal of a maskil and a symbol of the struggle against conservative trends in Jewish society. In his *Te'udah be'Yisrael* (*A Testimony in Israel*)[64] Isaac Baer Levinsohn (1788–1860), first and foremost among the *maskilim* of Czarist Russia, depicted Solomon as a link in a progression of figures in Jewish history who granted legitimacy to the acquisition and study of all forms of secular knowledge. Following in the footsteps of Abravanel, Levinsohn declared: "And we shall return to the wise king Solomon son of David who took pride in his wisdom, and more than he received from his father, he himself made an effort to acquire it and greatly excelled, until he became the father of all wisdoms and the head of all those seeking them among the scholars of his own time and thereafter: 'he spoke of trees, from the cedar tree that is in Lebanon even unto the hyssop that springs out of the wall'".[65]

The imaginary Solomon was brought into being to argue that Jews were the source of the ancient wisdoms (*prisca sapientia*), but Jewish apologists could not merely claim that Solomon was endowed with wisdom; they had to specify what that wisdom encompassed. At first, when the boundaries between occultism and science were not clear-cut,[66] Solomon would have functioned as the author of books of magic and as a master of both the natural and the occult "sciences",

---

61. See Kahana (2013a). Also see Kahana (2013b).
62. The book first appeared in 1797 in Brin, Moravia, and was translated into Yiddish and Ladino and printed in dozens of editions.
63. See I. Robinson (1989).
64. Written in 1823, printed in 1828.
65. At the same time, both Abravanel and Levinsohn noted that wisdom had not vanished after Solomon, and they did not mean to say that no men wiser than him would appear.
66. These boundaries were also glossed over by famous scientists such as Newton, Robert Boyle, and others. Newton is known to have been influenced by the book *The Compound of Alchemy or The Twelve Stones*, written by the alchemist George Ripley (c. 1415–1490). In other words, he regarded the ancient wisdom of Hermes Trismegistus and of Solomon as one and the same.

and eventually as a figure who inspired the "new science."[67] Because Aristotle, during that period, was regarded as the philosopher whose wisdom was "all-embracing", the need arose to claim that Solomon's wisdom was no less universal.

Solomon's Wisdom in Christian Literature
"If only I had great wisdom like that of Solomon"
    Francis of Assisi, *Testament of the Holy Father St. Francis*

Emperor Julian, as mentioned, mocked the wisdom of Solomon: "Can Solomon be compared to Phocylides or Theognis or Isocrates? Certainly not".[68] The target of his scorn was Christianity, which adopted the biblical description of Solomon's wisdom and its divine source.

The result of Christianity's ambivalent attitude toward Solomon's wisdom resulted in what Hattaway defines as the "Paradoxes of Solomon": on the one hand the king, in his wisdom and erudition, represented an advocate of sorts for the study of philosophy, while on the other hand the book of Ecclesiastes provided arguments against it. In the latter case, Solomon and Aristotle were seen as representing two diametrically opposed conceptions of wisdom and worthwhile study, which not only adopted the biblical portrayal of Solomon's wisdom but also embroidered upon it.

Bachiarius described Solomon as "that wondrous man who deserves to share in the wisdom that sits next to God",[69]—and in his treatise *On the Government of Rulers*, Thomas Aquinas extolled Solomon: "Not only did he [Solomon] receive from the Lord the wisdom that he requested, but also became praised for his wisdom more than all the kings",[70] "How can he be ignorant of anything that is, when he is Wisdom, the maker of the world, who brings all things to fulfillment and recreates all things, who is all that has come into being?"[71] Solomon, like Jesus, was said to know all.

According to Origen, "Solomon discovered and taught [...] by the wisdom that he received from God"; that is, his wisdom encompassed both moral philosophy and natural science,[72] and in Eusebius view, Solomon was a "pupil of the heavens"; and he discerned a resemblance

---

67. See Feiner (2002).

68. *Against the Galilieans*, 178b, p. 383.

69. "*Solomon ille mirabilis, qui meruit assistrici, Deo sapiencia*", in Behrends (1976, pp. 166–167).

70. *De regimine principum*, Chapter 9.

71. Eusebius (2002, pp. 560–561). The *Epistle of James* distinguishes between the "wisdom that descends from above", which is pure, loves peace, tolerance, is full of mercy, etc., and earthly wisdom, which "stems from instinct and the demons" and gives rise to envy, falsehood, and every evil deed (Eusebius 2002).

72. *The Song of Songs*, Origen (1957, pp. 40–41); see Chapter Three.

between Solomon's wisdom and the philosophy of Plato, who divided it into three branches—Physics, Ethics, and Logic.[73] According to him, Solomon, like Plato, drew a distinction between the contemplation of things abstract and incorporeal on the one hand, and the study of things observable through the senses—the natural sciences—on the other. In Ecclesiastes, Solomon explained the "nature of the fleeting substance of bodies" and arrived at the conclusion, saying "Vanity of vanities, all is vanity". This was Solomon's conclusion concerning corporeal substance. Clement of Alexandria quotes Proverbs 1,2, to reach the conclusion that wisdom is "a communicative and philanthropic thing". Solomon teaches that "the word that is sown is hidden in the soul of the learner, as in the earth, and this is spiritual planting". Gregory of Nazianzus prayed to possess Solomon's state of mind—"not to think or say anything about God that is simply my own. For when [Solomon] says, 'I am the most foolish of all people, and human prudence is not in me" [Prov. 20:2] it is not, surely, in recognition of his own lack of understanding that he speaks this way. For how could one say this who asked from God before all else—and who received—wisdom and contemplative vision and wideness of heart [...] Solomon said these things because he has no natural wisdom of his own, but is enlivened by more perfect wisdom that comes from God".[74] It was, therefore, possible to bring verses from Proverbs and Ecclesiastes to argue that philosophy is nonsense and evil on the one hand and claim that it helped faith on the other hand.

We have already seen that St. Anthony won out over the philosophers to whom he demonstrated the power of faith in Jesus and the cross, overcoming all those who were "blinded by the fog of secular wisdom and [...] most learned in all branches of philosophy"—this was a testament to his faith in the divine scriptures and in Jesus, the true God. "We Christians", he maintained, "keep the mystery of our life stored up, not in worldly wisdom, but in the power of faith which God has granted us through Christ".[75] Theologians and, later on, counter-Renaissance thinkers found that Ecclesiastes' dictum that "all is vanity", and the author's resulting exhortation to "fear God and keep his commands", supported their absolute preference for faith over wisdom and their conviction that the ability of wisdom and science to provide answers must be evaluated with humility and skepticism.

---

73. *Preparation for the Gospel Part 1*, Eusebius (2002, Book II and XI:VII, pp. 521, 644–562). He writes that Solomon, above all others, excelled in knowledge of the natural science "of things sensible".

74. Gregory of Nazianzus, *Oration 20: On Theology, and the Appointment of Bishops 5*, in Daley (2006, pp. 755).

75. C. White (1991, pp. 54–59).

However, "wisdom" is not only philosophy, but knowledge in many fields and, as we will see, it was difficult to reject.

Jesus' Wisdom

*"Wisdom is therefore queen of philosophy,
as philosophy is of preparatory of culture"*
        - Clement of Alexandria, *Stromata*, Book 1

Did Jesus learn from Solomon's wisdom and does his wisdom resemble Solomon's?

Jesus' wisdom is known only from the words and deeds attributed to him in the New Testament. In him "are hidden all the treasures of wisdom and knowledge";[76] he is "the power of God and the wisdom of God",[77] and the apostles reveal the concealed wisdom of God; they express it not in the words that human wisdom teaches, but in words that the Spirit teaches. It is God, not human wisdom, that truly understands a man's spirit: "For Jews demand signs and Greeks desire wisdom, but we proclaim Christ crucified [...] Christ the power of God and the wisdom of God".[78] In Colossians, Paul warns his listeners: "See to it that no one take you captive through philosophy and empty deceit, according to human tradition, according to the elemental spirit of the universe, and not according to Christ",[79] while 2 Timothy 2:7 promises that it is "the Lord [who] will give you understanding in all things." The sentiment is reflected by Augustine: "Christ is the wisdom of God [...] the word, co-eternal with the Father".[80] Christians do not consult any wise man but Wisdom Herself: "Let us then both give ear to Jesus Christ".[81]

Is "wisdom", only philosophy seemingly separated by a wide abyss from the wisdom of the gospels, Tertullian posed a rhetorical question—"What then has Athens to do with Jerusalem, or the academy and the church?" (*Quid ergo Athenis et Hierosolymis?*)[82]—

---

76. Colossians 2:3.

77. Paul adds: "My speech and my proclamation were not with plausible words of reason, but with a demonstration of the Spirit of power, so that your faith might rest not on human wisdom but on the power of God. Yet among the mature we do speak wisdom, though it is not wisdom of this age or of the rulers of the age, who are doomed to perish, but we speak God's wisdom, secret and hidden, which God decree before the ages for our glory". 1 Cor 2:4–7.

78. 1 Cor 1:22–24.

79. Colossians 2:8.

80. *City of God* XVII:20, Augustine (1984, p. 755).

81. Sermon X, in Schaff and Wace (1995, pp. 290–294).

82. Tertullian (1956, pp. 35–36). Away, he wrote, with the attempts to produce a mottled Christianity of Stoic, Platonists, and dialectical compositions. (See Roberts, (1924, pp. 63–78). Hyronimus wrote that he "made oath and called upon His name, saying, 'Lord, if ever again I possess worldly book, or if ever I read again such, I have

and again: "What there in common between the philosopher and the Christian, the pupil of Hellas and the pupil of the heavens".[83] Here Tertullian established a dichotomy between Aristotle and Solomon: "Unhappy Aristotle" (*miserum Aristotelen*) invented dialectics—"the art of building up and pulling down; an art so evasive in its propositions, so farfetched in its conjectures, so harsh in its arguments, so productive of contentions—embarrassing even to itself..."—while "our principles come from the Porch of Solomon, who himself taught that the Lord is to be sought in simplicity of heart". However, useful knowledge is desirable, and Augustine tried to work out *ab initio* what kinds of knowledge and expertise it might useful for Christian children to acquire", and claimed that rhetoric, history, medicine, astronomy, and even philosophy are divinely instituted discipline.[84]

However, although in early Christianity there were those who believed that philosophy was the creation of Satan or of demons,[85] more than a few Church Fathers nonetheless conceived of philosophy as a kind of "preparatory training to those who attain to faith through demonstration [...]. Philosophy, therefore, was [for those with a 'Hellenic mind'] a preparation, paving the way for him who is perfected in Christ".[86] Pelikan cites Gregory of Nazianzus, who was well acquainted with Platonic and neo-Platonic philosophy and argued that "Christians, many of them common people or even monks, were philosophically superior to Plato or Aristotle" since Christian philosophy "could be accommodated to the faith and understanding of simple believers. Such believers were now capable of becoming 'wise' in the fullest and truest sense of the word".[87] In the Song of Songs and Ecclesiastes, Gregory of Nyssa found a philosophy of apophatic restraint.[88]

In any event, what distinguished between pagan and Christian wisdom was that the former was "natural" wisdom and the latter was a product of supernatural (divine) revelation. Quite a few Church Fathers were familiar with HellenistRoman literature and, with some

---

denied you' (letter 22, 30; to Eustochium, 383 AD). One should not drink the cup of Christ, and at the same time, the cup of devils".

83. *Apologeticus* 46, 18. See Cochrane (1957, pp. 213–260), especially pp. 222–223.

84. See R.P. H. Green introduction to Augustine (2008, xiv–xv).

85. Daniélou (1973, pp. 62–64). Cyril of Jerusalem in his Fourth Catechetical Lecture (*On the Ten Points of Doctrine*) stated that knowledge of Christian doctrine was important "since there are many that make spoil through philosophy and vain deceit", in Schaff and Wace (1995, Vol. 7, pp. 19–28).

86. *Stromata*, v. In: Clement of Alexandria (1995, Vol. 2, p. 305).

87. Pelikan (1993, p. 180).

88. Pelikan (1993, p. 181).

reservations, permitted it to become part of standard Christian education, directing its students to a moral life.[89] And so both Solomon and Jesus were granted Divine wisdom, but Jesus was "wisdom itself", whereas Solomon, despite his wisdom, erred and sinned. The sin that is perceived to cast doubt on the value of human wisdom is another matter in which Jesus is "greater than Solomon". However, in another matter, Solomon is "greater than Jesus" in that Solomon's wisdom included subjects considered to be "human wisdom", thus making Solomon much closer to Aristotle than to Jesus.

From Thoth-Hermes to Aristotle

In the Middle Ages, Thoth reemerged in a new garb as Hermes Trismegistus. Hermetism[90] existed in fifteenth and sixteenth-century Italy side by side with various other occult traditions and theological and philosophic schools[91] including Neo-Platonism, Pythagoreanism, Stoicism, Aristotelianism, and Thomism.[92] Of all these, Hermetism is the most relevant to our subject.

In the 1460s, writings attributed to Hermes—namely the *Corpus Hermeticum*, a set of tracts said to have originated between 300–1000 C.E.—arrived in Florence. Hermetic or pseudo-Hermetic literature was widespread in Muslim culture; a ninth-century book by Abū Maʿshar, *Kitāb al-Ulūf* (The Book of Thousands), is one such text, summarizing the Hermetic occult science.[93] The *Corpus Hermeticum*, translated into Latin by Marsilio Ficino, and was printed in 1463;[94]

---

89. "This addition to the standard curriculum" was suggested by, among others, Basil of Caesarea (c.330–379, 12:233–234) See Basil of Caesarea (1970). On Augustinus, Classical literature, and the influence of Platonist Philosophy see Fox (2016).

90. See Garin (1983). A sign of Hermes' status may be found in the fifteenth-century floor mosaic in the Siena cathedral, where Hermes Mercurius Trismagistus is depicted as a contemporary of Moses ("*contemporaneous Moysi*") and harbinger of Christ. On Hermetic books in the Middle Ages, see Thorndike (1964, Vol. 2 , pp. 214–229). As far back as the tenth-century Byzantine encyclopedia *Suda* (*attributed to Sodas*) it was written that "He was called Trismegistus on account of his praise of the trinity, denying there is one divine nature in the trinity" (Thorndike 1964, xli). It was, of course, the Protestant scholar Isaac Casaubon who proved that the tracts were not ancient. See Grafton (1991). However, there were those who disagree with Casaubon's view and, as we have seen, they held that these philosophical and magic tracts have ancient Egyptian roots. In any case, the controversy is irrelevant to our discussion here.

91. Gibbons (2001).

92. Burke (1975); Shumaker, *The Occult Sciences in the Renaissance*: *A Study in Intellectual Patterns*, Berkeley, (1972, pp. 201–248).

93. See Carboni (2013).

94. In his *Kitāb Ṭabaqāt al-Umam* (Book of the Categories of Nations, 1068), a Muslim scholar from Andalusia, Ṣāʿid al-Andalusī, mentions several books written

parts of the corpus had been known to some Church Fathers,[95] and were accepted as the authentic ancient work of an Egyptian scholar who wrote primordial words of wisdom,[96] and became an influential school of thought.[97] Thus, the mythical Thoth was resurrected in the shape of Hermes Trismegistus, the *Pater philosophorum*, a super-sage and ancient prophet who represented *prisca theologia* and of whom Ficino wrote: "they called him Trismegistus because he was the greatest philosopher and the greatest priest and the greatest king".[98] Hermes' writings were regarded as presaging esoteric Christian wisdom; they both greatly preceded Jesus and foretold his coming. No less importantly, their existence was said to demonstrate that all "wisdoms" were born of a single ancient source and were, therefore, like Solomon's wisdom, universal.[99]

***

Jewish thinkers were also influenced by the Hermetic corpus,[100] and during the Renaissance, Solomon appeared in works by Jewish scholars as a parallel not only of Hermes Trismegistus but also of Apollonius of Tyana,[101] who was, we will recall, compared to Jesus (Eusebius, *Contra Hieroclem*) and accorded a semi-divine status. These two figures were linked in the Arabic pseudo-Aristotelian literature, which made its way into the West and was translated into Latin. The connection between the two originated mainly in the popular treatise *Kitāb Sirr al-Asrār*, a pseudo-Aristotelian work translated into Latin c. 1120 by John of Seville, who titled it *Secreta Secretorum* (the Secret of Se-

---

by Hermes of Babylon, "which proves his greatness as a scientist". See al-Andalusī (1991, pp. 19–20). See also: Ebeling (2007, p. 48); Celenza (2001, pp. 115–133).133–155.

95. Fowden (1993, pp. 198–202). Hermes is mentioned in *Cyranides*, a fourth-century compilation of magico-medical work, as a cosmologist and alchemist. Augustine, who was familiar with some part of the Hermetic literature, wrote that "Hermes says much of God according to the truth". See *City of God* VIII:23–24, Augustine (1984, pp. 332–337).

96. Najman et al. (2016).

97. Clement of Alexandria (1995) calls him Hermes, the false prophet (*Stromata*, xvii).

98. Copenhaver, Hermetica (1992, xlvii; 2003). See also: Yates (1979); Merkel and Debus (1988).

99. Celsus had also written that "There is an ancient doctrine which has existed from the beginning, which has always been maintained by wisest nations and cities and wise men" (I:14). He did not count the Jews and Solomon among these. See Origen (1965, I:17).

100. On Hermetic literature in the Geniza, see Eliyahu (2005). Wasserstrom (2000).

101. See Ellen (2014).

crets).¹⁰² It appeared in several versions and was translated into many languages, including Hebrew¹⁰³ and English (by Roger Bacon).¹⁰⁴ The text purports to be a letter sent by Aristotle to his pupil Alexander the Great; in substance, it is an encyclopedia on a broad range of subjects including astrology, alchemy, and medicine, and it was received as a genuine Aristotelian work.

Mahmoud Manzalaoui claims that the book "is an echo of the traditional notion that Aristotle's works were of two kinds, esoteric (acroamatic) and exoteric".¹⁰⁵ In the thirteenth century, the chapter that dealt with the occultic sciences began to be circulated separately as the book *Tabula Smaragdina* (The Emerald Tablet). It, too, was attributed to Hermes Trismegistus, and was discovered by Apollonius of Tyana, who learned from it "the reasons for all things". The *Tabula Smaragdina* was composed in Arabic between the sixth to eighth centuries and exists in several versions. Its author, or recorder, is supposedly Balinas/Balinus, the Arabic name of Apollonius of Tyana.¹⁰⁶ According to the story, Apollonius discovered the book in a vault under a statue of Hermes Trismegistus, where he found an old man seated on a throne of gold holding an emerald tablet containing the secrets of transmutation and its primordial substance. The first version of this pseudo-Aristotelian work, a product of Arab-Hermeticism that attributed to Apollonius hermetic books on astrology, alchemy, and cosmography,¹⁰⁷ was *Kitāb Sirr al-Khalīqa wa Ṣanʿat al-Ṭabīʿa* (Book of the Secret of Creation and the Art of Nature).¹⁰⁸ According to Jacob ben David Provençal, the content of this book was borrowed from *The*

---

102. A translation of its full name is *Book of the Science of Government, On the Good Ordering of Statecraft*. See Chapter Eight.

103. The translator from Arabic was Ibn Chasdai (1180–1240), a scholar, philosopher poet, and follower of Maimonides. The Hebrew translation (together with a translation into English and introduction by M. Gaster) of *Sod haSodot asher Katav oto Aristotolo el haMelekh haGadol Alexander* was printed in Venice in 1519 and published by Gaster (1907–1908), and reprinted in the third volume of Gaster (1925-1928, pp. 111–162). See also: Ryan and Schmitt (1982); S. J. Williams (1994b). The book deals with rhetoric, dialectics, arithmetic, geometry, and more. It was quoted in the fourteen-century Latin text *Secretum Philosophorum*, which originated in England c.1300–1359.

104. S. J. Williams (1994b). See Chapter Eight.

105. See his detailed monograph, Manzalaoui (1974). On the various versions of the book and its reception in the Christian West, see S. J. Williams (2003).

106. On the literature on this subject, see Ruska (1926); Steinschneider, (1891); Steele and Singer (1928).

107. Copenhaver (1992, xlvi, pp. 112–113).

108. An excerpt was translated by Newton, who wrote a commentary on the subject. From line 15: "And because of this they have called me Hermes Trismegistus since I have the three parts of the wisdom and Philosophy of the whole universe". See Weisser (1979).

Book of the Mystery of Nature, which in turn was attributed to Solomon;[109] Hermetic books were also attributed to Aristotle.

Was Hermes, then, a rival for Solomon, someone "greater than Solomon"? This question leads again to Johanan Alemanno, a scholar, philosopher, Kabbalist, and biblical exegete known mainly for having tutored Pico della Mirandola in Hebrew and Kabbalah. Alemanno connected between several legendary traditions about the source of magic, including the apocryphal *Book of Enoch* and *Sefer Raziel*, whose date of composition is unknown. According to the latter, Noah received from his forefathers a book of secrets that the angel Raziel had given to Adam, from which Noah learned how to construct his ark. That book finally reached Solomon, "who was very accomplished in all the secrets, sagacity, and parable, including all the spirits and all the objects and the harmful things roaming throughout the world, and prohibited them and permitted them and controlled them, and he built and did well, all from the wisdom in this book [...]".[110] According to Alemanno, each of the texts he addressed attributed the understanding of the secrets of creation to a heavenly source. He further mentioned unknown books of magic including "*Melekhet muskelet*" (English), attributed to Apollonius, whom Alemanno described as a "wise Christian", and from the Arab astronomer and mathematician from Seville, Abū Muḥammad Jābir ibn Aflaḥ (1100–1150). Primarily, Alemanno learned from Apollonius of Tyana that Solomon had composed twenty-four books on the occult sciences, in which he became, as a result, more proficient than Plato and Aristotle.[111] Alemanno claimed that he has in his possession a copy of the eleventh-century enigmatic mystical treatise *Sefer HaTamar* (The Book of the Palm) by a Muslim author from Syracuse, and he also quotes from it (see Chapter Eight). In that book, Suliman alYahud (Suliman the Jew), or the "ancient Suliman", is described as having taken an interest in the wisdom of religion when still a boy and having later studied the "scholarly wisdoms", becoming greater in wisdom than Plato and Aristotle and proposing five forms of study.[112]

---

109. The prolific translator from Greek to Arabic Yahya (Yuhanna) Ibn al-Bitriq (ca. 815) relates that while he was seeking philosophical texts, he arrived at the Temple of the Sun that the philosopher Asklepios had built and succeeded in convincing the priest to allow him to see the writings that were preserved there. These he then translated from Greek to Syriac and from Syriac to Arabic. See S. J. Williams (2003, pp. 8–9, and notes 5 and 6). Provençal was born in Mantua, engaged in maritime trade, and resided at the end of his life in Naples, where he served as a rabbi and wrote a commentary on the Song of Songs. See Carmoly (1844, p. 125).

110. Jellinek (1938, pp. 155–160).

111. Rosenthal (1977).

112. Gershom Scholem, who prepared the manuscript of *Sefer haTamar* for

It was Solomon, then, and not Hermes, who revealed the secrets of the occult (*secreta opera mundi*) to humanity.[113] Solomon "was wiser than any man and many perfect men who performed actions by intermingling various things and comparing qualities in order to create new forms in gold, silver, vegetable, mineral and animal [matter] which had never before existed and in order to create divine forms which tell the future and the laws and the *nomoi*, as well as to create the spirit of angels, stars and devils".[114] The lengthy introduction to the commentary on Song of Songs (mentioned in Chapter Three) was, in fact, Solomon's biography as a polymath and magus[115] proficient in all spheres of knowledge, both the theoretical and the practical;[116] Alemanno did find it "incredible, however, that King Solomon could have been wiser in the Torah than Moses himself".[117] Solomon was born as a "perfect man" with the "power of imagination, of assumption, intelligence, integrity of thought, the wisdom of logic"; he was accomplished "in the six verbal arts—grammar, humor, poetry, logic, incantations and combinations" as well as in "astrology, music, politics and the natural sciences". In a certain sense, he was wiser even than Moses, since Moses knew nothing of the wisdom of the nations, while Solomon did. From Plato, Alemanno learned that "desire" (1 Kings 9:1) was "the preparation of the soul and the way to ascend to human virtue", and Solomon did indeed desire the words of God.[118]

Hermetism was highly influential in shaping the figure of the Renaissance magus as one who dealt in the occultic sciences, and, in so doing, it contributed to Solomon's image as an occultist. Thus, an imaginary circle was closed: where Josephus had chosen the mythological god Thoth-Hermes as his model for Solomon, with the aim of glorifying the Jewish people (*ad maiorem gloriam Iudaeorum*) above Egypt,[119] the fifteenth and sixteenth centuries saw Solomon take the form of an ancient Jewish super-sage, greater in occultism

---

printing, wrote that Solomon is depicted in it as having opposed or even derided hermetic "even though he is very close to that literature". The Hebrew translation was printed in Jerusalem in 1926. Scholem also brought out a translation into German titled *Sefer Ha-Tamar*; *Das Buch von der Palme*, Scholem (1926). See Chapter Eight.

113. See also: Idel (1988); Hermann (1999). A demotic papyrus tells of the prince Khmawas, son of Ramses II and the high priest of the Petah temple, who heard of a book written by Thoth which recorded all the magic (*hekau*) in the world, including incantations with the power to rule nature. The book was placed in a silver box in Thoth's tomb.

114. Idel (1983b).
115. And as a Lorenzo de Medici-type figure.
116. See Lelli (2000, 2004); Idel (1988).
117. Quoted in Herrmann (1999, p. 73).
118. Alemanno (2019, p. 33).
119. See Conzelmann (1992).

than Hermes Trismegistus. Jewish culture could now boast not only an ancient magus of its own but one who could take his place among the other ancient magi in universal wisdom. Yet, Solomon, unlike Moses, was born too late to be regarded as the teacher of the legendary Hermes Trismegistus, who was believed to be a contemporary of Moses. Aristotle, on the other hand, postdated Solomon by centuries, and this made possible the invention of a tradition in which the Greek supersage became Solomon's pupil.

Solomon and Aristotle

The correspondence between Solomon and Hermes is marginal when compared to the correspondence drawn throughout the centuries between Solomon and Aristotle. It began, perhaps, in a fresco in the House of a Physician in Pompeii, in which Theodore Feder recognizes a depiction of the famous Judgment of Solomon and identifies the figures of two onlookers staring in astonishment at Solomon's wisdom as representing Socrates and Aristotle.[120] As to whence the creator, or commissioner, of the fresco might have drawn this connection, Feder cites a meeting between a Jewish sage and Clearchus of Soli, a pupil of Aristotle's, in Asia Minor (a meeting that could have occurred between 347–345 B.C.E.; based on Josephus' *Against Apion*,[121] an echo of the legendary tradition that Greek philosophy originated in Jewish wisdom.[122] However, Josephus and the Jewish-Hellenist writers appear to have been unfamiliar with Aristotle's writings, and in any event, did not rely on them.[123] Philo was the only Jewish Hellenistic writer who referred to Aristotle, whose cosmology he rejected. In the introduction to *De Opificio Mundi* (On the Creation), Philo wrote that "There are some people who, having the world in admiration rather than the Maker of the world, pronounce it to be without beginning and everlasting, while with impious falsehood they postulate in God vast inactivity".[124] There were probably Jewish sages who had heard of Aristotle, but in the tales that relate how Jewish sages (and even children) are wiser than the "sages of Athens",[125] Aristotle's name remains unmentioned.

---

120. Feder (2008).
121. See Bar Kochva (2010a). And see Chapter Eight.
122. On the antiquity of this tradition, see Bar Kochva (2008).
123. The *Greek Alexander Romance* tells about a letter he wrote to Aristotle on India, but Aristotle is not mentioned in the medieval Hebrew versions. See Gunderson (1980). Joseph Dan writes that the image of Alexander in the Hebrew versions as a philosopher king was influenced by his having been tutored by Aristotle; see Dan (1969, p. 17). But this is merely a hypothesis. See also: Yassif (2006).
124. 1 Philo, Trans. Francis Henry Colson (1994, I., LCL, MXMXX, p. 9).
125. *Bekhorot* 8b; *Midrash Lamentations* 1, 4F; *Derekh eretz rabba*, 5, 2.

One cannot truly speak of "Aristotelianism" in the singular since it constitutes a vast and enormously diverse corpus (*corpus Aristotelicum*); the plural "Aristotelianisms" would be more accurate.[126] It would be no less incorrect to focus on scholastic Aristotelianism alone, as beginning in the thirteenth century, the Christian West experienced an infusion of scientific literature via translations of Greek and Arabic texts into Latin.[127] In Chapter Four we saw that, in the fresco *Trionfo di san Thommaso d'Aquino*, Aquinas represented the importance of knowledge in the "various wisdoms" beyond merely the *trivium* and *quatrivium*; recall that the figures at the bottom of the fresco represent not only philosophy (Aristotle) but also astronomy, geometry (Euclid), arithmetic (Pythagoras), and so on. At Thomas Aquinas' request, a Dominican friar translated Ptolemy,[128] Hero of Alexandria, Galen, and others. Influenced by these translations, Roger Bacon wrote on the benefit of mathematics to the study of physics (*Mathematicae in Physicus Utilitas*) and on the subject of experimental knowledge (*De Scientia Experimentali*).[129]

Aristotle was revived in the Christian West hundreds of years after the Church excommunicated those who took an interest in the natural sciences.[130] He was almost forgotten from the fourth century C.E.[131] until his rediscovery in West via the translation of his works into Arabic and his appropriation by the Muslim world.[132] After 1255,

126. See Schmitt (1983).
127. By translators such as William of Moerbeke (c. 1120–1286).
128. Around the year 1230, Johannes de Sacrobosco (c. 1175-c. 1256), a French friar, scholar, and astronomer, published his book *Tractatus de Sphaera* (On the Sphere of the World), based on Claudius Ptloemy's influential *Almagestum* (second century C.E.), which had been translated into Latin in 1175 and studied for about four hundred years at European universities. That the combination of occultism and astronomy was not well received is demonstrated by the case of Cecco d'Ascoli (1257–1327), a physician and encyclopedist who wrote a commentary on the book in which addressed the subject of demonology; he was subsequently accused of heresy and finally burned at the stake in Florence.

129. See Rossi (1968).
130. See Sorabji (1990). On Aristotle and magic see Thorndike (1964, Vol. 1, p. 139). In Clement of Alexandria, there are allusions to the exoteric and esoteric writings of Aristotle. See Jean Daniélou (1973, Vol. 2, pp. 130–135). He writes that "the Aristotle of the second century was the Aristotle of exoteric writing".

131. In his *Confessions*, Augustine writes that when he was twenty, he read Aristotle's *Ten Categories* and derived no benefit from it. Augustine (1961, pp. 87–88).

132. The main work that introduced Aristotle's natural philosophy to the West is *Kitāb alMudkhal al-Kabīr fī 'Ilm Aḥakām al-Nujūm* (The Book of the Great Introduction to the Science of Judgement of the Stars) by the Persian astronomer al-Balkhi (787–886); it was translated into Latin in 1133 by John of Seville under the title *Introductorium in Astronomiam*. See also: Burnet (2001); Dod (1982).

it was impossible to halt the spread of Aristotelian philosophy, though its reception by the Roman Catholic Church was attended by acute internal controversy and the Pope had forbidden the study of Aristotle during the early thirteenth-century.[133] When the ban was lifted in the middle of the century and the full corpus of Aristotle's writings was translated into Latin, his reputation became that of the consummate philosopher and source of authority; Dante, in his *Paradiso*, described him as "*Maestro di color che sanno*" (the Master of Those Who Know) and situated him in Limbo.[134] Paul and Tertullian's declarations that an abyss separated "Athens" (Greek philosophy) from "Jerusalem" were quenched. The cardinal question that arose was whether it was possible to close the gap between what was perceived as Aristotle's most egregious error—namely his view that the world had always existed—and belief in a Creator, in the theology of creation and revelation, in miracles, in the ascension of Jesus to Heaven, and even in magic and witchcraft. This was no simple tension to resolve; we have seen how Marlowe's *Faust* ultimately chooses to burn his books, while Goethe's Faust recants his belief in occultism, and his despair of philosophy and theology, in a return to "reason".[135]

***

Thomas Aquinas was the major figure in Western Christianity who combined "Aristotelianism" and the Christian conception of the world[136] to synthesize a Christianized version of Aristotelianism, or perhaps an Aristotlized Christianity.[137] In H. Tirosh-Rothschild's perceptive formulation, "Aquinas was confident that Aristotle could be shaped to fit Christian perspectives and purposes, and that he, Aquinas, could create and supply the metaphysical teaching to accomplish that transformation. And this, not in order to Christianize the pagan thinker, but rather because some of his theories were valid and true […] unlike Maimonides, who reduced faith to reason, Aquinas asserted that

---

133. In 1210, the authorities of the University of Paris, instructed by Pope Gregory IX, ordered the burning of translations of Aristotle's work on physics and mathematics, but by 1255, it was impossible to halt the spread of Aristotelian philosophy, and all of Aristotle's writings were now studied at the university. See Copleston (1959, pp. 232–238).

134. Dante Alighieri, *Divine Comedy*: *Purgatorio*, Canto IV:131. In Dante's *Convitio* (The Banquet) III.5, Aristotle is "that glorious philosopher to whom nature most laid open".

135. Faust, Goethe (1963, I:354–385). See Ohly (1992, pp. 103–121). Roger Bacon ("doctor mirabilis") wrote the *Epistle on the Marvelous Power of Art and of Nature and Concerning the Nullity of Magic* (c.1270).

136. Markus (1961).

137. Elior (2010).

a qualitative difference exists between faith and knowledge with faith supreme".[138] The reconciliation that he proposed encountered harsh opposition by the Franciscans and he was condemned,[139] but once he and "scientific" theology had prevailed, the Catholic Church regarded any criticism of Aquinas or his interpretation of Aristotle as heresy.[140] However, Aquinas scarcely quotes from the books of wisdom attributed to Solomon. Only as a literary protagonist, escorting Dante to the fourth heavenly sphere in the *Divine Comedy*, does he describe Solomon's wisdom like the wisdom of good governance as well as the wisdom to know that there are questions to which the human intellect has no answers.[141]

***

---

138. Tirosh-Rothschild (1991, pp. 114–115). See also: Ducos and Giacomotto-Charra (2011).The Philosoper Ernst Bloch (1885–1977) writes "As far as Thomas may have pushed the substantial harmonization of faith and Knowledge, he was still unable to escape the real religious and, above all, genuinely Christian paradox that had confronted Paul as the Wisdom of the World" (1 Corinthians 3:119). See E. Bloch (2019, p. 7).

139. Thomas was not the only one. The thirteenth-century Spanish, or Portuguese, scholar Petrus Hispanus (Peter of Spain), whose identity is a matter of controversy, wrote in the book *Tractatus* (later titled *Summulae Logicale*) that Aristotelian logic was *scientia scientiarum*, the foundation of all study and inquiry, a declaration that led to his condemnation by the bishop of Paris in 1277. Peter Damian (c.1107–1072\3), Benedictine monk, cardinal, and reformer, held that philosophy must exist in the service of theology, since logic was concerned only with the formal validity of arguments.

140. A book by the Italian philosopher Pietro Pomponazzi (1462–1525), *De immortalitate animae* (On the Immortality of the Soul), which criticized Aristotle and Aquinas's commentary, was burned in Venice; the author's life came under threat as well. Pomponazzi addressed the difference between Platonism (and Hermetism) and Aristotelianism: "The Platonic method of philosophizing by means of enigmas, metaphors and images, which Plato used very frequently, was condemned by Aristotle who completely rejected it". Quoted in Garin (1983, p. 105). Martin Luther described the Catholic church as "Thomist", i.e., Aristotelian. Philosophy, he writes, could not encompass the notion of trans-substantiation; hence, "the divine spirit is stronger than Aristotle". See Luther, *De captivitate Babylonica ecclesiae praeludium* (1520), Weimarer Ausgabe, VI: 497–573. Luther regarded Aquinas as a man leading Christianity on a false path, and believed it was no wonder that the Thomist theologians in Paris called him "the enemy of science and philosophy". In this context, it is quite ironic that Tommaso Campanella (1568–1639) defended Galileo by means of the legend that held that Pythagoras was of Jewish origin, or, alternatively, had studied the Mosaic law. Campanella, in other words, argued that Galileo was following in the footsteps of Moses and Pythagoras rather than those of Aristotle, and that he was correct in maintaining that the sun was central in the celestial system. In relying on Aristotle, the Church was in fact deviating from the holy scriptures. Campanella (1622 [1994]), pp. 1–34, 119–121).

141. Dante, *Divine Comedy*: *Paradiso*, Canto XIII:97–123.

> "*Aristotle—is the ultimate of humans, save*
> *For those who received the divine over flow*".
> - Maimonides, "Epistle to Samuel Ibn Tibbon", 1199[142]

The Aristotelian corpus first entered Jewish culture in the first half of the thirteenth century, initially in the south of France and in Italy, and not only via Maimonides' *Guide for the Perplexed*.[143] This new influence provoked a serious controversy between "Aristotelian" and "anti-Aristotelian" thinkers (the former dubbed Aristotle "the philosopher", while the latter termed him "the Greek"). The controversy led to a ban on his books, which were labeled "books of heresy" in the communities of France and Spain.[144]

The Jewish opposition to Aristotelianism was multifaceted.[145] Its most radical critics were Kabbalists who regarded the philosophy of the "Greek sages" in general as the work of Satan and as "forbidden wisdom"; they viewed Aristotle as the most dangerous representative of this defilement.[146] Thus, for example, the editor of R. Judah Hayyat's commentary on *Ma'arekhet ha'Elohut* (The System of Divinity) issued a stark condemnation:

> "We have also seen that the books of Aristotle and his pupils have spread far and wide and that many of our people are abandoning the study of Torah and hastening to study these theories, though they contain fallacious views and though they who follow them have deviated from the ways of faith and though they are contradictory in the main [...] And we say raze it, raze it to its foundation".[147]

The commentator and preacher Gedaliah ben Joseph (c. 1515–1587) went even further. He relates the legendary tradition according to which Aristotle read Solomon's books, that Aristotle had ultimately discovered that philosophy was a sinister realm, that those who believed in philosophy would perish, and that the Torah, in contrast, was the wellspring of life. If Aristotle could, he would have gathered all of his books and burned them; better to suffocate than to allow his philosophical work to be disseminated.[148] Judah ben Solomon al Ḥarizi (c.

---

142. In Kraemer (2008, p. 443).

143. Mavroudi (2015, pp. 28–59); Freudenthal (2013). The archetype of a Jewish magus, or polymath, emerged during the Renaissance under the influence of the image of the Renaissance Man. See Borchardt (1990). Also see Bianchi et al. (2016).

144. The first polemic lasted from 1232–1235 and the second from 1303–1306.

145. See Schwartz (2018).

146. Idel (1983a, pp. 185–266.).

147. The book was printed in Mantua, and cited in Bar-Levav (2011, p. 316).

148. Gedaliah ibn Yahya, *Sefer Shalshelet ha-Kabbala* (1578). By 1962 the book had been printed six times, most recently in Jerusalem in 1961. The words quoted appear in an appendix on the genealogy of the Jewish people that deals with the history of the nations among which the Jews have dwelled.

1165–1234\5), who translated the *Maxims of Philosophers* into Hebrew, wrote that in their first year of study, pupils should learn the moral teachings of Aristotle; only in the tenth and final year should they be taught his philosophy.[149] The book claims to impart the rules of moral conduct that Aristotle advised Alexander the Great to adopt and follow.[150] Alexander's mother is said to describe Aristotle not only as exceptionally wise but as a guide towards goodness—a teacher of moral values devoid of skepticism. The book *Sefer haTapuach* (*Risālat al-Tuffāḥa*; *Tractatus de pomo et morte incliti principis philosophorum*; *The Book of the Apple*) is a Hebrew-language translation of a text originally written in Arabic and attributed to Aristotle; its translator, Abraham Ibn Ḥasdai, explains that he chose to bring the words of that philosopher—that great sage and master of all sciences—to the Hebrew-language reader, as they would persuade skeptical Jews who did not believe in the afterlife of the soul. Aristotle, after all, confessed on his deathbed that he believed in the afterlife and the Creation *ex nihilo*.[151]

The influence of the "Aristotelian sciences" constitutes an important chapter in Jewish intellectual history due to its place in the chronicles of Jewish philosophy[152] and science.[153] The sciences were introduced into the Jewish intellectual milieu not only through Maimonides but also via translations of Aristotle to Arabic and

---

149. *Sefer Shalshelet ha-Kabbala*, Part I, Chapter 11. On Maxims see Chapter Eight.

150. The Book, ascribed to Aristotle, was edited in Persian and English by David Samuel Margoliouth, 1892.

151. Maimonides wrote in his epistle that the Book of Apple belongs to "the spurious works ascribed to Aristotle and it is a "drivel, inane and vapid". See Kraemer (2008, p. 443).

152. The entry on Aristotelianism in the *Otzar Israel* encyclopedia writes about "Aristotle's aggressive government towards the Jews of that time" and remarks that "from the time that Aristotle's views became known to the sages of Israel, a terrible revolution occurred in their ways of thinking and modes of study, and even in our own time we sometimes find signs of that influence in the books of rabbis and the 'researchers' who unthinkingly use their true source", Kraemer (2008, p. 213). The historian Heinrich Graetz (1817–1891) wrote: "Once the supremacy of Aristotelian philosophy was finally broken by English naturalism and by the boost which philosophy got from the Cartesian principle of 'I think, therefore I am', Judaism also had to search around for another principle. The Aristotelian-Maimonidean system could no longer satisfy". Graetz (1975, p. 119).

153. Their influence on Jewish culture in general was minimal. This is demonstrated by, among other things, a comparison between the dissemination of philosophic literature and that of various types of religious literature at the beginning of the age of print via the reading culture of the Jews in the duchies of Mantua. See Baruchson (1993). Esti Eisenmann points out that even those who opposed rationalism in the Middle Ages used Aristotelian philosophy to explain natural phenomena, or to prove its limitations in arriving at an understanding of the world. See Eisenmann (2015).

Hebrew and through the corpus of Hebrew-language books written under the influence of the Aristotelian and anti-Aristotelian corpora.[154] This latter group includes, among others, *Ruah Hen*, a basic book for the study of Aristotelian sciences that appeared anonymously in the second half of the thirteenth century, apparently in the south of France, and was read for [several] generations thereafter.[155] For Rabbi David Messer Leon (c. 1470–1526), Thomas Aquinas modeled the successful merger of faith and *studia humanitatis*, or a secular curriculum (he was not alone in his interest: in 1490, the Talmudist Jacob ben David Provençal wrote to R. David about the importance of secular studies, particularly medicine). Johanan Alemanno suggested a four-stage curriculum of study—with each stage lasting seven years—in which Aristotle played a major role. Students would study rhetoric based on his *Organon*, and natural science and divinity (metaphysics) based on "Aristotle's Books of Nature and Divinity".[156]

***

Aristotle, whose "rediscovery" in the Latin West in the thirteenth century and subsequent "canonization" were perceived as a distinct manifestation of Catholic Europe's exit from the "Dark Ages" and its restoration of reason,[157] had become by the seventeenth century[158] a figure of great authority, and the fact that he was now championed by the Catholic church[159] began to obstruct the development of the new sci-

---

154. On the corpus see Zonta (2011). Some of the literature on this subject is addressed in Sela (2003); Glasner (2011).

155. The history of the book, its contents, and its readers are the subject of a comprehensive doctoral thesis: Elior (2010). Elior suggests that the author may be Yaacov Anatoli, who lived during the thirteenth century and was the first to translate Ibn Rushd's commentaries on the Aristotelian corpus.

156. Idel (1979). Alemanno's division of the sciences into different spheres was also based on the Aristotelian division, and at least in one case—that of Abraham Ibn Ezra (1089–1164), the poet, biblical commentator, astronomer, and neo-Platonic philosopher—the division into seven was in keeping with Proverbs 9:1: "Wisdom has built her house, she has hewn out her seven pillars". See Wolfson (1925) (reprinted in Wolfson (1973, pp. 493–545).

157. A one-dimensional picture of this sort is suggested in Rubenstein (2003); and C. Freeman (2002).

158. During the Renaissance there were already those who rejected Aristotle's absolute authority in every domain and instead advocated empiricism and reason.

159. Martin Luther wrote that in the universities, "the only one who rules is the idolatrous teacher who is blinder than Jesus"; he suggested discontinuing the study of the literature on physics, metaphysics, and ethics, from which nothing could learned about the soul or mind. He claimed this because he himself had carefully read, and thoroughly understood, Aristotle. He was prepared to reconcile himself to the study of Aristotle's books on logic, rhetoric, and poetics, but without commentaries. Luther, "An den christlichen Adel deutscher Nation von des christlichen Standes Besserung"

ence. The emerging challenges to the validity of Aristotelian science did not escape the notice of contemporary Jewish thinkers, whose need for a legendary tradition about Solomon as the source of Aristotle's wisdom lessened but was not entirely extinguished. Importantly, there was no need for a new legendary tradition in which yet another ancient philosopher would take Aristotle's place. On the contrary, seventeenth-century Christian philosophers could found support in the words of *Wisdom of Solomon* that God "has disposed of all things in number, weight and measure".[160] Other indirect references to Solomon and his books are also found in the work of Galileo Galilei (1561–1642), who asserted that Moses and King Solomon—not Aristotle—"knew the constitution of the universe perfectly". Francis Bacon quoted Ecclesiastes on the importance of wisdom and learning, through which one might gain release from the dictatorship of the Aristotelians and advance beyond the Greek philosopher.

Francis Bacon, in his revolutionary essay *The Advancement of Learning* (1804) presents Solomon as a model of a king who encourages and establishes free science: "By virtue of which grant or donative of God Solomon became enabled not only to write those excellent parables or aphorisms concerning divine and moral philosophy but also to compile a natural history of all verdure [...] Nay, the same Salomon the king, although he excelled in the glory of treasure and magnificent buildings, of shipping, and navigation [...], yet he maketh no claim to any of those glories, but only to the glory of inquisition of truth".[161] In his *Nova Atlantis*, Bacon described an academy called "Salomon's House" which contained a portion of his writings. Bacon mentions only one such book by name: *Natural History*, which Solomon composed on the subject of flora and fauna, from the cedar in Lebanon to the hyssop on the wall and all that lives and creeps upon the earth—a book, in other words, about zoology and botany, which fields belonged under Bacon's classification scheme to the sphere of "natural philosophy."[162] Bacon's "Salomon's House" was a "research institute" engaged in empirical research in all spheres, and did not represent its activity as miraculous or supernatural.[163]

It is not my intent here to detail the controversy regarding

(1520), Weimarer Ausgabe VI: 404–469. Though Luther rejected Thomist Aristotelianism, Aristotle played an important role in the development of Lutheranism and in the curricula of German universities—largely through the influence of the Lutheran theologian and "humanist" Philipp Melanchthon (1497–1560).

160. Cited in Shapin (1998, p. 46).
161. F. Bacon (1974, p. 40).
162. In Bruce (1999, pp. 167, 175).
163. See Lomas (2002). Newton, for his part, believed that Solomon used ancient esoteric doctrine in planning the Temple.

occultism, Hermetism, and empirical science, nor the differences between them. Thorndike finds the difference in, among other things, the fact that occultism has nothing new to say, while science advances and innovates constantly without need to rely on ancient authorities. To reinforce this view, he cites Roger Bacon's observation that many things known in his time were not yet known to Plato or Aristotle, to Hippocrates or Galen. Another source of support is Peter of Spain, who wrote that while the ancients were philosophers, he and his contemporaries were experimenters.[164] One must add that it is important to distinguish between occultism and speculative science, or science based on false assumptions. That's still empirical science though. In any event, in general, a scientist is not obliged to seek a correlation between a scientific theory and a sacred or authoritative text.

To return to Solomon, views such as those expressed by Bacon were incapable of undermining believers' faith in *prisca sapientia*, since any new theories, scientific discoveries, and inventions had already been encoded in his books. Jewish scholars faced the dilemma of deciding whether to change the strategy of their claims and assert that the "new science" was already known to Solomon— but they preferred to attribute that knowledge to the Sages, or to deny its validity. For example, a Jewish physician from Mantua, Abraham Portaleone (d. 1612), claimed in his book *Shiltei hagibborim* (Shields of the Heroes) that many of the new scientific theories had already been known in the time of Solomon. The paradox underlying this kind of claim is that only once the new science had formulated these theories and invented these inventions was it possible to "discover" that Solomon had gotten there first. Claims such as Portaleone's served primarily to justify the contemporary engagement in scientific activity, rather than to argue that the sciences were known in ancient times.

Wisdom versus Wit

"*But, one thing comforts me,*
when that I consider and see
there is so great a company,
me to sustain in my folly
of folks that to fore have be
of wonder great authority
as was King Solomon, and Virgil of great renown,
Cyprian, and Abelard,
And many another in this art"
    - Guillaume de Deguileville, *Pilgrimage of the Life of Man*,
       18729–18738

---

164. Thorndike (1964, Vol. 2, p. 979).

During the 16th century, numerous "Solomon plays" in which Solomon serves as a model of a perfect ruler were written in Germany. Among them are Baumgart's *Juditium Solomonis* (1561), and Sixtus Birck's (1501–1554) tragicomic play *Sapientia Solomonis* (The Wisdom of Solomon, Basel, 1547)[165] in which the eponymous king is described as "righteous, wise, knowledgeable, rich, and powerful (*"pius, sapiens, cortatus, dives est potensque"*), his wisdom unsurpassed by any other (*"quo nullus est sapientior"*). He earned his fame because of his reputation for wisdom. God sent Wisdom to be his life companion and to guide him, and she brought with her two companions: "Justice, Joined in sure alliance with Peace". The play was performed (in English) by the boys of Westminster School before Queen Elizabeth in January 1565/6.[166] The "lesson" the Queen was supposed to learn from Solomon's example was how a king should act:

> "Heavenly King, who rules magnificently by Thy virtue, who wieldest the scepters of justice, give sovereignty to the King; give him the government of the state an inviolable justice so that he may rule the people with fair laws; that he, as protector, may set free the good by justice and restrain the guilty by rigid law; that he may give charitable aid to those miserably effected [....] The king, just judge of the wretched, the distressed, judge of the poor, righteous judge of the needy, the King, Solomon, will give laws for the pious. The King will resolve any quarrel among fierce adversaries. There shall be no room from oppression in this King".[167]

---

165. Adapted to the stage by Hermann Kirscher of Marburg in 1591. See Beam (1920).

166. Payne (1938). In Friedrich Gottlieb Klopstock's play *Salomo* (1764), Solomon's wisdom is described as "boatful (*"verstiegene Weisheit"*). In Paul Heyse's play *Die Weisheit Solomons* (Berlin, 1896), Solomon acknowledged the love of Sulamit (from Song of Songs) for the shepherd Hadad, proclaiming that "the beginning of all knowledge is man's joy at the joy of others".

167. Paul Heyse, *Die Weisheit Solomons*, Act III, Scene viii, 95–96. In the epilogue, Solomon is "*Regis typus sapientis* "(the model of wise king): "he was pious and wholly dedicated to God. While he was serving Him faithfully and making a sacrifice, holy and sweet to the nostrils of God, he obtained his wish from heaven. Solomon sought wisdom alone; he achieved it. At the same time peace was given to him, and justice. He did not lack the bright ornaments of modesty. He knew /how to temper with mercy....", 128/129.

Fig. 3 King Salomon and Marcolphus © Wikimedia Commons

Solomon's wisdom was a frequent subject in popular literary works. The *Dialogus Solomonis et Marcolfi*, the first version of which appeared in the tenth century, exemplifies the trend: it is a parodic work[168] in which King Solomon and a peasant called Marcolfus (Marcolf),[169] who is no fool, engage in a comedic battle of verbal wit;[170] Marcolf's wit ultimately triumphs over Solomon's wisdom. In one version, Solomon describes himself as a lover of wisdom—*prudenciam semper amo*—exclaiming to Marcolf, "Your words are boorish, but mine are of wise men". To which Marcolf, who describes himself as "a trickster, base, defective, ignorant", replies, "You speak like a wise man, I speak like a man mocking. Wise men praise you, [the] unwise follow me".[171] In any event, Solomon's wisdom emerges intact and is actually enriched by the challenge Marcolf poses to it.[172] The story was adapted by the German mastersinger, poet, play writer (and shoemaker) Hans Sachs (1494–1576) and by Hans Folz (c. 1437–1513), both residents of Nuremberg. Sachs's version, *Fassnacht-Spiel—mit 4 Personen zu agiern: Von Joseph und Melisso, auch König Salomon* is about two residents who complain about their troubles and decide to seek Solomon's advice. The king advises the rich and unpopular one to seek love, and the other to beat his wife. In the interim, Solomon exchanges words with Marcolf and boasts of his books, achievements, and wis-

168. Bayless (1996).
169. The predecessor of the character Till Eulenspiegel, 1510–11, apparently based on earlier traditions. Luther refers to Marcolf as "Markolf the mocking bird".
170. On the book and its various incarnations, see Ziolkowski (2008); Paquet (1924); Duff (1892). In *Gargantua and Pantagruel*, Solomon is quoted as saying that "The man who ventures nothing wins neither horse nor mule", to which Marcolf (Malcon) replies: "The man who ventures too much loses both horse and mule". Rabelais (1976, p. 112). A modern version of that dialogue is also found in Paquet (1924).
171. Ziolkowski (2008, p. 286). See also: Bose (1996, pp. 193–197); Zemon Davis (1975, pp. 227–267).
172. Griese (2017), "Eine Autorität gerät ins Wanken: Markolfs Worte und Taten gegen Salomon in der Literatur des Mittelalter und der Frühen Neuzeit", in *Die Bibel in der Kunst* (BiKu), 2017; Payne (1938, pp. 30–39).

dom. Folz, in contrast, used the plot of his *Schwankhandlung, Fastnachtspiel Salomon und Markolf* to have Solomon voice doubts about the honesty of the Kaiser Maximillian I; his Marcolf represented the tension between the city and the village.[173] *The Dialogue of Salomon and Saturn* in Old English, which dates from the tenth or eleventh century, is an enigmatic dialogue between Solomon and a Chaldean prince who represents heathen wisdom. Here, I will only bring a few examples of the English text:

Solomon says: "in the embrace of flames \ most greedily bubbleth. \ Therefore hath the canticle \ over all Christ's books \ the greatest repute: \ it teacheth the scriptures, \ with voice it directeth, \ and its place it holdeth, \ heaven-kingdom's \ arms it wieldeth". Saturn says, "I will give thee all, / O Son of David, / King of Israel, / thirty pounds / of coined gold / and my twelve sons, / if thou wilt [will] bring me / that I may be touched, / through the word of the canticle, \ by Christ's lime[…]". To which Solomon answers, "Wretched is he on earth / useless in life, / devoid of wisdom, / like the neat he wandereth / that move over the plain, / the witless cattle,\ who through the canticle cannot / honour Christ." Later Saturn asks: "But how many shapes will the devil and Pater Noster taken when they are counted together?" "Thirty shapes," Solomon replies, and describes them at length.[174]

---

173. See Dietl (2001); Paquet (1924); Folz, Hans: *Das Spiel von dem König Salomon und dem Bauern Markolf*.

174. The quotations are from the translation by Kemble (1848). He writes that "it can hardly excite our surprise, when we find at time a most solemn and serious piece of mystical theosophy reappearing in another form of a coarse but humorous parody" (3). See also Anlezark (2009); Powell (2005).

Chapter Eight: Solomon, *Aristoteles Judaicus*, and the Invention of a Pseudo-Solomonic Library[1]

As the thirteenth century saw the rise of Aristotle as a new contender for the role of "the wisest, most learned man of all times, the very personification of all knowledge", Jewish scholars were faced with a new challenge: how to grapple with Aristotelian rationalist philosophy. One option was to declare it irrelevant, and present Judaism and Aristotelian philosophy as diametrically opposed; another option was to co-opt Aristotelian philosophy by depicting Aristotle as Solomon's pupil. The result of this latter approach was the emergence of a legendary tradition whose purpose was to legitimize Jews' study of philosophy, in general, and the influence of Aristotle, in particular.

What developed was in many ways a continuation of traditions dating from the Hellenistic and Roman periods. But Jewish-Hellenistic writers,[2] and later the Church Fathers, were concerned with the influence of the Jewish patriarchs, Moses, and the biblical prophets on the development of Egyptian and Greek wisdom—particularly that of Plato and Pythagoras. The new legendary tradition that emerged in medieval Jewish apologetics, on the margins of existing polemics between "Aristotelians" and "anti-Aristotelians", claimed in contrast that Jewish "wisdom", or Jewish "philosophy", had been appropriated specifically by Aristotle. Not only was Solomon, then, the wisest of all ancients, a teacher to kings who arrived from all four corners of the earth to hear him; he was also a teacher to that "greatest of all

---

1. See Shavit (2006); Melamed (2010). Melamed's work is an extremely comprehensive study on the subject, and I have learned a great deal from it.

2. Only Aristobulus (second century B.C.E.) was familiar with Aristotle (perhaps his *On Philosophy*). See A. Yarbro Collins (1985, p. 837).

philosophers," Aristotle, whose teachings, in turn, informed the Christian scholastics.[3] Seen through this lens, Aristotelian philosophy was no "Greek wisdom" extrinsic to Judaism, but rather a continuation of Jewish wisdom whose original form had been lost in the throes of history, only to be preserved in Greek garb. Its renewed reception into the bosom of Jewish culture was thus the restoration of what was lost to its former glory and rightful owner. Solomon was chosen for the role of Aristotle's teacher since no ancient figure in Jewish history more famous than he could better represent lost wisdom. And since Aristotle dealt not only in philosophy but in all spheres of knowledge, Solomon was the sole biblical figure whose intellectual scope could be considered comparable. This legendary tradition was born of necessity; it would not have emerged or appeared in so many texts had their authors not felt the need to legitimize their own engagement in theology, philosophy, and science, and to legitimize Aristotle.

This was a strategy of legitimizing cultural borrowing, in which an ancient figure of authority is invoked to make permissible the intercultural influence so widespread in the cultures of the ancient East as well as in Christianity and Islam. It sought to reframe such borrowing by claiming that Jewish culture was not only the source of all wisdom but also encompassed the whole of it, and hence no source was truly external. In the context of Solomon, according to this legendary tradition, not only was Aristotle Solomon's pupil, but it was Solomon's wisdom that led to Jesus' salvation.

This claim to universal scope is expressed in Judah Halevi's (1075–1141) book The Kuzari (*Kitāb al-Khazarī*):

> "And what is the opinion of Solomon's accomplishments? Did he not, with the assistance of divine intellectual and natural power, converse on all sciences? The inhabitants of all the earth travelled to him, in order to carry forth his learning, even as far as India. Now the roots and principles of all sciences were handed down from us first to the Chaldeans then to the Persians and Medians, then to Greece, and finally to the Romans. On the account of the length of this period and the many disturbing circumstances, it was forgotten that they had originated with the Hebrews, and so they were ascribed to the Greeks and Romans. To the Hebrews, however, belongs the first place as regards the nature and the languages and as to the fullness of meaning".[4]

---

3. Roth (1978).

4. II, 66. Trans. from the Arabic by Hartwig Hirschfeld, (Halevi 1905, p. 124). Elijah Hayyim ben Benjamin of Genazzano, a physician, theologian, and Kabbalist of the first half of the sixteenth century, suggested a different chain of transmission. There, the source for the idea of reincarnation was Abraham; the Chaldeans received it from him, and from them it passed to the Egyptians, the Persians, and the Indians. See Ogren (2009).

The idea that Solomon's wisdom was the source—direct or indirect—of some part of Greek wisdom appears even earlier in an introduction by the tenth-century Karaite scholar Yacob Qirqisani to the Book of Genesis. Therein he claimed that Solomon, the wisest of all, possessed what was known as "natural knowledge", which the Greek philosophers acquired from him (the Jewish sages too, he maintained, employed rationalist philosophical methods).[5]

The Arab tradition faced the same need for legendary legitimization when it came to translating Aristotle's writings into Arabic. *Kitāb al-Fihrist* (The Catalog) by Ibn al-Nadīm relates the tale of a dream dreamt by the Caliph al-Ma'mūn;[6] according to the story, Aristotle appeared in the dream and answered all the caliph's questions to his satisfaction. This granted him the approval for that interaction, al-Ma'mūn sent a delegation to Constantinople which returned to Baghdad with a convoy of camels laden with books.[7] This was a legendary tale that emerged against the background of a project of translation from Greek (as well as Persian and Indian) literature into Arabic, which began in the ninth and tenth centuries. It was, thus, a legendary appendage to the reality of the transmission of Greek philosophical literature from Alexandria to Baghdad. This transmission was at first mediated by the translation efforts of Syriac-speaking Nestorian and Monophysite Christians in Aleppo and Edessa; after the

---

5. Hirschfeld (1918, pp. 39–47). I am grateful to Prof. Yoram Erder for bringing this work to my attention.

6. The *Fihrist* was compiled in 987; Caliph al-Ma'mūn reigned from 813–833.

7. Ibn Abī Ya'qūb al-Nadīm (1970, Vol. 1, pp. 483–484); F. Rosenthal (1994, pp. 48–49). The Abbasid Caliph al-Manṣūr (755–759) asked the Emperor of Byzantium to send him books of mathematics; he was sent Euclid and several works on physics. His heir, al-Ma'mūn, would later bring translators to Byzantium to translate scientific literature into Arabic. According to another source, the Byzantine emperor opposed giving manuscripts to the Caliphate; only when alMa'mūn threatened to limit the religious freedom of the Christians under his rule was he forced to agree. Ibn Khaldūn wrote that al-Ma'mūn had a strong interest in science, and the collection he sent to Baghdad and its translation enabled Muslim scholars to devote themselves to the sciences and to excel therein. While they "might have been opposed to many of the views of the first and foremost teacher [*al-mu'allim al-awwal*] Aristotle," they regarded him as "the supreme authority insofar as the acceptance or rejection of a view was concerned, due to his great fame." In the *Muqaddimah*, Ibn Khaldūn (1958) writes: "The sciences of only one nation, the Greek, have come down to us, because they were translated through al-Ma'mūn's efforts", (*The Muqaddimah*, vii:18; Vol. 3, pp. 115–116, 328–330). According to al-Maqrīzī's *The Topography of Cairo* (*Kitāb al-Mawā'iẓ wa-l-I'tibār fī Dhikr al-Khiṭaṭ wa-l-Āthār*, 254), in 1070 al-Muntaẓir sold thousands of books from the Fatimid library in Cairo in order to pay the wages of his soldiers, and the books were borne to their destination on twenty-five camels. See el-Abbadi (1993, pp. 172–178); Abbou-Hershkovitz (2006). The prolific translator Ibn al-Baṭrīq wrote of having visited, as part of his search for materials, all the temples in which the philosophers placed had their books.

Orthodox bishop put an end to this work in 489, the translation efforts moved to Nisibis in south-east Anatolia and Jundishapur in north-west Persia,[8] mediated by the translations and exegetic work of the Sabians in Haran (today in southern Turkey). This translational activity was organized by the Abbasid caliphs themselves, who aspired to make Baghdad a cultural center that would inherit and build upon the legacy of Hellenistic Alexandria. For this purpose, the caliphs established a library and academy (*Bayt al-Ḥikma*) in their new capital and encouraged the project of translation into Arabic; such translations became widely available for sale in Baghdad.[9] Constantinople was not the sole source of the Greek-Hellenistic literature brought to Baghdad; it also arrived from Damascus, Alexandria, and other cities. Works by Aristotle were paramount in this translation project, and a large part of the Aristotelian corpus was translated as well as Aristotle's biographies (several works by Plato were also translated).[10] Nonetheless, the mythical tradition created to justify such borrowing was relatively marginal, since the Muslim culture of the time did not object in principle to the reception of "alien wisdom" in the way that Jewish culture did.

Jewish depictions linked Aristotle and Solomon (as well as "Solomon's library") because Aristotle represented the alien "Greek wisdom," and the legendary tradition, as we have seen, emerged as internal apologetics, namely, as an argument against the anti-Aristotelians, who described Aristotle as "the worst of the apostates, may his name be blotted out",[11] "an unbridled misguided philosopher" who disseminated "deviant theories", and similar derogatory expressions. This Jewish tradition regarding Aristotle, which developed gradually and in with a great deal of variety, is evident in many texts; below are few examples.[12]

---

8. Qadir (1991, pp. 31–34); Macy (1989).

9. On Muslim translational activity, the center in Baghdad, the libraries there, and the scope of the Aristotelian corpus in Arabic, see Lameer (1991); Daiber (1997, pp. 29–43); van Koningsveld (1998); Pinto (1929); Kraemer (1992); Mackensen (1932); Montgomery (2000, pp. 65–88); Moller (2019, pp. 59–98).

On the Harran Sabians and their translation activity, see Erder (1981, pp. 54–68); Stroumsa (1999). According to a Sabian tradition, their prophets were Pythagoras and Solon. Sabian literature was itself influenced mainly by neo-Platonic literature.

10. Peters (1968a, 1968b); Mavroudi (2015). See Chapter Seven.

11. Nachmanides (1962, p. 172).

12. For detailed, albeit incomplete, surveys, see Santer (1901); Zinberg (1960, pp. 394–398); Halevi Madlinger (1893, pp. 71–76); Eisenstein (1903, pp. 206–216); Rappel (1990, pp. 46–66); Fuss (1994). Micha Yosef Berdichevsky combined the contents of *Shevilei emunah*, *Shalshelet hakabalah*, and *Sefer hadorot* into one story; see Bin-Gorion (1952, pp. 162–163). The full description of the legendary tradition appears in Melamed (2010).

R. Abraham bar Ḥiyya wrote in the twelfth century that "all the scholars of the gentiles who are well-versed in the sciences learned that wisdom from our sages",[13] and Abraham Ibn Ezra (1089–1164) wrote that Hebrew science predated Greek science and had been pillaged by the Greeks;[14] neither, however, associated the transfer of knowledge with Aristotle. On the other hand R. Shem Tov ben Joseph ibn Falaquera (1225?-1290?) linked a second-century astronomer and mathematician, Claudius Ptolemy, to Solomon, and wrote in *Sefer haMa'alot* (The Book of Degrees) that "it is a well-known fact that in the days of Solomon people came from all four corners of the globe to hear his wisdom, as is written (1 Kings 10:24) and the whole land sought after Solomon and each who heard his speech or his name would write it in his own language as every nation copies that which it finds from the wisdoms of others, just as the Greeks copied all the books of the wisdoms into their language. And Claudius Ptolemy recalled that he sent to the priests in Jerusalem who would copy for him in his own language the books of wisdom that there were. And it is impossible that Solomon, may he rest in peace, did not write books of natural science and of divinity, but those books were lost in the Exile".[15]

In *Shevilei Emunah* (Paths of Faith), printed in Trento in 1518 (and published in several editions), R. Meir ben Isaac Aldabi (c.1310–1360) was probably the first to connect Solomon and Solomon's library to Aristotle: "And I found it written that Aristotle the Greek, who is followed by all the men of science, who draw upon his books, and who was the teacher of Alexander the Great who shook the whole world [...] when Alexander conquered Jerusalem, he took the treasure of Solomon for his teacher Aristotle; then Aristotle studied and interpreted all the books of Solomon and copied them in his own name and added to them his own errors, upon which he hid the books of Solomon[16] to cause the world to believe that Aristotle himself wrote

---

13. R. Abraham bar Hiyya, *Sefer ha'ibur* (Book of Intercalation), ed. Zvi Philipovski, London, 1851 (the first version of the book was printed in Verona in 1146), p. 73. On the identification of King Ptolemy Philadelphus with Claudius Ptolemy, see Sela (2003, p. 48).

14. See Sela (2003, pp. 304–313). Ibn Ezra adds an imaginary biographical story, which also appears in another version in the writings of the chronicler al-Bīrūnī, who assigned a Jewish sage the position of translator from Hindi to Arabic. The Caliph chose a Jew for this purpose not only because he knew both languages, but also because he was perceived as a "neutral" mediator who could serve as a kind of "inspector" and would also discern whether knowledge acquired from an Indian book might lead to heresy.

15. Falaquera (1894, p. 12). And see Malter (1910).

16. The source may be the *Book of Maccabees* 2 (2: 13–15): "The same things also were reported in the writings and commentaries of Nehemiah; and how he found

them of his own judgment".[17]

Aldabi, who relied on a source he left unnamed, composed his book in Jerusalem, where he died; perhaps it was for this reason that he felt the need to write of a library in Jerusalem, the seat of kings and home to a great Temple. The book devotes no consideration to the question of how Solomon's books (beyond those the Bible attributed to him) might have survived, or how Solomon's library (or the library of the First Temple) might have withstood the latter's destruction and the exile to Babylonia, and come to be found by Alexander in Jerusalem. In describing how "Aristotle studied and interpreted all the books of Solomon and copied them in his own name", Aldabi described the transfer, or translation, of a corpus of books representing the entirety of Jewish wisdom, from which Greek scholars would study: "these are the real words dispersed throughout the books of the foremost scholars". Aldabi also wrote that the Greeks added "many things from their lies that contradict the words of our sages, may their memories be blessed, since in what they did not learn from them they could not themselves arrive at the truth." What was true in Greek philosophy was what was borrowed from the wisdom of the Jewish people, all collected in Solomon's library. In Aldabi's worldview, it did not suffice to describe the "wisdom of Solomon" in general terms; rather, there was a need for a physical library to exist containing all the books written by Solomon—a complete corpus dealing with philosophy, metaphysics, and every natural science.

The Jewish legendary tradition about Aristotle and Solomon's library flourished in Spain, Provence, and Italy, and would reappear in quite a few works, some of them anonymous. Several claim that Aristotle received Solomon's wisdom by oral transmission, but, in the majority, he is described as having acquired it from Solomon's library.

Abraham ben Shem Tov Bibago, who lived in Spain in the fifteenth century and composed commentaries on Aristotle (including an exegesis on the *Posterior Analytics*, 1446), wrote in the third section of his book *Derekh ha'Emunah*[18] that the fame of Solomon's wisdom was widespread, his lost books having traveled broadly over time and been translated into the languages of other nations. Thus, he

---

a library that gathered together the acts of the kings, and the prophets, and of David, and the epistles of the kings concerning the holy gifts." Judah did the same, and "gathered together all those things that were lost by reason of the war we had" (the reference here is probably to several of the books of the Bible). On the question of whether there existed a library in the Second Temple, or whether a collection of books was preserved there and, if so, what it contained, see Haran (1994); Klijn (1977).

17. Ibn Aldaby (1988, p. 352). The book was written in 1440 and printed in Constantinople in 1552.

18. *Derekh ha'Emunah* (The Way of Faith), Bibago (1987, p. 56).

reasoned, "these are human, not Greek, wisdoms"—a useful distinction for a Jewish scholar who adhered to distinctly Aristotelian views. Like his predecessors, Bibago explained that all of these numerous wisdoms "which belong in our nation" had been lost in the darkness of exile. Bibago purported to quote Eusebius (whose work was translated into Latin in the fifteenth century, and who himself quotes Clearchus of Soli): "Most philosophy came to us [the Greeks] from the wise Aristotle, and if you wish I can tell you how it came to us and how we heard it from his lips". In this telling Aristotle was "a Jewish man from the seed of Israel, a Jerusalemite from the sons of Koliah, the tribe of Benjamin. He came to us from the distant islands in Asia and descended from the mountains and sat with us for many days. He studied our philosophy, and brought to us a greater philosophy of his own which we studied from him".[19]

The physician and philosopher Gedaliah Ibn Yaḥya ben Joseph (c. 1515–1587) added in his book *Sefer Shalshelet ha-Kabalah* (The Chain of Tradition), a Kabbalistic work, that not only Aristotle but many other scholars of Athens studied under Jewish sages in Jerusalem and elsewhere; Plato, for example, was Jeremiah's student. From the introduction to Bibago's commentary on the *Posterior Analytics*, Ibn Yahia learned that Aristotle had recanted his view of a pre-existing world and become a "convert." This new understanding, Aristotle wrote to Alexander, was courtesy of one of the wise Jews (Simeon the Just), who proved to him the futility of his philosophical concept of an "ancient, pre-existing world". Enlightened, Aristotle burned all his books, "since those who adhere to the Torah will walk through life by its light, while the adherents of philosophy will fall into the abyss of hell".[20] In other words, Ibn Yahya believed that truth was achieved not through rational inquiry, but only through divine revelation. He claimed to have learned of Aristotle's late conversion from an "old book" according to which the learned Don Abraham Ibn Zarzar had heard the story in Lisbon from an "Ishmaelite [Arab] sage", who in turn had seen a work in Cairo by Aristotle in which the latter retracted all his pronouncements regarding providence and the immortality of the soul. The source of this story was probably a book by the Muslim scholar Ibn Rushd (Averroes), *The Incoherence of the Incoherence* (Tahāfut al-Tahāfut, 1180), itself a response to Ibn al-Ghazālī's *The Incoherence of the Philosophers* (Tahāfut al-Falāsifa).[21]

---

19. Bibago (1987, pp. 195–198). See Wirszubski (1963, Appendix VI, pp. 72–75).

20. Ibn Yahya (1957, pp. 83–84). Over a period of two hundred years the book was printed four times, and a further dozen in the nineteenth century.

21. See Qadir (1991, pp. 31–69). The first part of al-Ghazālī's book, which was

This story recurs in different versions and texts, including *Sefer haMusar* (The Book of Moral Instruction) by the biblical exegete, philosopher, and grammarian Joseph ibn Kaspi (1280–1345); *Magen Avot* (Shield of the Faith) by the physician and scholar R. Simeon ben Ẓemaḥ Duran (1361–1444); Judah Abrabanel's (c.1465-c.1523) *Dialogi d'Amore* (Vikuah al Ahavah, Dialogues on Love); *Minhat Kana'ut* (Offering of Jealousy) by Yeḥiel of Pisa (1507–1574);[22] *Nefutzot Yehudah* (The Dispersed of Judah) by Judah Moscato (c. 1530–1589); *Kissot le-Beit David* (Chairs for the House of David) by R. Judah Asahel ben Eliezer Del Bene (1615–1678); and others.[23] Some of these stories are the source for Isaac Cardoso's (1603\4–1683) *Las excelencias de los hebreos* (Excellences of the Hebrews, Amsterdam 1679), in which Pythagoras, Plato, and other Athenian philosophers visit Egypt, Phoenicia, and Babylonia, learning on their journey of the wisdom of the Jews. (The book also relates that Aristotle arrived at the true understanding of things following a conversation with a "Jewish sage.") As a source for the story that Aristotle converted to Judaism late in life, Cardoso cites a work by the French Orientalist Jacques Gaffarel (1601–1681) and by the Italian philosopher Fortunio Liceti (1577–1657), *De Pietate Aristotelis erga Deum et homines*.[24] Both, in turn, acquired the story from a Jewish source, according to which Aristotle read the Jewish holy scriptures and was deeply influenced by them.[25]

There were scholars, however, who dismissed these traditions. Modena, for example, called them foolish; Azariah dei Rossi (1513–1578), in his *Sefer me'Or Einayim* (The Light of the Eyes), was similarly scornful. But this did not prevent their continued use in the coming generations. Among those who repeated the stories were R. Moses Isserles (referred to as Rema, 1520–1572), an eminent rabbi, posek (halakhic authority), and scholar in Poland, who wrote on the subject in his book *Torat ha'Olah* (On the Burnt Offerings, Prague, 1550).[26]

translated into Hebrew in the fourteenth century by Moshe Narboni, was also translated into Russian; one translation states that Aristotle learned from Zerubbabel, and from the prophets Ezra and Malachi.

22. Yeḥiel of Pisa was a banker and scholar who copied Ibn Rushd's translation of Aristotle's Metaphysics.

23. Three versions appear under the entry for Aristotle in *Bibliotheca magna rabbinica* by Giulio Bartolocci (1613–1687), who worked in the Vatican library.

24. Cardoso (1971, p. 36). See there, notes by the editor, 30, 31. See more on the claims of a Jewish source for Greek philosophy in Bonfil (1994, pp. 128–135).

25. See Del Soldato (2017).

26. Chapter 11 in Isserles (1854, pp. 39–50). R. Isserles, who studied philosophy and science, relied on *Sefer Ehad Yashan* and *Shevilei Emunah*, writing that Socrates had learned wisdom from Assaf and Ahitophel, while Aristotle derived his teachings

R. Jehiel Heilprin (1660–1745) repeats in his book *Seder haDorot* (The Book of Generations) the claims of Judah Halevi and added to them R. Meir Aldabi's account in *Shevilei Emunah* and Bibago's in *Derekh ha'Emunah*; Meier Eliezer Rapaport-Hartstein, in the introduction to his book *Sefer Chakhmei Yavano Divrei Chakhamim* (The Book of Greek Wisdom or the Words of Wise Men, Munkacs, 1905);[27] Isaac Baer Levinsohn[28] (1788–1860); and others.[29] He writes that it is written in *Shevilei Emunah*: when Alexander conquered Jerusalem,

from Solomon but added to Solomon's wisdom several "bad ideas" in order to conceal his theft: "the fundamental ideas of Aristotle were stolen from the wisdom of Solomon, of blessed memory. When Alexander of Macedonia conquered Jerusalem, he put Aristotle, his teacher, in charge of Solomon's library, and the latter put his name on all the good things he found there, and he added some bad ideas such as the eternity of the world" (trans. Fuss 1994, p. 109).

27. He also adds that "there are some among the first who wanted to find in Galen's book R. Gamliel's book of medicine", but also that many of the sages "abused and cursed Aristotle".

28. In Chapter 27 of his book *Teudah be'Yisrael* (1828 [1977 ed.]), Levinsohn repeats this tradition and adds earlier legendary traditions about Socrates who learned about the Creator of the world from Ahitophel and Assaf; about Plato who learned from the prophet Jeremiah; and about Aristotle who learned from Simeon the Just (1828, pp. 25–27).

29. The maskil Judah Leib ben Ze'ev (1784–1811) included in his popular reader *Beit haSefer*, Vol. II: *Mesilat halimud* (Vienna, 1820, 6th printing) sayings by Aristotle and episodes from his life and did not forget to mention the philosopher's "debt" to the Jews. "It was said of him that he spent many days in the company of a great sage, one of the wise men of the Jews, who taught him the wisdom of Egypt (the Kabbala) and their religion (and Jewish writers throughout the generations have told us that the name of the wise man is Simeon the Just, a great priest at the start of the construction of the Second Temple). Know now that two of the greatest wise men in the sciences, the most luminous among the sages of Greece, Plato and Aristotle, praised by the nations, learned their wisdom from the sages of Israel… and now this great, illustrious nation, where, where are they?" Of Aristotle's influence he writes that "Aristotle's fame spread throughout the land and his memory passed down through the generations, and his glory was known also in far-off isles, which possessed no books other than the books of their religion, and the ancient Ishmaelites [Muslims] studied his books that were in Hebrew, and the Persians in their language with Arabic commentaries, and to this very day his books are circulated and known to all. People followed him blindly, attentive to his every word, and Maimonides admired him greatly, and Moses Mendelsohn as well, so much so that they adhered to all of his teaching as if the Almighty had not given them eyes to see other than Aristotle, and no heart to know anything other than the son of Nicomachus". Ludwig Philippson (1875–1876) wrote a series of articles entitled "Moses und Aristoteles" in *Allgemeine Zeitung des Judenthums*, in which he compared Aristotle's political philosophy with Moses' Torah. While expressing his esteem for Aristotle, Philippson wrote that his philosophy was suitable for its time but that the Torah of Moses was universal, human, and atemporal. Considering the many testimonies about the way Aristotelianism penetrated the Jewish intellectual world, and the "rationalist" legitimization it received from the legendary tales, it is hard to accept Halbertal's view that the gate to Aristotelianism was esoterism. Halbertal (2007).

he took over the books of Solomon for his teacher Aristotle, and Aristotle copied philosophy from them and gave them his own name, and he was tongue-tied".[30] He quotes Yehudah Halevi as well as the story of Aristotle's conversion and the claim that in the latter's final book, Metaphysics,[31] he disavowed all his previous conclusions, writing late in life that if he could, he would have burned all the copies of the books he had written, though they be as numerous as the sand on the beaches: "And I would [rather] choose the strangulation of my soul than for my books to be widely distributed. For those that cling to the Torah go to light with the light of life. And those that cling to philosophy go to the pit of destruction [i. e., the grave] ... And even I am prepared to be punished". Aristotle, Heilprin claimed, wrote to Alexander the Great that God had opened his eyes: "He drew me out of this foolishness in which I was immersed all the days of my life in dealing with the teachings of philosophy... And therefore, my dear student—Alexander, my great king—do not put forward my works [for others to study]—neither you nor my fellow philosophers."[32]

---

30. Heilprin (1769, pp. 135–137). The book was printed a second time in Lwow in 1858 and a third time in Warsaw in 1878.

31. The book was translated into Hebrew for the first time in 1485 from a mediating translation in Latin. On translations of Aristotle in the Middle Ages, see Wolf (1715–1733, pp. 217–223); Steinschneider (1893).

32. A similar legend was told about Maimonides, namely that at the end of his life he cast aside Aristotelianism and turned to the Kabbala. See Scholem (1935). A tale about Aristotle and his student in medicine, Maimonides, had a long life. It relates that Aristotle told Maimonides that he could create a man who would live forever. They cast lots, and it was Maimonides' fate to be torn to bits, his limbs cut up and placed into a glass container. But Maimonides did not fulfill his part of the agreement; he did not allow Aristotle to be resurrected for fear that people would be misled by him and think him a god. The *maskil* Abraham Baer Gottlober (1810–1889) wrote that he heard the tale, like many others, from teachers, and regarded that as proof that they were filling their students' minds with "endless fantasies and nonsense" (A. B. Gottlober 1976).On the various sources and versions of the story, which apparently originated in the Middle Ages under the influence of legends about the Roman poet Virgil the Sorcerer, in popular and Yiddish pamphlets, see Yeshayahu Berger, "Maimonides in Folk Legends" *Masad—Maasef leDivrei Sifrut*, Tel Aviv, 1936. According to Berger's version, Maimonides' pupils suggested that he place a rooster in his home and tease it. He did as they suggested, and the rooster broke the glass case that held Aristotle's body parts. On Virgil's legends, see Comparetti (1895, pp. 326–327). In *maskilic* literature, Aristotle's name symbolizes a worldview opposed to Judaism. In *Divrei Shalom ve'Emet* (Berlin 1782–85, Vienna, 1826), Naphtali Herz Wessely wrote that Aristotle's metaphysics was based on "spiderwebs" and "emptiness", but that the fact that here and there "Aristotelian views" found their way into books on nature, and led to heresy, was not a reason to reject the views that originated in Jerusalem; these were universal views and no nation in the world existed in which these wisdoms were not employed (pg. 22–26). There was thus no all-encompassing prohibition against the study of the theory of nature or philosophy. In the nineteenth century, Mendele Mocher Seforim also wrote about Aristotle as a source of authority in his

This legendary tradition depicted Aristotle, rather than Plato, as the Greek philosopher who drew his doctrine from Jewish wellsprings. It was woven from five sources conjoined, in the context of Jewish intellectual history during the Middle Ages and the Renaissance, into a new tradition. These sources were: (1) the story of Alexander's visit to Jerusalem and his meeting with the High Priest there;[33] (2) Clearchus of Soli's account in his lost book, *On Sleep*, of Aristotle's meeting with a "philosopher" from Judea (Josephus, *Contra Apionem*, I.22, 177–182; Eusebius, *Preparatio Evangelica*; and Clement of Alexandria *Stromata* V, 66, 4–5).[34] This story was probably born against the background of Aristotle's stay in Assos in northwestern Asia Minor from 345–347 B.C.E., a period during which he discarded the views of his teacher Plato in regard to theological issues. An error in printing Eusebius' translation into Latin in 1470 engendered the story that Aristotle converted to Judaism;[35] (3) The numerous legendary accounts of the life of Aristotle (*Vitae Aristotelis*) and anecdotes from his life in Hellenistic, Syrian, and Arabic literature,[36] which included pseudo-epigraphical books of Aristotle's letters to Alexander the Great on political and other subjects, as well as Aristotle's "last will and testament". Muslim literature on this subject included details about Aristotle's life that did not appear in the Hellenistic literature; (4) The role played by Jews and Christians in disseminating stories about Aristotle, particularly by the Nestorian translator Hunain Ibn Ishak (c.808–873) novel "*Bayamim hahem*" (In Those Days). In the contest between the two autodidacts of the town, Lisaac and Isaac, the former cites Aristotle as an authority: "This is what Aristotle says, do you hear me, gentlemen, this is what Aristotle says!" The latter replies: "You frighten me! So what if Aristotle says? Is he a rabbi or a teacher in Israel?" Mendele, *Kol Kitvei Mendele Mocher Seforim*, (1963, p. 262).

33. Kasher (1993); Arnaldo Momigliano (1979). The legend about the encounter between the high priest Simeon the Just, the last member of the Great Assembly, "who was an extremely wise man in all the wisdoms and the sciences" (Yoma 69a), and Alexander the Great gave rise to the story that Simeon was the one who influenced Aristotle (who did not even accompany Alexander on his visit to Palestine). On this story in comparison with the version in Josephus, see Tropper (2013, pp. 113–156); Ben Shazar (2017).

34. Lewy (1938); B. Bar-Kochva (2010a).

35. The source for the re-emergence of this story about Aristotle's Jewish origins is a printing error in a 1448 Latin translation by a humanist from Crete, George of Trebizond, which was carried out for Pope Nicholas V (Eusebius *Preparatio Evengelica* 9, 5–6) This was a translation of Clearchus of Soli's story about the "meeting" between Aristotle and a Jewish sage. He translated the sentence "*Ille igitur unxit Aristoteles, Judeeus erat, et igitur*" and added "*e igitur subiunxit Aristoteles, Judaeus erat*".

36. See Aristotle (1957, pp. 258–265); Gunderson (1980); F. Rosenthal, *The Classical Heritage in Islam* (1994, pp. 116–118). Artmon collected and edited Aristotle's letters that were in Scepsis, including forged letters. See During (1957); and Gutas' criticism of During: Gutas (1986, pp. 15–36).

who wrote, among books, *Kitāb Nawādir al-Falāsifa* (Maxims of the Philosophers),[37] and by his son, Ashak, and their role in disseminating his teachings by translating the Aristotelian corpus into Arabic and thence into Latin, thereby reviving it in western culture;[38] (5) Aristotle's description in *Peri philosophies* of the "East" as a source of *Sophia* more ancient than that of Egypt, and therefore the birthplace of various inventions.[39]

Another source, which may have played a background role, was the legends regarding lost books of wisdom from antiquity (for example, the books of Enoch, to whom ancient traditions attributed 356 books), and legends of books hidden away in various locations. Such legends appear in a later form in the introduction by Yehia Altatrik, the "copying Ishmaelite", to the pseudo-Aristotalian book Secret of Secrets: "I did not leave any of the halls in which the philosophers placed their secrets. I entered them all and did not desist from any of the great monks there who professed to know them, until I came to a hall of the sun worshipper built by the great Hermes himself. There I

---

37. See A. Loewenthal (1896). Ḥunain Ibn Isḥak also quoted the words of the prayer that "Aristotle recited every morning": "Mighty, mighty, and ancient that departeth not / and emanates from all, save me from your great fire" (second section, Chapter 4, 27). In the polemic between Isserles and the Maharshal (R. Shlomo Yehiel Luria 1510–1574), the former was accused of having supported the words of Aristotle on a certain matter in his book *Torat ha'Olah*. In the polemic, the Maharshal's fear was that many students were abandoning the Torah and turning to Aristotle, whose words were the "wine of crocodiles". Isserles responded with the claim that "the wisdom of the scholars and the philosophers came to them from Israel and all of their wisdom is contained in the Torah... and it is written in *Shevilei Emunah* that most of the Aristotelian wisdom was stolen from the wisdom of Solomon, for when Alexander the Great conquered Jerusalem he took over the treasure of Solomon for his teacher Aristotle" (Isserles [1854]: *Torat ha'Olah* 1, 11, p. 39). One of Luria's accusations was that Isserles's students copied Aristotle's prayer into their own prayer books. See Ziv (1972); Elbaum (1990, pp. 156–165); Ben-Sasson (1984). According to Ben-Sasson, Aristotelianism arrived in Poland and, specifically, in Isserles' home Krakow, via Italy (mainly Padua), where the status of Ibn Rushd was preserved. The result was that Aristotelianism flourished in Krakow during the first decades of the fifteenth century, and perhaps for several generations thereafter. According to Jan Długosz (1415–1480), a Polish historian and cleric who would become the archbishop of Lwow, apocryphal stories about Aristotle were widespread in Poland in the fourteenth and fifteenth centuries. There are three Hebrew manuscripts of the pseudo-Aristotelian work *Problemata Physica*, translated by Ben Yitzhak, including one translated by Moshe Ibn Tibbon which quotes, *inter alia*, from the *Translation of Hunain Ibn Ishak* of Aristotle's book on "natural questions". See Filius (1999, LX-LXIV); Assaf (2001).

38. *Anecdotes of the Philosophers* (in German, *Sinnsprache der Philosophen*). Not only was Ḥunain a prolific translator—he translated 116 books from Greek, including those by Aristotle, Plato, and Galen—but he also authored thirty-six books in various areas of medicine.

39. On the fragments of the dialogue, see Ross (1955, pp. 73–96); Bywater (1877).

found a monk of great wisdom. I outsmarted him and grew near to him and used artifice until he gave me permission to peruse the books of the hall which had been placed there".[40]

Isaac Baer Levinsohn summed up what was known about the Jewish contribution to the dissemination of Greek philosophy in the world of Islam and Christianity in his book Te'udah beYisrael (1828). He wrote: "Know, learned reader! That the wisdom of Greek philosophers that is renowned today throughout all the nations of Europe, in the language of their countries, came to them from the Jews, who were the reason this wisdom spread and became known to their scholars, as well as the wisdom of later sages from among the Arabs and the Jews".[41]

In this apologetic literature, then, Solomon was not only Aristotle's teacher but also his counterpart; like him, he plumbed the depth and breadth of his wisdom in his many books.

The historical context in which this apologetic tale came into Jewish literature is the thirteenth century, a time when Christian theology in the West became re-acquainted with Aristotelian philosophy and Aristotelian science as a result of texts in these fields being translated into Latin via their translations into Arabic; these works

---

40. Gaster (1925–1928, London, pp. 2–3). On the St. Petersburg manuscript, see Hanah Yonah Gorland, "Yalkutei Katzir", in *HaShahar*, 3, 8, March 1872, pp. 451–456.

41. Levinsohn (1977, pp. 111–112). In this context, Levinsohn makes special mention of Aristotle ("the foremost philosopher") and of Clearchus's claim (which he attributed to Josephus) that Aristotle studied with a Jew, noting that "as a result many erred in this matter and thought that Aristotle was a Jew". (Levinsohn 1977, p. 114). He also writes that Greek scholars had learned the science of astronomy from Jewish sages, whose knowledge was lost during the time of the exile: "And the sages studied this science well and thoroughly, and perhaps they had access to our books from the Second Temple when they surpassed us" (Levinsohn 1977, p. 88). Levinsohn also repeats the tradition that Plato was a student of the prophet Jeremiah (p. 113). A contemporary use of this story is evident in an article by R. David Kleiner, "The Powerhouse of the Universe," published in the periodical *Et lahshov*, a Hebrew-language journal on Jewish thought (July 2002, pp. 36–39). The author repeats several of the claims noted above and quotes Isserles in *Torat ha'Olah* about the meeting between Jeremiah and Plato, during which Jeremiah answered Plato's questions about philosophy; he also cites Tommaso Campanella's claim that Pythagoras was a Jew and "a Hebrew." According to Campanella, Aristotle's teachings contradicted the holy scriptures (and reliance upon him furthermore impaired the "Italian" nature of the heliocentric doctrine); hence the Christians who relied on Aristotle were themselves denying the Holy Scriptures. The background to this is the tradition that the intellectual circle originally founded by Pythagoras in Calabria (where Campanella was born) acquired his heliocentric concept from a Jewish source; as a result, there was a continuity between heliocentrism (and Galileo's theory) and the Holy Scriptures. Campanella (1622 [1994], pp. 1–34, 119–121). The tradition according to which Pythagoras learned from the Jews (and from Solomon) also appears in Arabic literature.

soon assumed an incontrovertible authority. One may, of course, question whether the writers mentioned in this chapter or any others actually believed in this imaginary story and truly required it in order to legitimize Aristotle's reception into Jewish philosophy. It is entirely possible that the story simply drifted from text to text. However, the very fact that it did so and that its vitality was preserved beyond the era of Jewish intellectual syncretism demonstrates its power. On the other hand, medieval Christian literature, which until the eleventh century was familiar with some of Aristotle's writings through the translations of Porphyrios, Boethius, and Gaius Marius Victorianus, and later via translations created in Sicily in the twelfth century, required no such apologetics to legitimize his work. Albertus Magnus, Thomas Aquinas, and their students, for instance, needed no extrinsic justification in order to bring the "pagan" Aristotle into the tent of Christianity. Only when Aristotle's prestige declined in the mid-seventeenth century did a group of scholars come to his defense by using the Jewish legendary tradition to "baptize" Aristotle and describe him as owing his redemption to Solomon's wisdom.[42] On the other hand, Jewish culture did require a legendary tradition in order to overcome its objection to Aristotelian philosophy, and the continued vitality of the tradition reveals the value and status of philosophy and the sciences in Jewish culture. Nor is the tradition devoid of historical truth, if we interpret "Solomon" as a personification of the contribution of Jewish translators in transferring the Aristotelian corpus first from Greek to Arabic, and then into Latin, and thence to the emergence of scholasticism and Thomism.

In any event, what we have is a dual-edged sword: a legendary tradition that not only posited Aristotle as Solomon's pupil but shaped Solomon's image in the model of Aristotle, as a magus and an author of many books.

The Invention of a Pseudo-Solomonic Library
"*Auctoritatem litteris praestat antiquitas summa*"
- Tertullianus, *Apologeticum*, XIX[43]

In what manner was the wisdom of Solomon preserved, and where could it be found, apart from the three books attributed to him that were included in the Jewish and Christian bibles, and apart from the

---

42. This was an attempt, Del Soldato writes, to describe "the human, intellectual, and theological perfection of Aristotle, which could be saved by rejecting any dissonant voices, even those that were part of the same school and tradition". Del Soldato (2007, p. 546). And see Melamed (2010, p. 193), which relies on Chroust (1945).

43. "Extreme antiquity gives books authority", trans. Terrot Reaveley Glover, Tertullius (1984, pp. 92–93).

mentions made thereof in the Talmudic literature? Unlike Jesus, Solomon was no preacher, his teachings transformed into oral tradition. If indeed knowledge-seekers traveled the earth to hear him, where are the accounts they must surely have recorded upon return to their lands? That Solomon's fabled wisdom seemed to have left few marks was a gap the legendary tradition was called upon to fill, particularly as the middle ages saw parts of the Aristotelian and pseudo-Aristotelian corpus adopted into Western culture.

Solomon's afterlife began in the Hellenistic period, as various literary genres emerged. Libraries, both public and private, were established beyond the walls of temples and royal palaces;[44] and books became a sought-after, popular "commodity" via copiers and booksellers, to the extent that their very popularity became a subject of satire. Seneca (4 B.C.E.–65 C.E.), for example, wrote of the plethora of books suddenly in existence and of those who purchased them not in order to read but to impress others and decorate their homes.[45] Authors composed books on diverse subjects; according to Diogenes Laërtius, the Aristotelian corpus alone numbered 400 works. Nothing of this sort existed in the Jewish culture of the Hellenic and Roman periods, although books were accorded significant status in "sectarian" Jewish culture (the mythological Enoch, as we have seen, was said to have written 356 books under the guidance of the angel Uriel[46]—but this was strictly a legendary, or mythological, library). Jewish sources from these periods mention only a few prolific authors, and certainly none who wrote in a broad range of intellectual or literary spheres; nor have we evidence of the existence of Jewish libraries parallel to those established by the Romans, Greeks, and Christians, such as the library established by Pamphilus (d. 309) in Caesarea, which would later became the property of Eusebius.[47] Only in the Middle Ages do we find Jews who own large private libraries. A story in the sixteenth-century *Sefer haYashar* reflects the value ascribed to a collection of books as a reserve (and representation) of wisdom. The story relates that when Roman soldiers looted Jerusalem after its destruction by Titus, a general named Cidrus discovered a barrel full of books about religion, history and the like. He included these in his spoils, brought them

---

44. For example, it was said of Marcus Mettius Epaphroditus, a freed slave who wrote commentaries on Homer, that he owned 30,000 books (scrolls).

45. *De tranquillitate*, 9. In his satire, *Adversus indoctum et libros multos ementem* (The Ignorant Book-Collector), the second-century Lucian mocks a wealthy man who accumulates books but is incapable of reading them. Lucian of Samosata (1969, pp. 175–212).

46. 1 Enoch 2:10–11. These books were passed down from generation to generation; thus, for example, Enoch gives them to his son Methuselah (1 Enoch 1:1–2, 68).

47. See Grafton and Williams (2006).

to Seville, and from there several books found their way to Naples, where *Sefer haYashar* was written.[48] Such instances notwithstanding, the corpus of medieval Jewish manuscripts is meager compared to the great number of books and libraries in the Western culture of the period, or to the extensive project of manuscript reproduction the latter supported.

The relative lack of Jewish libraries does not signify an absence of literary activity: the Hellenic and Roman periods saw the development of Jewish apocryphal literature and Jewish Hellenistic literature, including the books of Josephus, Philo, and others whose work has not survived. During this lengthy period *The Wisdom of Solomon*, *Psalms of Solomon*, and *The Testament of Solomon* were added to Solomon's supposed oeuvre, as were books of magic such as the eleventh-century *Salomonis libri de gemmis et daemonibus* by the Byzantine historian Niketas (c.1155–1217), who enumerated other magical books by Solomon.[49]

The Middle Ages saw a growing perception within the Jewish cultures of Spain, Provence, Italy, and Ashkenaz of books, and collections of books, as an asset of great value.[50] The existing corpus of Hebrew-language books being small, a legendary tradition developed of ascribing to Solomon (who cautioned that "of making many books there is no end"[51]) the authorship of a nonexistent pseudo-Solomonic corpus relating to philosophy and science. Solomon, as we have seen in previous chapters, was a natural choice to be credited with (invented) work in those fields; still, such works were far outnumbered by the number of similarly invented books on matters arcane and magical that were attributed to him, and needless to say the total number of books ascribed to him is minuscule compared to those supposedly written by Aristotle, or various other Hellenist and Roman writers.

It would be an exaggeration—perhaps even an invention—to claim that the trend of attributing the authorship of invented works to Solomon emerged consciously from the desire to create a comprehensive "ancient" Jewish library that could equal the Aristotelian corpus. It does seem, however, that the invention of the pseudo-Solomonic corpus resulted from the fact that, without the background of

---

48. *Sefer HaYashar*, Dan (1986, pp. 37–38). Not to be confused with a popular thirteenth-century book of musar by this name, whose author is unknown, and which employs Aristotelian concepts. See also Bar-Levav (2006, 2011).

49. I have already mentioned (Chapter Seven) the *Ars Notoria*. For a list of magical manuscripts attributed to Solomon see Butler (1998, pp. 47–48).

50. This awareness was expressed in the interest taken in the process of creating a book, the ways of preserving it, the rules governing its lending and borrowing, etc. See in Vol. II, Book VI, pp. 421–433 of Dinur (1972).

51. Ecclesiastes 12:12.

a "written cannon", both the tradition relating to Solomon's wisdom and the legend that he was Aristotle's teacher lacked a vital element. Thus, the "books of Solomon" functioned as a substitute of sorts for the absent literature of the Second Temple period, which either never existed or had been lost and forgotten.

The Sages themselves attributed no books to Solomon other than the three mentioned in the Bible. They were unfazed by the absence of a Jewish "library" and felt no compulsion to credit books to Solomon other than those three. The sages of medieval times, however, were considerably more occupied with the question of his literary output. Judah Halevi explained the relative dearth of Jewish books written by Solomon by arguing that the king had indeed recorded all his wisdom, but that the books were translated into the language of the Chaldeans and the source was lost.[52] R. Levi ben Gershom (Gersonides, 1288–1344), the prolific Provençal scholar and rigid opponent of Aristotelian philosophy,[53] had a different explanation. According to him, Solomon had written only those books that were inspired by the divine spirit. Maimonides cited only *The Wisdom of Solomon*; R. Judah he-Ḥasid, the major figure in the Ashkenazi Chasidic movement, asserted in *Sefer Hasidim* that Solomon refrained from composing books for fear that those reading them would be distracted from their study of the Torah or—worse yet—come to rely on the sciences and abandon the Torah and its commandments. Yosef Taitazak, among those exiled from Spain, described ten books attributed to Solomon that had been hidden in earlier times for fear that non-Jewish scholars would claim them as their own; these books, he predicted, would reemerge with the coming of the Messiah.[54]

In contrast to this apologetic strategy, there developed a separate trend of attributing to Solomon the authorship of any number of books—a diverse pseudo-Solomonic corpus. Thus, R. Shem Tov Joseph Falaquera wrote in *Sefer haMa'alot* that Solomon had written sixty-five books, whose names he did not provide. One writer who claimed to know the identities of several of these was the Muslim writer Abū Aflaḥ of Syracuse, of whom little is otherwise known. In the enigmatic *Sefer haTamar* (Book of the Palem Tree), which was translated from Arabic into Hebrew, probably in Provence in the fifteenth century, Abū Aflaḥ wrote: "These are the articles called the articles of Saliman al-Yahud, one of the ancient kings: the *Book of Experiments, Book of Old Age, Book of Proverbs, Book of Perfection, Book of Exploits, Book of Uniqueness, Book of the Sermon, Book of*

---

52. *Kuzari* 1:63, 2:66.
53. Among his writings is *Milḥamot Ha-Shem* (The Wars of the Lord, 1325).
54. Scholem (1971–1978).

Calling for Security, *Book of Desire*, *Book of the Upright*, *Book of Medications*, *Book of Choices*, *Book of Maintaining Agility*, *Book of Sects of Scholars*, *Book of Purposes*";[55] he proceeded to cite excerpts from these books.

In his introduction to Abū Aflaḥ's work, Gershom Scholem wrote that the author objected to and even derided hermeneutics, contrasting that science with Solomon's wisdom, from which he cited twenty enigmatic maxims. Regarding Solomon, Abū Aflaḥ wrote that the former had delved into the wisdom of religion from his boyhood and "wrote renowned books about it", some of which were translated into Arabic, others of which appeared anonymously.

Part of another book by Abū Aflaḥ—*Mother of the King*—was included in a book by Gershon ben Solomon of Arles, Provence, entitled *Sha'arei Shamayim* (Gates of Heaven, printed in Venice in 1547). The latter book relates that the Queen of Sheba brought King Solomon a precious miraculous stone, which Solomon would later discuss in a book he composed titled *Sefer haMatzpen* (The Compass). In *Solomon's Desire*, a commentary on the Song of Songs, Johanan Alemanno provided a similar description of Solomon's books: "those that came out in our language [Hebrew] and those that did not. And those that did are not attributed to him, but he was the original author undoubtedly". He further mentioned 23 books about which he had allegedly learned from Apollonius of Tyana. Jacob ben David Provençal claimed that the Christians had stolen Solomon's great *Book of the Mystery of Nature*; while *Sefer haMeshiv* (Book of the Respondent), a Kabbalistic-mystic work demonizing philosophy that was written in Spain before the expulsion,[56] lists the names of ten secret books by Solomon, including *The Book of Correcting Traits*, *The Book of the Garden of Eden*, *The Secret of Hell*, and *The Wisdom of the Heavens in the Secret Knowledge of the Stars and Zodiac*.

This Jewish legendary tradition would eventually make its way into Western culture. Roger Bacon addressed it in his *Opus*, though he distorts Josephus' words when he writes that Solomon authored 4,005 books. Bacon's utopian novel *New Atlantis* (1627) describes an academy for scientific research named the "House of Solomon, wherein may be found "a few parts" of Solomon's books; these included a *Book of the History of Science*, which dealt with the subject of natural philosophy.

All the writers noted above supplied the names of books putatively written by Solomon in order to reinforce their various worldviews. The Jewish Italian philosopher and Kabbalist Abraham Jagel

---

55. Scholem (1926, p. 26).
56. Idel (1983c).

(1552–1623) solved the puzzle of how Solomon's many books made their way to other nations by claiming in his own Bet Ya'ar haLevanon that Solomon gifted books to those kings who came from far-off lands to hear his wisdom, and that "to this very day" some of these books exist in Armenia and the kingdom of Sheba. (The only book Yagel alludes to by name is the *Book of Medications*.) Yet the weakness of this legendary tradition lay in the fact that the most it could do was list the names of Solomon's lost books; little information could be supplied regarding their supposed content. Nor did it employ the tactic of fabrication, namely of presenting an existing text as a lost manuscript of Solomon's, miraculously discovered.[57] At any event, the tradition has not persisted into modern times; in this era no lost book in any sphere of science has been attributed to Solomon, although a claim has been made that since in his three books Solomon was writing for a broad contemporary public, he chose parables that would be comprehensible to that public and "concealed" his vast scientific knowledge. In the story "Solomon's Wisdom Excelled", which repeats these pretexts, S. Y. Agnon offers his own explanation. Solomon was apprehensive of commentators who stripped from texts their sacred meaning and cloaked them in fallacious interpretations. It was these ignorant, vulgar, and envious men who were to blame for the fact that we do not, today, possess Solomon's books; commentators of that ilk exist to this very day.[58]

---

57. Speyer (1970).
58. Agnon (1963). *Kol kitvei sipurav shel Shmuel Yosef Agnon*, v. 7: "*Ad Hena*" (To This Day), Jerusalem and Tel Aviv, pp. 299–304.

Afterword

The biblical King Solomon is "a king for all seasons", and he is the main character in the correspondence between the imagined trio not only because he predates the others, but because the many facets of his legendary image provided a wealth of raw material for the links that have been forged between him, the Greek philosopher, and the Christian messiah.

Solomon's "correspondence" with Jesus and Aristotle reflects the various aspects of the relationships between Judaism, Christianity, and Islam, but also between the three monotheistic religions and the cultural heritage of the classical world.

Solomon, Aristotle, and Jesus are not only historical figures; they are also meta-historical, trans-cultural, and symbolic. Solomon is more than a king, Aristotle transcends the philosophers, and Jesus is a son of God and the messiah. Solomon, of course, was unacquainted with the others; Aristotle never heard of Solomon; and Jesus was familiar with Solomon's biblical biography but was probably unaware of Aristotle. This correspondence occupies a textual expanse both broad and varied, as we have seen, and this study journeyed through a sea of textual worlds, some well-known and others esoteric, in which Solomon's identities have shifted from text to text and traversed cultures and religions, retaining their essentiality over the course of twenty-five hundred years, and maintaining, all the while, a correspondence with Aristotle and with Jesus. As such, it is a deeply rooted case study in trans-cultural transmission, cultural appropriation, and cultural debt.

Christianity's foremost concern with Solomon was the result of his description in the Bible as both a "son of god" and the son of David. It inspired a sense of competition between him and Jesus: thus, Christian Christology and tradition described Jesus as the "true Solomon"; identified in Solomon's life events that prefigured the life of Jesus; appropriated the three biblical books attributed to Solomon, interpreting them as referring to Jesus and the Church; and ascribed additional books to Solomon. The Church corresponded not only with the biblical but also the post-biblical Solomon—the Solomon of apocryphal literature and the *Aggadah*—and this latter image retains a place and status in Christian theology and culture. It is threaded throughout generations of Christian literature that appropriated the biblical and meta-historical Solomon and compared and contrasted him to Jesus.

Solomon would re-emerge in the thirteenth century as a magus—a philosopher well-versed in the occult sciences—and the correspondence between him and Aristotle was born. Jewish philosophy (including the *Kabbalah*) could not ignore the status and influence Aristotle gained in Latin Christianity, and the pro-Aristotelian stream in Judaism attempted to resolve the tension inherent in adopting the words of a pagan philosopher by inventing a legendary tradition in which Aristotle's wisdom derived from Solomon's. Though Christianity was generally not in need of legends or apologetics in order to accept Aristotle as an inspiration and influence, there were some Christian writers who found in this legendary tradition legitimization to adopt Aristotle's philosophy and create an "Aristotelian Christianity". Thus, in the imagined correspondence Jesus was seen both as the "true Solomon" and as "greater than Solomon", while Aristotle was described as a precursor of Jesus and a student of Solomon.

Solomon, Aristotle, and Jesus were utilized to personify various intangible phenomena such as inter-religious and intercultural transmissions and encounters; modes of reception and internalization of beliefs and customs; the boundaries between magic, occultism, the sciences, and philosophy; and more. Thus, this imaginary correspondence is not a history of texts from the distant past— theological writings, legends, bizarre composition, etc.,—but one that is present as well as relevant in our modern culture.

BIBLIOGRAPHY

The New Revised Standard Version (BRSV) (1989).

Muhammad M. Pickthall (Trans.) (1992): *The Glorious Qur'an*. Tahrike Tarsile Qur'an, Inc.

Abbou-Hershkovitz, Keren (2006): "The Mystery of the Alexandrian Library". In: Yosef Kaplan and Moshe Sluhovsky (Eds.): *Libraries and Book Collections*. Jerusalem: The Zalman Shazar Center, pp. 78–89. [Hebrew]

Abel, Ernest L. (1969): "The Virgin Birth: Was It a Christian Apologetic?". In: *Revue des Études Juives* 128-129, pp. 395–399.

Agnon, Shmuel Yosef (1963 edn.): *Kol Ktvei Agnon*. Jerusalem/Tel Aviv.

al-Kisā'ī, Muḥammad ibn ʿAbd Allāh (1997): *Tales of the Prophets* (Qiṣaṣ al-Anbiyā) (W. M. Thackston Jr., Trans.). Kazi Publications.

al-Thaʿlabī, Abū Isḥāq Aḥmad Ibn Muḥammad ibn Ibrāhīm (2002): *ʿArāʾis al-Majālis fī Qiṣaṣ al-Anbiyā* (*Lives of the Prophets*) (W. M. Brinner, Trans.). Leiden: Brill.

Abraham Bar Hiyya (1851 [1146]): *Sefer haʾibur* (Book of Intercalation) (Zvi Philipovski, Ed.). London.

Abramsky, Samuel (1982): "King Solomon as depicted by the Chronicles", Eretz Israel 14, pp. 3–14.

Agrippa von Nettesheim (Cornelius Heinrich): *Three Books on Occult Philosophy*, English trans., 1651.

Adler, Elkan N. (1926): "Aristotle and the Jews". *Revue Des Études Juives*, LXXXI, No. 163–164, pp. 91–102.

Akyol, Mustafa (2017): *The Islamic Jesus*: *How the King of the Jews Became a Prophet of the Muslims*. London: St. Martin Press.

al-Andalusī, Saʿid (1991): *Science in Medieval World*: *Book of the Categories of Nations* (S.I. Salem and A. Kumar, Trans.). Austin: University of Texas Press.

Alexander, Philip S. (1986): "Incantations and Books of Magic". In: Schürer, *The History of the Jewish People in the Age of Jesus Christ*, pp. 342–379.

Alemanno, Yohanan (2019): *Heshek Shelomo* (The Delight of Solomon) (Daphna Levin, Ed.). Tel Aviv: Idra. [Hebrew]

Allen, Garrick V., Kai Akagi, Paul Sloan, and Madhavi Nevader (Eds.) (2019): *Son of God*: *Divine Sonship in Jewish and Christian Antiquity*. Winona Lake, IN: Eisenbrauns.

Amir, Joshua (1968): "On King Solomon Image in Hellenistic Judaism". In: *Bet Mikra* 35. No. 4, pp. 16–22. [Hebrew]

Anlezark, Daniel (2009): *The Old English Dialogues of Solomon and Saturn*. Cambridge: D.S. Brewer.

Anonymous (1974 edn.): *Sir Gawain and the Green Knight* (Brian Stone, Trans.). Penguin Books.

Apuleius (1951 reprint): *The Golden Ass* (Robert Graves, Trans.). New York: Penguin Classics, pp. 62–63.

Aquinas, Thomas (1998): *Selected Writings* (R. McInerny, Ed. and Trans.). Penguin Books.

Aphrahat (2005 edn.): *Demonstrations II* (Kuriakose Valavanolickal, Trans.). Kottayam, India: St. Ephrem Ecumenical Research Institute.

Aristotle (1957): *Rhetoric ad Alexandrum* [Rhetoric to Alexander] (H. Rackham, Trans.). Cambridge, MA: Loeb Classical Library/Harvard University Press.

Arnheim, Michael (1984): *Is Christianity True?*. London: Duckworth.

Aron, Milton (1990): *Christianity versus Jesus*: *The Saga and Odyssey of a Postpagan Mystery Cult*. New York: Vantage Press.

Arye (Leon) of Modena (1960): *Clipeus et Gladuis* [*Sword and Shield*] (S. Simensohn, Ed.). Jerusalem. [Hebrew]

Asch, Sholem (1939): *The Nazarene*. New York: G.P. Putnam's Sons.

Ash, Paul S. (1999): *David, Solomon and Egypt*: A Reassessment. Sheffield Academic Press.

Ashkenazi, Shmuel (2000): "Aristo". In: Shmuel Ashkenazi: *Alpha Beta Dshmuel Zeira Tinggata*. Jerusalem, pp. 234–238.

Aslan, Reza (2014): *Zealot: The Life and Times of Jesus of Nazareth*. London: The Westbourne Press.

Assaf, David (2001): "The World of Torah in Poland during 16th-17th Centuries". In: Israel Bartal and Israel Gutman (Eds.): *The Broken Chain: Polish Jewry Through the Ages*. Jerusalem: The Zalman Shazar Center, pp. 69–111. [Hebrew]

Assmann, Jan (2003): *The Mind of Egypt: History and Meaning in the Time of the Pharaohs*. (Andrew Jenkins, Trans.). New York: Metropolitan Books, 2002.

Assmann, Jan (1997): "Magic and Theology in Ancient Egypt". In: Schäfer and Kippenberg, *Envisioning Magic*, pp. 1–8.

Astell, Ann W. (1990): *The Song of Songs in the Middle Ages*. Ithaca, NY: Cornell University Press.

Aston, Margaret (1993): *The King's Bedpost: Reformation and Iconography in a Tudor Group Portrait*. Cambridge University Press.

Attridge, Harold W. (1989): *Hebrews: A Commentary on the Epistle to the Hebrews*. Fortress Press.

Augustine (1961): *Confessions* (R. S. Pine-Coffin, Trans.). Penguin Classics.

Augustine (1984): *City of God* (H. Bettenson, Trans.). Penguin Classics.

Augustine. "On the Holy Trinity", in *Nicene and Post-Nicene Fathers*, Vol. 3, Book VI. Edited by Philip Schaff, Hendrickson, Peabody, Mass, 1995 (2nd edn.), pp. 97–103.

Augustine. "Sermon to the Catechumens on the Creed", in *Nicene and Post-Nicene Fathers*, Vol. 3, Bool VI. Edited by Philip Schaff, Hendrickson, Peabody, Mass, 1995 (2nd edn.), pp. 369–374.

Augustine (2008): *On Christian Teaching* (R. P. H. Green, Trans.). Oxford: Oxford University Press.

Avioz, Michael (2005): *Nathan's Oracle (2 Samuel 7) and Its Interpreters*. Bern: Peter Lang.

Bacon, Francis (1974): *The Advancement of Learning and New Atlantis* (A. Johnston, Ed.). Oxford: Clarendon Press.

Bacon, Roger (1988): *The Magical Letter of Roger Bacon: Concerning the Marvelous Power of Art and Nature and the Nullity of Magic*. Holmes Group.

Baines, John (1991): "Society, Morality, and Religious Practice". In: Byron E. Shafer (Ed.): *Religion in Ancient Egypt: Gods, Myths, and Personal Practice*. Ithaca: Cornell University Press.

Barb, Alphons Augustinus (1963): "The Survival of Magic Arts". In: Arnaldo Momigliano (Ed.): *The Conflict between Paganism and Christianity in the Fourth Century*. Oxford University Press, pp. 100–125.

Bar-Ilan, Meir (1995): "Exorcism by Rabbis: Talmudic Sages and Magic". In: *Daat* 34, pp. 17–33. [Hebrew]

Bar-Kochva, Bezalel (2008): "Pythagoras, Hermippus and the Jews: On the Question of the Myth about the Origin of Greek Philosophy in Jewish Wisdom". In: *Zion* 73, pp. 407–451. [Hebrew]

Bar-Kochva, Bezalel (2010a): "Aristotle, the Learned Jew and the Indian Kalaoni in Clearchus". In: *The Image of the Jews in Greek Literature: The Hellenistic Period*. Berkeley: University of California Press pp. 40–89.

Bar-Kochva, Bezalel (2010b): "The Anti-Jewish Treatise by Apollonius Molon". In: *The Image of the Jews in Greek Literature: The Hellenistic Period*. Berkeley: University of California Press, pp. 469–513.

Bar-Levav, Avriel (2006) "Between Library Awareness and the Jewish Republic of Letters". In: Yosef Kaplan and Moshe Sluhovsky (Eds.): *Libraries and Book Collections*. Jerusalem: The Zalman Shazar Center, pp. 201–224.

Bar-Levav, Avriel (2011): "The Sacred Space of the Portable Homeland: An Archeology of Unseen Libraries in Jewish Culture from the Medieval Period to the Internet". In: Yitzhak Hen and Iris Shagrir (Eds.): *Ut videant et Contingant: Essays on Pilgrimage and Sacred Space in Honour of Ora Limor*. Raanana: The Open University of Israel Press, pp. 279–320. [Hebrew]

Barnard, Leslie W. (1997): *St. Justin Martyr: The First and Second Apologies*. New York: Pauline Press.

Barrett, Charles Kingsley (1963): "The Bible in the New Testament Period". In: D. E. Nineham (Ed.): *The Church's Use of the Bible: Past and Present*. London: S.P.C.K., pp. 1–24.

Bartal, Ruth (2009): *Earthly Love—Divine Love: The Biblical Couple as Reflected in Western Art*. Jerusalem: Magnes University Press. [Hebrew]

Bartlett, John R. (1985): *Jews in the Hellenistic World*. Cambridge University Press.

Baruchson, Shifra (1993): *Books and Readers: The Reading Interests of Italian Jews at the Close of the Renaissance*. Ramat Gan: Bar-Ilan University Press.

Basil of Caesarea (1970): "Address to Young Men on Reading Greek Literature". In: R. J. Deferrari and M. R. P. Mcguire (Trans): *Saint Basil: The Letters* (Vol. 4). LCL. Cambridge, MA: Harvard University Press, pp. 365–435.

Battistini, Matilde (2004): *Astrology, Magic, and Alchemy in Art* (R. M. Giammanco, Trans.). Los Angeles, CA: J. Paul Getty Museum.

Baumgarten, Albert (2016): "Celsus and His Jew: Religious, Intellectual, and Cultural Horizons in the Ancient Jewish Diaspora". In: Geoffrey Herman, Aharon Oppenheimer and Meir Ben Shahar (Eds.): *Between Babylonia and the Land of Israel*. Jerusalem: The Zalman Shazar Center for Jewish History, pp. 147–167. [Hebrew]

Baumgarten, Joseph M. (1985): "The Qumran Songs Against Demons". In: *Tarbiz* 55, pp. 442–445. [Hebrew]

Bayless, Martha (1996): *Parody in the Middle Ages: The Latin Tradition*. Ann Arbor, MI: University of Michigan Press.

Beam, Jacob N. (1920): "Hermann Kirchner's 'Sapientia Solomonis'". In: *Modern Philology* 18, pp. 101–108.

Behrends, Frederik (Ed.) (1976): *The Letters and Poems of Fulbert of Chartres*. Oxford: Clarendon Press.

Benko, Stephen (1982): "Early Christian magical practices". In: *Society of Biblical Literature: Seminar Papers* 21, pp. 9–14.

Benoit, Pierre (1974): "The Inspiration of the Septuagint". In: Pierre Benoit: *Jesus and the Gospels*. London: Herder and Herder, pp. 1–10.

Ben-Sasson, Jonah (1984): *The Philosophical System of R. Moses Isserles*. Jerusalem: The Israeli Academy of Sciences and Humanities.

Ben Shazar, Meir (2017): "The High Priest and Alexander the Great". In: Ilan Tall, Vered Noam, Meir Ben Shahar; Daphne Baratz; Yael Fisch: *Josephus and the Rabbis*. Jerusalem: Yad Ben-Zvi Press, pp. 91–144. [Hebrew]

ben Ze'ev, Judah Leib (1820): *Beit haSefer* (Vol. 2: *Mesilat halimud*). Vienna. Berchman, Robert M. (2005): *Porphyry Against the Christians*. Leiden: Brill.

Berdyczewski, Micha J. [Micha Yosef Bin-Gorion] (1913): *From Jewish Sources, Stories, and Folk Tales* (*Aus dem jüdischen Sagenschatz*). Berlin: Achisefer. [Hebrew]

Berger, David (1997): "'The Wisest of All Men': Solomon's Wisdom in Medieval Jewish Commentaries on the Book of Kings". In: Yaakov Elman, Jeffrey S. Gurock, Hazon Nahum: *Studies in Jewish Law, Thought, and History*. New York: Yeshiva University Press, pp. 93–114.

Berger, Yeshayu (1936): "Maimonides in Folk Legends". In: Masad-Maase: *leDivrei Sifrut*. Tel Aviv. [Hebrew]

Bernard of Clairvaux (1981): *On the Song of Songs* [Sermons super Cantica canticorum] (K. Walsh, O.C.S.O., Trans.). Kalamazoo, MI: Cistercian Publications.

Bettenson, Henry (Ed.) (1963): *Documents of the Christian Church* (2nd ed.). Oxford: Oxford University Press.

Betz, Hans Dieter (Ed.) (1992): *The Greek Magical Papyri in Translation (Including the Demotic Spells)*. Chicago, IL: The University of Chicago Press.

Betz, Hans Dieter. "Jewish Magic in the Greek Magical Papyri (PGM VII-260–72)". In: Schäfer and Kippenberg: *Envisioning Magic*, pp. 45–63.

Bharyo, Siam and Catherine Rider (Eds.) (2017): *Demons and Illness from Antiquity to the Early-Modern Period*. Leiden: Brill.

Bialik, Chaim N. and Yehoshua Chana Ravnitzky (1931–1934): *Sefer Ha'aggadah*. Tel Aviv.

Bianchi, Lura, Simon Gilson, and Jill Kraye (Eds.) (2016): *Vernacular Aristotelianism in Italy from the Fourteenth to the Seventeenth Century*. London: The Warburg Institute.

Bibago, Abraham (1987): *Derekh ha'Emunah* (C. F. Goldschmidt, Ed.). Jerusalem: Bialik Institute.

Birkett, Kirsten (2015): *Spells, Sorcerers and Spirits: Magic and the Occult in the Bible*. London: Latimer Trust.

Birkhan, Helmut (2010): *Magie im Mittelalter*. München: C.H. Beck.

Bloch, Ernst (2019): *Avicenna and the Aristotelian Left* (L. Goldman and P. Thompson, Trans.). New York: Columbia University Press.

Bloch, Marc 1925: "La vie d'outre-tombe du roi Salomon". In: *Revue belge de philologie et d'histoire* 4. Nos. 2–3, pp. 349–377. [Reprinted in Bloch, Marc (Ed.) (1963): *Mélanges historiques* (Vol. 2). Paris, pp. 920–938.].

Boardman, John (2019): *Alexander the Great: From His Death to the Present Day*. Princeton University Press.

Boccaccio, Giovanni (1975): *Decameron* (G. H. McWilliam). Penguin Books.

Bock, Darrell L. (1991): "The Son of Man in Luke 5:24". In: *Bulletin of Biblical Research* 1, pp. 109–121.

Bohak, Gideon (2004): "Jewish Myth in Pagan Magic in Antiquity". In: Ithamar Gruenwald and Moshe Idel (Eds.): *Myth in Judaism: History, Thought, Literature*. Jerusalem: Zalman Shazar Center for Jewish History, pp. 97–122. [Hebrew]

Bohak, Gideon (2007): "Cross Cultural Contact in Ancient Magic", *Zmanim* 100 pp. 6–17. [Hebrew]

Bohak, Gideon (2008): *Ancient Jewish Magic: A History*. Cambridge: Cambridge University Press.

Bohak, Gideon (2015): "The Diffusion of the Greco-Egyptian Magic Literature Tradition in Late Antiquity". In: Ian Rutherford (Ed.): *Greco-Egyptian Interactions: Literature, Translation and Culture, 500 BC—AD 300*. Oxford University Press, pp. 354–384.

Bohak, Gideon (2016): "Manuals of Mantic Wisdom: From the Dead Sea Scrolls to the Cairo Genizah". In: Hindy Najman, Jean-Sébastien Rey and Eibert J.C. Tigchelaar (Eds.): *Tracing Sapiential Traditions in Ancient Judaism*. Leiden: Brill, pp. 191–216.

Bohak, Gideon (2017): "Conceptualizing Demons in Late Antique Judaism". In: Siam Bhayro and Catherine Rider (Eds.): *Demons and Illness from Antiquity to the Early-Modern Period*. Leiden: Brill, pp. 111–133.

Bohak, Gideon (2019): "How Jewish Magic Survived the Disenchantment of the World". In: *Aries—Journal for the Study of Western Esotericism* 19, pp. 7–37.

Bolin, Thomas M. (2017): *Ecclesiastes and the Riddle of Authorship*. London: Routledge.

Bonfil, Robert (1994): *As by a Mirror: Jewish Life in Renaissance Italy*. Jerusalem: The Zalman Shazar Center. [Hebrew]

Bonfil, Robert (2009): *History and Folklore in a Medieval Jewish Chronicle: The Family Chronicle of Ahima'az ben Paltiel*. Leiden: Brill.

Bonner, Campbell (1943): "The Technique of Exorcism". In: *Harvard Theological Review* 36, pp. 39–49.

Borchardt, Frank L. (1990): "The Magus as Renaissance Man". In: *The Sixteenth Century Journal* 21, pp. 57–76.

Borgen, Peder and Søren Giversen (Eds.): *The New Testament and Hellenistic Judaism*. Aarhus University Press.

Borland, Lois (1933): "Herman's 'Bible' and the 'Cursor Mundi'". In: *Studies in Philology* 30, pp. 427–444.

Bose, Mishtooni (1996): "From Exegesis to Appropriation: The Medieval Solomon". In: *Medium Aevum* 65. No.2, pp. 182–210.

Boureau, Alain (2013): *Satan the Heretic*: *The Birth of Demonology in the Medieval West*. Chicago: University of Chicago Press.

Boustan, Ra'annan, Klaus Herrmann, Reimund Leicht, Annette Y. Reed and Giuseppe Veltri (Eds.) (2013): *Envisioning Judaism*: *Studies in Honor of Peter Schäfer on the Occasion of His Seventieth Birthday*. Tübingen: Mohr Siebeck.

Boyarin, Daniel (1990): *Intertextuality and the Reading of Midrash*. Bloomington/Indianapolis: Indiana University Press.

Boylan, Patrick (1987 edn.): *Thoth the Hermes of Egypt*. Chicago: Ares Pub.

Bowman, John (1981): "Solomon and Jesus". *Abr-Nahrain* 23 (1981–1984). Leiden: Brill, pp. 1–13.

Bowersock, G. W. (2017): *The Crucible of Islam*. Harvard University Press..

Bremmer, Jan N. (2002): "The Birth of the Term 'Magic'". In: Jan N. Bremmer and Jan R. Veenstra (Eds.): *Metamorphosis of Magic from Late Antiquity to the Early Modern Period*. Leuven: Peeters, pp. 1–11.

Brezis, Davis (2018): *The Sages and their Hidden Debate with Christianity*. Jerusalem: Carmel. [Hebrew]

Bright, Pamela (Ed. and Trans.) (1999): *Augustine and the Bible*. Indiana: University of Notre Dame Press.

Brotton, Jerry (2017): *This Oriental Isle*: *Elizabethan England and the Islamic World*. Penguin Books.

Brown, Dan (2006): *The Da Vinci Code*. New York: Random House.

Brown, Peter (1970): "Sorcery, Demons, and the Rise of Christianity from Late Antiquity into the Middle Ages". In: Mary Douglas (Ed.): *Witchcraft: Confessions and Accusations*. London: Tavistok, pp. 17–46.

Bruce, Susan (Ed.) (1999): *Three Early Modern Utopias: Utopia, New Atlantis and The Isle of Pines*. Oxford: Oxford World's Classics.

Brueggemann, Walter (2005): *Solomon: Israel's Ironic Icon of Human Achievement*. University of South Carolina Press.

Brunner, Horst (2003): *Geschichte der deutschen Literatur des Mittelalters und der Frühen Neuzeit im Überblick*. Stuttgart: Reclam.

Bull, Christian H. (2018): *The Tradition of Hermes Trismegistus: The Egyptian Priestly Figure as a Teacher of Hellenized Wisdom*. Leiden: Brill.

Burger, Christoph (1970): *Jesus als Davidsshon: Eine traditionsgeschichtliche Untersuchung*. Göttingen: Vandenhoech & Ruprecht.

Burke, John G. (1975): "Hermeticism as a Renaissance World View". In: Robert S. Kinsman (Ed.): *The Darker Vision of the Renaissance: Beyond the Fields of Reason*. Berkeley/Los Angeles: University of California Press, pp. 95–117.

Burnett, Charles (2001): "The Coherence of the Arabic-Latin Translation Program in Toledo in the Twelfth Century". In: *Science in Context* 14, pp. 249–288.

Burnett, Charles (1986): "Arabic, Greek and Latin Works on Astrological Magic attributed to Aristotle". In: Kraye, Ryan and Schmitt, *Pseudo-Aristotle*, pp. 84–96.

Büschenthal, Lippmann Moses (1820): *Der Siegelring des Salomo*. Berlin.

Butler, Elizabeth M (1993): *The Myth of the Magus* (2nd edn.). Cambridge University Press. Butler, Elizabeth M. (1998): Ritual Magic. Sutton Publishing.

Byrne, Brendan (1979): *'Sons of God'—'Seed of Abraham': A Study of the Idea of the Sonship of God of All Christians in Paul Against the Jewish Background*. Rome: Pontificio Istituto Biblico.

Bywater, Ingram (1877): "Aristotle's Dialogue on Philosophy". In: *The Journal of Philology* 7, pp. 64–75.

Carrol, Scott (1989): "A Preliminary Analysis of the Epistle to Rehoboam". *Journal for the Study of Pseuodepigrapha* 4, pp. 91–103.

Campanella, Thomas (1622 [1994]): *A Defense of Galileo: the Mathematician from Florence* [Apologia pro Gallileo Matematico Fiorentino] (R. J. Blackwell, Trans.). Notre Dame, IN: University of Notre Dame Press.

Carboni, Stefano (2013): "The 'Book of Surprises' (Kitāb al-Bulhān) of the Bodleian Library". In: *La Trobe Journal* 91, pp. 22–34.

Cardoso, Isaac (Fernando) (1971): *Las Excelencias* (J. Kaplan, Trans,). Jerusalem: Zalman Shazar Center.

Carmoly, Eliakim (1844): *Histoire des médecins juifs anciens et modernes*. Brussels: Societé Encyclographique des Sciences Médicalles.

Cartlidge, David R. and David L. Dungan (Eds.) (1980): *Documents for the Study of the Gospels*. Philadelphia, PA: Fortress Press.

Carasik, Michael (1994): "Who were the 'Men of Hezekiah' (Proverbs XXV?)?". *Vetus Testamentum* XLIC, No. 3, pp. 289–301.

Cary, George (1956): *The Medieval Alexander* (D. J. A. Ross, Ed.). Cambridge University Press.

Cassel, Paulus (1888): *An Explanatory Commentary on Esther* (A. Bernstein, Trans.). Edinburgh: T&T Clark.

Celenza, Christopher S. (2001): "The Search for Ancient Wisdom in Early Modern Europe: Reuchlin and the Late Ancient Esoteric Paradigm". In: *The Journal of Religious History* 25, pp. 115–133.

Celsus (1987): *On the True Doctrine: A Discourse Against the Christians* (R. J. Hoffmann, Trans.) New York/Oxford: Oxford University Press.

Chadwick, Henry (1963): "The Bible and the Greek Fathers". In: D. E. Nineham (Ed.): *The Church's Use of the Bible: Past and Present*. London: S.P.C.K., pp. 25–34.

Chae, Young S. (2006): *Jesus as the Eschatological Davidic Shepherd: Studies in the Old Testament, Second Temple Judaism, and in the Gospel of Matthew*. Tübingen: Mohr Siebeck..

Charles, Robert H. (1908): *The Testament of the Twelve Patriarchs*. London: Adam and Charles Black.,

Charles, Robert H. (1913): *The Apocrypha and Pseudepigrapha of the Old Testament* (Vols. 1–2). Oxford: Clarendon Press.

Charles, Robert H. (1982 [1896]): *The Apocalypse of Baruch*. London.

Charlesworth, James H. (1961): *The Pseudepigrapha and Modern Research with Supplement*. Chico: Scholars Press (pp. 189–197).

Charlesworth, James H (1977): *The Odes of Solomon*. Missoula, MT: Scholars Press.

Charlesworth, James H. (1983): *The Old Testament Pseudepigrapha. Vol. 1: Apocalyptic Literature and Testaments*. Garden City: Doubleday.

Charlesworth, James H. (1985): *The Old Testament Pseudepigrapha. Vol. 2: Expansions of the "Old Testament" and Legends, Wisdom and Philosophical Literature, Prayers, Psalms, and Odes, Fragments of Lost Judeo-Hellenistic Works*. Garden City: Doubleday.

Charlesworth, James H. (1995): "The Son of David: Solomon and Jesus (Mark 10.47)". In: Peder Borgen and Søren Giversen (Eds.): *The New Testament and Hellenistic Judaism*. Aarhus University Press, pp. 72–87.

Chaucer, Geoffrey (1971): *Canterbury Tales* (A. Kent Hieatt and Constance Hieatt, Eds.). New York: Bantam Literature.

Chen, Zalman (1993): *His Life and Death (Jesus Son of Joseph)*. Tel Aviv: Reshafim Publishing. [Hebrew]

Childs, Wendy R. (Ed. and Trans.) (2005): *Vita Edwardi Secundi: The Life of Edward the Second*. Oxford: Oxford Medieval Texts.

Chilton, Bruce (1982): "Jesus ben David: Reflections on the Davidssohnfrage". In: *Journal for the Study of the New Testament* 4, No. 14, pp. 88–112.

Chroust, Anton Hermann (1945): "A Contribution to the Medieval Discussion:Utrum Aristoteles Sit Salvatus". In: *Journal of the History of Ideas* 6, pp. 231–238.

Chroust, Anton Hermann (1964): "A Brief Account of the Traditional Vitae Aristotelis". In: *Revue des Études Grecques* 77. Nos. 364–365, pp. 50–69.

Chroust, Anton Hermann (1973): *Aristotle: New Light on His Life and on Some of His Lost Works* (Vol. 1). Indiana: University of Notre Dame Press.

Clarke, Ernest G. (1973): *The Wisdom of Solomon—Commentary by Ernest G. Clarke* (The Cambridge Bible Commentary). Cambridge: Cambridge University Press.

Classen, Albrecht (Ed.) (2017): *Magic and Magicians in the Middle Ages and the Early Modern Time: The Occult in Pre-modern Sciences, Medicine, Literature, Religion, and Astrology*. Berlin: De Gruyter.

Clement of Alexandria (1960): *Stromata (Vol. 1)* (G. W. Butterworth, Trans.). LCL. Hendrickson Publishing.

Clement of Alexandria (1995): *The Stromata (Or Miscellanies)*. In: Alexander Roberts and James Donaldson (Eds.): *Ante-Nicene Fathers (Vol. 2)* (2nd ed.). Hendrickson Publishing.

Clement of Alexandria (1960 edn.): *The Exhortation to the Greeks* (G. W. Butterworth, Trans.) (Loeb Classical Library). Cambridge: Harvard University Press.

Clifford, Richard J. (Ed) (2007): *Wisdom Literature in Mesopotamia and Israel*. Atlanta, GA: Society of Biblical Literature.

Cochrane, Charles Norris (1957): *Christianity and Classical Culture: A Study of Thought and Action from Augustus to Augustine*. London: Oxford University Press.

Cohen, A. (Trans.) (1939): *Midrash Rabbah: Ecclesiastes*. London: Soncino.

Cohen, A. (1965): *The Minor Tractates of the Talmud (Vol. 1)*. London: Soncino Press.

Cohen, Jeremy (1999): *Living Letters of the Law: Ideas of the Jew in Medieval Christianity*. Berkeley: University of California Press.

Cohen, Jeremy (2001): "Raymundus Martini's Capistrum Iudaeorum Fleisher". In: Ezra Fleischer, Gerald Blidstein, Carmi Horowitz, and Bernard Septimus (Eds.): *Me'ah she'arim: Studies in Medieval Jewish Spiritual Life in Memory of Isadore Twersky*. Jerusalem: Magnes Press. [Hebrew]

Cohen Skalli, Cedric (2017): *Don Isaac Abravanel*. Jerusalem: The Zalman Shazar Center. [Hebrew]

Collins, John J. (1997 [1966]): *Jewish Wisdom in the Hellenistic Age*. Louisville, KY: Westminster John Knox Press.

Collins, John J. (2017): *The Invention of Judaism: Torah and Jewish Identity from Deuteronomy to Paul*. Oakland: University of California Press.

Colson, Francis Henry (Trans.) (1994 rep.): *Philo* (Vols. 1–10). Loeb Classical Library. Cambridge: Harvard University Press.

Comparetti, Domenico (1895): *Vergil in the Middle Ages* (E. F. Benecke, Trans.). New York: Swan Sonnenschein & Co.

Conway, Moncure D (1899): *Solomon and Solomonic Literature*.

Conybeare, Frederick C. (1898): "The Testament of Solomon". In: *The Jewish Quarterly Review* 11, pp. 1–45. [Recently reprinted as: Conybeare, Frederick C. (2007): "The Testament of Solomon". Gorgias Press.]

Conzelmann, Hans (1992): *Gentiles, Jews, Christians: Polemics and Apologetics in the Greco-Roman Era* (M. E. Boring, Trans.). Minneapolis, MN: Fortress Press.

Cooke, Gerald (1961): "The Israelite Kings as Sons of God". In: *ZAW* 73, pp. 202–225.

Cooperman, Bernard Dov (Ed.) (1983): *Jewish Thought in the Sixteenth Century*. Cambridge, MA: Harvard University Press.

Copenhaver, Brian P. (1992): *Hermetica*: *The Greek Corpus Hermeticum and the Latin Asclepius*. Cambridge: Cambridge University Press.

Copenhaver, Brian P. (2003): "Natural Magic, Hermetism, and Occultism in Early Modern Science". In: David C. Lindberg and Roberts S. Westman (Eds.): *Reappraisals of the Scientific Revolution*. Cambridge University Press, pp. 261–301.

Copleston, Frederick C. (1959): *A History of Philosophy*: *Medieval Philosophy (Part 1*: *Augustine to Bonaventure)*. New York: Doubleday.

Cordoni, Constanza and Gerhard Langer (Eds.) (2017): "*Let the Wise Man Listen and Add to Their Learning*" (*Prov. 1*:*5*): *Festschrift for Günter Stemberger on the Occasion of his 75th Birthday*. Berlin: De Gruyter.

Craffert, Pieter F. (2008): *The Life of a Galilean Shaman*: *Jesus of Nazareth in Anthropological-Historical Perspective*. Eugene, OR: Cascade Books.

Crenshaw, James L. (Ed.) (1976): *Studies in Ancient Israelite Wisdom*. New York, NY: Ktav Pub & Distributors Inc.

Cumaenus, Petrus (2006): *The Hebrew Republic* (P. Wyetzner, Trans.). Jerusalem/New York: Shalem Press.

Cyril of Jerusalem (1995): "Catechetical Lectures" (E. H. Gifford, Trans). In: Philip Schaff and Henry Wace (Eds.): *Nicene and Post-Nicene Fathers* (*Second Series*, *Vol. 7*). Peabody, MA: Hendrickson Publishing.

Cyril of Scythopolis (1991): *Lives of Monks of Palestine* (R. M. Price and J. Binns, Trans.). Kalamazoo, MI: Cistercian Publications.

Cyril of Scythopolis (2005): *Lives of the Judaea Desert* (Leah Di Sergi, Intro. and Trans.). Jerusalem: Yad Ben-Zvi Press. [Hebrew]

Dahan, Gilbert (Ed.) (1991): *Gersonide en son temps*: *Science et philosophie médiévales*. Louvain.Paris, Peters.

Daiber, Hans (1997): "Salient Trends of the Arabic Aristotle". In: G. Endress and R. Kruk (Eds.): *The Ancient Tradition in Christian and Islamic Hellenism*: *Studies on the Transmission of Greek Philosophy and Sciences*. Leiden: Brill, pp. 29–43.

Daley, Brian E. (Ed.) (2006): *Gregory of Nazianzus*. London/New York: Routledge.

Daley, Brian R. and Paul R. Kolbert (Eds.) (2015): *The Harp of Prophecy: Early Christian Interpretation of the Psalms*. South Bend, Notre Dame University Press.

Dan, Joseph (Ed.) (1969): *The Exploits of Alexander the Great*. Jerusalem: Bialik Institute. [Hebrew]

Dan, Joseph (Ed.) (1986): *Sefer HaYashar*. Jerusalem: Bialik Institute. [Hebrew]

Daniélou, Jean (1973): *Gospel Message and Hellenic Culture: A History of Early Christian Doctrine before the Council of Nicene*. London: Darton Longman & Todd/Philadelphia: Westminster Press.

Dante Alighieri (1981): *The Divine Comedy* (C.H. Sisson, Trans.). London: Pan Books.

Dante Alighieri (1985): *The Divine Comedy: Paradiso* (Charles S. Singleton, Trans.). Princeton: Princeton University Press.

Dante Alighieri (2017): *Paradiso* (H. W. Longfellow, Trans.). Mineola, NY: Dover Publications.

Day, Peggy L. (1988): *An Adversary in Heaven: Satan in the Hebrew Bible*. Scholars Press.

de Lange, Nicholas (2017): "Hebraists and Hellenists in the Sixth-Century Synagogue: A New Reading of Justinian's Novel 146". In: Constanza Cordoni and Gerhard Langer (Eds.): *"Let the Wise Listen and add to Their Learning" (Prov 1:5): Festschrift for Gunter Stemberger on the Occasion of his 75th Birthday*. Berlin: De Gruyter, pp. 217–226.

Delmedigo, Elijah (1984): *Sefer behinat hadat: A Critical Edition* (J. J. Ross, Ed.). Tel Aviv: The Chaim Rosenberg School of Jewish Studies. [Hebrew]

Del Soldato, Eva (2017): "Saving the Philosopher's Soul: The De pietate Aristotelis by Fortunio Liceti". In: *Journal of the History of Ideas* 78, pp. 531–547.

Deutsch, Yaacov (1997): *Toledot yeshu in Christian Eyes: the Dissemination of the Work and the Reactions to it in the Middle Ages and Early Modern Age* (M.A. thesis). Jerusalem: Hebrew University of Jerusalem. [Hebrew]

Deutsch, Yaacov (2011): "The Second Life of the 'Life of Jesus': Christian Reception of Toledot Yeshu". In: Peter Schäfer, Michael Meerson, and Yaacov Deutsch (Eds.): *Toledot Yeshu ("The Life Story of Jesus") Revisited*. Tübingen: Mohr Siebeck, pp. 283–295.

Dickie, Matthew W. (2001): *Magic and Magicians in the Greco-Roman World*. London: Routledge.

Dietl, Cora (2001): "Markolfs Klugheit und Salomons Weisheit: Hans Folz' neuer Zugang zu einem Traditionellen literarischen Thema". In: *European Medieval Drama* 15, pp. 31–46.

Dinur, Benzion (1972): *A Documentary History of the Jewish People from Its Beginning to the Present* (*Second Series*: *Israel in the Diaspora*). Jerusalem: Bialik Institute. [Hebrew]

Diogenes Laertius (1966): *Lives of Eminent Philosophers* (R. D. Hicks, Trans.). LCL. Cambridge, MA: Harvard University Press.

Dod, Bernard G. (1982): "Aristoteles Latinus". In: Norman Kretzmann, Anthony Kenny, Jan Pinborg, and Eleonore Stump (Eds.): *The Cambridge History of Later Medieval Philosophy*. Cambridge: Cambridge University Press, pp. 45–79.

Donaldson, Alexander and Donaldson, James (eds.). *Stromata*, v. In: *Ante-Nicene Fathers*, *Vol. 2*, Peabody, Mass., 1995.

Dorn, Erhard (1967): *Der sündige Heilige in der Legende des Mittelalters*. München: Fink.

Driscoll, Daniel (1977): *The Sworn Book of Honourius the Magician*. Heptangle Books.

Ducos, Joëlle and Violaine Giacomotto-Charra (Eds.) (2011): *Lire Aristotle au Moyen Âge et à la Renaissance: Réception du Traité Sur la Génération et la Corruption*. Paris: Honoré Champion Éditeur.

Duff, Edward Gordon (Ed.) (1892): *The Dialogue or Community Between the Wise King Salomon and Marcolphus*. London.

Duling, Dennis C. (1975): "Solomon, Exorcism, and the Son of David". In: *Harvard Theological Review* 68, pp. 235–252.

Duling, Dennis C. (1978): "The Therapeutic Son of David: An Element in Matthew's Christological Apologetic". In: *New Testament Studies* 24, pp. 392–410.

Duling, Dennis C. (1983): "Testament of Solomon". In: James H. Charlesworth (Ed.): *The Old Testament Pseudepigrapha* (*Vol. 1*). Duke University Press, pp. 935–987.

Duling, Dennis C. (1984): "The Legend of Solomon the Magician in Antiquity: Problems and Perspectives", *Proceedings*: *Eastern Great Lakes Biblical Society* 4, Westerville, OH, pp. 1–23.

Duling, Dennis C. (1985): "The Eleazar Miracle and Solomon's Magical Wisdom in Flavius Josephus 'Antiquitates Judaicae' 8:42–49)". In: *Harvard Theological Review* 78, pp. 1–25.

Duling, Dennis C. (1988): "The Testament of Solomon: Retrospect and Prospect". In: *Journal for the Study of Pseudepigrapha* 1, No. 2, pp. 81–112.

Dunn, James D.G. (2010): *Did the First Christians Worship Jesus?*: *The New Testament Evidence*. London: SPCK.

Dunn, James D. G. (2015): *Jesus, Paul and the Gospels* (C. Werman, Ed.). Ben-Gurion University of the Negev. [Hebrew]

Duran, Profiat (1520): *The Reproach of the Gentiles*. (See Talmage).

Düring, Ingemar (1957): *Aristotle in the Ancient Biographical Tradition*. Gothenburg: Gothenburg Institute of Classical Studies.

Ebeling, Florian (2007): *The Secret History of Hermes Trismegistus*: *Hermeticism from Ancient to Modern Times* (D. Lorton, Trans.). Ithaca: Cornell University Press.

Ego, Beate (1996): *Targum Scheni zu Ester*: *Übersetzung, Kommentar Und Theologische Deutung*. Tübingen: JCB Mohr (Paul Siebeck), pp. 59–137.

Ego, Beate (2001): "All Kingdoms and Kings Trembled Before Him: The Image of King Solomon in Targum Sheni on Megillat Esther". In: *Journal of the Aramaic Bible*, pp. 57–73.

Ehrman, Bart D. (2012): *Did Jesus Exist: The Historical Argument for Jesus of Nazareth*. New York: Harper Collins.

Ehrman, Bart D. (2019): *The Triumph of Christianity: How a Forbidden Religion Swept the World*. London: Oneworld Publications.

Eisenmann, Esti (2015): "Maharal's Use of Aristotelians Terms". In: Elchanan Reiner (Ed.): *Maharal, Overtures: Biography, Doctrine, Influence*. Jerusalem: Zalman Shazar, pp. 393–407. [Hebrew]

Eisenstein, Yudah (Ed.) (1903): *Encyclopedia of the Torah, Literature and History of the Jews* (*Vol. 2*) (2nd ed.). London.

el-Abbadi, Mostafa (1993): *The Life and Fate of the Ancient Library of Alexandria*. Paris: UNDP.

Elbaum, Jacob (1990): *Openness and Insularity: Late Sixteenth Century Jewish Literature in Poland and Ashkenaz*. Jerusalem: Magnes Press. [Hebrew]

Elior, Ofer (2010): *Ruah Hen as a Looking Glass: The Study of Science in Different Jewish Cultures as Reflected in a Medieval Introduction to Aristotelian Science and in its Later History*. PhD Diss. Beer Sheba: Ben-Gurion University of the Negev. [Hebrew]

Éliphas Lévi (Alphonse Louis Constant) (1982): *The History of Magic* (orig. 1913), Trans. Arthur Edward Rider-Waite. London.

Eliyahu, Ayala (2005): "Fragments of Hermetic Literature in the Genizah". In: *Ginzei Qedem* 1, pp. 9–29. [Hebrew]

Ellen, Michael J. B. (2014): "Pythagoras in the Early Renaissance". In: Carl A. Huffman (Ed.): *A History of Pythagoreanism*. Cambridge: Cambridge University Press, pp. 435–453.

Endress, Gerhard and Remke Kruk (Eds.) (1997): *The Ancient Tradition in Christian and Islamic Hellenism: Studies on the Transmission of Greek Philosophy and Sciences*. Leiden: Brill.

Erder, Yoram (1981): *The Penetration of Enoch Literature into Islam in Light of the Sources of Karaites and Sabians*. M.A. Diss., Tel Aviv University. [Hebrew]

Eshel, Esther (1999): *Demonology in Palestine during the Second Temple Period*. PhD Diss. The Hebrew University. [Hebrew]

Etkes, Emanuel (1995): "The Role of Magic and Ba'alei-Shem in Ashkenazi Society in the Late Seventeenth and Early Eighteenth Centuries". In: *Zion* 60, pp. 69–104. [Hebrew]

Eusebius (1985): Praeparatio Evangelica [Preparation for the Gospel] (A. Yarbro Collins, Trans.). In: James H. Charlesworth (Ed.): *The Old Testament Pseudepigrapha* (*Vol. 2*): New York, NY: Doubleday.

Eusebius (1989): *The History of the Church* (G. A. Williamson, Trans.). Penguin Books.

Eusebius (2002): *Preparation for the Gospel* [Praeparatio Evangelica] (E. H. Gifford, Trans.). Eugene, OR: Wipf and Stock Publishers.

Faerber, Rubin (1902): *König Salomon in der Tradition :Ein historische-kritischer Beitrag zur Geschichte der Haggada, der Tannaiten und Amoraer* (I–II). Vienna: Verlag von Jos & Schlesinger.

Falaquera, R. Shem Tov (1894): *Sefer haMa'alot*. Berlin. [Hebrew]

Falls, Thomas B. (1965): *Writings of Saint Justin Martyr*: "*The First Apology*". Washington D.C..

Fanger, Claire (1998): *Conjuring Spirits*: *Text and Traditions of Medieval Ritual Magic*. University Park, PA: Pen State University Press.

Feder, Theodore (2008): "Solomon, Socrates and Aristotle". In: *Biblical Archaeological Review* 34, pp. 32–36.

Feiner, Shmuel (2002): "Seductive Science and the Emergence of the Secular Jewish Intellectual". In: *Science in Context* 15, pp. 121–135.

Feiner, Shmuel (2017): *A New Age*: *Eighteenth-Century European Jewry 1700–1750*. Jerusalem: The Zalman Shazar Center. [Hebrew]

Feldman, Louis H. (1976): "Josephus as an Apologist to the Greco-Roman World: His Portrait of Solomon". In: Elisabeth S. Fiorenza (Ed.): *Aspects of Religious Propaganda in Judaism and Early Christianity*. Notre Dame University, pp. 69–98.

Feldman, Louis H. (1995): "Josephus' Portrait of Solomon": In: *Hebrew Union College Annual* 66, pp. 103–167.

Feldman, Louis H. (1997): "Josephus' View of Solomon". In: Lowell K. Handy (Ed.): *The Age of Solomon: Scholarship at the Turn of the Millennium*. Leiden: Brill, pp. 348–374.

Feldman, Louis H. (1998): *"Josephus's Interpretation of the Bible"*. University of California Press, Berkeley/Los Angeles/London: University of California Press.

Filius, Lourus Simon (1999): *The Problemata Physica Attributed to Aristotle: The Arabic Version of Hunain ibn Ishaq and the Hebrew Version of Moses Ibn Tibbon*. Leiden: Brill.

Finkelstein, Israel and Neil Asher Silberman (2006): *In Search of the Bible's Sacred Kings and the Roots of the Western Tradition*. New York: Free Press.

Fisher, Loren R. (1968) "'Can This Be the Son of David?'". In: F. Thomas Trotter (Ed.): *Jesus and the Historian. Written in Honor of Ernest Cadman*. Philadelphia: Westminster Press, pp. 82–97.

Fitzmyer, Joseph A. (2004): *The Genesis Apocryphon of Qumran Cave 1 (1Q20): A Commentary* (3rd ed.). Roma: Editrice Pontificio Istituto Biblico.

Fleg, Edmond (1959): *Solomon raconté par les peuples*. Paris: Albin Michel. [English translation: Fleg, Edmond (1929): *The Life of Solomon* (V. G. Garvin, Trans.). London: V. Gollancz.]

Flusser, David (1957): "Healing through the Laying-on of Hands in a Dead Sea Scroll". In: *Israel Exploration Journal* 7.

Flusser, David (1979): *Jewish Sources in Early Christianity: Studies and Essays*. Tel Aviv: Sifriat Poalim. [Hebrew]. [For the German edition: Flusser, David (1981): *Die rabbinischen Gleichnisse und der Gleichniserzähler Jesus (Vol. 1)*. Bern: Peter Lang.]

Flusser, David (2009): "The Son". In: Serge Ruzer and Arye Kofsky (Eds.): *Jesus*. Tel Aviv/ Jerusalem: Dvir and Magnes Press, pp. 153–163. [Hebrew]

Föhrer, Georg (1976): "Sophia". In: James L. Crenshaw (Ed.): *Studies in Ancient Israelite Wisdom*. New York, NY: Ktav Pub & Distributors Inc., pp. 63–83.

Förster, Niclas (2001): "Der Exorzist El'azar: Salomo, Josephus und das alte Ägypten". In: Jürgen U. Kalms (Ed.): *Internationales Josephus-Kolloquium Amsterdam 2000*. Münster: Lit, pp. 205–221.

Fowden, Garth (1993): *The Egyptian Hermes: A Historical Approach to the Late Pagan Mind*. Princeton, NJ: Princeton University Press.

Fox, Robin Lane (2016): *Augustine: Conversions and Confessions*. Penguin Books.

Frankel, Yonah (1994): "The History of the Literature of the Amoraim and the Late Midrash". In: Yonah Frankel: *Midrash and Aggadah: Unit 10*. Tel Aviv: The Open University. [Hebrew]

Fredriksen, Paula (2000): *From Jesus To Christ: The Origins of the New Testament Images of Christ* (2nd ed.). New Haven: Yale University Press.

Fredriksen, Paula (2018): *When Christians were Jews: The First Generation*. New Haven: Yale University Press.

Freely, John (2010): *Aladdin's Lamp: How Greek Science Came to Europe Through the Islamic World*. New York, NY: Vintage Books.

Freely, John (2015): *Light from the East: How the Science of Medieval Islam Helped to Shape the Western World*. London/New York: I.B. Tauris.

Freeman, Charles (2002): *The Closing of the Western Mind: The Rise of Faith and the Fall of Reason*. New York: Vintage Books.

Freeman, Margaret B. (1979): *The Story of the Three Kings*. New York: The Metropolitan Museum of Art.

Freudenthal, Gad (2013): "From Arabic to Hebrew: The Reception of the Greco-Arab Sciences in Hebrew (Twelfth-Fifteenth Centuries)". In: Abdelwahab Meddeb and Benjamin Stora (Eds.): *A History of Jewish-Muslim Relations: From the Origins to the Present Day*. Princeton/Oxford: Princeton University Press, pp. 796–815.

Frisch, Amos (1991): "Structure and Its Significance: The Narrative of Solomon's Reign (1 Kings 1:12–24)". In: *Journal for the Study of the Old Testament* 51, pp. 3–14.

Frisch, Amos (1997): "A Literary and Theological Analysis of the Account of Solomon's Sins (1 Kings 11:1–8)". In: *Shnaton: An Annual for Biblical and Ancient Near Eastern Studies* 11, pp. 167–179.

Fröhlich, Ida (2017): "Demons and Illness in Second Temple Judaism: Theory and Practice". In: Siam Bhayro and Catherine Rider (Eds.): *Demons and Illness from Antiquity to the Early-Modern Period*. Leiden: Brill, pp. 81–96.

Fuss, Abraham M. (1994): "The Study of Science and Philosophy Justified by Jewish Tradition". In: *The Torah U-Madda Journal* 5, pp. 101–114.

Gamble, Harry Y. (1995): *Book and Readers in the Early Church: A History of Early Christian Texts*. New Haven: Yale University Press.

Gammie, John G. and Leo G. Perdue (Eds.) (1990): *The Sage in Israel and the Ancient Near East*. Winona Lake, IN: Eisenbrauns.

Garber, Zeev (Ed.) (2001): *The Jewish Jesus: Revelation, Reflection, Reclamation*. Lafayette, IN: Purdue University Press.

Garin, Eugenio (1983): *Astrology in the Renaissance: The Zodiac of Life* (C. Jackson and J. Allen, Trans.). London: Routledge and Kegan Paul.

Gaster, Moses (1907–1908): "The Hebrew Version of the Secretum Secretorum: A Medieval Treatise Ascribed to Aristotle". In: *Journal of the Royal Asiatic Society* 39–40, pp. 879–911 (Vol. 39) and pp. 111–162, 1065–1084 (Vol. 40).

Gaster, Moses (1925–1928): *Studies and Texts in Folklore, Magic, Medieval Romance Hebrew Apocrypha and Samaritan Archaeology* (Vols. 1–3). London.

Gavin, Frank (1923): "Aphraates and the Jews: A Study of the Controversial Homilies of the Persian Sage in Their Relation to Jewish Thought". In: *Journal of the Society of Oriental Research Toronto* 7, pp. 95–166.

Geller, Markham J. (1974): *Joshua B. Perahia and Jesus of Nazareth: Two Rabbinic Magicians*. PhD Diss., Brandeis University.

Gevnents, Hans Joachim (Ed.) (1982): *Kleine Deutsche Gedichte*. Leipzig: Biblographisches Institut.

Gibbons, Brian J. (2001): *Spirituality and the Occult: From the Renaissance to the Modern Age*. London/New York: Routledge.

Gibson, Jeffrey B. (1995): *The Temptations of Jesus in Early Christianity*. London: Bloomsbury Publishing.

Ginzberg, Louis (2003): *Legends of the Jews (Vols. 1–6)*.

Giversen, Søren (1972): "Solomon und die Dämonen". In: Martin Krause (Ed.): *Essays on Nag Hamadi Texts*. Leiden: Brill, pp. 16–21.

Glasner, Ruth (2011): "The Peculiar History of Aristotelianism Among Spanish Jews". In: Resianne Fontaine, Ruth Glasner, Reimund Leicht and Giuseppe Veltri (Eds.): *Studies in the History of Culture and Science*. Leiden: Brill, pp. 361–381.

Goethe, Johann Wolfgang von (1963): *Faust* (W. Kaufmann, Trans.). New York: Doubleday.

Goldin, Judah (Trans.) (1955): *Avot de-Rabbi Nathan*. Yale University Press.

Gollancz, Herman (1903): *Clavicula Salomonis*. Minden.

Gooding, David W. (1965): "The Septuagint's Version of Solomon's Misconduct". In: *Vetus Testamentum* 14, pp. 325–335.

Goshen-Gottstein, Alon (1987): *God and Israel as Father and Son in Tannaitic Literature*. Phd Diss., Hebrew University of Jerusalem. [Hebrew]

Gottlober, Avraham (1858): *Anaf-etz-avot (kolel shalosh hashirim asher sharti likhvod adoneinu hakeisar Alexander II)*. Vilna.

Gottlober, Abraham Baer (1976): *Memoirs and Travels*. Jerusalem: Bialik Institute.

Grabbe, Lester L. (1997): *Wisdom of Solomon*. Sheffield: Sheffield Academic Press.

Grabbe, Lester L. (2019): "Jesus in Non-Christian Sources". http://www.asor.org/anetoday/2019/05/Jesus-in-Non-Christian-Sources, visited on April 14, 2020.

Graetz, Heinrich (1975): *The Structure of Jewish History and other Essays* (I. Schorch, Ed. and Trans.).New York: The Jewish Theological Seminary of America.

Grafton, Anthony and Megan Williams (2006): *Christianity and the Transformation of the Book: Origen, Eusebius and the Library of Caesarea*. Cambridge, MA: The Belknap Press of Harvard University.

Grafton, Anthony (1991): "Protestant versus Prophet: Isaac Casaubon on Hermes Trismegiscus". In: Anthony Grafton: *Defenders of the Text: The Tradition of Scholarship in the Age of Science 1450–1800*. Cambridge, MA: Harvard University Press, pp. 145–177.

Green, H. Benedict (1982): "Solomon the Son of David in Matthaean Typology". In: *Studia Evangelica* 7, pp. 227–230.

Greenbaum, Dorian Gieseler (2016): *The Daimon in Hellenistic Astrology*. Leiden: Brill.

Greg, Robert C (2015): *Shared Stories, Rival Tellings: Early Encounters of Jews, Christians, and Muslims*. Oxford University Press.

Gregory of Nyssa (1994): *Homilies on the Song of Songs* (R. A. Morris Jr., Trans.). Atlanta: Society of Biblical Literature.

Gribetz, Sarit Kattan (2013): "Jesus and the Clay Birds: Reading Toledot Yeshu in Light of the Infancy Gospels". In: Ra'anan S. Boustan, Klaus Herrmann, Reimund Leicht, Annette Y. Reed and Giuseppe Veltri (Eds.): *Envisioning Judaism: Studies in Honor of Peter Schäfer on the Occasion of His Seventieth Birthday*. Tübingen: Mohr Siebeck, pp. 1021–1048.

Griese, Sabine (2017): "Eine Autorität gerät ins Wanken. Markolfs Worte und Taten gegen Salomon in der Literatur des Mittelalters und der Frühen Neuzeit". In: *Die Bibel in der Kunst (BiKu) / Bible in the Arts (BiA)* 1.

Gronewald, Michael et al. (1997): *Kölner Papyri Band 8*. Westdeutscher Verlag.

Grossfeld, Bernard (1991): *The Two Targums of Esther*. Edinburgh: T & T Clark.

Grossfeld, Bernard (1994): *The Targum Sheni to the Book of Esther*. New York: Sepher Hermon Press.

Grossman, Abraham (2007): "The Gentiles in Rashi's Teaching: Polemical Trends in his Commentary on the Bible". In: Meir M. Bar-Asher et al (eds.). *A Word Fitly Spoke: Studies in Medieval Exegesis of the Hebrew Bible and the Qur'an*, pp. 97–124. [Hebrew]

Grossman, Avraham (2012): "Rashi as an Original Preacher". In: Kimmy Caplan et al. (Eds.): *Preachers, Sermons and Homiletics in Jewish Culture*. Jerusalem: Zalman Shazar, pp. 49–65. [Hebrew]

Guillaume de Deguileville (1975 [1426]): *The Pilgrimage of the Life of Man* (J. Lydgate, Trans.). New York.

Gunderson, Lloyd L. (1980): *Alexander's Letter to Aristotle about India*. Meisenheim am Glan: A. Hain.

Gutas, Dimitri (1986): "The Spurious and the Authentic in the Arabic Lives of Aristotle". In: Kraye, Ryan and Schmitt: *Pseudo-Aristotle*, pp. 15–36.

Guttman, Alexander (1947): "The Significance of Miracles for Talmudic Judaism". In: *HUCA* 20, pp. 383–406.

HaCohen, Ran (1994): *Bible Stories for Jewish Children during the Haskalah in Germany: The Bible, History and Models of German Children's Literature*, M.A. Diss., Tel Aviv University. [Hebrew]

Hadas-Lebel, Miraille (1999): "Hezekiah as King Messiah: Traces of an Early Jewish-Christian Polemic in the Tannaitic Tradition". In: Judit Targarona Borrás and Angel Sáenz-Badillos (Eds.): *Jewish Studies at the Turn of the Twentieth Century* (*Vol. 1*). Leiden: Brill, pp. 275–281.

Hagen, Kenneth (1974): *A Theology of Testament in the Young Luther: The Lectures on Hebrews*. Leiden: Brill.

Hagen, Susan K (1990): *Allegorical Remembrance: A Study of 'The Pilgrimage of the Life of Man' as a Medieval Treatise on Seeing and Remembering*. Athens, GA: University of Georgia Press.

Hägerland, Tobias (2012): *Jesus and the Forgiveness of Sins*: *An Aspect of his Prophetic Mission*. New York: Cambridge University Press.

Halbertal, Moshe (2007): *Concealment and Revelation*: *Esotericism in Jewish Thought and its Philosophical Implications* (J. Feldman, Trans.). New Jersey: Princeton University Press.

Halevi, Judah 1946 [1905]: *The Kuzari* [*Kitāb al-Khazarī*] (H. Hirschfeld, Trans.). New York: Paved Publishing House.

Halevi Madlinger, S. (1893): *The Life of Aristotle and His Philosophy*. Vienna. [Hebrew]

Halkin, Abraham and David Hartman (1985): *Crisis and Leadership*: *Epistles of Maimonides*. Philadelphia: Jewish Publication Society of America.

Halperin, David J. (1982): "The Book of Remedies, the Canonization of the Solomonic Writings, and the Riddle of Pseudo-Eusebius". In: *The Jewish Quarterly Review* 72, No. 4, pp. 269–292.

Hammer, Reuven (Trans.) (1986): *Sifre*: *A Tannaitic Commentary on the Book of Deuteronomy*. New Haven/London: Yale University Press.

Handy, Lowell K. (1997): *The Age of Solomon*: *Scholarship at the Turn of the Millenium*. Leiden: Brill.

Hanegraaff, Wouter J. (2013): *Western Esotericism*: *A Guide for the Perplexed*. London: Bloomsbury.

Hanig, Roman (1993): "Christus als 'wahrer Salomo' in der frühen Kirche". In: *ZNW* 84, pp. 111–134.

Haran, Menahem (1994): "Archives, Libraries, and the Order of the Biblical Books". In: *The Journal of the Ancient Near Eastern Society* 22, pp. 51–61.

Harari, Yuval (2017): *Jewish Magic before the Rise of Kabbalah*. Wayne State University Press.

Harris, J. Rendel and Alphonse Mingana (1916–1920): *The Odes and Psalms of Solomon*. Manchester University Press.

Harris, Jonathan (2016): *The Lost World of Byzantium*. New Haven: Yale University Press.

Ḥasdai Crescas (1990): *Sefer Bitul Iqqrei Ha-Nozriom* (J. S. Tov, Trans.) (D. A. Lasker, Ed.). Ramat-Gan and Beer-Sheva. [Hebrew]

Hattaway, Michael (1968): "Paradoxes of Solomon: Learning in the English Renaissance". In: *Journal of the History of Ideas* 29, No. 4, pp. 499–530.

Heilprin, Yehiel (1769): *Sefer Seder haDorot—Kore haDorot miRosh Yemot Olam* [The Book of Generations]. Karlsruhe.

Hengel, Martin (1976): *The Son of God: The Origins of Christology and the History of Jewish-Hellenistic Religion* (J. Bowden, Trans.). Philadelphia: Fortress Press.

Hermann, Klaus (1999): "The Reception of Hekhalot Literature in Yohanan Alemanno's Autograph MS Paris 849". In: Joseph Dan and Klaus Herrmann (Eds.); *Studies in Jewish Manuscripts*. Tübingen: Mohr Seibeck, pp. 19–88.

Herrin, Judith (2008): *Byzantium: The Surprising Life of a Medieval Empire*. Penguin Books.

Heyd, Michael (2011): "'Train Up the Child According to His Way': Authoritarian Education or Training for Autonomy? Early Modern English Translations, Commentaries, and Sermons on Proverbs 22:6 as a Case Study". In: Immanuel Etkes, Tamar Elor, Michael Heyd and Baruch Schwarz (Eds.): *Education and Religion: Authority and Autonomy*. Jerusalem, pp. 101–144. [Hebrew]

Heywood, W. (1924): *The Little Flowers of the Glorious Messer St. Francis and His Friars* [Actus beati Francisci et Sociorum eius]. London.

Highet, Gilbert (1970): *The Classical Tradition: Greek and Roman Influences on Western Literature*. Oxford University Press.

Hildegard of Bingen (2001): *Selected Writings* (M. Atherton, Trans.). Penguin Classics.

Hill, Christopher (1994): *The English Bible and the Seventeenth-century Revolution*. Penguin.

Hirschfeld, Hartwig (1918): *Qirqisâni Studies*. London: Jews' College.

Hirshman, Mark (Ed.) (2016): *Midrash Kohelet Rabbah*. Jerusalem: Schehter Institute of Jewish Studies.

Hirshman, Marc (1988): "The Greek Fathers and the Aggada on Ecclesiastes: Forms of Exegesis in Late Antiquity," *Hebrew Union College Annual*, pp. 137–165.

Hogeterp, Albert L. A. (2012): "Solomon in the New Testament and Jewish Tradition". In: Joseph Verheyden (Ed.): *The Figure of Solomon in Jewish, Christian an Islamic Tradition*. Leiden: Brill, pp. 144–154.

Horbury, William (2006 [1998]): *Jews and Christians in Contact and Controversy*. Edinburgh: Bloomsbury Publishing.

Hornung, Erik (2001): *The Secret Lore of Egypt: Its Impact on the West* (D. Lorton, Trans.). Ithaca, NY: Cornell University Press.

Horovitz, Hayyim Saul and Israel Abraham Rabin (Eds.) (1960). *Mekhilta Pisha 15* (2nd ed.). Jerusalem, pp. 59–60.

Hurowitz, Victor Avigdor and Shamir Yona (Eds.) (2011): *Wisdom: Its Seven Pillars*. Beer Sheva: Ben-Gurion University Press. [Hebrew]

Hübner, Johann (1986 [1714]: *Zweymahl und fünfzig Auserlesene Biblische Historien Aus dem Alten und Neuen Testament, Der Jugend zum Besten abgefasset*. Zurich/New York: Hildesheim.

Huffman, Carl. A. (Ed.) (2014): *A History of Pythagoreanism*. Cambridge: Cambridge University.

Hull, John M. (1974): *Hellenistic Magic and the Synoptic Tradition*. London: SCM Press.

Hurtado, Larry W. (2005): *How on Earth did Jesus Become a God? Historical Questions about Earliest Devotion to Jesus*. Grand Rapids, MI: Eerdmans.

Ibn Abī Yaʿqūb al-Nadīm (1970): *The Fihrist of al-Nadim: A Tenth-Century Survey of Muslim Culture* (B. Dodge, Trans.). New York: Columbia University Press.

Ibn Aldaby, Meir (1988): *Sefer Shevilei Emunah*. Jerusalem: Bakal.

Ibn Khaldūn (1958): *The Muqaddimah: An Introduction to History* (F. Rozenthal, Trans.). New York: Pantheon Books.

Ibn Yahya, Gedaliah (1957): *Sefer Shalshelet ha-Kabbala*. Venice.

Idel, Moshe (1979): "The Study Program of R. Yohanan Alemanno". In: *Tarbiz* 48, pp. 303–331.

Idel, Moshe (1983a): "Inquiries into the Doctrine of 'Sefer ha-Meshiv'". In: *Sefunot* 17, pp. 185–266. [Hebrew]

Idel, Moshe (1983b): "The Magical and Neoplatonic Interpretations of the Kabbalah in the Renaissance". In: Bernard Dov Cooperman (Ed.): *Jewish Thought in the Sixteenth Century*. Cambridge, MA: Harvard University Press, pp. 186–242.

Idel, Moshe (1988): "Hermeticism and Judaism". In: Ingrid Merkel and Allen G. Debus (Eds.): *Hermeticism and the Renaissance: Intellectual History and the Occult in Early Modern Europe*. Washington, pp. 59–76.

Idel, Moshe (1994): "The Lost Books of Solomon: On the Attitude to Science in the Book of the Responding Entity". In: *Daat* 32–33, pp. 235–246. [Hebrew]

Idel, Moshe (1995): "On the King as Magician: Several Lines". In: Rachel Milstein (Ed.): *King Solomon's Seal*. Jerusalem: Tower of David Museum of the History of Jerusalem, pp. 15–17. [Hebrew]

Idel, Moshe (1997): "On Judaism, Jewish Mysticism and Magic". In: Schäfer and Kippenberg, *Envisioning Magic*, pp. 195–214.

Idel, Moshe (2007): *Ben: Sonship and Jewish Mysticism*. London/New York: Continuum.

Ilan, Tal (2013): "Jesus and Joshua ben Perahiah: A Jewish-Christian Dialogue on Magic in Babylonia". In: Ra'anan S. Boustan, Klaus Herrmann, Reimund Leicht, Annette Y. Reed and Giuseppe Veltri (Eds.): *Envisioning Judaism: Studies in Honor of Peter Schäfer on the Occasion of His Seventieth Birthday* (Vol. 2). Tübingen: Mohr Siebeck, pp. 985–995.

Illes Johnston, Sarah (2003): "The Testament of Solomon from Late Antiquity to the Renaissance". In: Jan N. Bremmer and Jan R. Veenstra (Eds.): *The Metamorphosis of Magic* (Groningen Studies in Cultural Change, Vol. 1). Leuven, pp. 30–35.

Isidore of Seville: *Allegoria quaedam sanctae Scriptura*, Migne, Patrologia Latina, Vol. 98, cols. 97–130.

Israel, Jonathan (1995): "Spinoza, King Solomon and Frederik Van Leenhof's Spinozistic Republicanism". In: *Studia Spinozana* 11, pp. 303–317.

Israelowich, Ido (2015): *Patients and Healers in the High Roman Empire*. Baltimore, MD: Johns Hopkins University Press.

Isserles, Moshe R. (1854): *Sefer Torat ha'olah*. Königsberg.

James, Montague Rhodes (Ed.) (1893): *Apocrypha Anecdota*. Cambridge: Cambridge University Press.

Jankrift, Kay Peter (2005): *Mit Gott und schwarzer Magie*: *Medizin in Mittelalter*. Stuttgart: Wissenschaftliche Buchgesellschaft.

Jasnow, Richard and Karl-Theodor Zauzich (2005): *The Ancient Egyptian Book of Thoth*: *A Demotic Discourse on Knowledge and Pendant to the Classical Hermetica*. Wiesbaden: Harrassowitz Verlag.

Jayne, Walter A. (1962): *The Healing Gods of Ancient Civilizations*. New York: Kessinger Publishing.

Jellinek, Adolph (1873): *Bet ha-Midrasch*. Vienna.

Jellinek, Adolph (1938): *Beit Hamidrash, Sammlung kleiner Midraschim und Vermischter Abhandlungen aus der Ältern Jüdischen* (*Vol. 3*). Jerusalem: Bamberger & Wahrmann. [Hebrew]

Jenkins, Claude (1953): "Saint Augustine and Magic": In: Edgar Ashworth Underwood (Ed.): *Science, Medicine and History*: *Essays on the Evolution of Scientific Thought and Medical Practice* (Vol. 1). London: Oxford University Press, pp. 131–140.

Jensen, Robin M. (2017): *The Cross*. Cambridge, MA: Harvard University Press.

Johannes of Würzburg (1971): *Description of the Holy Land* (A. Stewart, Trans.). New York: AMS Press.

John of Salisbury (2007): *Policraticus* (C. J. Nederman, Ed. & Trans.). Cambridge University Press.

Jordan, David R. and Roy Kotansky (1997): "A Solomonic Exorcism". In: Michael Gronewald, Klaus Maresch and Cornelia Römer (Eds.): *Papyrologica Coloniensia* (*Vol. 7.8*). pp. 53–69.

Josephus (1963): *Jewish Antiquities* (3rd ed.) (R. Marcus, Trans.).

Julian (1980): *The Works of Emperor Julian* (W. C. Wright, Ed. and Trans.). Cambridge/London.

Justin Martyr (2003): *Dialogue with Trypho* (T. B. Falls, Trans.). Washington D.C.: The Catholic University Press.

Kahana, Maoz (2013a): "An Esoteric Path to Modernity: Rabbi Jacob Emden's Alchemical Quest". In: *Journal of Modern Jewish Studies* 12, pp. 253–275.

Kahana, Maoz (2013b): "The Scientific Revolution and the Encoding of Sources of Knowledge: Medicine, Halakhah, and Alchemy in Hamburg-Altona, 1736". In: *Tarbiz* 8, pp. 165–212. [Hebrew]

Kalimi, Isaac (2012): "King Solomon: His Birth and Names in the Second Temple Period Literature". In: *Biblica* 93, pp. 481–499.

Kalimi, Isaac (2017): *Fighting Over the Bible*: *Jewish Interpretation, Sectarianism and Polemic from Temple to Talmud and Beyond*. Leiden: Brill.

Kalimi, Issac (2019): "Writing and Rewritung the Story of Solomon in Ancient Israel". ASOR 7, No. 7.

Kalugila, Leonidas (1980): *The Wise King*: *Studies in Royal Wisdom as Divine Revelation in the Old Testament and its Environment*. Lund, Sweden: CWK Gleerup.

Kamin, Sarah (2008a): "Rashi's Commentary on the Song of Songs and Jewish-Christian Polemic". In: Sarah Kamin: *Jews and Christians Interpret the Bible*. Jerusalem: Magnes Press, pp. 22–57. [Hebrew]

Kamin, Sarah (2008b): "The Relation of Nicolas de Lyre to Rashi in his Commentary on the Song of Songs". In: Sarah Kamin (2008): *Jews and Christians Interpret the Bible*. Jerusalem: Magnes Press, pp. 58–68. [Hebrew]

Kara-Ivanov Kaniel, Ruth (2014): *Holiness and Transgression: Mothers of the Messiah in The Jewish Myth*. Tel Aviv: Hakibbutz Hameuchad Publishing.

Kartschoke, Dieter (1990): *Geschichte der deutschen Literatur im frühen Mittelalter*. München: Deutscher Taschenbuch Verlag.

Kasher, Aryeh (1993): "The Journey of Alexander the Great in Eretz-Yisrael". ASOR 7, No. 7. In: Rappaport and Ronen, *The State of the Hasmoneans*. Jerusalem/Tel Aviv, pp. 13–35.

Katz, David (2007): *The Occult Tradition: From the Renaissance to the Present Day*. London: Jonathan Cape.

Kee, Howard Clark (1986): *Medicine, Miracle and Magic in New Testament Times*. Cambridge: Cambridge University Press.

Kellner, Menachem (1991): "Gersonides' Commentary on Song of Songs: Why He Wrote it and to Whom it was Addressed". In: Gilbert Dahan (Ed.): *Gersonide et son temps*: Science et philosophie médiévales. Louvain-Paris: Peters, pp. 81–107.

Kelly, Henry Ansgar (2006): *Satan: A Biography*. Cambridge: Cambridge University Press.

Kelly, John Norman Davidson (1963): "The Bible and the Latin Fathers". In: D. E. Nineham (Ed.): *The Church's Use of the Bible: Past and Present*. London: S.P.C.K., pp. 41–56.

Kemble, John M. (Ed.) (1848): *The Dialogue of Salomon and Saturnus*. London.

Khalidi, Tarif (Ed. and Trans.) (2001): *The Muslim Jesus: Sayings and Stories in Islamic Literature*. Cambridge: Harvard University Press.

Kieckhefer, Richard (1990): *Magic in the Middle Ages*. New York: Cambridge University Press.

Kimhi, David (Radak) (1967): *The Complete Commentary on Psalms* (A. Darom, Ed.). Jerusalem: Mossad Harav Kook. [Hebrew]

Kiperwasser, Reuven and Serge Ruzer (2013): "The Holy Land and Its Inhabitants in the Pilgrimage Narrative of the Persian Monk Bar Sauma". *Cathedra* 148, pp. 41–71. [Hebrew]

Kippenberg, Hans G. (1997): "Magica in Roman Civil Discourse: Why Rituals Could be Illegal". In: Schäfer and Kippenberg, *Envisioning Magic*, pp. 137–163.

Klausner, Joseph (1955): "The Jewish Messiah and the Christian Messiah". In: Joseph Klausner: *Judaism and Humanism (Vol. 2)*. Jerusalem. [Hebrew]

Klein-Braslavy, Sara (2007): *King Solomon and Philosophical Esotericism in the Thought of Maimonides*. Jerusalem: Magnes Press. [Hebrew]

Klein-Braslavy, Sara (2005): "The Alexandrian Prologue Paradigm in Gersonides's Writings". *Quarterly Review* 90, No. 2, pp. 257–289.

Klijn, Albertus F. J. (1977): "A Library of Scriptures in Jerusalem?". In: K. Treu (Ed.): *Studia Codicologica 124*. Berlin: Technische Universitat, pp. 265–272.

Klutz, Todd (Ed.) (2004): *Magic in the Biblical World: From the Rod of Aaron to the Ring of Solomon*. London: Bloomsbury Publishing.

Klutz, Todd E. (2005): *Rewriting the Testament of Solomon: Tradition, Conflict and Identity in a Late Antique Pseudepigraphon*. London: Bloomsbury Publishing.

Knight, Christopher and Alan Butler (2007): *Solomon's Power Brokers: The Secrets of Freemasonry, the Church, and the Illuminati*. London: Watkins Publishing.

Knoppers, Gary N. (1995): "Images of David in Early Judaism: David as Repentant Sinner in Chronicles". *Biblica* 76, pp. 449–470.

Kofsky, Aryeh and Serge Ruzer (2018): *Early Christian Beliefs: Challenges, Transformations, Polemics*. Tel Aviv: IDRA Publishing. [Hebrew]

Kohs, Michael (2017): "The Interplay of Images and Writing in Mafteah Shelomoh: Two Experiments for Escaping from Prison". In: *European Journal of Jewish Studies* 11, pp. 1–23.

Kotansky, Roy (1995): "Greek Exorcistic Amulets". In: Meyer and Mirecki, *Ancient Magic and Ritual Power*, pp. 243–277.

Kraemer, Joel L. (1992): *Humanism in the Renaissance of Islam: The Cultural Revival during the Buyid Age* (2nd ed.). Leiden: Brill.

Kraemer, Joel L. (2008): *Maimonides: The Life and World of One of Civilization's Greatest Minds*. New York: Doubleday.

Kraft, Robert Allan (2009): "The Dialogue of Timothy and Aquila and Its Echoes of Judaism". In: Supplement to the *Journal for the Study of Judaism* 137, pp. 173–196.

Kraus, Samuel (1995): *The Jewish-Christian Controversy: From the Earliest Times to 1789* (W. Horbury (Ed.). Vol. 1. Tübingen: J.C.B. Mohr.

Kraye, Jill, William Francis Ryan and Charles B. Schmitt (Eds.) (1986): *Pseudo-Aristotle in the Middle Ages: The Theology and Other Texts*. London: The Warburg Institute, University of London.

Kushelevsky, Rella (2011): *Penalty and Temptation: Hebrew Tales in Ashkenaz*. Jerusalem: Magnes Press.

Lahey, Lawrence L. (2001): *The Dialogue of Timothy and Aquila: Critical Greek Text and English Translation of the Short Recension with an Introduction including a Sourcecritical Study*. University of Cambridge. Ph.D. dissertation.

Lakoff, George and Mark Johnson (2003): *Metaphors We Live By*. University of Chicago Press.

Lameer, Joep (1991): "From Alexandria to Baghdad: Reflections on the Genesis of a Problematic Tradition". In: G. Endress and R. Kruk (Eds.): *The Ancient Tradition in Christian and Islamic Hellenism: Studies on the Transmission of Greek Philosophy and Sciences*. Leiden: Brill, pp. 181–191.

Langer, Gerhard (2013): "Solomon in Rabbinic Literature": In: Joseph Verheyden (Ed.): *The Figure of Solomon in Jewish, Christian and Islamic Tradition. King, Sage and Architect*. Leiden: Brill, pp. 127–142.

Lasker, Daniel J. and Sarah Stroumsa (1996): *The Polemic of Nestor the Priest*. Jerusalem: Yad Ben Zvi.

Lasker, Daniel J. (1997): "Jewish Polemics against Christianity in Thirteenth-Century Italy". In: Yaakov Elman and Jeffrey S. Gurock (Eds.): *Hazon Nahum: Studies in Jewish Law, Thought, and History*. New York: Ktav, pp. 251–263.

Lasker, Daniel J. (2017): *Jewish Philosophical Polemics Against Christianity in the Middle Ages: With a New Introduction*. Liverpool University Press.

Lasker, Daniel J. (2019): "Jewish Anti-Christian Polemics in Light of Mass Conversion to Christianity". In: Mercedes García-Arenal and Gerard Wiegers (Eds.): *Polemical Encounters: Christians, Jews and Muslims in Iberia and Beyond*. Penn State University Press.

Lassner, Jacob (1993): *Demonizing the Queen of Sheba: Boundaries of Gender and Culture in Post-Biblical Judaism and Medieval Islam*. Chicago, IL: University of Chicago Press.

Lassner, Jacob (2007): "Additional Riddles From the Riddler's File of King Solomon and the Queen of Sheba". In: Y. Tzvi Langermann and Josef Stern (Eds.): *Adaptations and Innovations: Studies on the Interaction between Jewish and Islamic Thought and Literature from the Early Middle Ages to the Late Twentieth Century*, Dedicated to Professor Joel L. Kraemer. Paris/Louvain/Dudley, MA: Peeters, pp. 249–287.

Lebensohn, Micah Joseph (1972): *Shirei Michal: Sifriyat Dvir La'am*. Tel Aviv.

Lehrich, Christopher I. (2005): *The Language of Demons and Angels: Cornelius Agrippa's Occult Philosophy*. Leiden: Brill.

Leithart, Peter J. (2008): *Solomon Among the Postmoderns*. Grand Rapids, MI: Brazos Press.

Lelli, Fabrizio (2000): "'Prisca Philosophia' and 'Docta Religio': The Boundaries of Rational Knowledge in Jewish and Christian Humanist Thought". In: *The Jewish Quarterly Review* 91, pp. 53–99.

Lelli, Fabrizio (2004): "Jews, Humanists, and the Reappraisal of Pagan Wisdom Associated with the Ideal of Dignitas Hominis". In: Allison P. Coudert and Jeffrey S. Shoulson (Ed.): *Hebraica Veritas? Christian Hebraists and the Study of Judaism in Early Modern Europe*. Philadelphia, PA: University of Pennsylvania Press, pp. 49–70.

Levinsohn, Isaac Baer (1977 [1829]): *Teudah beYisrael* [A Testimony in Israel]. Jerusalem: Zalman Shazar Center.

Levinson, Joshua (2006): "Enchanting Rabbis: Contest Narratives between Rabbis and Magicians in Rabbinic Literature of Late Antiquity". In: *Tarbiz* 75, pp. 295–328. [Hebrew]

Lewy, Johann Hans (1938): "Aristotle and the Jewish Sage according to Clearchus of Soli". In: *The Harvard Theological Review* 31, pp. 205–235.

Lichtheim, Miriam (1975): *Ancient Egyptian Literature* (*Vol. 1*: *The Old and Middle Kingdoms*). Berkeley, CA: California University Press.

Lienhard, Joseph T. (1970): "The Christology of the Epistle to Diognetus". In: *Vigiliae Christianae* 24, pp. 280–289.

Limor, Ora and Guy Stroumsa (Eds.) (1966): *Contra Iudaeos*: *Ancient and Medieval Polemics between Christians and Jews*. Tübingen: J. C.B. Mohr (Paul Siebeck).

Limor, Ora (1998a): " The Polemic of Nestor the Priest and Sefer Toledot Yeshu". In: *Pe'amim*: *Studies in Oriental Jewry* 75, pp. 109–128. [Hebrew]

Limor, Ora (1998b): *Holy Land Travels*: *Christian Pilgrims in Late Antiquity*. Jerusalem: Yad Ben Zvi. [Hebrew]

Linder, Amnon (Ed. and Trans.) (1987): *The Jews in Roman Imperial Legislation*. Detroit: Wayne State University Press / Jerusalem: The Israel Academy of Sciences and Humanities.

Locke, John (1993): *Two Treatises of Government* (M. Goldie, Ed.). London: Everyman.

Loewenthal, Albert (1896): *Honein ibn Ishâk, Sinnsprüche der Philosophen*, Nach der hebräischen Uebersetzung Charisi's ins Deutsche übertragen und erläutert. Berlin: Calvary.

Lomas, Robert (2002): *The Invisible College*: *The Royal Society, Freemasonry and the Birth of Modern Science*. London, Headline Book Publishing.

Long, Anthony A. (1982): "Astrology: Arguments Pro and Contra". In: Jonathan Barnes, Jacques Brunschwig, Myles Burnyeat and Malcolm Schofield (Eds.): *Science and Speculation: Studies in Hellenistic Theory and Practice*. Cambridge/Paris: Cambridge University Press and Éditions de la Maison des Sciences de l'Homme, pp. 165–192.

Lucas, Leopold (1993): *The Conflict between Christianity and Judaism: A Contribution to the History of the Jews in the Fourth Century*. Warminster: Aris & Phillips. [German orig., 1910].

Lucian of Samosata (1969): *Lucian (Vol. 2)* (A. M. Harmon, Trans.). LCL. Cambridge, MA: Harvard University Press.

Lur'e, Jakov Solomonovič (1964): "Une légende inconnue de Salomon et Kitovras dans un manuscrit du XVe siècle". In: *Revue des Études Slaves* 43, pp. 7–11.

Luther, Martin (2015): *On The Jews and Their Lies* [Von den Juden und Iren Lügen] (D. d'Abruzzo, Ed.). Princeton: Eulenspiegel Press.

Lutz, Cora E. (1975): "The letter of Lentulus Describing Christ". In: *The Yale University Library Gazette* 50, pp. 91–97.

Macgregor Mathers, Samuel Liddell (2006 [1888]): *The Key of Solomon the King*. New York: Cosimo Classics.

Mackensen, Ruth Stellhorn (1932): "Four Great Libraries of Medieval Baghdad". In: *Library Quarterly* 2, pp. 279–299.

McGlynn, Moyna (2010): "Solomon, Wisdom and the Philosopher-Kings". In: Géza G. Xeravits and Jo´zsef Zsengelle´r (Eds.): *Studies in the Book of Wisdom*. Leiden: Brill, pp. 61–81.

MacMullen, Ramsay (1975): *Enemies of the Roman Order: Treason, Unrest, and Alienation in the Empire* (2nd ed.). Cambridge, MA: Harvard University Press.

Macy, Jeffrey (1989): "Hellenistic Influences on Islam and Judaism in the Middle Ages". In: Yosef Kaplan and Menahem Stern (Eds.): *Acculturation and Assimilation: Continuity and Change in the Cultures of Israel and the Nations*. Jerusalem: The Zalman Shazar Center. [Hebrew]

Maguire, Henry (Ed) (1995): *Byzantine Magic*. Washington DC: Dumbarton Oaks Research Library and Collection.

Maimonides (1904): *The Guide for the Perplexed* (2nd ed.) (M. Friedlander, Trans.). New York.

Maimonides (2002): *The Guide of the Perplexed* (M. Schwarz, Trans.). Tel Aviv University Press.

Malter, Harry (1910): "Shem Tov Ben Joseph Palquera: A Thinker and Poet of the Thirteenth Century". In: *The Jewish Quarterly Review* 1, pp. 151–181.

Mandelbaum, Bernard (Ed.) (1962): Pesiqta de-Rab Kahana. New York: The Jewish Theological Seminary of America. [For the English edition: Braude, William G. and Israel James Kapstein (1975): *Pesiqta de-Rab Kahana*. Philadelphia.]

Manzalaoui, Mahmoud (1974): "The Pseudo-Aristotelian 'Kitāb Sirr al-Asrār': Facts and Problems". In: *Oriens* 23–24, pp. 147–257.

Map, Walter (1988): *De nugis curialium: Courtier's Trifles* (M. R. James, C. N. L. Brooke, and R. A. B. Mynors, Eds.). Oxford: Clarendon Press.

Margalioth, M. (1966): *Sefer ha-Razim: A newly Discovered Book of Magic from the Talmudic Period Collected from Genizah Fragments and Other Sources*. Jerusalem: American Academy for Jewish Research. [Hebrew]

Margoliouth, David Samuel (Ed.) (1892): The Book of the Apple (ascribed to Aristotle). In: *The Journal of the Royal Asiatic Society of Great Britain and Ireland*, pp. 197–252.

Markus, Robert Austin (1961): "The Impact of Aristotle on Medieval Thought". In: *Blackfriars* 42, pp. 96–102.

Martin, Lois (2010): *A Brief History of Witchcraft: Demons, Folklore, and Superstition*. London: Constable & Robinson.

Martin, Ralph P. (1964): "A Footnote to Pliny's Account of Christian Worship". In: *Vox Evangelica* 3, pp. 51–57.

Martin, Vincent (1995): *A House Divided: The Parting of the Ways between the Synagouge and Church*. Paulist Press.

Matthews, Alastair (2010): "'Ich pin der haid Aristotiles. ein exempel nemend des': Performing Aristotle's Lessons". In: Manuele Gragnolati and Almut Suerbaum (Eds.): *Aspects of the Performative in Medieval Culture*. Berlin/Boston: De Gruyter, pp. 245–276.

Mavroudi, Maria (2015): "Translations from Greek into Latin and Arabic During the Middle Ages: Searching for the Classical Tradition". In: *Speculum* 90, pp. 28–59.

McCown, Chester Charlton (1922a): "The Christian Tradition as to the Magical Wisdom of Solomon". In: *Journal of the Palestine Oriental Society* 2, pp. 1–21.

McCown, Chester Charlton (1922b): *The Testament of Solomon*. Leipzig: J.C. Hinrichs'sche Buchhandlung.

McLeod, Frederick (2009): *Theodore of Mopsuestia*. Routledge.

Meerson, Michael and Peter Schäfer (Eds. and Trans.) (2014): *Toledot Yeshu*: *The Life Story of Jesus*: *Two Volumes and Database*. Tübingen: Mohr Siebeck.

Meggitt, Justin J. (2006): "Magic, Healing and Early Christianity; Consumption and Competition". In: Amy Wygant (Ed.): *The Meanings of Magic*: *From the Bible to Buffalo Bill*. New York/Oxford: Berghahn Books, pp. 89–114.

Meggitt, Justin J. (2015): *The Madness of King Jesus*: *The Real Reasons for his Execution*. London: I.B. Tauris.

Meir, Yaacov Z. (2014): "Handles for the Torah". In: *Ha'aretz*, 18 April 2014, Culture and Literature supplement.

Melamed, Abraham (2003): *On the Shoulders of Giants*: *The Debate Between Moderns and Ancients in Medieval and Renaissance Jewish Thought*. Ramat-Gan: Bar-Ilan University Press. [Hebrew]

Melamed, Abraham (2010): *The Myth of the Jewish Origins of Science and Philosophy*. Haifa University Press. [Hebrew]

Mendele Mocher Sforim (1962): *The Works of Mendele Mocher Sforim*. Tel Aviv: Dvir. [Hebrew]

Merback, Mitchell B. (Ed.) (2008): *Beyond The Yellow Badge*: *Anti-Judaism and Anti-Semitism in Medieval And Early Modern Visual Culture*. Leiden: Brill.

Merchavia, Chen-Melech (1970): *The Church Versus Talmudic and Midrashic Literature (500–1248)*. Jerusalem: Bialik Institute. [Hebrew]

Merkel, Ingrid and Allen G. Debus (Eds.) (1988): *Hermeticism and the Renaissance: Intellectual History and the Occult in Early Modern Europe*. Washington, DC: Folger Institute.

Meyer, Marvin and Paul Mirecki (Eds) (2002): *Ancient Magic and Ritual Power*. Leiden: Brill.

Milikowsky, Chaim (Ed.) (2013): *Seder Olam*. Jerusalem: Yad Ben Zvi. [Hebrew]

Milstein, Rachel (Ed.) (1995): *King Solomon's Seal*. Jerusalem: Tower of David Museum of the History of Jerusalem. [Hebrew]

Milton, John (1994): *The Works of John Milton* (C. N. L. Brooke, Ed.). Hertfordshire: Thee Wordsworth Poetry Library.

Minnis, Alastair (2009): *Medieval Theory of Authorship: Scholastic Literary Attitudes in the Later Middle Ages*. University of Pennsylvania Press.

Moller, Violet (2019): *The Map of Knowledge: How Classical Ideas Were Lost and Found: A History in Seven Cities*. London: Picador.

Momigliano, Arnaldo (1979): "Flavius Josephus and Alexander's Visit to Jerusalem". In: *Athenaeum* 57, pp. 442–448.

Monroe, Elizabeth (2007): "'Fair and Friendly, Sweet and Beautiful': Hopes for Jewish Conversion in Synagoga's Song of Songs Imagery". In: Merback, *Beyond the Yellow Badge*, pp. 33–61.

Montesquieu (1973): *Persian Letters* (C. J. Betts, Trans.). Penguin Books.

Montgomery, Scott L. (2000): *Science in Translation: Movements of Knowledge through Cultures and Time*. Chicago, IL: University of Chicago Press.

Morgan, Michael A. (Trans.) (1983): *Sefer Ha-Razim* [The Book of Mysteries]. Chico, CA: Scholar Press.

Muntner, Sussmann (1958): *Rav Shem Tov ben Yitzchak miTortosa alChayey haRofe haIvri uMusaro beEuropa*. Jerusalem: Sinai/ Sefer HaYovel and Mossad HaRav Kook. [Hebrew]

Na'aman, Nadav (2017): "Was an Early Edition of the Book of Kings Compost during Hezekiah's Reign?". In: *Scandinavian Journal of the Old Testament* 31, pp. 80–91.

Na'aman, Nadav (2018): "Game of Thrones: Solomon's 'Succession Narrative' and Esarhaddon's Accession to the Throne". In: *Tel Aviv* 45, pp. 89–119.

Na'aman, Nadav (2019): "Hiram of Tyre in the Book of Kings and in the Tyrian Records". In: *Journal of Near Eastern Studies* 78, pp. 75–85.

Nachmanides (1962): "Sermon on Ecclesiastes". In: Charles Ber Chavel (Ed.): *The Writings of Nachmanides. Jerusalem*. [Hebrew]

Najman, Hindy, Jean-Sébastien Rey and Eibert J. C. Tigchelaar (Eds.) (2016): *Tracing Sapiential Traditions in Ancient Judaism*. Leiden: Brill.

Natali, Carlo (2013): *Aristotle: His Life and School* (D. S. Hutchinson, Ed.). Princeton University Press.

Neusner, Jacob (1987): *Sifre to Deuteronomy: An Analytical Translation*. Atlanta, GA: Scholars Press.

Neusner, Jacob (Trans.) (1989): *Song of Songs Rabbah* (*Vol. 1*). Atlanta, GA: Scholars Press.

Neusner, Jacob (Trans.) (1997): *The Components of the Rabbinic Documents. From the Whole to the Parts* (*Vol. 11*: *Pesiqta deRab Kahana, Part One*). Atlanta, GA: Scholars Press.

Newbold, W.R. (2019): *The Descent of Christ in the Odes of Solomon* (Analecta Gorgiana 51). Piscataway, NJ: Gorgias Press.

Nitsche, Martin (2017): "Salomo". https://www.bibelwissenschaft.de/stichwort/25919/, visited on April 14, 2020.

Nitzan, Bilha (1985): "Hymns from Qumran 'To Frighten and to Confuse' Evil Spirits". In: *Tarbiz* 55, pp. 19–46. [Hebrew]

Norman, Diana (1995): "The Art of Knowledge: Two Artistic Schemes in Florence". In: Diana Norman (Ed.): *Siena, Florence and Padua: Art, Society and Religion 1280–1400* (*Vol. II: Case Studies*). New Haven, CT: Yale University Press.

Noth, M. and D. Winton Thomas (Eds.) (1955): *Wisdom in Israel and in the Ancient Near East*. Leiden: Brill.

Oeming, Manfred (2007): "Salomo-Christologie im Neuen Testament". In: Günter Thomas and Andreas Schüle (Ed.), *Gegenwart des lebendigen Christus*, Leipzig: Evangelische Verlagsanstalt, pp. 57–76.

Ogren, Brian (2009): "Elia Hayyim Ben Binyamin of Genazzano, Prisca Theologia, and the Two Ancient Paths to Metempsychosis". In: Brian Ogren (Ed.): *Renaissance and Rebirth*. Leiden: Brill, Leiden, pp. 163–184.

Ohly, Friedrich (1992): *The Damned and the Elect: Guilt in Western Culture* (L. Archibald, Trans). Cambridge: Cambridge University Press.

Origen (1921): *Homilien zu Numeri 20/3* (GCS [*Die griechischen christlichen Schriftsteller*] 30). Leipzig.

Origen (1957): *The Song of Songs: Commentary and Homilies* (R. P. Lawson, Trans.). New York: Newman Press.

Origen (1965): *Contra Celsum* (H. Chadwick, Trans.). Cambridge University Press.

Orleans, Lorens of (1270): *Somme le Roi*. [English: The Book of Vices and Virtues].

Ovid (1986): *Metamorphoses* (A.D. Melville, Trans.). Oxford University Press.

Paffenroth, Kim (1999): "Jesus as Anointed and Healing son of David in the Gospel of Matthew". In: *Biblica* 80, pp. 547–554.

Page, Sophie (2004): *Magic in Medieval Manuscripts*. London: British Library.

Pagels, Elaine and Karen L. King (2007): *Reading Judas: The Controversial Message of the Ancient Gospel of Judas*. Penguin.

Paquet, Alfons (1924): *Marcolph oder König Solomon und der Bauer*. Frankfurt am Main.

Papadopoulos-Kerameus, Athanasios (1963, orig. 1891): *Analekta Hierosolymitikes Stachyologias* (edition of mainly unpublished Greek texts). Brussels: Anastatic Impression.

Parker, Kim Ian (1992): "Solomon as Philosopher King? The Nexus of Law and Wisdom in Kings I-II." *JSOT* 53, pp. 75–91.

Parkes, James W. (1934): *The Conflict of the Church and the Synagogue: A Study in the Origins of Antisemitism*. London: Soncino Press.

Parpola, Simo (1997): *Assyrian Prophecies*. Helsinki University Press.

Patai, Raphael (1994): *The Jewish Alchemists: A History and Source Book*. Princeton, NJ: Princeton University Press.

Patai, Shaily (2017): *Magical Practices and Discourses of Magic in Early Christian Traditions: Jesus, Peter, and Paul*. Ph.D. dissertation, University of North Carolina—Chapel Hill.

Parrinder, Geoffrey (2013): *Jesus in the Qur'an*. London: Oneworld Books.

Pastis, Jacqueline Zacarie (1994): *Representation of Jews and Judaism in 'The Dialogue of Timothy and Aquila': Construct or Social Reality?*. PhD. Diss., University of Pennsylvania.

Payne, Elizabeth Rogers (Ed.) (1938): *Sapientia Solomonis*. New Haven, CT: Yale University Press.

Pelikan, Jaroslav (1993): *Christianity and Classical Culture: The Metamorphosis of Natural Theology in the Christian Encounter with Hellenism*. New Haven: Yale University Press.

Pelikan, Jaroslav (1999): *Jesus Through the Centuries: His Place in the History of Culture*. New Haven/London: Yale University Press.

Pelikan, Jaroslav (2005): *Whose Bible Is It?: A Short History of Scriptures*. Penguin Books.

Pellech, Christine (1997): *Die ersten Entdecker Amerikas: der Kulturdiffusionismus*. Frankfurt am Main: Peter Lang.

Perkins, Larry (1998): "Greater than Solomon' (Matthew 12:42)". In: *Trinity Journal* 19, pp. 207–217.

Peters, Francis E. (1968a): *Aristotle and the Arabs*: *The Aristotelian Tradition in Islam*. New York: New York University Press.

Peters, Francis E. (1968b): *Aristoteles Arabus*: *The Oriental Translations and Commentaries of the Aristotelian Corpus*. Leiden: Brill. Philostratus (1912): *The Life of Apollonius of Tyana* (F. C. Conybeare, Trans.). LCL.

Philostratus (1995): *Vita Apollonii* (*The Life of Apollonius of Tyana*) (C. P. Jones, Trans.). LCL. Cambridge.

Ritter, Hellmut and Martin Plessner (Trans.)(1962): *"Picatrix"— Das Ziel des Weisen von Pseudo-Marğitī*. London: University of London—The Warburg Institute.

Pick, Bernhard (1911): "The Attack of Celsus in Christianity". In: *The Monist* 21, pp. 223–266.

Pinch, Geraldine (1994): *Magic in Ancient Egypt*. London: British Museum Press.

Pinson, Yona (1996): "The Iconography of the Temple in Northern Renaissance Art". In: *Assaph: Studies in Art History*. Section B., 2, pp. 147–174.

Pinto, Olga (1929): "The Libraries of the Arabs During the Time of the Abbasids". In: *Islamic Culture*: *The Hyderabad Quarterly Review* 3, pp. 210–248.

Plutarch (1958): *Plutarch's Lives* (B. Perrin, Trans.). LCL.

Plutarch (1973): *The Age of Alexander* (I. Scott-Kilvert, Trans.). Penguin Classics.

Pomykala, Kenneth E. (1995): *The Davidic Dynasty in Early Judaism*: *Its History and Significance for Messianism*. Atlanta, GA: Scholar Press.

Pope Benedict XVI (2007): *Jesus of Nazareth* (A. J. Walker Trans.). New York: Doubleday.

Potter, Rev. Dr. Charles Francis (1962): *The Lost Years of Jesus Revealed*. New York: Fawcett.

Powell, Kathryn (2005): "Orientalist Fantasy in the Poetic Dialogues of Solomon and Saturn". In: *Anglo-Saxon England* 34, pp. 117–143.

Preisendanz, Karl (1957): *Ein Wiener Papyrusfragment zum Testamentum Salomonis*. Varsaviae—Vratislaviae: Ossolineum.

Preisendanz, Karl (2001): *Papyri Graecae*: *Griechischen Zauberpapyri*. Münden—Leipzig.

Prudentius (2011): *The Origin of Sin*: *an English Translation of Hamartigenia* (M. A. Malamud, Trans.). Ithaca/London: Cornell University Press.

Prudentius (Trans. H.J. Thomson) (1979): *Prudentius, Vol. II, Dittochaeon* (Loeb Classical Library). Cambridge: Harvard University Press.

Qadir, Chaudry Abdul (1991): *Philosophy and Science in the Islamic World*. London/New York: Routledge.

Raba, Joel (1986): *The Land of Israel in Descriptions of Russian Travelers* (12th–17th *Centuries*). Jerusalem: Yad Ben Zvi. [Hebrew]

Raba, Joel (2014): *The Gift and Its Wages*: *The Land of Israel and the Jewish People in the Spiritual Life of Medieval Russia*. Turnhout: Brepols Publishers.

Rabbi Judah ben Samuel (1998): *Sefer Hasidim*. Jerusalem.

Rabelais (1976): *Gargantua and Pantagruel* (J. M. Cohen, Trans.). Penguin Books.

Rappaport, Uriel and Israel Ronen (Eds.) (1993): *The State of the Hasmoneans*. Jerusalem/Tel Aviv: Yad Ben-Zvi/Open University. [Hebrew]

Rappel, Dov (1990): *The Seven Wisdoms*: *The Dispute about Secular Studies in Judaism*. Jerusalem. [Hebrew]

Redford, Donald B. (1986): *Pharaonic King-Lists, Annals and Day-Books*: *A Contribution to the Study of the Egyptian Sense of History*. Mississuga, Ontario: Benben Publications.

Richards, E. Randolph (2004): *Paul and First-Century Letter Writing*: *Secretaries, Composition and Collection*. Downers Grove, IL: InterVarsity.

Ritner, Robert K. (1993): *The Mechanics of Ancient Egyptian Magical Practice*. Chicago: The Oriental Institute of the University of Chicago.

Ritner, Robert K. (1995a): "The Religious, Social, and Legal Parameters of Traditional Egyptian Magic". In: Meyer and Mirecki, *Ancient Magic and Ritual Power*, pp. 43–60.

Ritner, Robert K. (1995b): "Egyptian Magical Practice under the Roman Empire: The Demotic Spells and their Religious Context". In: Wolfgang Hasse (Ed.): *Aufsteig und Niedergang der römischen Welt* 18, No. 5, Berlin: De Gruyter, pp. 3333–3379.

Roberts, Alexander and James Donaldson (Eds.) (1955): *Ante-Nicene Fathers, Vol. II (Clement of Alexandria) & Vol. III (Tertullian)*. Oxford University Press.

Roberts, Robert Edward (1924): *The Theology of Tertullian*. Epworth Press, Methodist Publishing House.

Robertson, Robert Gerald (Trans.) (1986): *The Dialogue of Timothy and Aquila: A Critical Text Introduction to the Manuscript Evidence, and an Inquiry into the Sources and Literary Relationships*. PhD Diss, Harvard Divinity School.

Robinson, Ira (1989): "Kabbalah and Science in Sefer Ha-Berit: A Modernization Strategy for Orthodox Jews". In: *Modern Judaism* 9, pp. 275–288.

Robinson, James M. (Ed.) (1988): *The Nag Hammadi Library in English* (3rd ed.). San Francisco: Harper & Row.

Robinson, Ian Stuart (1983): "'Political Allegory' in the Biblical Exegesis of Bruno of Sergi". In: *Recherches de théologie ancienne et medieval* 50, pp. 69–98.

Rokeah, David (1969): "Ben Stara ls Ben Pantera: Towards the Clarification of a PhilologicalHistorical Problem". In: *Tarbiz* 39, pp. 9–18.

Rokeah, David. (1980): "The Church Fathers and the Jews in Wiritings Designed for Internal and External Use". In: Shmuel Almog (Ed.): *Antisemitism Through the Ages*. Jerusalem, pp. 55–87. [Hebrew]

Rokeah, David (1982): *Jews, Pagans and Christians in Conflict*. Jerusalem: Magness Press; Leiden: Brill.

Rokeah, David (2012): "The Septuagint and Christian Theology". In: *Te'uda* 25, pp. 445–489.

Rosenberg, Yudel (1914): *Sefer Divrei haYamim asher leShlomo Alav haShalom* [The Chronicles of the Life of Solomon, Peace Be Upon Him]. Piotrków. [Hebrew]

Rosenthal, Erwin I. J. (1960): "Anti-Christian Polemic in Medieval Bible Commentaries". In: *Journal of Jewish Studies* 11, pp. 115–135.

Rosenthal, Erwin I. (1977): "Yohanan Alemanno and Occultic Science". In: Yasukatsu Maeyama and Walter G. Salzer (Eds.): *Prismata: Naturwissenschaftsgeschichtliche Studien*. Wiesbaden: Franz Steiner, pp. 349–361.

Rosenthal, Franz (1994 repr.): *The Classical Heritage in Islam* (Emile and Jenny Marmorstein, Trans.). London/New York: Routledge.

Rosenthal, Franz (Trans.) (1958): *The Muqaddimah, An Introduction to History*. New York: Pantheon Books.

Ross, Sir David (Ed.) (1955): *Aristotelis Fragmenta Selecta*. Oxford: Clarendon Press.

Rossi, Paolo (1968): *Francis Bacon: From Magic to Science*. Chicago: University of Chicago Press.

Rotman, David (2016): *Dragons, Demons and Wondrous Realms: The Marvelous in Medieval Hebrew Narrative*. Hevel Modi'in/Beer-Sheva: Kinneret, Zmora-Bitan, Dvir—Publishing House Ltd. and Heksherim Institute, Ben Gurion University of the Negev. [Hebrew]

Roth, Norman (1978): "The 'Theft of Philosophy' by the Greeks from the Jews". In: *Classical Folia: Studies in the Christian Perpetuation of the Classics* 32, pp. 56–77.

Rowe, Nina (2008): "Idealization and Subjection at Strasbourg Cathedral". In: Merback, *Beyond the Yellow Badge*, pp. 179–202.

Royce Moore, Kenneth (Ed.) (2018): *Brill's Companion to the Reception of Alexander the Great*. Leiden: Brill.

Rubenstein, Richard E. (2003): *Aristotle's Children: How Christians, Muslims, And Jews Rediscovered Ancient Wisdom and Illuminated the Middle Ages*. Orlando, FL: Harcourt.

Rückert, Friedrich (1841): *Gedichte (Mit dem Bildnis und Facsimile des Verfassers)*. Frankfurt.

Ruska, Julius (1926): *Tabula Smaragdina: Ein Beitrag zur Geschichte der hermetischen Literatur*. Heidelberg: Carl Winter.

Russell, James (1995): "The Archaeological Context of Magic in the Early Byzantine Period". In: Maguire (Ed.), *Byzantine Magic*, pp. 35–50.

Russell, Jeffery Burton (1984): *Lucifer: The Devil in the Middle Ages*. Ithaca, NY: Cornell University Press.

Russell, Jeffrey Burton (1991): *Satan: The Early Christian Tradition*. Ithaca, NY: Cornell University Press.

Rutgers, Leonard V (2009): *Making Myths: Jews in Early Christian Identity Formation*. Leeuven, Belgium: Peeters.

Ruzer, Serge (2006): "Son of God as Son of David: Luke's Attempt to Biblicize a Problematic Notion". In: *Babel und Bibel* 3. Winona Lake, IN: Eisenbrauns, pp. 321–352.

Ruzer, Serge (2007): "Who Was Unhappy with the Davidic Messiah?". In: Serge Ruzer (Ed.): *Mapping the New Testament: Early Christian Writings as a Witness for Jewish Biblical Exegesis*. Leiden: Brill, pp. 101–129.

Ruzer, Serge (2012): "Jesus' Messianic Biography as Response to Second Temple Jewish Beliefs". *Zmanim* 120, pp. 40–51. [Hebrew]

Ruzer, Serge (2016): "Review of Jörg Frey, The Gospel According to John: From the Jews and the World, edited by Cana Werman, Ben-Gurion University of the Negev Press, 2014". In: *Zion* 81, pp. 109–122.

Ruzer, Serge and Yair Zakovitch (2016): *God's Word is Powerful: Eight Conversations on the Epistle to the Hebrews*. Jerusalem: Magnes Press. [Hebrew]

Ryan, William Francis and Charles B. Schmitt (Eds.) (1982): *Pseudo-Aristotle, The "Secret of Secrets": Sources and Influences*. London: The Warburg Institute.

Ryan, William Francis (1986): "Aristotle and Pseudo-Aristotle in Kievan and Muscovite Russia". In: Kraye, Ryan and Schmitt, *Pseudo-Aristotle*, pp. 3–14.

Saint Ambrose (1972): *Seven Exegetical Works* (M. P. McHugh, Trans). The Catholic University of America Press.

Saint Bonaventure (2010): *The Life of St. Francis of Assisi*. TAN Books.

Salzberger, George (1907): *Die Salomonsage in der semitischen Literatur*. Berlin: Mayer & Müller.

Salzberger, George (1912): *Salomos Tempelbau und Thron in der semitische Sagenliteratur*. Berlin: Mayer & Müller.

Salzmann, Marcus (Trans.) (1966): *The Chronicle of Ahimaaz*. New York: Columbia University Press.

Samostz, David (1837): *Nahar me-'Eden*. Breslau.

Santer, Nathan (1901): "Der Jude Aristoteles". In: *Monatsschrift für Geschichte und Wissenschaft des Judentums* 45, pp. 453–459.

Sapir, Shaul (1931): *Shlomo haMelekh: Historischer Roman*. New York: United Publishing Co. [Yiddish].

Särkiö, Pekka (2004): "Solomon und die Dämonen". In: *Studia Orientalia Electronica* 99, pp. 305–322.

Şarlak, Eva and Ruhiye Onurel (2014): "Depictions of Prophet Solomon in Christian Icons and Ottoman Miniature Art". In: *Mediterranean Archaeology and Archaeometry* 14, pp. 321–345.

Sarton, George (1930): "Aristotle and Phyllis". In: *Isis* 14, pp. 8–19.

Sarton, George (1993): *Hellenistic Science and Culture in the Last Three Centuries B.C.*. New York, NY: Dover Publications.

Sasson, Gilad (2003): *A King and Layman: The Sages' Attitude toward King Solomon*. Tel Aviv: Resling. [Hebrew]

Schäfer, Christian (Ed.) (2008): *Kaiser Julian "Apostata" und die philosophische Reaktion gegen das Christentum*. Berlin: De Gruyter.

Schäfer, Peter (1990): "Jewish Magic Literature in Late Antiquity and Early Middle Ages". *Journal of Jewish Studies* 41, no. 1, pp. 75–91.

Schäfer, Peter (1997): "Magic and Religion in Ancient Judaism". In: Schäfer and Kippenberg, *Envisioning Magic*, pp. 19–43.

Schäfer, Peter and Hans G. Kippenberg (Eds.) (1997): *Envisioning Magic: A Princeton Seminar and Symposium*. Leiden: Brill.

Schäfer, Peter (2007): *Jesus in the Talmud*. Oxford/Princeton: Princeton University Press.

Schäfer, Peter, Michael Meerson and Yaacov Deutsch (Eds.) (2011): *Toledot Yeshu (The Life Story of Jesus) Revisited: A Princeton Conference*. Tübingen: MohrSiebeck.

Schäfer, Peter (2012): *The Jewish Jesus: How Judaism and Christianity Shaped Each Other*. Princeton University Press.

Schäfer, Peter (2016): *Jüdische Polemik gegen Jesus und das Christentum: Die Entstehung eines jüdischen Gegenevangeliums*. München: Carl Friedrich von Siemens Stiftung.

Schaff, Philip (Ed.) (1995): *Nicene and Post-Nicene Fathers (First Series)*. Peabody, MA: Hendrickson Publishers.

Schaff, Philip and Henry Wace (1995): *Nicene and Post-Nicene Fathers (Second Series)*. Peabody, MA: Hendrickson Publishing.

Schechter, Solomon (1890): "The Riddles of Solomon in Rabbinic Literature". In: *Folk-lore* 1, pp. 349–358.

Schlauch, Margaret (1939): "The Allegory of Church and Synagogue". In: *Speculum* 14, pp. 448–464.

Schmeling, Gaylin R.: "The Typological Interpretation of the Old Testament". http://bibleresearcher.com/schmeling.html, visited on 20 November 2019.

Schmitt, Charles B. (1983): *Aristotle and the Renaissance*. Cambridge, MA: Harvard University Press.

Scholem, Gershom (1926): *Sefer Ha-Tamar; Das Buch von der Palme des Abu Aflah aus Syracus*. Berlin.

Scholem, Gershom (1935): "From Philosopher to Cabbalist (A Legend of the Cabbalists on Maimonides)". In: *Tarbiz* 3, pp. 334–342. [Hebrew]

Scholem, Gershom (1971–1977): "The Magid of R. Yosef Taitazak and the Revelations Attributed to him". In: *Sefunot* 11, pp. 67–112. [Hebrew]

Schürer, Emil (Ed.) (1986): *The History of the Jewish People in the Age of Jesus Christ* (G. Vermes, F. Millar and M. D. Goodman, Eds.): Edinburgh: T&T Clark.

Schwartz, Dov (1993): "Ethics and Ascetism in the Neoplatonic School of the 14th Century". In: Avi Sagi and Daniel Statman (Eds.): *Between Religion and Ethics*. Ramat Gan: BarIlan University Press, pp. 185–208. [Hebrew]

Schwartz, Dov (2004a): *Amulets, Properties and Rationalism in Medieval Jewish Thought*. Ramat Gan: Bar-Ilan University Press. [Hebrew]

Schwartz, Dov (2004b): *Astral Magic in Medieval Jewish Thought* (2nd ed.). Ramat Gan: BarIlan University Press. [Hebrew]

Schwartz, Dov (2005): *Studies on Astral Magic in Medieval Jewish Thought*. Leiden: Brill. (English)

Schwartz, Dov (2016): *Jewish Thought in Byzantium in the Late Middle Ages*. Jerusalem: Magnes Press. [Hebrew]

Schwartz, Dov (2018): *The Clash of Paradigms: Medieval Science and Jewish Theology*. Jerusalem: Magnes Press. [Hebrew]

Schwarz, Sarah L. (2007): "Reconsidering the Testament of Solomon". In: *Journal for the Study of Pseudepigrapha* 16, pp. 203–237.

Scott, R. B. Y. (1969): *Solomon and the Beginnings of Wisdom in Israel*. Leiden: Brill.

Segal, Alan F. (1977): *Two Powers in Heaven: Early Rabbinic Reports about Christianity and Gnosticism*. Leiden: Brill.

Segal, Moshe (1953): *Sefer ben Sira ha-shalem*. Jerusalem: Bialik Institute.

Sela, Shlomo (1999): *Astrology and Biblical Exegesis in Abraham Ibn Ezra's Thought*. Ramat Gan: Bar Ilan University Press. [Hebrew]

Sela, Shlomo (2003): *Abraham Ibn Ezra and the Rise of Medieval Hebrew Science*. Leiden: Brill.

Sela, Shlomo (1999): *Astrology and Biblical Commentary in the Thought of Abraham Ibn Ezra*. Ramat Gan: Bar Ilan University Press. [Hebrew]

Seligsohn, Max (1925): "Solomon in Rabbinical Literature and Legend". In: *The Jewish Encyclopedia* (*Vol. 2*). New York, pp. 438–441.

Sergi, Omer (2010): "The Composition of Nathan's Oracle to David (2 Samuel 7:1–17) as a Reflection of Royal Judahite Ideology". In: *Journal of Biblical Literature* 129, pp. 261–279.

Seymour, John D (1924): *Tales of King Solomon*. Oxford University Press.

Shaked, Shaul, James Nathan Ford and Siam Bhayro (Eds.) (2013): *Aramaic Bowl Spells*: *Jewish Babylonian Aramaic Bowls*. Leiden: Brill.

Shaked, Shaul (1999): "Jesus in the Magic Bowls: Apropos Dan Levene's '…and by the name of Jesus…'". In: *Jewish Studies Quarterly* 6, pp. 309–319.

Shalev-Eyni, Sarit (2006): "Solomon, his Demons and Jongleurs: The Meeting of Islamic, Judaic and Christian Culture". In: *Al-Masāq* 18. No. 2, pp. 147–160.

Shapin, Steven (1998): *The Scientific Revolution*. Chicago, IL: The University of Chicago Press.

Shavit, Yaacov (1999): *Athens in Jerusalem*: *Classical Antiquity and Hellenism in the Making of the Modern Secular Jew*. London: The Littman Library of Jewish Civilization.

Shavit, Yaacov (2006): "Stolen Libraries: The Transformation and Functions of the Legendary Tradition of King Solomon's Library and Aristotle as Its Main Protagonist". In: Yosef Kaplan and Moshe Sluhovsky (Eds.): *Libraries and Book Collections*. Jerusalem: The Zalman Shazar Center, pp. 423–445. [Hebrew]

Shavit, Yaacov (2013): "'He was Thoth in Everything': Why and When King Solomon Became Both Magister Omnium Physicorum and Master of Magic". In: Ra'anan S. Boustan, Klaus Herrmann, Reimund Leicht, Annette Y. Reed and Giuseppe Veltri (Eds.): *Envisioning Judaism: Studies in Honor of Peter Schäfer on the Occasion of His Seventieth Birthday*. Tübingen: Mohr Siebeck, pp. 599–600.

Shavit, Yaacov (2018): "Aristotle the Greek Philosopher Kneels on All Fours While the Wife of Alexander the Great Rides Him and Urges Him on With Her Whip". In: *Haaretz Literary Supplement*.

Shimoff, Sandra R. (1997): "The Hellenization of Solomon in Rabbinic Texts". In: Lowell K. Handy (Ed.): *The Age of Solomon*. Leiden: Brill, pp. 457–469.

Shimoff, Sandra R. (1987): "Hellenization Among the Rabbis: Some Evidence from Early Aggadot Concerning David and Solomon". *Journal for the Study of Judaism* 17, no. 2, pp. 169–187.

Shumaker, Wayne (1972): *The Occult Sciences in the Renaissance: A Study in Intellectual Patterns*. Berkeley: University of California Press.

Siker, Jeffrey S. (1987): "Abraham in Graeco-Roman Paganism". In: *Journal for the Study of Judaism* 18, pp. 188–208.

Silberman, Lou (1974): "The Queen of Sheba in Judaic Tradition". In: James B. Pritchard (Ed.): *Solomon and Sheba* London: Phaidon, pp. 65–84.

Silverman, Arthur J. (1976): "Censorship of Medical Works: Hezekiah and 'The Book of Remedies'". In: *Dine Israel* 7, pp. 151–157. [Hebrew]

Skehan, Patrick W. (Trans.) and Alexander A. Di Lella (Intro. and Comm.) (1987): *The Wisdom of Ben Sira* (The Anchor Bible). New York: Doubleday.

Smalley, Beryl (1983): *The Study of the Bible in the Middle Ages* (3rd ed.). Oxford University Press.

Smith, Morton (1978): *Jesus the Magician*. New York: Harper and Row.

Snyder, H. Gregory (2001): *Teachers and Texts in the Ancient World: Philosophers, Jews and Christians*. London/New York: Routledge.

Sorabji, Richard (Ed.) (1990): *Aristotle Transformed: The Ancient Commentators and Their Influence*. Ithaca, NY: Cornell University Press.

Soucek, Priscilla (1976): "The Temple of Solomon in Islamic Legend and Art". In: Joseph Gutman (Ed.): *The Temple of Solomon: Archaeological Facts and Medieval Tradition in Christian, Islamic and Jewish Art*. Missoula, MT: Scholars Press, pp. 73–123.

Sperber, Daniel (1994): *Magic and Folklore in Rabbinic Literature*. Ramat-Gan: Bar Ilan University Press.

Speyer, Wolfgang (1970): *Bücherfunde in der Glaubenswerbung der Antike*. Göttingen: Vandenhoeck & Ruprecht.

Spinoza, Benedict (Baruch) (1883 [1677]): *Tractatus Theologico Politicus* (G. H. M Elwes, Trans.). George Routledge and Sons.

Schröder, Werner (1971): *Zur Form des 'Lob Salomonis'*. München: Wilhem Fink.

Stamm, Johann Jakob (1960): "Der Name des Königs Salomo". In: *Theologische Zeitschrift* 16, pp. 285–297.

Staniforth, Maxwell (Trans.) (1968): *Early Christian Writings: The Apostolic Fathers*. Penguin Books.

Steele, Robert and Dorothea Waley Singer (1928): "The Emerald Table". In: *Proceedings of the Royal Society of Medicine* (*Section of the History of Medicine*) 21, pp. 485–501.

Stein, Dina (1993): "The Queen of Sheba vs. Solomon—Riddles and Interpretation in Midrash Mishle A". *Jerusalem Studies in Jewish Folklore* 15, pp. 7–36. [Hebrew]

Steinschneider, Moritz (1891): "Apollonius von Thyana (oder Balinas) bei den Arabern". In: *Zeitschrift der Deutschen Morgenländischen Gesellschaft* 45, pp. 439–446.

Steinschneider, Moritz (1893): *Die Hebräischen Übersetzungen des Mittelalters und die Juden als Dolmetscher*. Berlin.

Stevenson, David (1988): *The Origins of Freemasonry: Scotland's Century, 1590–1710*. New York: Cambridge University Press.

Stone, Michael E. (1978): "Concerning the Penitence of Solomon". In: *The Journal of Theological Studies* 29, pp. 1–19.

Stoneman, Richard (Trans.) (1991): *The Greek Alexander Romance*. Penguin Books.

Strabo (1930): *Geography*, (H. L. Jones, Trans.). LCL. Cambridge.

Strobel, Lee (2013): *The Case for Christ: A Journalist's Personal Investigation of the Evidence for Jesus*. London: Zondervan.

Stroumsa, Sarah (1999): "The Ṣabians of Ḥarrān and the Ṣabians of Maimonides: on Maimonides' Theory of the History of Religions". In: *Sefunot* 22, pp. 277–295.

Sweet, Ronald F. G. (1990): "The Sage in Akkadian Literature: A Philological Study". In: John G. Gammie and Leo G. Perdue (Eds.) (1990): *The Sage in Israel and the Ancient Near East*. Winona Lake, IN: Eisenbrauns, pp 45–66.

Swift, Jonathan (Ed. David Womersly) (2013): *Gulliver's Travels*. Cambridge: Cambridge University Press.

Tacitus (1969): *Vol 3: Histories* (C. H. Moore, Trans.). LCL. Cambridge, MA: Harvard University Press..

Talmage, Frank (ed.) (1983): *The Polemical Writings of Profiat Duran: The reproach of the Gentiles and 'be not like unto thy fathers'*. Jerusalem: The Zalman Shazar Center. [Hebrew]

Tanman, Gülru and Brigitte Pitarakis (2018): *Life is Short: The Art of Healing in Byzantium*. Istanbul: Istanbul Arastirmalari Enstitüsü.

Tertullian (1956): De praescriptione haereticorum (On the Prescriptions of the Heretics). In: S. L. Greenslade (Ed.): *Early Latin Theology: Selections from Tertullian, Cyprian, Ambrose, and Jerome*. Westminster: John Knox Press.

Tertullian (1984): *Apology de Spectaculis XIX* (T. R. Glover, Trans.). Loeb Classical Library. Cambridge: Harvard University Press, pp. 11–46.

Theissen, Gerd (1983 [1974]): *The Miracle Stories of the Early Christian Tradition* (F. McDonagh, Trans.). Philadelphia, PA: Fortress Press.

Theophilos, Michael P. and A. M. Smith (2013): "The Use of Isaiah 28:11–12 in 1 Corinthians 14:21". In: Wendy Mayer and Bronwen Neil (Eds.): *Religious Conflict from Early Christianity to the Rise of Islam*. Berlin: De Gruyter, pp. 51–70.

Thomas, Keith (1973): *Religion and the Decline of Magic: Studies in Popular Beliefs in Sixteenth and Seventeenth-century England*. Penguin Books.

Thompson, James W. (2008): *Hebrews*. Grand Rapids, MI: Baker Academic.

Thompson, Thomas L. (1999): *The Mythic Past: Biblical Archaeology and the Myth of Israel*. New York: Basic Books.

Thorndike, Lynn (1964): *A History of Magic and Experimental Science During the First Thirteen Centuries of Our Era* (Vols. 1–8). New York: Columbia University Press.

Thräde, Kurt (1962a): "Erfinder, II (geistesgeschichtlich)". In: T. Klausner (Ed.): *Reallexikon für Antike und Christentum* (Vol. 1). Stuttgart: Hiersemann, pp. 1191–1278.

Thräde, Kurt (1962b): "Exorzismus". In: T. Klausner (Ed.): *Reallexikon für Antike und Christentum* (Vol. 3). Stuttgart: Hiersemann, pp. 44–117.

Throntveit, Mark A. (1997): "The Idealization of Solomon as the Glorification of God in the Chronicler's Royal Speeches and Royal Prayers. In: Lowell K. Handy (Ed.): *The Age of Solomon: Scholarship at the Turn of the Millennium*. Leiden: Brill, pp. 411–427.

Tirosh-Rothschild, Hava (1991): *Between Worlds: The Life and Thought of Rabbi David ben Judah Messer Leon*. Albany, NY: State University of New York.

Torijano, Pablo A. (2002): *Solomon the Esoteric King: From King to Magus, Development of a Tradition*. Leiden: Brill.

Tränkle, Hermann (Ed.) (1964): *Q. S. F. Tertulliani Adversus Iudaeos*. Wiesbaden: Steiner.

Trebilco, Paul (2004): *The Early Christians in Ephesus from Paul to Ignatius*. Tübingen: Mohr-Siebeck.

Troiani, Lucio (2017): "Paul's Preaching and the Jewish Communities". In: Constanza Cordoni and Gerhard Langer (Eds.): *Let the Wise Listen And Add To Their Learning (Prov 1:5): Festschrift For Günter Stemberger on the Occasion of his 75th Birthday*. Berlin/Boston: De Gruyter, pp. 447–456.

Tropper, Amram (2011): *Like Clay in the Hands of the Potter: Sage Stories in Rabbinic Literature*. Jerusalem: Zalman Shazar Center for Jewish History. [Hebrew]

Tropper, Amram (2013): *Simeon the Righteous in Rabbinic Literature: A Legend Reinvented*. Leiden: Brill.

Trotter, Thomas (Ed.) (1968): *Jesus and the Historian*. Philadelphia: The Westminster Press.

Trumbower, Jeffrey (2001): *Rescue for the Dead: The Posthomous Salvation of Non-Christians in Early Christianity*. Oxford University Press.

Turner, Robert (2007 [1657]): *Ars Notoria: the Notery Art of Solomon*. London: Teitan Press.

Twelftree. Graham H. (2007): "Jesus the Exorcist and Ancient Magic". In: Michael Labahn and Bert Jan Lietaert Peerbolte (Eds.): *A Kind of Magic: Understanding Magic in the New Testament and its Religious Environment*. London: T&T Clark, pp. 57–86.

Tyler, Thomas (1990): "M. D. Conway's 'Solomon'". In: *The Jewish Quarterly Review* 12, 4, 745–749

Tzfatman, Sarah (2016): *Be gone, foul thing: The Exorcism of Spirits in Ashkenazi Judaism in Modern Times*. Jerusalem: Magnes Press. [Hebrew]

Ullman, Walter (1965): *A History of Political Thought: The Middle Ages*. Penguin Books.

Underwood, Edgar Ashworth (Ed.) (1953): *Science, Medicine and History: Essays on the Evolution of Scientific Thought and Medical Practice (Vol. 1)*. London: Oxford University Press.

Urbach, Ephraim E. (1961): "Sermons by the Sages and Commentaries of Origen to Song of Songs and the Jewish-Christian Dispute". In: *Tarbiz* 30, pp. 148–170. [Hebrew]

Urbach, Ephraim E. (2006): *The Sages: Their Concepts and Beliefs* (I. Abrahams, Trans.). New York, NY: Varda Books.

Van de Vliet, Jacques (2013): "Solomon in Egyptian Gnosticism ". In: Verheyden, *The Figure of Solomon in Jewish, Christian and Islamic Tradition: King, Sage and Architect*. Leiden: Brill, pp. 197–198.

Van Dam, G. Raymond (1993): *Saints and Their Miracles in Late Antique Gaul*. Princeton, NJ: Princeton University Press.

van Keulen, Percy (2004): *Two Versions of the Solomon Narrative: An Inquiry into the Relationship between MT 1 Kgs. 2–11 and LXX 3 Reg. 2–11*. Leiden: Brill.

Van Koningsveld, P. S. (1998): "Greek Manuscripts in the Early Abbasid Empire: Fictions and Facts About Their Origin, Translation and Destruction". In: *Bibliotheca Orientalis* 55, pp. 345–372.

Van Leeuwen, Raymond C. (2007): "Cosmos, Temple, House: Building and Wisdom in Mesopotamia and Israel". In: Richard J. Clifford (Ed.): *Wisdom Literature in Mesopotamia and Israel*. Atlanta, GA: Society of Biblical Literature, pp. 67–90.

van den Broeck, R., and Maarten Jozef Vermaseren (Eds.) (1981): *Studies in Gnosticism and Hellenistic Religions: Presented to Gilles Quispel on the Occasion of His 65th Birthday*, Leiden: Brill.

Van Winden, J.C.M. (1971): *An Early Christian Philosopher: Justin Martyr's Dialogue with Trypho Chapters One to Nine*. Leiden: Brill.

Vanning, Stewart (2002): *Medieval Christian and Jewish Approaches to the Sins of King Solomon and his Salvation or Damnation with Special Reference to the Treatise of Philip of Harvengt.* PhD Diss., Bar-Ilan University.

Varner, William (2004): *Ancient Jewish-Christian Dialogues*: *Athanasius and Zacchaeus, Simon and Theophilus, Timothy and Aquila. Introduction, Text, and Translations.* Lewiston, N.Y.: E. Mellen Press.

Verheyden, Joseph (Ed.) (2013a): *The Figure of Solomon in Jewish, Christian and Islamic Tradition*: *King, Sage and Architect.* Leiden: Brill.

Verheyden, Joseph (2013b): "Josephus on Solomon". In: Joseph Verheyden (Ed.): *The Figure of Solomon in Jewish, Christian and Islamic Tradition*: *King, Sage and Architect.* Leiden: Brill.

Verheyden, Joseph (1995): "Josephus on Solomon". In: Louis H. Feldman: "Josephus' Portrait of Solomon", Hebrew Union College Annual 66, pp. 103–167.

Vermes, Geza (1987): *The Dead Sea Scrolls in English* (3rd ed.). Penguin Books.

Ville-Patlagean, Evelyne (1962): "Une image de Salomon en basileus Byzantin". In: *Revue des Études Juives* 121, pp. 9–33.

Vilozny, Naama (2017): *Lilith's Hair and Ashmedai's Horns*: *Figure and Image in Magic and Popular Art*: *Between Babylonia and Palestine in Late Antiquity.* Jerusalem: Yad Ben-Zvi. [Hebrew]

Visotzky, Burton L. (1990): *Midrash Mishle*: *A Critical Edition Based on Vatican Ms. Ebr. 44, With Variant Readings From All Known Manuscripts and Early Editions, and With an Introduction, References and a Short Commentary.* New York, NY: The Jewish Theological Seminary of America.

Visotzky, Burton L. (1992): *The Midrash on Proverbs.* New Haven, CT: Yale University Press.

Von Hochwart, Ludwig August Frankl Ritter (1876): *Tragische Könige.* Vienna: Hölder.

Wacholder, Ben Zion (1974): *Eupolemus*: *A Study of Judeo-Greek Literature.* Cincinnati: Hebrew Union College.

Wälchli, Stefan (1999): *Der weise König Salomo: Eine Studie zu den Erzählungen von der Weisheit Salomos in ihrem alttestamentlichen und altorientalischen Kontext.* Stuttgart: Verlag W. Kohlammer.

Walker, Daniel Pickering (1975 [1958]): *Spiritual and Demonic Magic, from Ficino to Campanella.* University of Notre Dame Press.

Wasserstrom, Steven (2000): "The Unwritten Chapter: Notes Towards a Social and Religious History of Geniza Magic". In: *Pe'amim* 85, pp. 43–63. [Hebrew]

Weisser, Ursula (Ed.) (1979): *Buch über das Geheimnis der Schöpfung und die Darstellung der Natur von Pseudo-Apollonios von Tyana.* Aleppo: The Institute for the History of Arabic Science, University of Aleppo.

Weitzman, Steven (2011): *Solomon: The Lure of Wisdom.* New Haven: Yale University Press.

Wessely, Naphtali Herz (1826 [1782–1785]): *Divrei Shalom ve'Emet.* Berlin/Vienna.

West, Gerald D (1954): "L'Uevre Salemon". In: *The Modern Language Review 49*, No. 2, pp. 176–182.

White, Aaron, David Wenham and Craig A. Evans (Eds.) (2018): *The Earliest Perceptions of Jesus in Context.* T&T Clark.

White, Carolinne (Trans.) (1991): *Early Christian Lives.* Penguin Books.

Wighatman, Gregory J. (1990): "The Myth of Solomon". *BASOR 277*, No. 8, pp. 5–22.

Wilken, Robert (1979): "Pagan Criticism of Christianity". In: William R. Schoedel and Robert Wilken (Eds.): *Early Christian Literature and the Classical Tradition.* Paris: Éditions Beauchesne.

Wilkinson, John (1999): *Egeria's Travels.* Warminster: Aris & Phillips.

Williams, A. Lukyn (1935): *Adversus Judaeos: A Bird's Eye View of Christian Apologiae until the Renaissance.* Cambridge: Cambridge University Press.

Williams, Steven J. (1994a): "Roger Bacon and His Edition of the Pseudo-Aristotelian Secretum Secretorum". In: *Speculum* 69, pp. 57–73.

Williams, Steven J. (1994b): "The Early Circulation of the Pseudo-Aristotelian 'Secret of Secrets'". In: *Micrologus* 2, pp. 127–144.

Williams, Steven J. (2003): *The Secret of Secrets: The Scholarly Career of a Pseudo-Aristotelian Text in Latin Middle Ages*. Ann Arbour: University of Michigan Press.

Winston, David (Trans.) (1979): *The Wisdom of Solomon, Anchor Bible*. Garden City, NY: Doubleday.

Wirszubski, Chaim (Ed.) (1963): *Flavius Mithridates: Sermo de Passione Domini*. Jerusalem: The Israeli Academy of Sciences.

Wolf, Johann Christoph (1715–1733): *Bibliotheca Hebraica*. Hamburg.

Wolfson, Harry A. (1925): "The Classification of Sciences in Medieval Jewish Philosophy". In: David Philipson et al. (Eds.): *Hebrew Union College Jubilee Volume*, pp. 263–315.

Wolfson, Harry A. (1973): *Studies in the History of Philosophy and Religion* (I. Twersky and G. H. Williams, Eds.). Cambridge, MA: Harvard University Press.

Wright, Benjamin G. (2013): "The Wisdom of Ben Sira". In: Louis H. Feldman, James L. Kugel and Lawrence H. Schiffman (Eds.): *Outside the Bible: Ancient Jewish Writings Related to Scripture*. Philadelphia: Jewish Publication Society.

Wright, Robert (Ed.) (2007): *The Psalms of Solomon: A Critical Edition of the Greek Text*. New York: T&T Clark.

Wygant, Amy (Ed.) (2006): *The Meanings of Magic: From the Bible to Buffalo Bill*. New York/ Oxford: Berghahn Books.

Yarbro Collins, Adela (1985): "Aristobulus: A New Translation and Introduction". In: James H. Charlesworth: *The Old Testament Pseudepigrapha (Vol. 2)*. Garden City, NY: Doubleday.

Yarbro Collins, Adela (1999): "Mark and His Readers: The Son of God among Jews". In: *Harvard Theological Review* 92, pp. 393–408.

Yarbro Collins, Adela and John J. Collins (2008): *King and Messiah as Son of God: Divine, Human, and Angelic Messianic Figures in Biblical and Related Literature*. Grand Rapids, MI: Eerdmans.

Yassif, Eli (2004): *The Hebrew Collection of Tales in the Middle Ages*. Tel Aviv: HaKibbutz. [Hebrew]

Yassif, Eli (2006): "The Hebrew Traditions About Alexander the Great: Narrative Models and Their Meaning in the Middle Ages". In: *Tarbiz* 75. [Hebrew]

Yates, Frances A. (1979): *Giordano Bruno and the Hermetic Tradition*. Chicago/London: The University of Chicago Press.

Yates, Frances A. (1984): *The Art of Memory*. London: Ark Paperbacks.

Young, Frances M. (2002): *Biblical Exegesis and the Formation of Christian Culture*. Peabody, MA: Hendrickson Publishers.

Yuval, Israel Jacob (2008): *Two Nations in Your Wombs: Perception of Jews and Christians in Late Antiquity and the Middle Ages*. Berkeley: University of California Press.

Zakovitch, Yair (1982): "Poor And Riding On an Ass (Zechariah 9:9–10)". In: *The Messianic Idea in Jewish Thought*. Jerusalem: The Israel Academy of Science and Humanities, pp. 7–17. [Hebrew]

Zakovitch, Yair (2015): "'Solomon Must Have a Thousand' (Songs of Songs 8:12)". In: Avihu Zakaki, Paul Mendes-Flohr and Zeev Gries (Eds.): *Fields in the Wind: A Tribute to Avraham Shapira, in Friendship and Appreciation*. Jerusalem: Carmel, pp. 255–263. [Hebrew]

Zambelli, Paola (2012): *Astrology and Magic from the Medieval Latin and Islamic World to Renaissance Europe: Theories and Approaches*. Farnham, Surrey/ Burlington, VT: Ashgate Variorum.

Zemon Davis, Natalie (1975): "Proverbial Wisdom and Popular Errors". In: Natalie Zemon Davis: *Society and Culture in Early Modern France*. Stanford University Press, pp. 227–267.

Zer-Kavod, Mordechai (1977): "The Wisdom of Solomon in the Legends of the Sages". *Beit Mikra* 23, pp. 203–207. [Hebrew]

Zinberg, Israel (1960): *History of Jewish Literature (Vol. 2)*. Tel Aviv. [Hebrew]. [For the English translation: Martin, Bernard (Trans.) (1973): *A History of Jewish Literature (Vol. 2)*. Cleveland: Case Western Reserve University Press.]

Ziolkowski, Jan M. (Trans.) (2008): *Solomon and Marcolf*. Cambridge: Harvard University Press.

Ziv, Asher (1972): *Rabbi Moses Isserles (Remo)*. New York: Yeshiva University.

Zonta, Mauro (2011): "Medieval Hebrew Translations of Philosophical and Scientific Texts: A Chronological Table". In: Gad Freudenthal (Ed.): *Science in Medieval Jewish Cultures*. New York: Cambridge University Press, pp. 17–73.

www.ingramcontent.com/pod-product-compliance
Lightning Source LLC
Chambersburg PA
CBHW042113100526
44587CB00025B/4039